Toolkit for Organizational Change

Dedicated to our mentors, Dick Hodgson and Ron Burke.

Toolkit for Organizational Change

Tupper Cawsey • Gene Deszca

Wilfrid Laurier University

SAGE Publications
Los Angeles • London • New Delhi • Singapore

For information:

Sage Publications, Inc.
2455 Teller Road
Thousand Oaks, California 91320
E-mail: order@sagepub.com

Sage Publications India Pvt. Ltd.
B 1/I 1 Mohan Cooperative Industrial Area
Mathura Road, New Delhi 110 044
India

Sage Publications Ltd.
1 Oliver's Yard
55 City Road
London EC1Y 1SP
United Kingdom

Sage Publications Asia-Pacific Pte. Ltd.
33 Pekin Street #02-01
Far East Square
Singapore 048763

Printed in the United States of America

Library of Congress Cataloging-in-Publication Data

Cawsey, T. F.
Toolkit for organizational change / Tupper Cawsey, Gene Deszca.
    p. cm.
Includes bibliographical references and index.
ISBN 978-1-4129-4106-8 (pbk.)
1. Organizational change. I. Deszca, Gene. II. Title.

HD58.8.C39 2008
658.4′06—dc22   2007002081

This book is printed on acid-free paper.

09 10 11 10 9 8 7 6 5 4 3 2

Acquisitions Editor:	Al Bruckner
Associate Editor:	Deya Saoud
Production Editor:	Denise Santoyo
Copy Editor:	Cheryl Rivard
Typesetter:	C&M Digitals (P) Ltd.
Indexer:	Kathy Paparchontis
Cover Designer:	Michelle Lee Kenny
Marketing Manager:	Nichole M. Angress

Brief Contents and Chapter Summaries

Chapter 1 sets out the orientation of this book: to assist change managers or potential change managers to be more effective in making change. Organizational change is defined as "planned alteration of organizational components to improve the effectiveness of organizations." The chapter outlines the social, demographic, technological, political, and economic forces affecting change today and discusses four types of organizational change: tuning, adapting, reorienting, and re-creating. It concludes with a description of key change roles found in organizations, the difficulties in creating successful change, and the characteristics of successful change leaders.

Chapter 2 differentiates between **HOW** to create organizational change (the process) and **WHAT** should be changed (the content) but focuses on **HOW** to change. The chapter begins with Lewin's classic "Unfreeze-Change-Refreeze" model, and then describes a modified version of Beckhard's and Harris's change management process. The model asks the following questions: (1) What is our initial analysis of the organization? (2) Why change? (3) What is the gap between the existing and desired states? (4) What plans need to be implemented to close this gap and manage during the transition? and (5) How do we measure and control the change process? These models will help change leaders articulate their implicit assumptions about the ways organizations work and how to change their organization.

Chapter 3 deals with **WHAT** needs to change and how we can develop our skills at organizational diagnosis. The chapter outlines six models, three to provide organizational frameworks and three to assist change agents to think about the complex, nonlinear, interactive, multilevel, and time-dependent nature of organizations. It considers the usefulness of each model and the circumstances under which it might be useful. It explains why we use the Nadler and Tushman model as the overarching framework in this book.

Chapter 4 asks the question "Why change?" and develops a framework for understanding the need for change. It describes what makes organizations ready for change and provides a questionnaire to rate an organization's readiness for change. It outlines how change leaders can create an awareness for change and concludes by outlining the importance of the change vision and how change leaders can create a meaningful vision that energizes and focuses action.

Chapter 5 examines how formal organizational structures and systems can foster or impair change initiatives. It considers the role of systems and structures in obtaining approval for change initiatives, in gaining acceptance of the change, and in creating more adaptive systems and structures.

Chapter 6 addresses the importance of change agent's understanding the sources of support for and resistance to change and the sources of power. The chapter introduces Force Field Analysis and Stakeholder Analysis as two key tools in developing a better understanding of the informal organizational system and how to work with it and change it.

Chapter 7 explores the ways in which people respond to change, from eager acceptance to resistance. It introduces the notion of ambivalent feelings toward the change and how mixed feelings can be used by change leaders to influence attitudes toward the change. The chapter includes a discussion of the psychological contract between the organization and the employees and how this contract affects change. Chapter 7 concludes by asking change leaders to consider how to minimize the negative effects of change, in part by making change the norm and by encouraging recipients to become change leaders or change implementers themselves.

Chapter 8 discusses the characteristics of successful change agents. The chapter describes four change agent types: the emotional champion, the intuitive adapter, the developmental strategist, and the continuous improver. Finally, the chapter considers two situational factors for change agents: whether they are internal or external change agents, and the nature of the change team.

Chapter 9 emphasizes that change leaders need to take action and learn from the results. Change initiators have a "do it" attitude. Action planning involves making the right decisions, planning the work, organizing the team, and working the plan.

Action planning deals with encouraging people to move from initial **awareness** of the change, to being **interested**, to **desiring** the change, and finally to taking **action** (AIDA). Change agents learn to specify who does what, when, and how to make change happen. Responsibility charts are key tools in successful action planning. The chapter concludes by addressing how successful change managers build a change team, develop detailed communications plans, and manage the change transition.

Chapter 10 addresses measurement of change and how measurement systems can facilitate or hinder change management. It describes four types of control systems: diagnostic/steering controls, belief systems, boundary systems, and interactive controls. Finally, four measurement tools are presented that can assist change agents: strategy maps, the balanced scorecard, the risk exposure calculator, and the Duration, Integrity, Commitment, and Effort (DICE) model.

This chapter presents an expanded summary model of organizational change and applies the model to a case situation. It outlines our thoughts on the future of organizational change and organizational change agents. The chapter ends with questions on how to orient yourself to organizational change and what questions change agents need to ask as they manage the process.

Detailed Contents

Preface

This text is the product of over ten years of working with executives, managers, and senior MBA students to develop a toolkit for organizational change. Our intent is to be pragmatic, realistic, and useful. Our initial image was a book that managers would grab off the shelf when faced by an organizational change—whether they were initiating change, implementing it, or on the receiving end. We wanted readers to access the tools quickly and easily, using what they found helpful and leaving the rest until needed. Based on the feedback we have received from our MBA students and the managers we have worked with, we think we have succeeded.

The motivation for the book was to fill a gap we saw in the marketplace. Our challenge was to develop a book that not only gave prescriptive advice, "how-to-do-it lists," but one that also provided up-to-date theory without getting sidetracked by academic theoretical complexities. We hope that we have captured the management experience with change so that our manuscript assists all those who must deal with change, not just senior executives or organization development specialists. Although there is much in this book for the senior executive and organizational development specialist, our intent was to create a book that would be valuable to a much broader cross section of the workforce.

When we examined the literature on change management, we were concerned with the dominance of a rational, linear model of change. When we talked to those on the firing line, we saw a complex, dynamic reality that was not easily captured by linear thinking. While our book is organized in a linear fashion, we hope that we have integrated the interactive, dynamic processes involved in complex change.

As we worked on the book, the role of middle managers in creating change came back into the literature. Again, this fit our experience of organizations and management. The very best leader-managers at the top of organizations encourage and support initiatives throughout the organization. They use their power to support worthy change initiatives created by those in touch with customers and employees. Those in the middle still need to act—otherwise things languish, regardless of the level of supportiveness of the environment. As a result, our book became oriented toward helping to develop change agent capacities among those who find themselves in the middle of the organization, rather than just those at its apex.

Finally, our personal beliefs form the basis for the book. Even as academics, we have a bias for action. We believe that "doing is healthy." Taking action creates influence and demands responses from others. While we believe in the need for excellent analysis, we know that action itself provides opportunities for feedback and learning that can improve the action. Finally, we have a strong belief in the worth of people. In particular, we believe that one of the greatest sources of improvement is the untapped potential to be found in the people of the organization.

We owe a significant debt to MBA students and managers who gave us feedback and tolerated our early drafts of this book. We knew that we could rely on them to keep us on track with our pragmatic approach. If they couldn't use it or didn't understand it, they quickly let us know. Our faith in their abilities as knowledgeable change agents and as critics has been justified time and again.

We have emphasized a pragmatic approach. While we believe that the book captures the most up-to-date concepts in the field, we have included those straightforward models that shed light on change situations. We usually opt for dealing in depth with one model rather than a comparison of the intricacies of several models. A key feature of the book that emphasizes the practical is the many toolkit exercises that provide the opportunity for students to apply the models and develop their thinking. There are four major case studies that will help integrate thinking and practice. In the Instructor's Resource, you will find references or links to other lengthy cases, shorter cases, and relevant articles and other Web sites. For instructors, PowerPoint slides are available, as well as instructor's notes for cases, and course outlines and exercises. We hope you will enjoy the book, and we welcome comments or feedback that will help our practice of change.

Acknowledgments

We would like to acknowledge all who have helped to make this book possible. Our students, who suffered its growing pains cheerfully, have been a source of inspiration. The managers that we have known have provided insights and applications while keeping us focused on what is useful and relevant. Many of our colleagues have provided guidance and feedback. In particular, Cheryl Harvey, our colleague at Laurier, has given us support, feedback, and wisdom.

Of special note are our wives, Bertha and Heather, who tolerated our moods and encouraged us when we were discouraged. Special thanks to Heather and Kathy Cawsey and their editing skills. Never a passive verb shall go unnoticed.

Our editors at Sage have been excellent. They moved this project along and made it easy. Thank you, Deya Saoud, Al Bruckner, and Cheryl Rivard. Our special thanks go to John Szilagyi, who first decided that this book was worthy of publication and who ensured that we had the chance to make it a success.

Finally, we would like to recognize the reviewers who plowed through the early versions of this book, made excellent suggestions, and gave us the positive feedback to keep the project going. They are: Jeanne Aurelio, Bridgewater State College; Peter Diplock, University of Connecticut; Marion Harris, Bowie State University; Rolf Holtz, Ball State University; Carol Napoli, Synergies, Inc.; W. Scott Sherman, Texas A&M University, Corpus Christi; Joan Sylvester, Dominican University; and Ely Weitz, Tel Aviv University.

Our thanks go to all who made this possible.

Organizational Change in Our Complex World

Nothing endures but change.

—Heraclitus (540 BCE–480 BCE)

Chapter Overview

- Chapter 1 defines organizational change as "planned alteration of organizational components to improve the effectiveness of organizations."
- Organizational development and change management are differentiated. The orientation of this book is to assist change managers or potential change managers to be more effective in their change activities.
- Four change roles found in organizations are described: change initiators, change implementers, change facilitators, and change recipients. The terms *change leader* and *change agent* are interchangeable and could mean any of the four roles.
- The social, demographic, technological, political, and economic forces affecting change today are outlined.
- Four types of organizational change: tuning, adapting, reorienting, and re-creating—are discussed.
- The difficulties in creating successful change are highlighted, and some of the characteristics of a successful change leader are described.

Our world is filled with organizations. We put our children into daycare organizations. We work at for-profit or not-for-profit organizations. We rely on organizations to deliver the services we need: food, water, electricity, and sanitation. We depend on health organizations when we are sick. We use religious organizations to help our spiritual lives. We assume that most of our children's education will be delivered by formal education organizations. In other words, organizations are everywhere. Organizations are how we get things done.

And these organizations are changing—adapting to meet the shifting demands of their environments. What exactly is organizational change? What do we mean in this book when we talk about it?

What Is Organizational Change?

When we think of organizational change, we think of major changes: mergers, acquisitions, buyouts, downsizing, restructuring, the launch of new products, and the outsourcing of major organizational activities. We can also think of lesser changes: departmental reorganizations, installations of new technology and incentive systems, and shutting down particular manufacturing lines or opening new branches in other parts of the country—tuning changes to improve the efficiency and operations of our organizations.

In this book, when we talk about **organizational change,** we are referring to *a planned alteration of organizational components to improve the effectiveness of the organization.* By **organizational components,** we mean the *organizational mission and vision, strategy, goals, structure, process or system, technology, and people in an organization.* When organizations enhance their effectiveness, they increase their ability to generate value for those they are designed to serve.

Note that, by our definition, organizational change is intentional and planned. Someone in the organization has taken an initiative to alter a significant organizational component. This means a shift in something relatively permanent. Usually, something formal has been altered. For example, a new customer relations system may be introduced that captures customer satisfaction and reports it to managers; or a new division is created and people are allocated to that division in response to a new organizational vision.

We need to recognize what is *not* considered to be organizational change in this book. Simply doing more of the same, such as increasing existing sales efforts in response to a competitor's activities, would not be classified as an organizational change. However, the restructuring of a sales force into two groups (key account managers and general account managers) would be an organizational change, even though this restructuring could well be in response to a competitor's activities and could well lead to increased sales effort.

Some organizational components are concrete and thus easier to understand when contemplating change. Shifts in structure, systems, and/or processes fall into these categories. For example, assembly lines can be reordered. The change is definable, and the end point clear when it is done. Similarly, the alteration of a reward system or job design is concrete and can be clearly documented. The creation of new positions, subunits, or departments is equally obvious. Such organizational changes are tangible and easier to enact.

When the change management target lies more deeply imbedded in the organization, the change challenge is magnified. For example, a shift in an organization's culture is more difficult to engineer. We can plan a change from an authoritarian to a more participative culture, but the initiatives required to bring about the change and their sequencing are trickier to get hold of than more concrete change initiatives. Simply announcing a new strategy or vision does not mean that anything significant will change. As someone said, "You need to get the vision off the walls and into the halls."[1] A more manageable way to think of such a cultural change is to see it as the result of more concrete changes. If management alters reward systems, shifts decision making downward, and creates participative management committees, they increase the likelihood that they will create cultural change over time. Sustained behavioral change occurs when people in the organization understand, accept, and act. Through their actions, the new vision or strategy becomes real.[2]

The focus of change needs to be considered carefully. Often managers choose concrete tangible changes because they are easiest to plan for and can be seen. For example, it is relatively easy to focus on pay and give monetary incentives in an attempt to address morale issues. But the root cause of these issues might be managerial styles or processes—much more difficult to recognize and address. Intervening through compensation may have unanticipated consequences and worsen the problem. The following is an example of what might happen:

> In a mid-size social service agency, family services division, turnover rates climbed to over 20% causing serious issues with service delivery and quality of service. The manager of the division argued that staff were leaving because of wages. According to him, children's aid societies' wages were higher and that caused the turnover. Upon investigation, senior management learned of morale problems arising from the directive, noninclusive management style of the manager. Instead of altering pay rates, which would have caused significant budgetary and equity problems throughout the organization, senior management replaced the manager and moved him to a project role. Within months, turnover rates dropped to under 10% and the manager decided to leave the agency.[3]

If the original analysis had been accepted, turnover rates might have declined. Staff may have been persuaded to stay for financial reasons—even though they were dissatisfied. Not only would the agency be facing monetary issues, they would have had a morale problem that was festering!

In summary, the focus of this book is on organizational change as a planned activity designed to improve the organization's effectiveness. Changes that are random (occur simply due to chance) or unplanned are not the types of organizational change that this book intends to explore. Similarly, changes that may be planned but do not have a clear link to attempts to improve organization effectiveness are not considered. That is, changes made solely for personal reasons—for personal gain, for example—fall outside the intended focus of this book.

The Roots of Organizational Change

Managers have long voiced an interest in improving their organizations. Writings on the topic can be found throughout recorded history. Early religious texts provide many examples of advice and action related to enhancing effectiveness (e.g., Moses' actions related to the Diaspora from Egypt, and the advice of major religious figures on how life should be led). Likewise, early philosophers such as Plato offered advice on how change should be promoted and managed (e.g., "One of the penalties for refusing to participate . . . is that you end up being governed by your inferiors.").[4]

The founder of the Han Dynasty, Liu Bang (256 BC–195 BC), attributed his success at defeating his opponent and founding his Dynasty to his policy of using the right people in the right position. He said: "In strategic planning of warfare Chang Liang is better than I; in logistics administration for the battlefield Shoa is better than I; and in deployment of a million troops to win the battles Han Sin is better than I. All three of these people are elite. I can look for their strength and put it to work. That's why I could be the founder of a new Dynasty."[5]

Liu Bang's thinking is similar to that of many managers: They are concerned with making their organization effective, and they are focused on improving their position or role within that organization.

Modern thinking about organizational change has its roots in organization development.[6] French and Bell describe four stems of organization development:

1. The Small Group Training stem, which focused on creating change by improving self-awareness and the group's dynamics

2. The Survey Research and Feedback stem, which intervened with sophisticated surveys and analysis to create the need for change

3. The Action Research stem, which encouraged the use of action, based on research, in continuous cycles (in essence, learning by doing, followed by observation, doing, and more learning)

4. The Sociotechnical stem, which focused on the interaction between the sociological and technical subsystems of the organization and described change in more holistic terms

Worren, Ruddle, and Moore have differentiated organization development from change management.[7] Table 1.1 outlines this shift according to Worren.

The field of organizational change has developed to become more integrative and strategic. There is a shift from considering personal and group outcomes to organizational ones. Organizational change is broader based, and action often requires a change team to make change happen. Organizational change is focused on the business—using an understanding of human relationships to improve organizational results.

Change capability has become a core managerial competence. Without change management skills, individuals cannot operate effectively in today's fluctuating,

Table 1.1   Organizational Development Versus Change Management

	Organizational Development	Change Management
Underlying Theory and Analytical Framework	Based primarily on psychology Individual/group functioning *org learning resilance STS —*	Includes principles and tools from sociology, information technology, and strategic change theories *STRATEGY* Individual/group functioning AND systems, structures, work processes (congruence model)
Role of Change Agent	Facilitator or process consultant	Content expert (organization design and human performance) AND process consultant *STRATEGY* Member of cross-functional team, which includes strategists and technologists Part of project organization, which includes client managers/employees
Intervention Strategies	Not directly linked to strategy Focus on one component at a time Normative-re-educative (change attitudes to change behavior)	Driven by strategy *STRATEGY* Simultaneous focus on several components (strategy, human resources, organization design, technology) Action-oriented (change behavior before attitudes)

Source: From Worren, N., Ruddle, K., & Moore, K. (1999). From organizational development to change management. *Journal of Applied Behavioral Science, (35)*3, 280.

shifting organizations.[8] Senior management sets the organizational direction, and in this decentralized organizational world, it is up to managers to shift the organization to accomplish the new goals and objectives. To do this, change management skills are paramount.

This is about pushing the leverage of change to the mid-mgr level. So culture can be changed w/o changing the management?

The rapid growth in the volume of formal research about organizational change is a relatively recent phenomenon, and the volume of literature on organizational change is overwhelming.* Despite this literature, management's ability to deliver successful change is modest at best. One study reports that 7 of 10 change efforts fail to achieve their intended results; for major corporate systems investments, 28% are abandoned before completion, 46% are behind schedule or over budget, and 80% are not used in the way intended or not used at all after 6 months.[9]

---

*A Google search yielded over 110 million hits; "Ask.com," 7.5 million hits; Harvard Business School site, 1,024 hits; Proquest Search, 15,530 articles; Fast Company Web search yielded 3,120 hits.

Pfeffer is a late comer to this....

Clearly, change management is more difficult than we anticipate. We believe, as does Pfeffer, that there is a Knowing-Doing gap.[10] Knowing the concepts and understanding the theory behind organizational change are not enough. This book is designed to provide practicing and prospective managers with the tools they will need to be more effective change agents.

The Orientation of This Book

There is a story of two stonecutters. The first, when asked what he was doing, responded, "I am shaping this stone to fit in that wall." The second, however, said, "I am helping to build a cathedral."

This is not aspirational "I'm building a big thing" not "I'm having an impact. People in NFP + some service orgs would find this insufficient

While the organizational contribution of each stonecutter might well be the same in terms of productivity, their perspectives are dramatically different. The personal outcomes in terms of satisfaction and organizational commitment will likely be much higher for the visionary stonecutter than for the "just doing my job" stonecutter. Finally, the differences in satisfaction and commitment may well lead to different organizational results. After all, if you are building a cathedral, you might have the motivation to stay late, to take extra care, to find ways to improve things, and to help others when help is needed.

In other words, the organizational member who has a "grander perspective" on their contribution and on the task at hand is likely to be a better, more satisfied employee. As a result, we take a perspective that encourages change leaders to take a holistic perspective on the change and to be widely inclusive in letting employees know what changes are happening.

If employees have no sense of the intended vision and see themselves as "just doing a job," it is likely that any organizational change will be difficult to understand, be resisted, and cause personal trauma. On the other hand, if employees sense the vision of the organization and understand the direction and perspective of where the organization is going and why, they are much more likely to understand their role in the future organization—even when that future includes their exiting the organization.[11]

Without a sense of vision, purpose, and engagement, it is easy to become the passive recipient of change. As a passive recipient, you see yourself as subject to the whims of others, as relatively helpless, perhaps even as a "victim." As a passive recipient, your self-esteem and self-efficacy may feel as if they are under attack.[12] Your perception of power and influence will diminish and you will feel acted on. Years ago, Jack Gordon talked about "aligning employees." That is, once top management has decided on the strategic direction, employees need to be aligned with that direction. We cannot help but think that if you are the recipient of change, "being aligned" just won't feel very good.[13]

This book is aimed at those who want to be involved in change and wish to take positive action. One of the messages of this book is to encourage readers to escape from a passive, negative change recipient position and to move into more active and healthy roles, those of change initiators, change facilitators, and change implementers. Readers may be in middle manager roles or may be entering management.

Or they may be leaders of change of an organization or a subunit. The book is also aimed at the informal leaders in organizations who are driving change, sometimes in spite of their bosses. They might believe that their bosses "should" be driving the change but don't see it happening, and so they see it as up to them to make change happen regardless of the action or inaction of their managers.

Organizational Change Roles

Who are the participants in organizational change? Many, perhaps most of us, will end up making the change work. We will be the change implementers, the ones implementing what others, the change initiators, have promoted. Or we could be on the receiving end of change, change recipients. Some will play a role in facilitating change—they won't be the ones responsible for implementing the change, but they will assist initiators and implementers in the change through their contacts and consultative assistance. Or a person might be the change initiator or champion, framing the vision for the change and/or providing resources and support for the initiative.

Of course, one person might play multiple roles. That is, you might have a good idea and talk it up in the organization (change initiator), take action to make the change occur (change implementer), talk to others to help them manage the change (change facilitator), and be affected yourself by the change you have proposed (change recipient). Clearly, you are acting as change leader. In this book, we use the terms *change leader* and *change agent* interchangeably. Change initiators, change implementers, and change facilitators represent different roles played by the change leader or change agent. At any given moment, the person leading the change may be initiating, implementing, or facilitating. Table 1.2 outlines the four roles of organizational change.

Change Initiators

Change initiators get things moving, take action, and stimulate the system to react. They are the ones constantly seeking change to make things better. They identify the need for change, see the vision of the better future, take on the change task, and champion the initiative. Change initiators may face considerable risk in the organization. To use a physical metaphor, action creates movement, movement creates friction, and friction creates heat! And creating heat may hurt your career. We don't encourage foolish initiation, one that will get you into trouble quickly with no chance of success. We do encourage calculated action taken by knowledgeable individuals who are prepared to undertake the work needed to create and support the powerful arguments and coalitions needed to effect change in organizations, be it from the top or the middle of the organization.

Change initiators will find useful aids for change in this book. We can't supply the passion or powerful vision needed by the initiators, but we can point out the requirements of successful change: planning, persuasion, and perseverance. And we can provide frameworks for analysis that will enhance the likelihood of successful change.

Change initiators need to be dogged in their desire and determination—those who succeed will have earned reputations for realistic, grounded optimism, for a good sense of timing, and for not giving up. If nothing else, the opposition may tire in the face of their persistence. Better yet are those who have the uncanny ability to creatively combine with others into a coalition that turns resisters into allies and foot draggers into foot soldiers for change.

Change Implementers

Many would-be and existing managers find themselves as change implementers. Others (including their bosses) may initiate the change, but it is left to the implementers to make it work. We do not want to diminish this role and the contribution that implementers make. Pfeffer argues that effectiveness doesn't come from making the critical decision but rather managing the consequences of decisions and creating the desired results![14] As he says, "If change were going to be easy, it would already have happened." The change implementer role is important and is needed in our organizations.

Change implementers will find much in this book to assist them. They will find guidance in creating and increasing the need for the changes that change initiators are demanding. They will find tools for organizational diagnosis and for identifying and working with key stakeholders. And they will find concepts and techniques to improve their change/action planning and implementation skills.

At the same time, we encourage and challenge change implementers to become more active and to initiate change themselves. Oshry identifies the dilemma of "middle powerlessness" where the middle manager feels trapped between tops and bottoms and becomes ineffective as a result.[15] Many middle managers transform their organizations by recognizing strategic initiatives and mobilizing the power of the "middles" to move the organization in the direction needed.

Change Facilitators

Today's complex organizational changes can run into roadblocks because parties lock into positions or because perspectives get lost in personalities and egos. In such cases, an outside view can facilitate change. Change facilitators understand change processes and assist the organization to work through change issues. As such, they sometimes formally serve as consultants to change leaders and teams. However, many of those who act as change facilitators do so informally, often on the strength of their existing relationships with others involved with the change. They have high levels of self-awareness and emotional maturity and are skilled in the behavioral arts—using their interpersonal skills to work with teams or groups.

In this book, change facilitators will discover conceptual frameworks that will help them to understand change processes. With these frameworks, they will be able to translate concrete organizational events into understandable situations and so ease change. And their knowledge will provide change perspectives that will allow managers to unfreeze their positions.

Change Recipients

Change recipients are those who find themselves on the receiving end of change. Their responses will vary from active resistance to passivity to active support, depending on their perceptions of the change, its rationale, and its impact. When they are feeling acted upon and have little or no voice or control in the process, dissatisfaction, frustration, alienation, absenteeism, and turnover are common responses to change demands.[16]

This book provides guidance that will help recipients to better understand what is happening to them and their organizations. Further, it will identify strategies and approaches that will help them to take a more active role and increase the amount of control they have over what will happen to them.

Regardless of your role in the organization—change recipient, change implementer, change initiator, or change facilitator—we believe that this book contains useful food for thought. Change recipients will understand what is happening to them and will learn how to respond positively. Change implementers will develop their capacity to use tools that increase their effectiveness. Change initiators will learn to take more effective actions to lever their change programs. And change facilitators will find themselves with new insights into easing organizational change.

Gary Hamel of Harvard talks about "leading the revolution"—anyone can play the change game. They can seek opportunities, ask questions, challenge orthodoxies, and generate new ideas and directions![17] And in doing so, individuals from virtually anywhere in an organization (or even outside of it) can become change leaders. Change leaders foment action. They take independent action based on their analysis of what is best for the long-term interests of their organizations. And they recognize the many faces of change and what the crucial next steps are toward

Table 1.2   Managerial Roles and Organization Change

Roles	Role Description
Change Initiator	The person who identifies the need and vision for change and champions the change.
Change Implementer	The person who has responsibility for making certain the change happens, charting the path forward, nurturing support, and alleviating resistance.
Change Facilitator	The person who assists Initiators, Implementers, and Recipients with the change management process. They identify process and content change issues and help resolve these, foster support, alleviate resistance, and provide other participants with guidance and counsel.
Change Recipient	The person who is affected by the change. Often the person who has to change his or her behavior to ensure the change is effective.

their long-term change goal. Finally, they recognize who needs to play what roles in order to advance needed change. As such, at different points in time, they fulfill the roles of change initiator, implementer, and facilitator, depending on the needs of the situation, their skills and abilities, and their beliefs about what is required at that point in time to advance the change.

What Is Driving Change Today?

Much change starts with shifts in an organization's environment. Government legislation dealing with employment law pushes new equity concerns through hiring practices. Globalization means that production and other parts of the organization (e.g., customer service through call centers) can be outsourced and/or moved around the world, so your organization's competition becomes worldwide rather than local. New technology means that purchasing can be linked to production within the supply chain so that supplier–customer relationships are forever changed. A competitor succeeds in attracting your largest customer and upsets your assumptions about the marketplace.

Sometimes organizations are caught by surprise by these environmental shifts, while at other times organizations have anticipated and planned for these eventualities. For example, management may have systems to track the perceived quality of its products versus the competition. That benchmarking data might show that its quality is beginning to lag behind a key competitor. This early warning system allows for action before customers are lost.

This book is not the place for an in-depth treatment of all the various trends and alterations in the environment. However, we will highlight some of the more important trends to sensitize readers to their environments. Today, organizations find themselves influenced by several fundamental forces: changing social, cultural, and demographic patterns; spectacular technological achievements that are transforming how we do business; a global marketplace that sends us competing worldwide and brings competition to our doorsteps; and continued political uncertainty in many countries that have the potential to introduce chaos into world markets.

You Need to Understand the Risks of Not Understanding Your Organizational Environment!

A group of senior executives attending Stanford University's advanced management program decided to escape the boot camp pace by visiting Napa Valley. They hired a limo service to make the day free of driving responsibilities. Throughout the day they chatted to the limo driver and learned of his background. He was an ex-CEO of a dot.com "success" story. This ex-CEO/limo driver had raised millions of dollars for his organization, burned through the money, and crashed when the market crashed. And now, he says you get work where and when you can!

> The driver and his fellow executives had no sense of their organization's external environment. They assumed that their success could be attributed to their efforts rather than luck. They assumed that the halcyon days would continue. And they spent freely without concern for building long term. Even a virtual organization needs more than virtual cash flow.[18]

The Changing Social, Cultural, and Demographic Environment

The social, cultural, and economic environment will be dramatically altered by demography. Demographic changes in the Western world mean that aging populations will alter the face of Europe, Canada, and Japan. The financial warning bells are already being sounded. Standard and Poor's predicts that the average net government debt-to-GDP ratio for industrialized nations will increase from 33% in 2005 to 180% by 2050, due to rising pension and healthcare costs,[19] if changes are not undertaken.

Although the United States will age slightly, Europe will face a dependency crisis of senior citizens requiring medical care and pension support. By 2050, the median age in the United States is projected to be 36.2 versus 52.7 in Europe. The United States will keep itself younger through immigration and a birth rate that is close to replacement level.[20] Even with this influx, the U.S. governmental debt-to-GDP ratio is expected to grow to 350% of GDP by 2050, due mainly to pension and healthcare costs.[21]

Europe's population is projected to peak in 2015 at around 400 million, while the United States passes that number in 2020 and continues to grow thereafter. Although this is far in the future, the economic implications for business are significant. Imagine 400–500 million relatively wealthy Americans and the impact that will have on global economic power, assuming that pension and healthcare challenges are effectively managed. Consumer spending in emerging economies is expected to more than double from $4 trillion to over $9 trillion in the next ten years.[22] And, also imagine the impact of graying Europe and Japan with declining workforces.* Some estimates put the fiscal problems in providing pensions and health care for senior citizens at 250% of national income in Germany and France.[23]

Pension costs can become a huge competitive disadvantage at the company level as well. At General Motors, there were 2.5 retirees for every active worker in 2002, and these so-called "legacy" costs were $900 per vehicle at that time, due to pension and healthcare obligations. These costs were estimated to have risen to $1,600 by 2005 and $1,800 by 2006.[24] At the same time, an aging population provides new market opportunities—who would believe that the average age of a Harley-Davidson purchaser is 52![25]

Other demographic issues will provide opportunities and challenges. In the United States, Latinos will play a role in transforming organizations. The numbers of Latinos jumped from 22.4 million to 35.3 million during the 1990s, and at 12.5% of the population, they are the largest ethnic/racial group in the United States.[26]

---

*Already, the impact of the "graying of Europe" is being seen as the governments of Germany and France met significant resistance as they attempt to reduce retirement and unemployment benefits for their citizens.

Significantly, the largest growth often is in "hypergrowth" Latino destinations that have seen over a 300% increase in Latino populations since 1980. This growth will continue due to the economic activity in these areas, and one of the outcomes will be an imbalance of Latino males and females. In the non-Latino population, the ratio of males to females is 96:100, but in the Latino population, it switches to 107:100 and to 118:100 in the hypergrowth destinations (peaking at 188:100 in Raleigh, North Carolina).[27] While the specific implications for business are unclear, the general need for response and change is not. Our notions of cultural norms (including those around English literacy) and markets could be shattered by such demographic shifts.

With aging populations, organizations can expect pressures to manage age prejudice more effectively. Subtle discrimination on age will not be acceptable. Innovative solutions such as those by Joe Pesce will be welcomed:

> "There is no mandatory retirement age at Baycrest (a large geriatric care facil-ity in Toronto, Canada), where roughly 35 of the center's 2,000 employees are now over 65," said Mr. Pesce, Vice-President of Human Resources.
>
> Mr. Pesce is putting together a list of "retiree alumni"—a pool of retired employees who might be willing to come back on a part-time or temporary basis as needed—and is also looking at other ways to make Baycrest a more "elder-friendly" workplace."[28]

Clearly, Joe Pesce has become a change initiator in this important area of demo-graphic change.

Our assumptions about families and gender will continue to be challenged in the workplace and marketplace of the future. Diversity, inclusiveness, and equity issues will continue to challenge organizations with the results being unpredictable. For example, the liberal initiatives in California are now subject to some backlash according to Diamond: "Immigration, affirmative action, multilingualism, ethnic diversity—my state of California was among the pioneers of these controversial policies and is now pioneering a backlash against them."[29] Signs of this were appar-ent in the heated debates that occurred in the United States in 2006, concerning leg-islation related to illegal or undocumented emigrants and workers. The language used to describe the target group shifts, depending on your position on the matter.

As the nature and variety of relationships change, organizations will have to respond. Flexible systems will become vital to attract and keep the knowledge work-ers of the future. Already we see multinationals such as IBM viewing workforce diversity management as a strategic tool for sustaining and growing the enterprise.[30]

New Technologies

In addition to demographic changes in the workplace and marketplace, the trite but true statements about the impact of technological change must be embraced by organizations and their change managers. To broaden your perspective on technol-ogy, here are some of the newer technologies that can be found in the literature:

- Energy engineers are talking about "clean coal" technology being on the brink of commercialization.

- Ultra-Wide Band devices can beam flawless video and audio clips at 100 megabits per second.
- An implantable syringe-on-a-chip will inject minute quantities of drugs at precise intervals over months.[31]
- Disease-detecting biochips are being developed where chips are encoded with DNA patterns of viruses and programmed to look for matching samples.[32] Hospitals will detect infectious diseases in hours rather than in days.
- Prisoners will be tracked with tamperproof wristbands,[33] and guards can monitor when they get too close to things they should be staying away from.
- Nanotechnology promises to produce a host of products that will transform industries—from TV monitors to fuel cells to drug delivery systems.[34]

Wieners claims that there will be eight technologies that will change the world:

1. Biointeractive materials—high-tech sensors for living systems

2. Biofuel production plants—where genetically engineered crops produce fuel to replace coal and oil

3. Bionics—artificial systems to replace lost or disabled body parts

4. Cognitronics—where there are interfaces between the computer and the brain

5. Genotyping—where we classify people based on their genetics

6. Brute-force R&D—where powerful computers crunch data to identify and test random solutions for positive results

7. Molecular manufacturing—building complex structures atom by atom

8. Port-a-Nukes—which will provide portable, safe, nonpolluting nuclear power[35]

Technology has woven our world together—the number of international air passengers rose from 75 million in 1970 to 142 million in 2000. The cost of a 3-minute phone call from the United States to England dropped from over $8 to less than 36¢ from 1976 to 2000, and the number of transborder calls in the United States increased from 200 million in 1980 to 5.2 billion in 1999.[36] The emergence of VoIP (voice over the Internet) is poised to disrupt long-distance telephone markets dramatically, reducing the cost of international calls to pennies per minute or zero, if one has the right equipment. At the same time, security concerns related to viruses and hacking are raised.[37] On a business-to-business level, supply chains are woven together and software allows them to operate effectively and be responsive to the marketplace.[38]

With the establishment of the World Wide Web, high school students can have access to the same quality of information that the best researchers have! At the same time that technology has brought us closer, it has also produced a technological divide between have and have-nots that has the potential to produce social and political instability.* Lack of access to clean water, sufficient food, and needed medication is far less likely to be tolerated in silence when media images tell us that

---

*The effects are not straightforward as shown by the move of MIT's media lab to create a $100 laptop computer for disadvantaged youth in Africa, Asia, and around the world. (See: http://laptop.media.mit.edu).

others have an abundance of such resources and lack the will to share. Technology transforms our relationships—blogging is commonplace; in 2005, over 12% of U.S. newlyweds met online.[39]

Our purpose is not to catalogue all new and emerging technologies. Rather, our intent is to signal to change leaders the importance of paying attention to technological trends and the impact they may have on organizations, now and in the future. As a result of these forces, product development and product life cycles are shortened and managers are driven to respond in a time-paced fashion. Competition can leapfrog your organization in quantum leaps and drop your organization into obsolescence through a technological breakthrough. The advantages of vertical integration can vanish as technical experts in one segment of the business drive down the costs and then migrate the technology through outsourcing to other segments that have not anticipated such changes. The watchwords for change leaders are to be aware of technological trends and to be proactive in your consideration of how to respond to organizationally relevant ones.

Political Changes

The external political landscape of an organization is a reality that change leaders need to figure out how to respond to. Even the largest of multinationals has minimal impact on the worldwide alteration of national boundaries and the focus of governing bodies.[40]

The collapse of the Soviet Empire gave rise to optimism in the West that democracy and the market economy were the natural order of things, the only viable option for modern society.[41] With the end of communism, there was no serious competitor to free-market democracy, and the belief existed that the world would gradually move to competitive capitalism with market discipline. The American hegemony would rule the world.

Of course, this optimism was not fully realized. Nationalistic border quarrels (India-Pakistan, for example) became huge issues. Some African countries have become less committed to democracy (Zimbabwe and the Sudan). Nation-states have dissolved into microstates (remember Yugoslavia?). The definition of the free market has been challenged by Tony Blair and others in the European community. And while American power may be dominant worldwide, September 11, 2001 (9/11), demonstrated that even the dominant power may not be able to guarantee safety. Non-nation-states and religious groups have become actors on the global stage. The Middle East and Central Asia continue to be in turmoil creating political and economic uncertainty. At the same time, the markets of China and India are on a "tear."[42]

Though their markets retain significant elements of state control, Russia and China have become new and more open markets. Kazakhstan offers promise of oil opportunities. The events of 9/11 shut down significant corporate air travel for months and have organizations rethinking the need for face-to-face meetings. Security concerns of nation-states have altered the flow of goods and people among nations, and regional rivalries continue to be a topic that must be kept in mind. Organizations have had to respond to these shifts.

As organizations become global, they need to clarify their own ethical standards. Not only will they need to understand the law, they will have to determine what norms of behavior they will work to establish for their organization members. Peter Eigen, chairman of Transparency International, states, "Political elites and their cronies continue to take kickbacks at every opportunity. Hand in glove with corrupt business people, they are trapping whole nations in poverty and hampering sustainable development. Corruption is perceived to be dangerously high in poor parts of the world, but also in many countries whose firms invest in developing nations."[43] This political corruption becomes imbedded in organizations. Transparency International finds bribery most common in public works/construction and arms and defense as compared with agriculture.[44] The accounting and governance scandals of 2001–2002 (Enron, WorldCom) created a demand for both new regulation and an emphasis on ethical role models.

The politics of globalization and the environment have created opportunities and issues for organizations. The Kyoto Accord will change the costs of operating for businesses in nations that sign on to the accord. At the same time, they may develop new technologies that will bring profits in the future. Earlier experiences with environmental initiatives such as acid rain and ozone depletion show a strikingly similar pattern: corporate resistance and doom-and-gloom predictions, followed by innovation and growth. Senge from MIT argues that the new environmentalism will be driven by innovation and will result in radical new technologies, products, processes, and business models.[45]

In fall 1999 the sustainability consortium was hosted by the Xerox "Lakes" team that had developed the Document Center 265 copier. Already aware of the team's innovations in design for remanufacture (more than 500 patents came from the Lakes project) and the product's success in the marketplace, we learned about how the team's zero-waste vision translated into a manufacturing facility with virtually no waste.

We had all heard the Lakes motto, "Zero to landfill, for the sake of our children."[46]

The politics of the world are not the focus of many managers, but change leaders need to understand their influence on market development and attractiveness, competitiveness, and the resulting pressures on boards and executives. A sudden transformation of the political landscape can trash the best-laid strategic plan. Successful change leaders will have a keen sense of the opportunities and dangers involved in political shifts.

What Are the Implications for Change Management of Worldwide Trends?

The economic globalization of the world, the demographic shifts in the Western world's population, technological opportunities, and upheaval and political uncertainties form the reality of organizational environments. Predicting specific short-run changes is a fool's errand. Nevertheless, change leaders will have a keen sense of just how those external events may impact internal organizational dynamics. "How will external changes drive strategy and internal adjustments and investments?" will become a critical question that change leaders will want to address.

Barkema suggests that macro changes will change organizational forms and competitive dynamics and in turn lead to new management challenges.[47] (Table 1.3 summarizes Barkema's article.) He describes three macro changes facing us today: (1) digitization of information, (2) integration of nation-states and the opening of international markets, and (3) the geographic dispersion of the value chain. These are leading to the globalization of markets. This globalization, in turn, will drive significant shifts in organizational form and worldwide competitive dynamics.

The new management challenges of greater diversity, greater synchronization and time-pacing requirements, faster decision making, more frequent environmental discontinuities, faster industry life cycles, increased obsolescence, and more competency traps all suggest more complexity and a more rapid organizational pace. Barkema argues that much change today deals with middle-level change—change

Table 1.3   New Organizational Forms and Management Challenges Based on Environmental Change

Macro Changes and Impacts	New Organizational Forms and Competitive Dynamics	New Management Challenges
Digitization leading to: Faster information transmission Lower-cost information storage and transmission Integration of states and opening of markets Geographic dispersion of the value chain All leading to: Globalization of markets	Global small and medium-sized enterprises Global constellations of organizations (i.e., networks) Large, focused global firms All leading to: Spread of autonomous, dislocated teams Digitally enabled structures Intense global rivalry Running faster while seeming to stand still	Greater diversity Greater synchronization requirements Greater time-pacing requirements Faster decision making, learning, and innovation More frequent environmental discontinuities Faster industry life cycles Faster newness and obsolescence of knowledge Risk of competency traps where old competencies no longer produce desired effects Greater newness and obsolescence of organizations

Source: Adapted from Barkema, Harry G., et al. (2002). Management challenges in a new time. *Academy of Management Journal*, (*45*)5, 916.

that is more than incremental but not truly revolutionary. As such, middle managers will play increasingly significant roles in making change effective in their organizations in both evolutionary and revolutionary scenarios.

What Types of Organizational Change Exist?

Earlier we mentioned common types of organizational change: mergers, acquisitions, buyouts, downsizing, restructuring, outsourcing the human resource function of our computer services, departmental reorganizations, installations of new incentive systems, and shutting down particular manufacturing lines or opening new branches in other parts of the country. All of these describe specific organizational changes. The literature on organizational change classifies different changes into two types, episodic/discontinuous change and continuous change. That is, change can be dramatic and sudden—the introduction of a new technology that makes your business obsolete or new government regulations that immediately shift the competitive landscape; or change can be much more gradual—the alteration of core competencies of an organization through training and adding key individuals.

Under dramatic or episodic change, organizations are seen as having significant inertia. Change is infrequent and discontinuous. Reengineering programs are examples of this type of change and can be viewed as a planned example of injecting quantum or significant change in an organization. On the other hand, under continuous change, organizations are seen as emergent and self-organizing where change is constant, evolving, and cumulative.[48] Japanese automobile manufacturers have led the way in this area with *kaizen* programs focused on encouraging continuous change.

Further, change can occur in a proactive, planned, and programmatic fashion, or it can happen reactively, in response to shifts in external events. Programmatic or planned change occurs when managers anticipate events and shift their organizations as a result. For example, Intel anticipates and appears to encourage a cycle of computer chip obsolescence.[49] As a result, their organization has been designed to handle that obsolescence. Alternately, shifts in an organization's external world lead to a reaction on the part of the organization. For example, the emergence of low-cost airlines has led to traditional carriers employing reactive strategies, cutting routes, costs, and service levels in an attempt to adapt.[50]

Nadler and Tushman provide another way of thinking about the scope of changes. They have developed a useful model to illustrate different types of change (see Table 1.4). They start with a systems perspective and argue that changes can vary from evolutionary, incremental, and adaptive changes to ones that are much more revolutionary and strategic in nature. Typically, incremental changes focus on the individual components in the systems model and have as their goal the improvement of performance through regaining, maintaining, or incrementally enhancing the congruence of those elements within the organization. For example, realigning the information system so that customer service representatives can provide customers with more accurate and timely product information is an incremental change. More revolutionary or strategic changes involve many, or potentially all, organizational systems and require us to substantially reshape our frames of reference concerning how the organization should operate. For example, low-cost airlines are transforming the airline business by changing how we think about the organization of airlines. No longer do we think of "hub and spoke" routes, full-service trips (economy to first class), and multiple plane types. Instead we focus on "point to point" routes, single service level (economy class), and single plane types.[51]

Tuning is defined as small, relatively minor changes made on an ongoing basis in a deliberate attempt to improve the efficiency or effectiveness of the organization.

Table 1.4   Types of Organizational Change

	Incremental/Continuous	*Discontinuous/Radical*
Anticipatory	*Tuning* • Incremental change made in anticipation of future events • Need is for internal alignment • Focuses on individual components or subsystems • Middle management role • Implementation is the major task • E.g., a quality improvement initiative from an employee improvement committee	*Redirecting or Reorienting* • Strategic proactive changes based on predicted major changes in the environment • Need is for positioning the whole organization to a new reality • Focuses on all organizational components • Senior management creates sense of urgency and motivates the change • E.g., a major change in product or service offering, in response to opportunities identified
Reactive	*Adapting* • Incremental changes made in response to environmental changes • Need is for internal alignment • Focuses on individual components or subsystems • Middle management role • Implementation is the major task • E.g., modest changes to customer services, in response to customer complaints	*Overhauling or Re-Creating* • Response to a significant performance crisis • Need to reevaluate the whole organization, including its core values • Focuses on all organizational components to achieve rapid, systemwide change • Senior management create vision and motivate optimism • E.g., a major realignment of strategy, involving plant closures and changes to product and service offerings, to stem financial losses and return the firm to profitability

Source: Adapted from Nadler, D., & Tushman, M. (1989). Organizational frame bending: Principles for managing reorientation. *Academy of Management Executive, (3)*3, 196.

Responsibility for acting on these sorts of changes typically rests with middle management. Most improvement change initiatives that grow out of existing quality improvement programs would fall into this category. Adapting is viewed as relatively minor changes made in response to external stimuli—a reaction to things observed in the environment such as competitors' moves or customer shifts. Relatively minor changes to customer servicing that are stimulated by reports of customer dissatisfaction or defections to a competitor provide an example of this sort of change, and once again, responsibility for such changes tends to reside within the role of middle managers.

Redirecting or reorientating involves major, strategic change resulting from planned programs. These frame-bending shifts are designed to provide new perspectives and directions in a significant way. For example, a shift in a firm to truly develop a customer service organization and culture would fall here. Finally, overhauling or re-creation is the dramatic shift that occurs in reaction to major external events. Often there is a crisis situation that forces the change—thus, the emergence of low-cost carriers is forcing traditional airlines to re-create what they do. Likewise, many domestic consumer manufacturing firms, facing brutal price competition, are having to radically realign themselves and their activities in the marketplace.

The impact of the change increases in intensity as we move from minor alterations and fine-tuning to changes that require us to reorient and re-create the organization. Not surprisingly, these latter forms of change are much more difficult and time-consuming to effectively manage because of the increasing complexity attached to them. They also have a greater impact on individuals who must reorient themselves correspondingly.

An examination of the history of British Airways (BA) provides a classic example of a single organization facing both incremental and discontinuous change while both anticipating issues and being forced to react.[52] Todd Jick's case study describes the crisis of 1981. BA's successful response in the 1980s was revolutionary in nature. The slow decline in the 1990s occurred as the systems and structures of BA became increasingly incongruent with the new deregulated environment and the successful competitors that were spawned by it. Since then, major upheavals in international travel have pushed BA into a reactive mode, and the results of management's attempts to develop new strategies are unclear. A strike in the summer of 2003 created more uncertainty for the firm.[53] While profits have recovered, pension obligations and a new boss continue that uncertainty.[54]

Nadler and Tushman's model raises the question, "Will incremental change be sufficient or will radical change be necessary in the long run?" Suffice it to say that this question has not been answered. However, the Japanese provided a profound lesson in the value of incremental, daily changes. Interestingly enough, it was a lesson the Japanese industrialists learned from North American management scholars such as Duran and Deming. When you observe employee involvement and continuous improvement processes effectively employed,[55] you also see organizational team members that are energized, goal directed, cohesive, and increasingly competent because of the new things they are learning. They expect that tomorrow will be a little different from today. Further, when more significant changes have to be embraced, team members are likely to be far less resistant and fearful of them, because of their earlier experiences with facilitating change within group structures. Organizational change appears to be easier for them.

Many of us tend to think of incremental/continuous change and discontinuous/radical change as states rather than a perspective or a spectrum of change size. From the organization's point of view, a departmental reorganization might seem incremental. However, from the department's perspective, it will seem discontinuous and radical. As Gareth Morgan puts it,

> A mythology is developing in which incremental and quantum change are presented as opposites. Nothing could be further from the truth ... True, there is a big difference between incremental and quantum change when we talk of results (but) incremental and quantum change are intertwined. As we set our sights on those 500% improvements, remember they're usually delivered through 5, 10, and 15% initiatives.[56]

Morgan's observations deserve more than passing attention. We saw earlier that organizations seek stability and predictability and attempt to manage things with that goal in mind. Incremental changes help to advance that agenda and assist the organization in adjusting to the internal and external pressures that build over time. However, is it inevitable that there will be times when incremental changes are simply not sufficient to cope with the magnitude of needed alterations? If so, this leads to the need for more revolutionary and radical changes.

The perception of the magnitude of the change lies in the eye of the beholder. Incremental changes at the organization level may appear disruptive and revolutionary at a department level. However, as noted earlier, those who are accustomed to facing and managing incremental change on a regular basis will likely view more revolutionary changes in less threatening terms. Those who have not faced and managed change will be more likely to view even incremental changes as threatening in nature.

Organization members need to learn to accept and value the perspectives of both the adaptor (those skilled in incremental change) and the innovator (those skilled in more radical change).[57] As a change agent, personal insight regarding your abilities and preferences for more modest or more radical change is critical. The secret to successful organizational growth and development over time lies in the capacity of organization members to embrace both approaches to change at the appropriate times and to understand that they are, in fact, intertwined.

Planned Changes Don't Always Produce the Intended Results

To this point, we have accepted the premise that change—even radical reconstruction—is becoming a necessary prerequisite to organization survival. However, successful change is extremely difficult to execute. Many types of change initiatives have failed: reengineering, total quality management, activity-based costing, joint optimization, strategic planning, and network structures.[58] If we were to fully consider these failure rates when designing interventions or acquisitions, we might be too terrified to act.

As one manager put it, "The opportunity has turned out to be 10 times what I thought it would be. The challenges have turned out to be 20 times what I thought they were!"[59] Unfortunately, inaction and avoidance are no solution. Maintenance of our organization's status quo typically does not sustain or enhance competitive advantage, particularly in troubled organizations. Delays and halfhearted efforts that begin only after the problems are critical increase the costs and decrease the likelihood of a successful transformation. As Hamel and Prahalad put it, "No company can escape the need to re-skill its people, reshape its product portfolio, redesign its process and redirect resources."[60] Organizations that consistently demonstrate their capacity to innovate, manage change, and adapt over the years are the ones with staying power.[61]

Hamel and Prahalad believe that restructuring and reengineering, on their own, do little to increase the capabilities of the firm. These two "r's" increase profitability and can enhance competitiveness, but "in many companies . . . re-engineering (and restructuring) . . . are more about catching up than getting out in front."[62] Hamel and Prahalad argue that companies need to regenerate their strategy and reinvent their industry by building their capacity to compete.

Radical solutions both terrify and fascinate managers. Often managers are comfortable with relatively small technological fixes as the source of products, services, efficiency, and effectiveness. However, they tend to fear interventions that seem to reduce their control over situations, people, and outcomes. We argue that when we embrace technology but not people, we pay a steep price. We reduce the likelihood that the change will produce the desired results, and we fail to take advantage of the collective capacity of organization members to improve operations, products, and services. To say the least, this practice is extremely wasteful of human capacity and energy, causing it to atrophy over time. And recent evidence suggests that true productivity increases come only when the forms are reorganized, business practices reformulated, and employees retrained. Investment in infrastructure alone is insufficient.[63]

Table 1.5 highlights common sources of difficulty that change initiators, implementers, and facilitators face when attempting to implement planned changes. There are many external factors that can frustrate or divert progress in unanticipated and undesirable directions, but this table does not address these. They will be dealt with later in the book. This table focuses on ways in which change leaders can act as their own worst enemies, self-sabotaging their own initiatives. They stem from predispositions, perceptions, and a lack of self-awareness. The good news is that they also represent areas that a person can do something about if they become more self-aware and choose to take off their blinders.

What Is Required to Be a Successful Change Leader?

Successful change leaders will balance keen insight with a driving passion for action. They will have that sensitivity to the external world described above and will be skilled "anticipators" of that world. They will have a rich understanding of organizational systems—their system in particular—and the degree to which continuous or strategic

Table 1.5   Common Managerial Difficulties in Dealing With Organizational Change

1. Managers are action oriented and assume that other rational people will see the inherent wisdom in the proposed change and will learn the needed new behaviors (or managers will be able to replace them).

2. Managers assume they have the power and influence to enact the desired changes, and they underestimate the power and influence of other stakeholders.

3. Managers look at the transition period as a cost, not an investment.

4. Managers are unable to accurately estimate the resources and commitment needed to facilitate the integration of the human dimension with other aspects of the change (e.g., systems, structures, technologies).

5. Managers are unaware that their own behavior (and that of other key managers) may be sending out conflicting messages to employees and eventually customers.

6. Managers find managing human processes unsettling (even threatening) because of the potential emotionality and the difficulties they present with respect to prediction and quantification.

7. Managers simply lack the capacity (attitudes, skills, and abilities) to manage complex changes that involve people.

8. Managers' critical judgment is impaired due to factors related to overconfidence and/or group-think.

Source: Russo, J. E., & Shoemaker, P. J. H. (1992). Managing overconfidence. *Sloan Management Review,* (*33*)2, 7–18.

changes are appropriate. They will have a deep understanding of themselves, their influence and image, in their organizational context. They will have personal characteristics—a tolerance for ambiguity, emotional maturity, self-confidence, comfortableness with power, a keen sense of risk assessment, a need for action and results, and persistence grounded in reasoned optimism and tenacity. Finally, while they will be curious and have a strong desire to learn, they will have a deep and abiding distrust of organizational fads and will recognize the negative impact of fad surfing in organizations.[64] Change leaders who see the world in simple, linear terms will have more difficulty creating effective change.[65]

Change leaders will understand the rich tapestry that forms the organizational culture. They understand the stakeholder networks that pattern organizational life. They recognize the impact and pervasiveness of organizational control systems (organizational structures, reward systems, measurement systems). They know and can reach key organization members—both those with legitimate power and position and those with less recognizable influence. And they understand which tasks are key at *this* point in time, given *this* environment and *this* organizational strategy.

Successful change leaders will know their personal skills, style, and abilities and how those play throughout the organization. Their credibility will be the bedrock on which change actions are taken. Because change recipients will be cynical and will examine how worthy the leaders are of their trust, change leaders must be aware of their personal blind spots and ensure that these are compensated for whenever needed.

Change leaders will also embrace the paradoxes of change:

They will be involved in both driving change and enabling change. Change leaders will understand the need to persist and drive change through their organization. Without such determination, organizational inertia will slow change and other organizations will race ahead. At the same time, change leaders will recognize that getting out of the way might be the most helpful management action to be taken. When those around a manager are following a passion, the best thing might be to help in whatever way possible or to provide resources to make things happen.

They will recognize that resistance to change is both a problem and an opportunity. Change resistance happens in planned change. Overcoming such resistance is frequently necessary to make progress. However, change leaders recognize that there are often good reasons for resistance—the person resisting is not just being difficult or oppositional, they often know things or have perspectives that cast doubt on the wisdom of change. Change leaders need to recognize this and work actively to overcome this paradox.

Good change leadership focuses on outcomes but is careful about process. Far too often change programs get bogged down because a focus on results leads change implementers to ignore good process. At the same time, too much attention to process can diffuse direction and lead to endless rituals of involvement and consultation. Good change leaders learn how to manage this balance well.

Change leaders recognize the tension between "getting on with it" and "changing directions." The environment is always changing. We can always modify our objectives and respond to the environment. But if we do this repeatedly, we never settle on a design and direction and as a result will fail to get things done. Keeping the focus on the overall long-term direction while making adjustments can make sense. The trick is to understand and balance this tension.

Change leaders understand the need to balance patience and impatience. Impatience may prove very helpful in overcoming inertia and fear, generating focus, energizing a change, and mobilizing for action. However, patience can also prove a valuable tool in reducing tension and establishing focus and direction, by providing time for people to learn, understand, and adjust to what is being proposed.

Finally, today's change leader knows that in today's global competition, what matters is not the absolute rate of learning but rather the rate of learning compared to the competition. And if your organization doesn't keep pace, it loses the competitive race.

The Outline of This Book

In this chapter, we have introduced organizational change and our orientation to that change. Throughout the book, we take an applied action orientation, encouraging readers to embrace change to make things happen. To facilitate this, we will lay out a sequence of steps and tools that systematically lead people to successful organizational change.

Chapter 2 begins this by providing a process model for change. This model focuses on how change agents can think about change: the need for change, the gap between what exists and what is desired, and the action steps necessary to close that gap. Chapter 3 deals with what needs to change by providing organizational models that give us a better understanding of organizations. Chapter 4 deals with both the need for change and the creation of a compelling change vision. Chapters 5, 6, 7, and 8 expand this understanding by examining organizational systems and structures, stakeholders, change recipients, and change leaders. Chapter 9 takes these insights to develop logical, systematic action plans. Finally, Chapter 10 focuses on the measurement of change to enable us to better manage the change process, consider what changes have been accomplished, and help identify what is needed next.

Summary

This chapter defines organizational change as a planned alteration of organization components to improve the effectiveness of the organization. It outlines the change roles that exist in organizations: change initiator, change implementer, change facilitator, and change recipient. Change leaders or change agents could be any of the four roles: initiator, implementer, facilitator, or recipient.

The forces that drive change today are classified under social, demographic, technological, economic, and political forces. Environmental shifts create the need for change in organizations and drive much organizational change today. Four types of organizational change—tuning, reorienting, adapting, and re-creating—are outlined.

Finally, the nature of change leaders is discussed, and some of the paradoxes facing them today are examined.

Glossary of Terms

Organizational Change—For the purposes of this book, organizational change is defined as a planned alteration of organizational components to improve the effectiveness of the organization. By organizational components, we mean the organizational mission and vision, strategy, goals, structure, process or system, technology, and people in an organization. When organizations enhance their effectiveness, they increase their ability to generate value for those they are designed to serve.

The **Open Systems View of Organizations** looks at the web of structures, systems, and processes that underpin the organization. They are interrelated and affect one another and are also influenced by what happens in the external environment they are situated in.

Organizational Development is based in psychology and is focused on bringing about organizational improvement, with primary attention to human factors.

Roots of Change—Organization Development Perspective

Small-Group Training focuses on creating change by improving self-awareness and the group's dynamics.

Survey Research and Feedback uses the analysis and feedback of sophisticated surveys, combined with employee participation, to create the need for change.

Action Research encourages the use of action, based on research, in continuous cycles. In essence, one learns by doing, followed by observation, doing, and more learning.

Sociotechnical Systems Change focuses on the interaction between the sociological and technical sub-systems of the organization and describes change in more holistic terms.

Change Management is based in a broad set of underlying disciplines (from the social sciences to information technology), tends to be strategy driven, with attention directed to whatever factors are assessed as necessary to the successful design and implementation of change.

Change Initiator—The person who identifies the need and vision for change and champions the change.

Change Implementer—The person responsible for making certain the change happens, charting the path forward, nurturing support, and alleviating resistance.

Change Facilitator—The person who assists Initiators, Implementers, and Recipients with the change management process. They identify process and content change issues and help resolve these, foster support, alleviate resistance, and provide other participants with guidance and counsel.

Change Recipient—The person who is affected by the change. Often the person who has to change his or her behavior to ensure the change is effective.

Change Leader or Change Agent—These two terms are used interchangeably in the text to describe those engaged in change initiator, implementer, or facilitator roles. All those involved in providing leadership and direction for the change fall within their broad coverage.

PEST Factors—The political, economic, social, and technological environmental factors that describe the environment or context in which the organization functions.

Macro Changes—Large-scale environmental changes that are affecting organizations and what they do.

Incremental/Continuous Change—Organizational changes that are relatively small in scope and incremental in nature. They may stem from the tuning of existing practices or represent an incremental adaptation to environmental changes.

Discontinuous/Radical Change—Changes that are broad in scope and impact and that may involve strategic repositioning. They usually occur in anticipation of or reaction to major environmental changes and are discontinuous in that they involve changes that are NOT incremental in nature and are disruptive to the status quo.

END-OF-CHAPTER EXERCISES

TOOLKIT EXERCISE 1.1

Change Roles in Your Organization

Pick an organization that you are familiar with—an organization you have worked for either full-time or part-time, a school you have attended, or a voluntary association you know such as a baseball league.

Who plays what change roles in the organization? How do individuals work at those roles? What are the consequences of their roles? How do individuals achieve effective change? Take a moment to identify people in your organization who play each of the roles: change recipient, change initiator, change facilitator, and change implementer.

What roles do you play? Think of a time when you have been involved in change. What role did you play? How comfortable were you with each of those roles?

Think back on your personal organizational history. When did you fill the role of:

Change Initiator?

Change Implementer?

Change Facilitator?

Change Recipient?

How did each of these roles feel? What did you accomplish in each role?

TOOLKIT EXERCISE 1.2

Analyzing Your Environment

Select an organization you are familiar with. What are the key environmental issues affecting the organization? List these and their implications for the organization.

The organization:

Political Factors:

Implications:

Economic Factors:

Implications:

Social Factors:

Implications:

Technological Factors:

Implications:

Legal Factors:

Implications:

Notes

1. A version of this quote can be found in Wheatley, M. J. (1994). *Leadership and the new science* (p. 55). San Francisco: Berrett-Koehler.

2. Miles, R. H. (1997). *Leading corporate transformation.* San Francisco: Jossey-Bass.

3. Personal experience of the authors.

4. Plato, 427 BC–347 BC. www.wikiquote.org.

5. Chenglieh, P. (1985). In search of the Chinese style of management. *Malaysian Management Review, (20)*3. http://mgv.mim.edu.my/MMR/8512/851210.Htm. Professor of Management, Tsing Hua University of China, Deputy Secretary General China Enterprise Man Professor.

6. French, W., & Bell, C. (1995). *Organization development* (5th ed., ch. 3). Englewood Cliffs, NJ: Prentice Hall.

7. Worren, N., Ruddle, K., & Moore, K. (1999). From organizational development to change management. *Journal of Applied Behavioral Science, (35)*3, 273–286.

8. 2000 change management conference: Increasing change capability. *The Conference Board of Canada,* November 2000. See also Higgs, M., & Rowland, D. (2005). All changes great and small: Exploring approaches to change and its leadership. *Journal of Change Management, (5)*2, 121–151.

9. Miller, D. (2002). Successful change leaders: What makes them? What do they do that is different? *Journal of Change Management, (2)*4, 359–368. See also Higgs, M., & Rowland, D. (2005). All changes great and small: Exploring approaches to change and its leadership. *Journal of Change Management, (5)*2, 121–151.

10. Pfeffer, J., & Sutton, R. (1999). Knowing "what" to do is not enough: Turning knowledge into action. *California Management Review, (42)*1, 83–108.

11. Appelbaum, S. H., Henson, D., & Knee, K. (1999). Downsizing failures: An examination of convergence/reorientation and antecedents—processes—outcomes. *Management Decision, (37)*6, 473–490.

12. Van Yperen, N. W. (1998). Informational support, equity and burnout: The moderating effect of self-efficacy. *Journal of Occupational and Organizational Psychology, (71)*1, 29–33.

13. Gordon, J. (1993). Employee alignment? Maybe just a brake job would do. *Wall Street Journal,* February 13, 1989, as reported in T. Jick, *Managing change.* (1993). Homewood, IL: Irwin.

14. Pfeffer, J. (1995). Managing with power: Politics and influence. *Executive Briefings.* Stanford Videos.

15. Oshry, B. (1990). Finding and using a manager's power to improve productivity. *National Productivity Review, (10)*1, 19–33.

16. Mishra, K. E., Spreitzer, G. M., & Mishra, A. K. (1998). Preserving employee morale during downsizing. *Sloan Management Review, (39)*2, 83–95.

17. Hamel, G. (2000). *Leading the revolution.* Boston: Harvard Business School Press.

18. Personal communication, 2003.

19. Sovereign creditworthiness could be undermined by age-related spending trends. (2006, June 5). *Standard and Poor's.* www.standardandpoors.com.

20. Half a billion Americans? (2002, August 22). *The Economist.*

21. Sovereign creditworthiness could be undermined by age-related spending trends. (2006, June 5). *Standard and Poor's.* www.standardandpoors.com.

22. Davis, I., & Stephenson, E. Ten trends to watch in 2006. (2006, January). *McKinsey Quarterly; The Online Journal.* http://www.mckinseyquarterly.com/article_print.aspx?12=18&L3=30&ar=1734.

23. Ibid., p. 5. Also, Davis, I., & Stephenson, E. (2006, January). Ten trends to watch in 2006. *McKinsey Quarterly; The Online Journal*. http://www.mckinseyquarterly.com/article_print.aspx?12=18&L3=30&ar=1734.

24. Revell, J. GM's slow leak. (2002, October 28). *Fortune;* Why GM's plan won't work . . . and the ugly road ahead. (2005, May 9). *BusinessWeek Online;* Maynard, M. (2006, March 7). US: G.M. to freeze pension plan for salaried workers. *New York Times,* Business Section.

25. Marketing to the old: Over 60 and overlooked. (2002, August 8). *The Economist* (print ed.).

26. Suro, R., & Singer, A. (2002, July). *Latino growth in metropolitan America.* Center on Urban & Metropolitan Policy and The Pew Hispanic Center, The Brookings Institution.

27. Ibid., Table 4, p. 9.

28. Galt, V. (2002, October 16). What am I, chopped liver? *The Globe and Mail* (print ed., p. C1).

29. Diamond, J. (1999). *Guns, germs and steel* (p. 322). New York: W. W. Norton & Co.

30. Thomas, D. A. Diversity as strategy. (2004). *Harvard Business Review, (82)*9, 98–109.

31. The technology quarterly. (2002, September 21). *The Economist.*

32. Livingston, A. D., Campbell, C. J., Wagner, E. K., & Ghaza, P. (2005). Biochip sensors for the rapid and sensitive detection of viral disease. *Genome Biology, (6)*6, 112. Published online May 26, 2005.

33. Roberti, M. (2002, September 30). Big brother goes behind bars, high-tech tracking in prisons. *Fortune.*

34. Nanotechnolgy, The Tech Outlook. (2002, Spring). *BusinessWeek Online.*

35. Wieners, B. 8 Technologies that will change the world (2002, June). *Business 2.0,* 79.

36. Yergin, D., & Stanislaw, J. (2002). *The commanding heights: The battle for the world economy* (p. 405). New York: Touchstone.

37. Mullen, R. Security issues lurking beyond VolP's cost saving promise. (2005, March 11). *Silicon Valley/San Jose Business Journal* (print ed.). Http://www.sanjose.bizjournals.com/sanjose/stories/2005/03/14/smallb3.html.

38. Violino, B. Fortifying supply chains. (2004, July). *Optimize,* 73–75. http://www.optimizemag.com/article/showArticle.jhtml?articleId=22101759; Huyett, W. I., & Viguerie, S. P. (2005). *McKinsey Quarterly, 1,* 46–57.

39. Davis, op. cit., p. 2.

40. Others believe otherwise. Note the protests whenever the WTO meets, for example.

41. False heaven. (1999, July 29). *The Economist* print ed.).

42. Farrell, D., Khanna, T., Sinha, J., & Woetzel, J. R. (2004). China and India: The race to growth [Special edition]. *McKinsey Quarterly,* 110–119.

43. Transparency international corruption perceptions index. (2002). *Transparency International Secretariat,* Otto-Suhr-Allee 97–99, 10585 Berlin, Germany.

44. Bribe payers index. "(2002)."? *Transparency International Secretariat,* Otto-Suhr-Allee 97–99, 10585 Berlin, Germany.

45. Senge, P., & Carstedt, G. (2001). Innovating our way to the next industrial revolution. *Sloan Management Review, (42)*2, 24–38.

46. Ibid., p. 31.

47. Barkema, H. G., Baum, J. A. C., & Mannix, E. A. (2002, October). Management challenges in a new time. *Academy of Management Journal, (45)*5, 916–930.

48. Weick, K. E., & Quinn, R. E. (1999). Organizational change and development. *Annual Review of Psychology, 50,* 361–86.

49. Savyas, A. (2005, March 8). Intel points to convergence. *Computer Weekly,* 12.

50. Lam, J. (2005, March 1). Continental sets tentative accords for cutting costs. *Wall Street Journal* (Eastern ed.), p. A2.

51.   Charlemagne. (2005, January 27). Low-cost founding fathers: How cheap air flights are bringing Europeans together. *The Economist* (print ed.).

52.   Peiperl, M. (2003). Changing the culture at British Airways; and British Airways update, 1991–2000. In T. Jick, *Managing change* (pp. 26–44). New York: McGraw-Hill Higher Education.

53.   One strike and you're out: British Airways. (2003, August 2). *The Economist*, 64.

54.   Lining up for profits: After losing $43 billion in five years, airlines are at the beginning of a massive boom. (2005, November 10). *The Economist* (print ed.).

55.   An interesting comparison of TQM and employee involvement is contained in Lawler, E. E., III. (1994). Total quality management and employee involvement: Are they compatible? *Academy of Management Executive*, (*8*)1, 68–76.

56.   Drawn from Morgan, G. Quantum leaps, step by step (1994, June 28). *Globe and Mail*, p. B22.

57.   Kirton, M. J. (1984). Adaptors and innovators—why new initiatives get blocked. *Long Range Planning*, (*17*)2, 137–143; Tushman, M. L., & O'Reilly, C. A., III (1996). Ambidextrous organizations: Managing evolutionary and revolutionary change. *California Management Review*, (*38*)4, 8–30.

58.   The life cycle of interventions is readily apparent in the management literatures. First comes the concept, accompanied or followed closely by examples of successful implementation. Next are cautionary notes, examples of failure, and remedies. As the luster fades, new approaches emerge in the literature and the process recurs, hopefully building upon earlier learning. For example, see Miles, R. E., & Snow, C. C. (1992). Causes of failure in network organizations. *California Management Review*, (*34*)4, 53–72.

59.   Helyar, J. (2003). *Wall Street Journal*, August 10, 1998. In T. Jick, *Managing change* (p. 503). New York: McGraw-Hill Higher Education.

60.   Hamel, G., & Prahalad, D. K. (1994, October). Lean, mean and muddled. *Globe & Mail Report on Business Magazine*, 54–58.

61.   Voelpel, S. C., Liebold, M., & Streb, C. K. (2005, March). The innovation meme: Managing innovation replicators for organizational fitness. *Journal of Change Management*, (*5*)1, 57–69.

62.   Hamel, G., & Prahalad. C. K. (1994, October). Lean, mean and muddled. *Globe & Mail Report on Business Magazine*, 57.

63.   The new "new economy." (2003, September 13). *The Economist*, 62.

64.   Shapiro, E. C. (1996). Fad surfing in the boardroom: Managing in the age of instant answers. Cambridge, MA: Perseus.

65.   Higgs, M., & Rowland, D. (2005). All changes great and small: Exploring approaches to change and its leadership. *Journal of Change Management*, (*5*)2, 121–151.

CHAPTER 2

Change Frameworks for Organizational Diagnosis

How to Change

> *Change is.*
>
> —Anonymous

Chapter Overview

- The chapter differentiates between **how** to create organizational change, its process, and **what** should be changed, the content. Change leaders must understand both.
- Lewin's classic "Unfreeze-Change-Refreeze" model is discussed.
- A modified version of Beckhard and Harris's change management process is developed in depth. The model asks: (1) What is going on in the organization? (2) Why change? (3) What is the gap between the existing and desired states? (4) How do we close this gap? and (5) How do we manage during the transition phase?
- These explicit models will help change leaders articulate their implicit models of how organizations work and how to change their organizations.

Sweeping demographic changes, technological advances, geopolitical shifts, and pressures to be more sensitive to our physical environment are combining with concerns for security and organizational governance to generate significant pressure for organizational change. Awareness of the political, economic, sociological, and technological (PEST) aspects of any organization's external environment forewarns us of the need to pay attention to such factors. Furthermore, it alerts managers to a need to have some means in place to attend to their organization's relevant environmental contexts and to decide whether they need to take some action as a result.

McDonald's is one of many organizations scanning its environment and making decisions about changes to its products as a result of changes in its environment.

Des Moines, Iowa—McDonald's Corp. is working on an alternative for parents who wish their kids would lay off the french fries in Happy Meals—apple slices that can be dipped in caramel. William Whitman, a spokesman for the fast-food giant, Tuesday said a three-market test of the item, called "Apple Dippers," is planned for later this summer. Whitman said it would cost an additional 20 cents to exchange the fries for Apple Dippers. The test comes as food manufacturers and restaurant chains are under increased pressure to improve nutritional values. McDonald's restaurants in the United Kingdom already offer fresh fruit in Happy Meals. Those in Sweden have baby carrots and juice as options.[1]

McDonald's provides an interesting example for change managers to think about. To make these product decisions, McDonald's managers had to evaluate environmental shifts and assess their relevance to the organization's strategy and the probability of its continued effectiveness. The healthy food trend meant that McDonald's needed different products and different approaches to developing and sustaining their markets. McDonald's managers examined the trends and decided that product changes were necessary. We can take the McDonald's example and generalize it to all managers—changes in the internal and external environments provide the important clues and cues for change leaders. Diagnosing and understanding those clues and cues provide the basis for the vision and direction for change.*

In this chapter, we focus on the process of organizational change. **How** may a change agent think about making change happen? The chapter sets out frameworks that can help you understand organizations and how you might approach the change challenge. These frameworks, or models, provide explicit, if somewhat simplified, views of organizations. Using these models makes it easier to understand how our organizations work. Then, with this understanding, change is easier to plan and promote.

Each of us has ideas about how our own organization works. For some of us, this *model* is explicit—that is, it can be written down and discussed with others. However, many managers' views of organizational functioning are complex, implicit, and based on their personal experiences. Deep knowledge and intuition about the functioning of your organization is invaluable. However, such knowledge or intuitions are intensely personal, difficult to communicate, and almost

---

*For more on McDonald's changes, see Big Mac's makeover. (2004, October 14). *The Economist*; Reuters: http://www.reuters.com/newsArticle.jhtml?storyID=8253292; and Carpenter, D. (2006, January 24). *McDonald's profit sizzles*. Associated Press.

impossible to discuss and challenge rationally. As a result, we argue for a much more explicit approach. This chapter and the next will provide you with the means to articulate your unspoken models of how organizations work and to use other models to think systematically about how to change your organization.

Van de Ven and Poole categorize four types of change models that managers use implicitly when thinking about change.[2] These models are (1) life cycle, (2) evolutionary, (3) debate-synthesis, and (4) goal setting.˙ In other words, many of the assumptions that managers make about change can be captured by these four types. Life-cycle change models assume that there is a prescribed series of steps or stages that must happen. The metaphor of a biological organism helps to explain the concept. Biological entities are born, grow, mature, decline, and die. Organizations can be viewed similarly. Under a life-cycle perspective, change involves natural, linear steps and is beyond the control of the changing entity. That is, change happens.[3] An organization starts as an entrepreneurial venture, grows, becomes mature, and eventually declines under this model.

Evolutionary change is based on Darwin's notions of survival. The conflict between types results in a natural selection process as the organism adapts to its environment. This recurrent competition notion can be seen in some of the literature describing organizational populations and survival rates.[4] Venture capital firms often operate under these assumptions. They know they must fund a number of start-ups. Many or most start-ups will fail, but the few that are significant successes make up for the failures. The conflict between North American automakers and the Japanese ones can also be seen in this context.

Debate-synthesis models suggest that there are opposing sides that are in conflict. When the conflict is resolved, synthesis equilibrium is established until another conflict arises. An example in an organization could be the conflict between an older and younger generation in a family business. Eventually, the younger generation takes over. This new stability lasts until a further conflict occurs. Other examples could involve departments with conflicting goals or the organization itself with goals that collide with other organizations' intentions.[5]

Goal-setting change involves defining gaps between where the organization is and where you want it to be, setting goals and taking action to reduce those gaps, and measuring the results to identify new gaps. Since this book is oriented around planned organizational change, much of the content, particularly the action-planning chapter, relies heavily on goal-setting-related themes. Because of environmental changes, there is a recurring pattern of goal setting followed by action.[6] Many performance management systems are based on a "gap-analysis/goal-setting/action" frame.

These frameworks capture how organizations change, or at least how we think about such change. The personalities of many managers often lead them to follow a goal-setting frame. Their need for power and achievement drives them to action to close perceived gaps in performance and effectiveness. Life-cycle and evolutionary change have an element of fatalism (what will happen will happen)

˙Goal setting is named teleological in the literature. Debate-synthesis is called dialectic.

about them, which does not fit easily with an active hands-on approach to change.

While the goal-setting model is simple and appealing, Higgs and Rowland found in one study that having a simple, linear model of change is not as effective as having a more complex view.[7] They claim that there is "relatively clear evidence to support the view that recognition of the complexity of change is important to the formulation of effective change strategies."[8] In this chapter, we move from a relatively simple model of change, Lewin's, to a more complex one, a modification of Beckhard and Harris's model.

While the analysis of the change is complex and often emergent, the type of actions that change leaders may take can be categorized fairly simply into eight sets: (1) changes in mission/purpose; (2) redefinition of strategy; (3) shifts in objectives or performance targets; (4) alterations in organization culture, values, or beliefs; (5) organizational restructuring; (6) technology changes; (7) task redesign; and (8) changing people.[9] Changes in mission/purpose and strategy involve a realignment of the organization with its environment. Alterations in the organization culture, values, or beliefs (including its informal systems and processes) may just be a shift in the internal workings of the organization but could also be in response to environmental demands. Organizational restructuring includes the redesign of formal systems and processes and is perhaps the most common perspective on organizational change where new reporting relationships are developed. Technology changes and task redesign are changes inside the organization affecting how the work is accomplished. People can be changed by altering key competencies; shifting attitudes, values, and/or perspectives; or through adding and/or removing key people from the organization. These broad categories of action suggest simplicity. We caution change leaders against assuming this as the dynamic nature of the organization, and its components make it far from simple.

Can We Differentiate How to Change From What to Change?

The complexity of change can be simplified somewhat by recognizing that there are two distinct aspects of change that must be addressed in any change management situation. Managers must decide both **how** to change and **what** to change. In this chapter, we look at **how** to change, using Lewin's three-stage model of organizational change and a version of Beckhard and Harris's model of change. Then, in the next chapter, we develop an appreciation of **what** to change, describing three models of organizational analysis: the McKinsey 7-S model, the Burke-Litwin model, and Nadler and Tushman's congruence framework. As well, we outline Sterman's systems dynamic model, Quinn's "Competing Values Model," Greiner's model of organizational growth, and Nadler and Tushman's differentiation of incremental and strategic change.

The example below highlights the difference between the **how** and **what** of change. Imagine that you are the general manager of a major hotel chain and you received the following customer letter of complaint:

A Letter of Complaint

Dear Sir,

As a customer of yours, I wanted to provide you with our experiences at ATMI, your London, England, hotel.[*] Since that time, I have reflected on my experience and finally decided I needed to provide you with feedback—particularly given your promise on your Web site—the Hospitality Promise Program.

My wife and I arrived around 10 PM after a flight from North America and the usual tiring immigration procedures, baggage check, and finding our way to your hotel. The initial greeting was courteous and appropriate. We were checked in; the desk person asked if we wished a room upgrade. After I clarified that this would cost money, I declined that proposal.

We then went to our room on the 3rd floor, I believe, and discovered it was a disaster, totally not made up. I phoned the switchboard and was put through to reception immediately. There were profuse apologies and we were told that someone would be up immediately with another key.

Within 5 minutes, someone did meet us with a key to a room on the 5th floor, a quick, fast response. However, when we got to the new room, it was not made up!

Again I phoned the switchboard. The operator said, "This shouldn't have happened. I will put you through to the night manager." I said that was not necessary, I just wanted a room. However, the operator insisted and I was put through to the night manager. Again, there were profuse apologies and the manager said, "This shouldn't have happened. I will fix this and get right back to you." I indicated that I just wanted a room—I didn't want the organization fixed, just a room. The manager repeated, "I will get right back to you."

We waited 5, 10, 15 minutes. Inexplicably, the manager did not return the call even though he said he would.

Finally, around 20 minutes later, I phoned the switchboard again. I said we were waiting for a room and that the night manager had promised to call me back. The operator said, "This is probably my fault as I was doing work for the assistant manager." I did not and do not understand this part of the conversation, but again, I was told that they would call right back. Again, I repeated that "I just need a room."

I waited another 5 minutes—it was now 11PM at night and we were quite tired—there was no return phone call.

My wife and I went down to reception and after a brief time were motioned forward by the person who registered us initially. I explained that we needed a room. He said, "You were taken care of. You got a room." I stated that no, I did not have a room, I just had two rooms that were not made up and we needed a clean one for the night.

Again there were profuse apologies. The reception person then said, "Excuse me, just for a moment, so I can fix this." I said, "Really, I just would like a room." The person at the reception desk went around the corner and began to berate someone working there. This went on for several minutes. He then returned to his station, called me forward again, apologized again, and located a third room for us. As well, he gave us coupons for a complimentary breakfast.

(Continued)

---

[*] The hotel name is disguised.

(Continued)

> This third room was made up. It was "more tired" than the previous rooms, but it was clean and we were delighted to find a spot to sleep.
>
> In the middle of the night, as is the norm in many places, the invoice was delivered to our room. To our surprise, a 72 £ charge was added to the price of the room for a "room change."
>
> Of course, early the next morning, I queued up to discuss this charge. The same reception person was still on duty. He motioned me forward and then immediately left to open up all the computer stations in the reception area. He had a tendency to not make eye contact. This may have been a cultural phenomenon, or it may have been his dismay at having to deal with me again. I cannot say.
>
> I showed him the invoice. He said, "Oh, there will be no charge for that room." I said that I was concerned as the invoice did show the charge. He said, "It is taken care of." I said, "Regardless, I would like something to prove that there will not be another charge to my credit card." After one further exchange and insistence on my part, he removed the charge from my invoice.
>
> My wife and I had a pleasant breakfast and appreciated it being complimentary.
>
> We thought that you would want to know of our experience. Customer service is a critical part of the hospitality industry, and I am certain that ATMI would wish feedback on experiences such as these.
>
> I am interested in such things and look forward to your reply.
>
> Yours truly,

The list of things done wrong and the organizational issues that exist are extensive. Identifying this list of **what** needs attention is relatively easy. The desk clerk has twice assigned rooms that were unmade. This implies system issues—the system to capture the state of the rooms is either nonexistent or not working. One wonders if there is a quality-control person signing off on rooms. There are managerial issues—a manager promises to get back to a customer and doesn't. There are organizational culture issues—the excuses by the switchboard operator and yelling by the reception person. There are further system issues or customer service problems as indicated by the 72 £ charge for a room change. There are some service-training issues—the responses by the reception person were variable. He was quick to send up a second room key but left the customer standing while he turned on computers. And he was reluctant to reverse the extra room charge. There is some hint that there may be other cultural issues that are pertinent. Perhaps you could list more things that are organizationally wrong.

What is not clear is **how** the general manager should proceed with needed changes. If the computer system for tracking room availability does not exist, then it is relatively simple to create and install one. However, if the system exists but is not being used, how does the general manager create change? Closer supervision might work, but who can do that and who will pay for it? Even more difficult are the organizational and other cultural issues. The norm appears to be to make excuses and to "berate" others when things go wrong. You can tell people that these behaviors are inappropriate, but how does one persuade employees not to respond this way—particularly when employees have been acting in this way and found it satisfactory? And how will the general manager know if and when the changes are implemented? Is there a system in place to track customer satisfaction? Employee satisfaction? Are these systems worth the cost they impose on the organization?

Clearly, managers must know what needs to change. However, how to go about making change happen requires careful thought and planning. The models provided below will help us think about change and how we can make it happen.

How to Change

As suggested above, many leaders know what they need to achieve; they just don't know how to get there. An examination of competitor initiatives and accomplishments provides cues as to what is needed—but moving one's own organization to successfully addressing these needs often defeats us.

Why is it so difficult to accomplish change? One of the common causes lies in practices that have proven effective in the past, and this is often referred to as the "failure of success." Organizations learn what works and what doesn't. They develop systems that exploit those learnings. They establish rules, policies, procedures, and decision frameworks that capitalize on the success. Further, they develop patterned responses (habits), assumptions, attributions, and expectations that influence the ways they think about how the world works.[10] These beliefs and engrained responses form a strong resistant force, which encourages organizations and people to maintain old patterns regardless of feedback or input suggesting that they are inappropriate. In many respects, this is where the questions of what to change and how to change intersect.

Charles Handy describes some of these dilemmas by examining the pattern of success over time.[11] As he so aptly describes, too often "by the time you know where you ought to go, it's too late." He describes a "sigmoid" curve that outlines where you should begin changing and where it becomes obvious you need to change. (See Figure 2.1.) This curve depicts the outcomes or outputs of a system—a curve that increases during early-stage development and growth phases, flattens at maturity, and shifts into decline over time. Consider the path tracked by successful technological innovations. Once they can demonstrate their value to key early adopters, sales take off, as others see the benefits of the innovation and begin to adopt it as well. Patents and proprietary knowledge provide some protection, but over time, competitors launch similar products, profit margins become squeezed, and sales growth slows due to increased competition and the level of market saturation. This leads to a flattening of the curve, referred to as the maturity phase. Decline follows, as the market becomes increasingly saturated and competitive, and this decline accelerates with the arrival of a new, disruptive innovation that attracts customers away from the existing product. Think of what happened to the VCR players when DVD players arrived on the scene, and consider how prices have fallen for DVD players in the face of competition.

The costs of change are real, while the benefits of change are uncertain. By holding off investing in change, you can improve your profit in the short run. However, if conditions change and you fail to adjust in a timely fashion, you can quickly find yourself lagging your competitors, scrambling to adapt and catch up. If you wait too long, you may find it impossible to do so.

By the time the system reaches point A, the need for change is obvious, but it may also be too late for the organization to survive without experiencing significant trauma. Positive planned change needs to be commenced sooner in the process—before things deteriorate to a crisis or disaster stage. Unfortunately, change typically comes with costs that appear to lessen the positive outcomes in the short run. As many of us know, convincing anyone that they should incur short-run costs for longer-run benefits is a difficult selling task—particularly when things are going well. This is depicted as the shaded space between the solid and dotted lines beginning at B in Figure 2.1. The costs of change appear certain and are tangible. But the benefits are uncertain and often vaguely defined. The time after point B is a time of two competing views of the future—and people will have difficulty abandoning the first curve (the one they are on) until they are convinced of the benefits of the new curve. In concrete terms, creating change at point B means you must convince others, including your boss, about the wisdom of spending time and money now for an uncertain future return.

How to change is difficult because identifying and demonstrating the need for change is not obvious. If you have a system that appears to be working, why on earth change for an unproven new one that promises something better? Many of us have experience adopting new technologies or approaches that fail to deliver on the explicit or implied promises—is it any wonder we are skeptical?

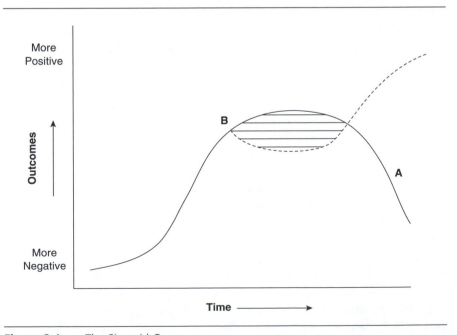

Figure 2.1   The Sigmoid Curve

Lewin's Model of Change

Sixty years ago, Kurt Lewin[12] wrote about the problem of how to bring about change. He described a three-stage model of change:

Unfreeze ⟶ **Change** ⟶ **Refreeze**

Lewin stated that we need to understand the situation and system as a whole as well as the component parts that make up the system. Before change can occur, an unfreezing process must happen within that system. This focuses on the need to dislodge or upend the beliefs and assumptions of those required to participate in the change, and engage in systemic alterations to the status quo. The unfreezing process might occur because of some crisis. For example, a major government cutback to a funded social service agency or new competitive products that are attacking the major profit producers of a private enterprise might be sufficient shocks to these organizations to "unfreeze" the patterns. In both examples, the balance in the system must be disrupted or broken in order to permit conditions for change to develop. Some top managers even talk about "creating a crisis" in order to develop the sense of urgency around change.[13]

When this unfreezing occurs, the systems and the people who are embedded in those systems become susceptible to change. Systems and structures, beliefs and habits, become fluid and thus can shift easier.

To illustrate Lewin's model, refer back to the Letter of Complaint above and examine the comments below.

Unfreeze

Will this letter of complaint be sufficient to "unfreeze" the general manager and move her to action? If this is a single letter, it is highly unlikely that change will occur. If complaints are common for this hotel, this may be seen as just one more letter in a pile—background noise in running the hotel. The letter suggests that this may be an airport hotel in London, England. The location of the hotel may be such that customer service shortfalls may not make a difference to occupancy rates, whereas minimizing costs would be crucial to the hotel's profitability. In all the above scenarios, no unfreezing would take place.

However, this letter may represent an initiative that captures managerial attention and promotes action. The general manager may be facing declining occupancy and view this letter as a signal of where problems may lie. A comparison with other hotels on measures of profitability and customer satisfaction may demonstrate a dramatic need for change that the letter foreshadowed. In this situation, the general manager's views on the existing system are more likely to be unfrozen and she would be ready to change.

Note that the unfreezing must take place at many levels. The general manager may be ready for change, but the person at the reception desk may think things are just fine. His perceptions need unfreezing as well! The integration and interdependence of systems and people require us to think about the unfreezing of the organizational system as a whole.

Change

Assume that the general manager accepts the need to improve the specific system that indicates that rooms are ready. She must now decide on what needs to be changed to bring about the needed improvements. She could begin by using the options mentioned earlier in this chapter. For example, she could hire a quality-control person who is charged with inspecting and certifying all rooms before they are entered into the system as "ready to use." Some computer programming may need to be done so that rooms are flagged when they are ready or not ready, and the quality-control person may be given responsibility for managing that flag subsystem. The quality-control person will have to be recruited, hired, and trained if he or she cannot promote an appropriate person from within. Once the room-quality system has been designed and needed procedures are in place, all reception people will have to be trained. This change could be done participatively with the involvement of staff, or the general manager could have it designed and order its implementation. The change process would be reasonably complex, involving a number of people and systems.

During this phase, there would be considerable uncertainty. The new system could well be ready before the quality-control person is hired and trained. Or the reverse—the person may be hired and trained but the room-quality system is not ready. Employees may see opportunities to improve what is being proposed and make suggestions regarding those improvements. Regardless of the specifics, the system would be in flux.

In addition to a quality-control person alternative, many other possible solutions exist—some may be much more participative and job enriching than the above. The questions the general manager must answer are which alternatives will be selected, why, and how will they be implemented (who will do what, when, where, why, and how).

Refreeze

Once the changes are designed and implemented, employees will need to adapt to those changes and develop new patterns and habits. The new flag system will alter how those at reception and in housekeeping do their work. They may informally ask the quality-control person to check certain rooms first, as these are in higher demand. The general manager will follow up to see how the system is working and what people are doing. New reporting patterns would be established, and the quality-control person may begin passing on valuable information to hotel maintenance and housekeeping regarding the condition of particular rooms. At this point, the system settles into a new set of balances and relative stability. With this stability comes refreezing, as the new processes, procedures, and behaviors become the new "normal" practices of the organization.

What do we mean by this notion of relative stability and predictability that comes with refreezing? It stems from the observation that organizational systems, composed of tasks, formal systems, informal systems, and individuals, develop an interdependent state of balance over time called homeostasis. Perturbations or shifts in one part of the system are resisted, or swings away from balance are countered and balance is regained. As we have suggested earlier, managers may introduce change initiatives only to have those initiatives fail because of existing systems, processes, or relationships that work against the change. Planned changes in structures and roles may be seen as decreasing the power and influence of informal groups, and these groups may react in complex ways to resist change. For permanent change, a reconfiguration is needed and new points of balance or homeostasis developed.

The image of a spider's web can help to picture the phenomenon. That is, view the organization as a complex web of systems, relationships, structures, assumptions, habits, processes, and so on that become interconnected and interdependent over time. Altering one strand of the web is not likely to significantly alter the pattern or overall configuration. What is needed is a breaking of many interconnected items—the "unfreezing" in Lewin's terms.

This simple model has stood the test of time. Change agents find it useful both because of its simplicity and because it reminds us forcefully that you can't expect change unless the system is unfrozen first! We may need other, more complex models of the organization to be able to think through what must be unfrozen and changed, but Lewin forces us to recognize the rigidity that comes with stability and interconnectedness within existing systems, relationships, and beliefs.

However, several concerns prevent us from wholeheartedly embracing this model. First, the model suggests that change is simple and linear. The reality is that change tends to be complex, interactive, and emergent. Second, the creation of the need for change deserves more attention. It is not merely moving individuals away from their assumptions that are required. Rather, they need to have a vision of a future desirable state. Finally, the model implies that refreezing is acceptable as a frame of mind. This seems problematic. In today's rapidly changing world, organizations find that pressures to adapt mean they are never "refrozen"—and if they are, they are in trouble. However, at one level, leaders know that without a degree of refreezing, that is, some stability, efficiency is impossible. Without stability, it is difficult to establish coherence of direction and purpose. Each organization member could claim primacy of direction for their local area without regard for an overarching vision (particularly, as they do know local conditions best). On the other hand, organizations that freeze too firmly may fail to thaw when new markets and customers appear. They may refuse to incorporate feedback in making useful changes. Continuous improvement programs may appear faddish, but they reflect a realistic view of what is needed for a dynamic environment because they enhance an organization's adaptive capacity. Thus, there is concern with the image created by the word "refreeze" as this is likely too static a condition for our long-term organizational health.*

Beckhard and Harris's Change Management Process

An alternate model of **how** to change is outlined by Beckhard and Harris.[14] We have modified their model slightly as shown in Figure 2.2. The change process begins with an assessment of why change is needed. Following the recognition of the need for change, change leaders are faced with the task of defining and describing

---

*In discussions with managers and students, we often find the phrase "regelling" to have some appeal as a compromise between total fluidity and excess rigidity.

the desired future state in contrast to the organization that exists now (the present state, in their terms). This allows leaders to identify the gap between where we are now and where we want/need to go. The vision, contrasted against the present, allows change leaders to address how they propose to close the gap. This discussion of how to get from the present to the desired future state represents the action or implementation stage. The final step in the change process is to manage the transition. As presented, this model provides a framework for this into which the chapters in this book can be slotted.

Determining the need for change is the unfreezing part of Lewin's model. Note that Beckhard and Harris challenge the assumption that change is required—that is, they ask, "Is there a choice about making a change?"

The Initial Organizational Analysis
Understanding the Forces for Change and the
Organizational Situation
Chapter 3

Why Change?
Determining the Need for Change, Determining the Degree of
Choice About Whether to Change, Developing the Change Vision
Chapter 4

Defining the Desired Future State	 Gap Analysis – Chapters 5, 6, 7, 8 	Describing the Present State

Action Planning and Implementation
Assessing the Present in Terms of the Future to Determine the
Work to Be Done, Doing the Work
Chapter 9

Measuring the Change
Designing Effective Control Systems
Chapter 10

Figure 2.2   The Change Management Process

Many assume that the need for change is easily recognizable, obvious, and evident from the environment. Of course, nothing could be further from the truth. Things are as they are because people have found that, in general, the situation works. Perhaps it is a statement of the obvious, but if people were really dissatisfied with the situation, they would recognize the need for change strongly enough to begin searching for some form of action. If they are prepared to accept or tolerate the status quo, then they are likely in one of four conditions: (1) relatively satisfied, (2) not dissatisfied to the point of being provoked to look for alternatives, (3) believing that nothing can be done, or (4) believing that the costs of changing are such that they choose not to make those changes. Many workers at Wal-Mart have voiced unhappiness about such things as pay levels and hours of work for years, but most have never taken the steps required to unionize. The costs and risks seem to have been viewed as too high relative to the potential benefits.*

It is important to understand that the perception of the need for change is exactly that—a perception. And just because we hold that perception does not imply that others will hold it or agree. We often fall into the trap of thinking that the other person simply does not understand the situation. Thus, we believe that if we explain things, that person will change his or her mind. That might work, but the other person could well have a different set of objectives or a set of experiences, assumptions, and beliefs that leads him or her to a different view of the situation. As a result, it is dangerous to assume that what they want (or believe needs to be done) will be achieved by achieving the change you want. They may see no need for change or believe that they don't have to change.

Managers sometimes make the mistake of assuming that once they are convinced, others will easily understand and be convinced as well. Even if others in the organization could be convinced, it ignores the lag that will occur as the message moves through the organization. For example, senior managers may well be aware of a significant competitor threat, a new product, or service delivery model that will hit the market soon. They begin to respond with change plans. However, most employees may not have any awareness of what the competitor is doing. From their perspective, things are fine—in fact, they may well be very busy meeting current product demand. Asking them to think about changing what they are doing will be a hard sell. The lags in information flows require change managers to recognize the need to bring employees along with them, persuade them of the importance of changing now—not continuing with previous patterns and procedures.

The description and analysis of the present state and the definition of the future state lead to a gap analysis—an image of the differences in specific terms. Too often, our analysis results in nonhelpful gaps. For example, a manager may conclude that morale is low. This description does not lead easily to action plans. Instead, the root causes of the morale issue need to be understood. Why is morale low? Is it pay? Is it management style? Working conditions? Each of these descriptions is more powerful and useful in moving to change, and each suggests a different course of action.

---

*One of the risks is that Wal-Mart will close the store that unionizes. The closing of the Jonquiere, Quebec, store is an example of this. You can find more on this at: http://www.economist.com/displaystory.cfm?story_id=3706455.

In Chapter 3, several frameworks are described that will help us to develop a more sophisticated checklist for organizational diagnosis. If we get the diagnosis wrong, it is highly likely that we will take inappropriate action. The gap analysis allows change leaders to more clearly address the question of why change is needed and to articulate the vision for the change (Chapter 4). The analyses of formal and informal dimensions of the organization, the various stakeholders, the recipients of the change, and the change agents themselves (Chapters 5 to 8) help to complete our understanding of the situation and the gaps we need to pay attention to.

Beckhard and Harris's "getting from here to there" and "managing during the transition state" phases of the change model involve action planning and implementation. These topics are dealt with explicitly in Chapter 9. Action planning appears linear and straightforward. Unfortunately, in today's complex organizations, most change is neither linear nor straightforward. Managing change while one is operating the organization is difficult. As a result, transition management is an important subject.

Understanding the success of the particular organizational changes we are trying to achieve depends on our ability to measure such change. In Chapter 10, we examine the difficulty of change measurement and suggest how change agents can improve in this area.

If we return to our hotel case example, we can apply the Beckhard and Harris model.

Why Change?

The general manager who received the above letter may have very good reasons for not responding and changing. The hotel may be in the midst of a computer systems modification and is overwhelmed with other changes. Or the general manager may have a tracking system that indicates that most hotel guests are very satisfied and that this is an unusual occurrence. Or there may be personal reasons—the general manager may have a set of cost objectives and view change as leading to increased costs. Or the general manager may see himself or herself as exiting the organization and believe that such change efforts could have an adverse impact on her career.

Even if the general manager accepts the need for change, the employees may not. At this point in time, they know nothing about the letter. They likely feel that their performance is good and no change is needed. They may have a manager who doesn't follow up on directives, and thus, they could believe that no action is necessary. Or they may be involved with learning other aspects of their job and don't have time to attend to these customer issues. The challenge for the change leader is to articulate "why change" in ways that increase the likelihood that key stakeholders will understand why change is needed. Gap analysis and visioning are important tools in addressing this challenge.

Gap Analysis

The present state has several dimensions that could be addressed. The following gaps seem to exist:

- A gap in information of room readiness between what is actually ready and what is showing
- A gap between what managers say they will do and what they actually do
- A gap between the appropriate bill and the bill given to the customer
- A gap between the desired interpersonal relationships between employees and that which seems to exist
- A gap between the desired handling of hotel guests and that which occurred

Each of these gaps could require different action plans for change. And careful analysis may demonstrate that there is a more fundamental underlying issue that needs to be dealt with. For example, if the organization culture has evolved to one that is not focused on customer care and relationships, the individual gaps may be difficult to correct without a more systematic approach. This gap analysis then needs to be used by change leaders to frame the vision for the change. This vision plays a critical role in helping others understand the gap in concrete terms by contrasting the present state with the desired future state.

Getting From Here to There

This section in the Beckhard and Harris model is similar to the "change" section under Lewin's model. Here, we specify the specific actions needed for the change. Several planning tools could be used (see Chapter 9). If we, as general manager in our hotel case example, decided that the issue to be tackled was a computer systems issue, we may plan the following steps:

- Discuss the need for change, the gap analysis, and the vision for change with involved staff to develop a consensus concerning the need for action.
- Form a users' task force to develop the desired outcomes and usability framework for the new system.
- Contact internal information systems specialists for advice and assistance on improving the organization information system.
- Identify the costs of systems changes, and decide which budget to draw on or how to find the capital funds needed for the system changes.
- Approach Purchasing in order to submit a "request for proposal" so that systems suppliers could bid on the proposed system.
- Contact Human Resources to begin staffing and training plans.

This example list lays out the actions needed to accomplish the change. In Chapter 9, tools will be identified that will help you in your planning. For example, there are tools to assign responsibilities for different aspects of projects, and others will ask you to consider contingency plans.

In Chapter 9, you are also asked to consider how to manage during the transition. Organizations usually don't stop what they are doing because they are changing! That is, if you are manufacturing something, that often has to continue in spite of modifications being made to assembly lines. In our hotel example, rooms will need to be made up, allocated, and assigned while the system is being modified.

In particular, receptionists will need to ensure a seamless transition from the old to the new system. In many system changes, parallel systems are run until the bugs in the new system are found and corrected. Hotel receptionists need to be trained on the new system. How and when that will be done in this transition is part of the managerial challenge during the transition state.

The final aspect of the model deals with the measurement of change and the metrics used in that measurement. How will the general manager know that the changes implemented are working? You can measure inputs easily—the number of hotel receptionists who are trained on the new system. But management will also need to track the number of times rooms are misallocated. This is a more difficult problem because the staff could be motivated to pervert such a system if the results of the system could put the staff in a negative light.

Models such as the Beckhard and Harris one improve change managers' abilities to plan and implement organizational change. They provide a straightforward framework that lays out a linear process for change. It helps us to think in causal terms—if I do this, it will result in what I want. Underlying the model are goal-setting assumptions flowing from the gap analysis. The power dynamics of an organization may be such that a top-down, traditional managerial approach is not appropriate. Perhaps a more decentralized, emergent approach would work better. Careful analysis will be needed to recognize the biases inherent in the model.

At the same time, the model risks having change managers oversimplify the challenge. Cause-effect analysis is complex because organizations are nonlinear, complex entities. An overreliance on straightforward linear thinking can lead to errors in judgment and unpleasant surprises. Organizations are more surprising and messier than we often assume. The subsequent chapters of this book, particularly Chapter 3, will help change leaders to avoid thinking simplistically.

Coordination and control of change appears straightforward using the Beckhard and Harris model. The reality is that organizations often undertake multiple change projects simultaneously. For example, a factory may be shifted toward a focused factory model while a continuous improvement process is being developed, while other parts of the organization are being restructured. Different managers are working on different change projects to make things better. Under such complexity, control is difficult and likely involves multiple layers of authority and systems.

The models of Chapter 3 will help us to think in more complex, anticipatory ways to avoid those negative surprises. Nevertheless, outlining clear stages in the change process by using the Beckhard and Harris or a similar model assists in our own logic.

Summary

This chapter outlines four categories of models used to understand thinking about organizational change: life cycle, evolutionary, goal setting, and debate-synthesis.

Successful change management therefore requires attention to both process and content. To focus on this, the chapter differentiates **what** needs to be changed from **how** change should be accomplished.

Lewin's unfreeze-change-refreeze model is described as a process model of change and is applied using a customer complaint letter received by a hotel general manager. The Lewin model emphasizes the need to unfreeze the organizational system before change is possible. While the Lewin model is straightforward and simple, these characteristics make the model less suitable for the complex, dynamic emergent processes that organizational change normally entails.

As a result, a modified version of the Beckhard and Harris model is presented as a process model that will help change leaders to plan how to make organizational changes. The model forms the framework for this book, and the chapter sequence is laid out in the model. The Beckhard and Harris model is elaborated, and the same hotel case situation is analyzed to enable the reader to contrast the two models.

Glossary of Terms

The How and What of Change

The **"How"** of change relates to the process one uses to bring about change.

The **"What"** of change relates to the assessment of what it is that needs to change—in other words, the content of the change.

Sigmoid Curve

The Sigmoid Curve describes the normal life cycle of something. If we think of it in terms of a product or service, the initial or lag phase is the time at which it attempts to gain traction through market acceptance. Once it becomes accepted, a period of growth occurs, characterized by acceleration, and than deceleration as the market becomes more competitive and it reaches maturity. As competition mounts and the market becomes saturated, decline ensures. Decline can also be precipitated by the arrival and acceptance of a superior product or service. The only things that will differ are the slope and height of the curve and the time required to get to different points on the curve.

Lewin's Model of Change: Unfreeze-Change-Refreeze

Unfreeze—The process that awakens a system to the need for change—in other words, the realization that the existing equilibrium or the status quo is no longer tenable.

Change—The period in the process in which participants in the system recognize and enact new approaches and responses that they believe will be more effective in the future.

Refreeze—The change is assimilated and the system reenters a period of relative equilibrium.

Beckhard and Harris's Change Management Process

Organizational Analysis—The stage in the process used to understand the forces for change and the reasons why the organization is performing as it currently does.

Why Change—The stage of the process in which the need for change is determined and the nature of the change or vision is characterized in terms others can understand.

Gap Analysis—The identification of the distance between the desired future state and the present state at which the system operates.

Action Planning and Transition Management—The stage of the process in which plans are developed for bridging the gap between the current mode of operation and the desired future state and the means by which the transition will be managed.

Measuring the Change—The measures you will use to help you know where you are in the change process and the level of success achieved.

END-OF-CHAPTER EXERCISES

TOOLKIT EXERCISE 2.1

Interview a manager who has been involved in change in his or her organization. Ask him or her to describe the change, what he or she was were trying to accomplish, and what happened.

After the interview, describe the processes of the change. That is, **how** did the managers work to make things happen? Who did they involve? How did they persuade others? What resources did they use?

As well, describe **what** was being changed. Why were these things important? How would it help the organization?

Which was more important: how things were changed or what was changed?

Be prepared to share the results of your interview with others.

Notes

1. Retrieved July 16, 2003, from http://www.theday.com/eng/web/newstand/re.aspx?reIDx=056526B1-C70A-41FE-85EF-8D977206E591.

2. Van de Ven, A. H., & Poole, M. S. (1995). Explaining development and change in organizations. *Academy of Management Review, (20)*3, 510–540.

3   Szamosi, L. T. (1999, June). *A new perspective on the organizational change process: Developing a model of revolutionary change and a measure of organizational support for revolutionary change* (p. 15). Unpublished PhD Thesis, Carleton University.

4. Carroll, G., & Hannan, M. T. (1989). Density delay in the evolution of organizational populations: A model of five empirical tests. *Administrative Science Quarterly, (34)*3, 411–430.

5. Szamosi, op. cit., p. 19.

6. Burke, W. W. (2002). *Organization change: Theory and practice* (p. 148). London: Sage.

7. Higgs, M., & Rowland, D. (2005, June). All changes great and small: Exploring approaches to change and its leadership. *Journal of Change Management, (5)*2, 121–151.

8. Op. cit., p. 144.

9. Part of this categorization is drawn from Robbins, S., & Langton, N. (2003). *Organizational behavior* (3rd ed., p. 530). Toronto: Pearson Education Canada.

10. Sull, D. N. (1999). Why good companies go bad. *Harvard Business Review, (77)*4, 42–52.

11. Handy, C. (1994). *The age of paradox* (p. 50). Boston: Harvard Business School Press.

12. Lewin, K. (1951). *Field theory in social science.* New York: Harper & Row.

13. A recent discussion of Lewin's contribution can be found in Rosch, E. (2002). Lewin's "field theory as situated action in organizational change." *Organization Development Journal, (20)*2, 8–14.

14. Beckhard, R., & Harris, R. T. (1987). *Organizational transitions: Managing complex change.* Reading, MA: Addison-Wesley.

CHAPTER 3

Change Frameworks for Organizational Diagnosis

What to Change

There is nothing so practical as a good theory.

—K. Lewin

Chapter Overview

- Change leaders need to understand both **how** to go about change (the process of making the change) and **what** changes need to be made (the content of those changes). Understanding **what** needs to change is the focus of this chapter. Knowing **what** to change depends on your skill in organizational diagnosis.
- Change leaders' abilities to determine **what** needs changing require them to have a clear organizational framework that they can use for analysis. They need to understand how complex and interactive organizational components are, how analysis can occur at different levels, and how organizations and their environments will shift over time.
- This chapter outlines three models that provide organizational frameworks: the McKinsey 7-S model, the Burke-Litwin causal model, and Nadler and

---

Tushman's organizational congruence model. While each of these models is useful, this book uses the Nadler and Tushman model as its framework because it balances the complexity needed for organizational analysis and the simplicity needed for action planning and communication.

- The complexity of organizations is highlighted by Sterman's systems dynamics model. It helps us to think of the nonlinear and interactive nature of organizations.
- Quinn's competing values model provides a framework that bridges individual and organizational levels of analysis.
- Organizational changes over time are highlighted by Greiner's five phases of organizational growth model.
- Complexity theory is introduced to highlight the interactive, time-dependent nature of organizations and organizational change.

In Chapter 2, we considered **how** to change. That is, we outlined a process approach to effective change. In this chapter, we deal with the content of change, or **what** to change. Change leaders need to understand and be skilled in both the **what** and the **how.** Differentiating the process from the content is sometimes confusing, but the rather unusual example below will highlight the difference.

Bloodletting is a procedure that was performed to help alleviate the ills of mankind. . . . In the early nineteenth century adults with good health from the country districts of England were bled as regularly as they went to market; this was considered to be preventive medicine.[1]

The practice of bloodletting was based on a set of assumptions about how the body worked—bloodletting would diminish the quantity of blood in the system and thus lessen the redness, heat, and swelling that was occurring. As a result, people seemed to get better after this treatment—but only in the short term. The reality was that they were weakened by the loss of blood. As we know today, the so-called science of bloodletting was based on an inaccurate understanding of the body.

It is likely that bloodletting professionals worked to improve their competencies and developed reputations based on their skills in bloodletting. They worked hard at the **how** aspects of their craft. Advances in medicine prove that they did not really understand **what** they were doing.

Similarly, a highly gifted change leader may be able to shift the organization. But the usefulness of that shift is determined by what they choose as well as how they do it. For example, a change leader might embark on developing a customer relations focus for the organization when it is really the computer system that needs fixing—being nice to customers isn't helpful if you are working with the wrong data. This is highlighted by the following:

Magna Corporation, a $22 billion revenue company, designs, develops, and manufactures automotive components and vehicles primarily for sale to original equipment manufacturers worldwide.

Magna International Inc. had for over 10 years spun off divisions when they reached sufficient size for an initial public offering. This was based on the assumption that focusing on special parts and components achieved efficiencies and higher profits. Clearly, by 2004, this diagnosis was incorrect. As Magna shifted to making complex modules and entire vehicles, the need for coordination soared. This was increasingly difficult given the independence of each spun-off division.[2]

Magna had transformed its organization from 1994 to 2004. They may have been good at **how** they did things, but by 2004, there was concern that **what** to change had shifted. Magna's approach was increasingly out of alignment with what was needed in the marketplace. As has been stressed, effective change leaders need both: a good understanding of **what** to change and excellent skills at **how** to go about achieving those changes. Further, they need to understand that the **what** and the **how** will change over time as the environmental conditions shift.

Bruch and Gerber differentiate the **what** and the **how** into a leadership question: "What would be right? and a management question: "How do we do it right?"[3] They analyze a strategic change program at Lufthansa's from 2001 to 2004. This program successfully generated over one billion euros in sustainable cash flow. While the **how** questions focussed on gaining acceptance of the change—focusing the organization, finding people to make it happen, and generating momentum—the **what** questions were more analytical, asking what change was right, what should the focus be, and what can be executed given the culture and situation. They conclude that a focus on implementation is not sufficient. A clear grasp of the critical needs, the change purpose, or vision is essential.[4]

Underlying our understanding of what needs to change in an organization is the set of assumptions and beliefs about the organization and how it works. In our example above, barber-surgeons believed that the body consisted of humors that needed to be in balance. Bloodletting could restore that balance. Today's physicians have a much more complex, science-based, systemic view of the body. The parallel is clear. Determining **what** should change in an organization relies heavily on the models we have of how organizations work and our skill in using them to identify appropriate, needed changes.

In this chapter, we outline three models that provide a framework for organizations.[*] As well, we provide other models that highlight the need to understand organizational dynamics, the level of analysis, and how organizations shift over time. The models help us to understand the underlying patterns of causation within an organization. Market intelligence gathering, news reports, benchmarking studies, and the like can be excellent sources for ideas, but they are not a substitute for the careful thinking and detailed organizational analysis that is needed.

---

[*]We provide three models as examples of frameworks for analysis. Many other models exist, of course. However, the focus for this book is on helping change leaders to be effective rather than helping them to understand the differences and intricacies of many models. Thus, we limit the numbers covered.

Consider the following account of employee reactions to the introduction of new uniforms for cabin staff at Air Canada. It was part of a rebranding effort for the airline that occurred within the backdrop of bankruptcy proceedings, layoffs, organizational restructuring, and significant compensation and benefit reductions that resulted from the renegotiation of existing collective agreements.

Negative Union Reaction to Air Canada's New Uniforms[†]

New uniforms for Air Canada's flight attendants were introduced in the fall of 2004. Celine Dion's star power was used to showcase the new look—one designed to promote a fresh look as Air Canada emerged from bankruptcy protection. The uniforms were to be introduced in 2005. The union representing the flight attendants, the Canadian Union of Public Employees, filed a grievance. The union reported that their members had not had access to prototypes and they needed more time to consider the matter, including the design, cost, quality, and durability. Previous discussions on uniform changes took up to three years, much more than the one-year introduction Air Canada wanted. The union reported that it was led to believe there would be meaningful consultations around the development of the uniform, but did not believe this had occurred. All of these discussions were in the context of an employee group that had been asked to take pay and benefit cuts and other sacrifices for the airline. Employees viewed the new uniform introductions as lavish, high-handed, and inappropriate in light of all the cutbacks. As well, employees would have to pay for these garments![5]

Air Canada considered the matter a redesign of the uniform and missed the dynamics that gave rise to this predictable reaction. Change agents need to understand the webs of relationships and multiple systems that are involved. They need to recognize the role that external environmental factors and history play. In Air Canada's case, these included customers, competitors, the media, government, and a mature, highly competitive market. The history of sour employee–employer relationships at the airline anchored the perceptions that the parties had of one another. The change agent needs a framework that will help to capture the complex pattern of relationships.

In Chapter 2, a framework for the change management process was presented. In this chapter, we are concentrating on providing frameworks to do both an initial organizational analysis and a deeper gap analysis as shown in Figure 3.1. The gap analysis tools are discussed in more detail in Chapters 5, 6, 7, and 8.

Figure 3.1 allows change leaders to combine the **what** of change with the **how** of change by linking the content of the chapters of the book with the model.

Below are three models that allow change agents or leaders to classify information and to improve their understanding of their organization's dynamics.

[†]Air Canada is Canada's largest domestic and international full-service airline. During 2005, Air Canada and its subsidiary, Jazz, operated, on average, approximately 1,200 scheduled flights each day with a combined fleet of 322 aircraft.

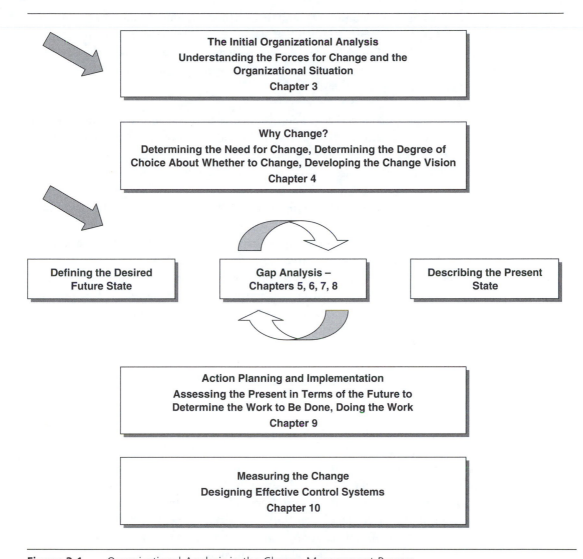

Figure 3.1   Organizational Analysis in the Change Management Process

How Do We Analyze Organizations?

Models of Organizational Analysis

The McKinsey 7-S model, the Burke-Litwin model, and the Nadler and Tushman model are presented. Each model gives a framework for organizational analysis that helps us to structure our thinking and improve the quality of our analysis. While all models are useful, we use the Nadler and Tushman model as a framework for this book. The Nadler and Tushman model has a reasonably complete set of variables and presents them in a way that encourages straightforward analysis. It specifically links environmental input factors to the organizational components and outputs. As well, it provides a useful classification of internal organizational components while showing the interaction among them.

Regardless of model, organizations are assumed to interact with their environments in a complex and dynamic way. This **open-systems perspective** is based on the following assumptions:[6]

- Open systems exchange information, material, and energy with their environment. As such, a system interacts with and is not isolated from its environment.
- A system is the product of its interrelated and interdependent parts and represents a complex set of interrelationships, rather than a chain of linear cause-effect relationships.
- A system seeks equilibrium, and one that is in equilibrium will change only if some energy is applied.
- Individuals within a system may have views of the system's function and purpose that differ greatly from the views held by others.
- Things that occur within and/or to open systems (e.g., issues, events, forces) should not be viewed in isolation but rather should be seen as interconnected, interdependent components of a complex system.

The adoption of an open-systems perspective allows managers to identify areas of misalignment and risk points. Open-systems analysis helps us to develop a much richer appreciation for the current condition of the organization and the plausible alternatives and actions that could be considered for improvement. For example, we know that when systems have been isolated from the environment for extended periods of time, they risk becoming seriously incongruent with the external environment.[7] We also know that when the environment changes rapidly, the results can prove disruptive and, in some cases, disastrous. Consider what happened with the deregulation of electrical utilities[8] in the United States, the impact of the fall of the Berlin Wall on existing East German organizations, or the impact of the removal of protective tariffs on North American garment manufacturers.[9] Each of these led to significant disruption and change. Disruptions can shake organizations to their foundations, but they also have the potential to sow the seeds for renewal (hence the term "creative destruction," coined by Joseph Schumpeter[10]).

In summary, organizations should not be analyzed as if they exist in a bubble, isolated from the environment.

The McKinsey 7-S Model

One way of thinking about organizational components and their alignment with the environment can be found in the McKinsey 7-S model. It was developed by Peters and Waterman when they were consultants with McKinsey, a consulting firm with a strong, positive global reputation.[11] Table 3.1 describes the components of the model.

The seven elements in the model vary in the ease with which they can be understood and evaluated. Structures, systems, and strategy are normally easier to track because they tend to leave a visible trail (e.g., organization charts, documents detailing policies and systems, strategic plans, and implementation strategies). However, there is always the question of whether such data reflect the actual practices of the firm. One of the

Table 3.1   Components of the 7-S Model

Strategy	A plan or course of action undertaken in response to or in anticipation of changes in the external environment. It leads to the allocation of the organization's finite resources to reach specific goals.
Structure	How people and the work are formally organized. It relates to the nature of the formal hierarchy, reporting relationships, and other design factors that go into the formal structure (e.g., span of control, degree of centralization).
Systems	The formal and informal processes and procedures used to flow information and facilitate decision making and action.
Style	How the managers behave (their style, what they pay attention to, how they treat others) in the pursuit of organizational goals. At a more macro level, it means the nature and strength of the culture (norms, shared beliefs, and values) that develops over time and influences behavior.
Staff	How human resources are developed and categorized over time.
Shared Values	Longer-term vision and shared values that shape what organization members do and the destiny of the firm.
Skills	The dominant attributes and distinctive competencies that exist in key personnel and the organization as a whole.

Source: From "Structure is Not Organization," by R. Waterman, Jr. *Business Horizons, 23*(3), copyright © 1980. Reprinted with permission from Elsevier.

reasons that actual practices differ from what is espoused often lies in the influence that the other S's in the model have on what occurs—the skills, staff, style (managerial style and culture), and the shared values and superordinate goals of the organization.

The underlying thesis of the model is that organizational effectiveness is a function of the degree of fit achieved among these factors and the environment. When organizations experience change, the degree of fit is affected, and the challenge of change management is to make changes so that high levels of fit among the seven elements can be achieved.

Changes to one of the components can affect all the other components. Therefore, those implementing change need to understand these components as an interconnected set of levers. For example, if changes are being made to the information system in order to make the organization more customer responsive, those making such changes need to carefully consider the implication on the other components and be prepared to manage the change in a more holistic fashion. Making changes to one of the components while ignoring the implications on the others is a recipe for failure. Enhancing internal and external congruence or alignment is the key to developing organizational effectiveness (see Figure 3.2).

The 7-S approach to organizational analysis tells us first to think about the external environment and the alignment of the key organizational dimensions. The

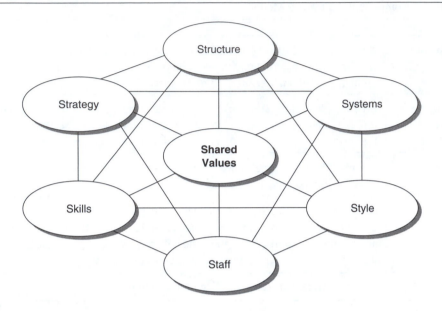

Figure 3.2   The McKinsey 7-S Model

environment does not appear as a variable in the model. However the author's use of the model suggests that the organization should be considered as embedded in the environment. Second, it assists in identifying areas of strong alignment and support and areas of misalignment or nonalignment that will need to be addressed in order to increase the prospects for success. It does not emphasize the informal side of organizations—the politics and power and connections between people based on trust and friendships. Additionally, while it focuses on the interactions among components, it does not explicitly address organizational outcomes.

Table 3.2 provides a template for thinking about change and the components of the 7-S model.[12] First, one must address the question, "Why is change needed?" This may be triggered by competitor actions, public complaints, or the fact that organization members are no longer happy with how the organization is performing. When change is undertaken, the table helps the change leader to identify where congruence and incongruence exist and consider what options are available. Then the impact is considered on other variables. When a change leader uses this model, the goal is to develop a change approach that will lead to high levels of congruence among all the organizational factors and the environment, because this will result in heightened organizational performance.

Applying the Magna Corporation example (from earlier in the chapter) to Table 3.2, the analysis would show that the alignment between its strategy and structure has slipped. The decentralized structure did not fit the strategy requirements of making entire vehicles. Only by creating new coordinating mechanisms could Magna regain alignment. As a second example, values of the Air Canada staff were not aligned with the strategy that management was pursuing. Management believed that new uniforms would represent the revitalized organization as it came

Table 3.2   Identifying Areas of Alignment and Misalignment That Will Need to Be Managed and Actions That Need to Be Taken

Degree of Alignment:	Environment	Style	Shared Values	Skills	Staff	Systems	Structure	Strategy
Strategy								
Structure								
Systems								
Staff								
Skills								
Shared Values								
Style								
Environment								

out of bankruptcy. Staff believed that the uniforms were an unnecessary expenditure. A third example would be the gap between what employees perceived to be the authoritarian management style of many corporate executives and the organization's espoused values of the importance of people and their development.

As the situation changes, the analysis must change as well. Environmental and organizational analysis and alignment represent an ongoing challenge that is facilitated by openness to new ideas, experimentation, organizational learning, and the capacity to implement and refine.

The 7-S model provides change agents with a checklist of critical variables that need to be analyzed. It focuses on their connectedness and the need for alignment among variables. However, the role of the environment is implicit. The model does not suggest a flow from environmental variables to organizational ones that then lead to performance outcomes. As well, while the model emphasizes interconnections and congruence, it does not suggest cause-effect relationships that lead to increased understanding by change agents.

The Burke-Litwin Causal Model

A second model that can be used to analyze organizational situations is the Burke-Litwin causal model.[13] The Burke-Litwin model contains variables similar to other open-system models. However, it seeks to address more directly the question of change management. As Burke notes, the combination of double-headed arrows and multiple variables creates a messy, complex picture; however, it is one that is also reflective of the reality that those interested in change must deal with (see Figure 3.3).

Variables located in the top half of the model (environment, leadership, mission and strategy, and organizational culture) are identified as the ***transformational factors***. Changes to these organizational factors are seen as likely caused by interactions with the external environment. Initiatives in this area are difficult to manage because they challenge core beliefs and assumptions about the organization and what it should be doing. They entail significantly new behavior by organization members and major alterations to other variables in the model. However, when fundamental reorientation and re-creation are a necessity, they may represent the only viable approach to organizational rejuvenation and long-term success.[14]

The remaining variables are identified as the ***transactional factors*** because they are more directly involved in the day-to-day activities of the organization. Changes of an incremental or evolutionary nature can occur without necessarily triggering changes in the transformational factors. We see this in ongoing quality improvement initiatives, management development programs, work realignment, and other incremental interventions aimed at refining and improving internal practices in order to enhance fit, and, therefore, performance.[15]

As Burke notes, transactional factors can also, at times, be used to help trigger changes of a more transformational nature. For example, organizational assessments that lead to alterations in reward systems, team management processes, or a new product/service initiative may trigger questions about culture and strategy. This creates awareness of the need for transformational changes that then could migrate back to other transactional factors. Collins reports that transformations in companies that went from "good to great"[16] often began their journey by trying to sort out how

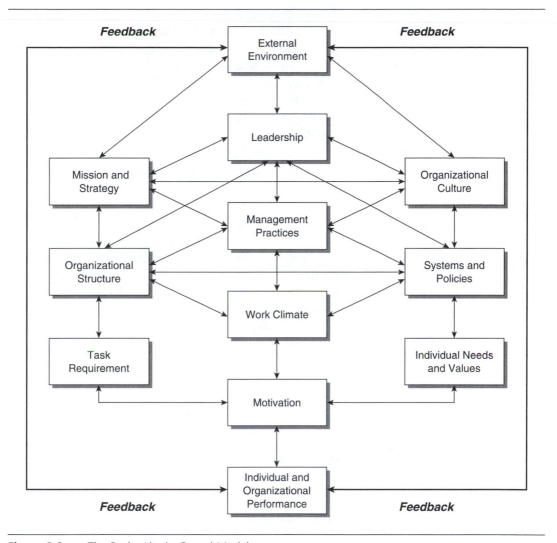

Figure 3.3   The Burke-Litwin Causal Model

Source: From *Organizational Change:* Theory and Practice by W. Warner Burke, copyright © 2002. Reprinted with permission of Sage Publications, Inc..

to better align their internal systems and processes with their customers. They ended up with transformational changes through having the right people engage in disciplined evaluations, followed by a disciplined, steady, committed course of action.[17] As noted elsewhere in this book, an understanding of timing, trigger points, catalysts, and leverage can be used to stimulate self-assessment, organizational learning, and change that have proven very difficult to initiate, energize, and implement.

The Burke-Litwin model enriches our conceptual map of the organization. It provides a complex set of variables that will help explain organizational dynamics. By separating variables into transformational and transactional, the model gives us a way of examining the impact of changes of different variables. However, this complexity makes it more difficult to keep track of all variables and develop clear action plans. Additionally, while it does have both the environment and individual/organizational performance as variables in the model, these are viewed as just 2 of the 12 variables. As a result, there is no apparent flow from environment to organization to performance.

Both the 7-S and the Burke-Litwin models are useful analytical tools. The choice of model is often one of personal preference—both can help a change agent. However, because of the limitations that we see in the 7-S model and the Burke-Litwin model, this book relies on the Nadler and Tushman model, outlined below. In our view, Nadler and Tushman offer a relatively complex organizational analysis while maintaining an action focus.

The Nadler and Tushman Organizational Congruence Model

Nadler and Tushman[18] provide a conceptual scheme that describes an organization and its external environment. The model focuses on how the organization's parts fit or don't fit[19]. We have adapted their model as depicted in Figure 3.4 and use the model as a framework for this book. Inputs are transformed to outputs, but the feedback links make the model dynamic and the components highly interdependent.

The major components of the model are the following:

The External Environment, History, and Resources of the Organization

These include the competitive situation faced by the organization, the trends in society, and other environmental factors that have an impact on the organization's

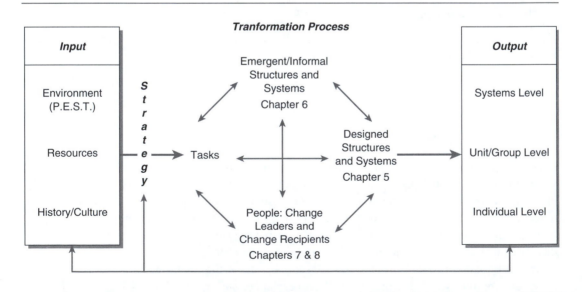

Figure 3.4   The Nadler and Tushman Organizational Congruence Model

ability to be effective and efficient. The past history of the organization provides us with some insight into the organization's culture and its emergent structure. Finally, the human, technological, and capital resources available also impact an organization's strategy and, ultimately, its outputs. In thinking about what to change, all of these inputs may be sources of opportunity and constraint.

The Strategy

An analysis of the organization's competencies, strengths, and weaknesses, in light of the environmental threats and opportunities, leads to the strategy that the organization decides to pursue. Sometimes this is consciously decided on. At other times, it may be a reflection of past actions and market approaches that the organization has drifted into. When there is a gap between what they say their strategy is and what they do (i.e., the actual strategy in use), one needs to pay close attention to the strategy in use.

For change leaders, the change strategy is a critical focus of their analysis. What are the purposes and objectives of the planned change in the context of the organizational strategy?

The Tasks

In order to carry out the strategy, a set of tasks is defined. Some of these tasks are *key success factors* that the organization must execute in order to successfully implement its strategy. An organization's tasks may be described in a very discrete way, listing, for example, the duties of a particular position or, at the polar extreme, the basic functions such as marketing, production, and so on that the organization performs in its transformation processes.

For change situations, change leaders need to think through the shift in key tasks caused by the change. This will enable a specific gap analysis.

The Designed Structure and Systems

This includes any formal structure or system that management creates to produce desired outcomes. Once the tasks are identified and defined, they are grouped to form reporting relationships, the formal organizational chart of roles, responsibilities, departments, divisions, and so on. The purpose of this structure is to enable efficient and effective task performance. The systems of an organization are the formal mechanisms that help the organization accomplish its tasks and direct the efforts of its employees. These include an organization's human resource management systems (recruitment and selection, reward and compensation, performance management, training and development), information systems, measurement and control systems (e.g., budget, balanced scorecard), production systems, and so forth.

For some changes, the formal organizational hierarchy will be a critical variable—particularly if formal power needs to be used. For other changes, the decision process or approval system will be critical in effecting change. Chapter 5 deals with designed systems and structures.

The Emergent or Informal Structure and Systems

The informal relationships among people and groups in the organization and the informal way things get done form the emergent or informal structure. While managers define the tasks necessary to accomplish the strategy and then structure those tasks in formal ways, many things occur that are unplanned or unanticipated. For example, friendly relationships between individuals often ease communications, groups form and provide support or opposition for the accomplishment of tasks, and individuals adapt procedures to make things easier or more productive.[*] The informal system will include an organization's culture, the norms or understandings about "how we do things around here," values (e.g., about the importance of customer service), beliefs (e.g., about why the organization is successful), and managerial style (e.g., a "tough boss" style). Culture is a product of both the organization's history and its current organizational leadership. It acts as a control system in the sense that it defines acceptable and unacceptable behaviors, attitudes, and values, and will vary in strength and impact, depending on how deeply held and clearly understood the culture is. Other elements of the emergent organization that are important to analyze when considering how to create change include power relationships, political influence, and informal decision-making processes.

Change leaders need to recognize the key individuals that can facilitate or block change. Some of them will be from these emergent structures and systems. Identifying those individuals and bringing them onside will be a critical activity. Understanding the emergent structures and systems that have the potential to influence and at times derail change is critical to increasing the likelihood of a successful change initiative. Chapter 6 deals with emergent and informal systems and structures.

People

The people in an organization perform its tasks, using both the organization's designed and emergent systems and structures. It is important that the knowledge, skills, and abilities of each person match what the organization needs. Understanding the individuals in the organization and how they will respond to the proposed change will be significant in managing the change situation. The role of change recipients is dealt with in detail in Chapter 7.

Within every organization, certain *key individuals* are critical to its success. Often we think of the formal leaders as those who are most important in terms of accomplishing the mission, but others may be crucial. These people might have special technical skills or might be informal leaders of a key group of employees. People such as these, acting as change leaders, are described in Chapter 8.

---

[*]For an interesting perspective on the informal system, see either Hutt, M., et al. (2000, Winter). Defining the social network of a strategic alliance. *Sloan Management Review*, (*41*)2, 51–62; or Krackhardt, D., & Hanson, J. R. (1993). Informal networks: The company behind the chart. *Harvard Business Review*, (*74*)4, 104–111.

The Outputs

The outputs of an organization are the services and products it provides to generate profitability or, especially in the case of public sector and nonprofit organizations, to meet other goals. Additional outputs are also important: the satisfaction of organization members, the growth and development of the competencies of the organization and its members, and customer satisfaction (to name just three). These outputs need to be defined and measured as attentively as profitability, return on investment (ROI), or numbers of clients served. The success of the organization in producing desired outputs becomes part of a feedback loop that updates the history and resources components of the model, potentially reinforces or modifies thinking about the organization's strategy, and reinforces or modifies the nature of what goes on in the transformation portion of the Nadler and Tushman model.

In their work, Nadler and Tushman argue three critical things. First, the system is dynamic. This means that your diagnosis will change over time and with different concerns and objectives. Second, the "fit" or congruence between components is significant in diagnosing why the organization performs as it does. And third, the better the "fit" between components, the more effective is the organization. The organizational change challenge is to align the system components to respond to changing external and internal conditions.

The system is dynamic. If your organization's environment shifts, so must your diagnosis. For example, when inflation was running at 1,100% per year in Brazil,[20] the influence of financial executives soared, because financial management played the pivotal role in sustaining the firm. When inflation slowed and stabilized in the range of 10%–20%, power shifted away from finance and toward sales, marketing, and production. If the internal organization alters significantly, your diagnosis must also change. While this may seem like a statement of the obvious, it often goes unobserved in practice. Managers develop patterns of thinking about organizational performance that serve them well, but over time, these patterned approaches may impair their ability to see when conditions change. As a result, the assumptions we make about how things work may come to be just plain wrong!

As systems change over time, different parts of the system become more or less important. For example, if we introduce a new system, training for that system is an issue. Once the training is complete, the significance of that issue is less and our focus shifts. As well, your view of the system depends on who you are and what you wish to diagnose. Thus, a senior executive will examine the entire organization with the factors drawing the greatest attention being the ones critical to achieving his or her aims. A department manager will focus at a more specific level and examine what his or her department must do and how it is structured, and so on.

The "fit" between organizational components is critical. We need to understand the various components of the organization and how they fit together and influence one another. Executives in an organization who restructure and ignore the informal groupings do so at risk. Or if managers create structures to fit several key people and then those people leave, there will be a significant loss of fit between the structural component and the key people within Nadler and Tushman's model. In our earlier example of Magna International, the fit between Magna's strategy and the external environment had been strained as the environment shifted. Magna's strategy of decentralizing operations and spinning them off into independent companies became incongruent with the need for coordination between units. As a result, Magna had to alter its strategy and repurchase those same companies.

Organizations with good fit are more effective. Nadler and Tushman and others argue that effective organizations have excellent "fit" or "congruence" between components. Further, they argue that the strategy needs to flow from an accurate assessment of the environment and respond to the changes occurring in that environment. Similarly, the strategy fits the organization's capabilities and competencies. If all of these are not aligned reasonably, the strategy will fail or be less effective. Inside the organization, the four components (tasks, designed structure and systems, emergent structure and systems, and people) must fit each other. For example, if we hire motivated, skilled individuals and assign them routine tasks without challenge or decision-making opportunities, there will be a lack of fit and productivity will suffer. Or if the strategy demands the adoption of new technology and employees are not provided with the necessary training, fit is lacking. There can be a lack of fit between the emergent structure of the organization and other components. Within categories, elements might not fit. For example, an organization might decide to "empower" its employees. If it fails to adjust the reward system, this lack of fit could easily lead to a failure of the empowerment strategy.

Overall, lack of fit leads to a less effective organization. Good fit means that components are aligned and the strategy is more likely to be attained.

For many managers, the notion of "fit" is easiest to understand as they follow the flow from strategy to key tasks to organizing those tasks into formal structures and processes to accomplish the desired objectives. This is a rational approach to management and appeals to the logic in all of us. At the same time, the reality of organizations as represented by the needs of individuals and by the existing informal structures often means that what appears to management as "logical" and "necessary" is not logical to employees. Managerial "logic" is viewed by employees as against their interests or unnecessary. Peters recognizes the importance of the so-called nonrational aspects of organizations.[21] He argues that managers should tap into the power of teams to accomplish results, that individuals can be challenged to organize themselves to accomplish tasks. Thus, while "fit" is easiest to picture in logical terms, we also need to consider it in terms of the informal system and the key individuals in the change process.

In a typical scenario, changes in our environment lead us to rethink the organization's strategy. This, in turn, results in changes in key tasks and how we structure the organization to do those tasks. In developing our new strategy and in redesigning our organization's systems and structures, managers need to become aware of and understand the influence of key individuals and groups.

This congruence framework helps us in three important ways. First, it provides us with a template to assist us in our organizational analysis. Second, it gives us a way of thinking about the nature of the change process—environmental factors tend to drive interest in the organization's strategy, which in turn propels the transformational processes. These then determine the results. Third, the congruence framework emphasizes that for organizations to be effective, a good fit between all elements in the process is required—from environment to strategy through to the transformation process. Fit is also necessary within the transformation process—a constant challenge for incremental change initiatives such as continuous improvement programs. An emphasis on the internal fit between organizational components often focuses on efficiency. An emphasis on the external fit between the organization and its environment is an effectiveness focus.

An Example Using the Nadler and Tushman Organizational Congruence Model

In Chapter 2, we gave an example of a change that McDonald's restaurants were making to its children's Happy Meals in the United States. This change was in response to environmental pressures perceived by McDonald's. These pressures include an enhanced requirement for nutrition on the part of parents, the threat of litigation and legislation involving "fat" foods, adverse publicity, and the availability of more nutritious alternatives offered by competitors. The pressures and McDonald's slowness in responding led to poor performance over the past several years.

McDonald's stock had declined over 60% in the three years leading up to its Apple Dipper proposal in mid-2003. It reported its first quarterly loss in its 47-year history in 2002. Consumer surveys reported that service and quality were less than its competitors. It had failed at several initiatives, including an attempt at pizza (the container wouldn't fit through drive-through windows), discounting (below cost prices, which upset franchisees), and a standardized restaurant kitchen upgrade that slowed service. McDonald's tried to respond but did not identify solutions that fit with its new environmental demands.

To revitalize itself, the company brought back retired Vice Chairman James R. Cantalupo as CEO. He had steered McDonald's successful international expansion earlier, but faced a very different challenge when he returned in December 2002. That year, 126 franchisees left the chain. Sixty-eight of those were poor performers and were forced out. Simultaneously, McDonald's continued to add stores in less than optimal locations. Sales growth was closer to 2% than to the expected 15%. Investors were unhappy.

Franchisees were finding that margins had declined rapidly. McDonald's discounting practices, new menu items that didn't sell (its low-fat burgers, for example), and expensive renovations did not rejuvenate the company. Customers continued shifting to competitors that offered fresher, better-tasting, and more nutritious food in restaurants that were cleaner and gave faster service than McDonald's. Operating an additional store, the traditional reward to franchisees, was no longer attractive.[22]

Using the congruence model of analysis, we can see that McDonald's had become poorly aligned. The company tried to rely on the ingredients of its past success and either ignored or was slow in responding to changes in both customer desires and its competition. It kept expanding, opening more outlets offering more of the same product. Internally, its aggressive expansion led to a de-emphasis on inspection and grading of restaurants' service and cleanliness. When these tasks were no longer rigorously monitored and rewarded, franchise performance declined on these dimensions. Although individual franchisees had created two of McDonald's best-selling products, the Big Mac and the Egg McMuffin, product innovation by franchisees was discouraged. Corporate product initiatives failed. The outputs, at the store level and corporately, measured by sales, profits, and share price all declined. Individual franchisees left for a chance at success in other restaurant chains or retired after seeing their futures turn bleak. New franchisees were not as profitable as they had been. At the same time, a wave of low-fat, low-carbohydrate diets became popular, and McDonald's suffered adverse publicity from being sued (unsuccessfully, so far) for making people fat.[23]

A different set of tasks became key to matching the changed environment. Management focused on the traditional success keys of quality, service, cleanliness, and value but emphasized the new tasks of innovation and expanding margins. The task of expanding the number of franchises was moved to a nonstrategic position.

Key people were changed. Cantalupo, a long service executive, was appointed CEO, and two individuals were promoted from McDonald's younger corporate staff, one as COO (and who became CEO when Cantalupo died suddenly in April 2004) and the other to develop new products and McDonald's new growth strategy.

Systems were modified and strengthened. The store inspection system became more high-tech with handheld units used to ensure store rounds were made and key performance measures assessed in an expeditious manner. Franchisees were asked for their ideas. Local franchises were encouraged to experiment with pricing and new food types (e.g., teriyaki burgers). New cooking systems were tried.

Cantalupo and his replacement, as longtime employees, knew the informal systems at McDonald's and were able to use these systems to identify key talent and to persuade franchisees to use the new systems and adopt new practices. They were also able to extricate themselves from the immediate past practices that had led to franchise difficulties.

These efforts to introduce new key people, redesign organizational systems, modify the company's strategy, and alter the product mix have shown superb initial success and may reverse McDonald's slide (at the time of the writing of this book, it is too early to tell). However, it is clear that the steps taken have improved the congruence between key variables in at least the short term, and the results are showing this.

The Nadler and Tushman model enables us to think systematically about the organization. It acts as a checklist to ensure that we consider the critical components that must be matched with the strategy and environmental demands. Note that as was pointed out earlier, the system is dynamic. The environment, the people, the competition, and other factors change over time, and part of that change is due to how the components interact with each other. Second, the "fit" between organizational components is critical. McDonald's products, organization, systems, and culture were becoming misaligned with the new environment. Finally, organizations with good fit are more effective. The moves that Cantalupo made improved the fit and led to a turnaround in sales and margins.

Like any living entity, an organization survives by acting and reacting effectively to the external environment it faces. Unless it adjusts with appropriate changes to its strategy and/or its transformational process, it reduces its capacity to thrive. When one part of the organization is changed, the other parts also need to adapt to establish the congruence or "fit" that leads to effectiveness. In managing organizational change, ignoring that the organization is a social system and forgetting to take care of fit is a recipe for failure. Cantalupo and his replacement (Charlie Bell) have begun the realignment at McDonald's. Whether they have made the right changes and enough changes for the long term will be demonstrated by McDonald's performance in the future. Critical to this will be McDonald's ability to innovate and change in the face of shifts in its environment.

Evaluating the Nadler and Tushman Organizational Congruence Model

Are the assumptions made by the Nadler and Tushman organizational congruence model reasonable ones? For example, should strategy always dictate or lead to the organization's structure and systems? While that is one of the traditional views of strategy, it is not unusual to see changes in the transformational process drive alterations to strategy (note our earlier comments on the Burke-Litwin model). Yetton and his colleagues showed that changes in information technology produced changes in strategy as the organization learned about and took advantage of new technology.[24] Thus, while we think that the implied direction of the Nadler and Tushman model is appropriate, any analysis must recognize how dynamic and interactive these factors are. For many change agents, particularly those in middle management, the strategy of their organization will be a given and their role will be to adapt internal structures and systems. Alternatively, they may attempt to influence the strategy directly (e.g., participation in a strategic task force) and/or indirectly (initiate activities that lead to the development of new internal capacities that make new strategies viable).

Has the importance of fit been overstated? We think not. For example, in an investigation into the mixed results achieved by Total Quality Management (TQM) initiatives, Grant, Shani, and Krishnan (1994)[25] found that "TQM practices cannot be combined with strategic initiatives, such as corporate restructuring, that are based on conventional management theories. The failure of one or both programs is inevitable" (p. 25). Thus, they found that the strategy, the structure, and new TQM processes need to fit with each other. More recently, as a result of September 11, 2001, a new superintelligence agency was created, presumably to control the dozen or so intelligence agencies in the United States. However, reports that have emerged suggest that the new intelligence czar has none of the levers needed to do his job—the formal structure has been created but not the systems and processes that give him leverage to be successful.[26] In both these examples, a lack of fit creates issues that impair success.

The need for change may not always be identified by looking only at an organization's environment. Problems surface in a variety of ways. There might be some signs in the organization's outcomes, indicating that some aspect of performance needs to be addressed. Further, there is the question of the magnitude of the change. The organization may decide to change its strategy, its culture, or some other core element. Generally, the more fundamental the change, the more other elements of the organization will have to be adjusted or modified to support the desired change. For example, a change to an organization's culture often creates a domino effect, requiring multiple changes to its structure, systems, and people.

Finally, does better fit always mean more effectiveness? This depends on the measure of effectiveness. In the short run, fit might mean increased profits as the organization reduces costs and becomes efficient. However, an innovation measure might show that fit has led to declining innovation. It can be argued that in the long run, tight congruence in a stable environment leads to ingrained patterns inside the organization. Individuals develop habits and systems and structures are made routine. Such patterns can be very change resistant and can be hugely ineffective when the environment does change radically. Perhaps McDonald's suffered from this prior to Cantalupo's changes. A similar argument would hold that the pace of change is so rapid that an overemphasis on congruence can lead to too static an analysis. Approximations are appropriate given the rate of change—"don't make it perfect, get it acceptable" and move on. Nevertheless, for most of our purposes, the assumption that an increasing fit is a good objective is appropriate.

As with other congruence or alignment-oriented models, the Nadler and Tushman model must deal with the criticism that "too much emphasis on congruence potentially (could have) an adverse or dampening effort on organizational change."[27] The key lies in balancing the need for flexibility and adaptiveness with the need for alignment. This balance point shifts as environmental conditions and organizational needs change. To emphasize the dynamic nature of organizations, this chapter examines Sterman's systems dynamics model.

How Can We View Organizational Systems as Dynamic Models?

Sterman's Systems Dynamics Model[28]

Successful change agents will have a dynamic and complex view of organizations. They will avoid a static and linear view. While the Nadler and Tushman model can be viewed as dynamic, the model does not focus on the nature of dynamic systems. Sterman (2001, p. 10) suggests that "our mental models are limited, internally inconsistent, and unreliable." Managers handle increased complexity by increasing the number of variables considered. Much more important in Sterman's view is the dynamic nature of those variables and the interactions over time between those variables—particularly when those interactions are counterintuitive.

He describes how many will take a linear view of the world—a rational causative model where managers identify a gap between what is and what is desired, make a decision, and take action, expecting "rational" results. If sales are low, we increase advertising and sales will flow! However, because of complex, interactive, nonlinear, and history-dependent variables, this linear view is inaccurate and limiting. What we get are counterintuitive results that are often policy or change resistant. Increasing advertising may lead to competitive responses—others may increase their advertising as well. The result may be increased costs and static revenues. Figure 3.5 provides a framework for Sterman's model.

Often because of the goals we have and our perception of the environment, we make decisions following a rational model. However, we fail to anticipate the side effects of our decisions and often don't comprehend the goals of others and other environmental factors. This leads to different actions by others as they seek to optimize their outcomes.

Consider the following example. We change the incentive structure for employees anticipating that this will lead to higher productivity. However, employees may see increased productivity as likely to lead to layoffs—and thus resist increasing outputs. Or this move to change rewards may lead employees to focus on quantity and neglect crucial quality concerns. This, in turn, may create negative customer reactions that cause management to create new control systems around quality. Such control systems take additional paperwork and effort, which will increase costs and potentially defeat the original objective of increasing productivity.

According to Sterman, many of the issues result from time lags and delays, inventories and buffer stocks in the system, and attribution errors. Thus, in our above example, employees may increase their efforts to generate new sales as the result of the changed rewards. However, there could well be a significant lag before new sales result. Some sales cycles take months and even years before producing

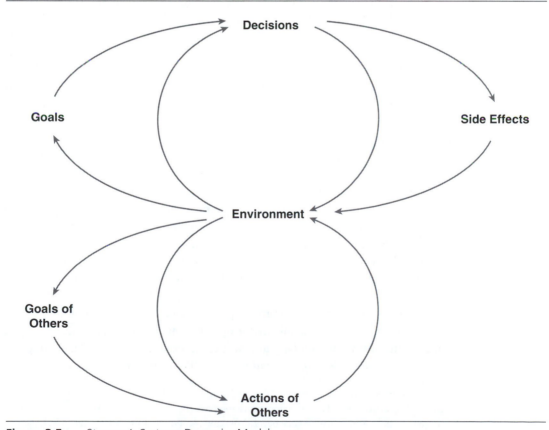

Figure 3.5   Sterman's Systems Dynamics Model

Adapted from Sterman, J. (2001, Summer). Systems dynamic modelling. *California Management Review, (43)*4, 13, copyright © 2001 by the Regents of the University of California. Reprinted by permission.

firm results. Thus, management's initial observation might be that the rewards system change did not work. Small changes in demand may get exaggerated because of inventory buffers that automatically adjust. And finally, humanity's need to attribute cause can create issues. We may assume causal links that don't exist.

Sterman's model heightens our awareness of the complexity involved with change and the challenges involved in developing alignments that will produce desirable results in the longer term and not result in very unpleasant surprises. As such, it builds on the work of Argyris and Schön,[29] identifying the importance of organizational analysis through double-loop and triple-loop learning.* It is also consistent with the work of Senge[30] on how organizations should be designed and managed in order to enhance organizational learning, innovation, and change.

It is too easy to get stuck in old patterns and comfortable ways of thinking because they worked in the past. Life is more predictable when living in a single-loop world. However, when we do so, we fail to open our minds and hearts to environmental threats and opportunities, to new ways of assessing situations, and to potentially more potent approaches to innovation and organizational improvement.

In Figure 3.5, the decisions lead to side effects as well as intended effects. These interact with the environment and the goals of others to create a much more complex set of responses than were anticipated.

In the McDonald's example described earlier, management's early initiatives to increase the number of stores and decrease costs led to a decreased focus on store cleanliness. In the short term, this led to positive outcomes. With more stores, overall revenues increased. With less time and effort spent focusing on cleanliness, costs would be lower and profits higher. However, over time, cleanliness would slide in the absence of sufficient attention; customers would be aware of the lack of cleanliness and would stop going to McDonald's. These side effects would create more pressures for short-term profits as sales declined. The cycle would repeat until management became aware that the cycle was self-defeating.

When a firm lowers price in order to increase market share and profitability, they may do so without thinking through the implications of their decision. Their actions may lead to competitor responses that lower prices further and sweeten sales terms and conditions (e.g., no interest or payments for 12 months, improved warranties) in an effort to respond to their competitor and win market share back. Thus, the planned advantages coming from the price cuts may end up adding few new sales, shrink margins, condition customers to see the product in primarily price terms, and lock the organization into a price-based competition cycle that is difficult to escape.[31]

Sterman reminds us to avoid the trap of thinking in a static, simplistic way. We need to understand the dynamics of the operation. Increasingly, successful managers are resorting to systems thinking and more complex, nonlinear modeling to improve their diagnostic skills. *The Economist* argues, "Better understanding is the key" to

---

*Single-loop learning is essentially adaptive learning within the organization's operation. Internal data are assessed and modifications are made, but the original objectives are not questioned. Double-loop learning goes beyond making incremental modifications and challenges the assumptions, standards, policies, values, and mode of operation that gave rise to the standards and objectives. Triple-loop learning extends this analysis and exploration of possibilities further and questions the underlying rationale for the organization and why it exists.

improved productivity.[32] They provide examples where a deep understanding led to major productivity gains: Procter & Gamble developed a counterintuitive conclusion to distribute their products in "less than full" trucks; Delta Airlines analyzes engine data to anticipate problems and correct potential failures before they occur.

In doing our diagnosis, we need to recognize the assumptions and values we bring that underlie our implicit understandings of organizational dynamics and the nature of the environment and the marketplace. Picture marketing people in a meeting with operations or R&D people—you can imagine the value clashes. Marketing people are often externally oriented, while operations people are concerned with internal dynamics. A model by Quinn helps to frame and understand some of these issues and points to the value of a diversity of perspectives when approaching organizational and environmental analysis.

How Can We Focus on the Different Levels of Organizational Systems?

Quinn's Competing Values Models Framework

How we think about our organization will determine what we think needs changing. The focus or level of analysis will determine many of our perspectives. An economist's view using econometric models will be very different than a psychologist's, which would be at the individual and group levels. Each of the components of the Nadler and Tushman model allows us to include many different models at different levels of analysis. For example, formal structures and systems could include the organizational structure, the formal information system, or the reward system. The informal system would include models of group behavior or of organizational culture. Quinn provides a model that bridges the organizational level with the individual level.[33] His framework is appropriate for both organizational-level and individual-level analysis.

Quinn's competing values model outlines four different ways of thinking about organizations. Each of these ways is based on a set of values and assumptions about the organization and how it works. He argues that two dimensions underlie our view of organizations: an internal-external dimension and a control-flexibility dimension. Underlying our perceptions of organizations are assumptions about the importance of both **internal versus external** and **control versus adaptability** aspects of organizations. These two dimensions form four quadrants, each of which provides a different "frame" or view of the organization.

As a manager, do you think more about the organization in internal terms and how it operates, or do you think of the organization's environment and the fit between that environment and the organization? Do you focus your attention on how the organization adapts and changes, or is your emphasis more on ensuring that the direction is under control and that people do what is needed? Quinn argues that these dimensions form the four value orientations (Open-Systems View, Rational Economic View, Internal Processes View, and Human Resources View) that underlie how we think. Further, he states that while all orientations are needed in an organization, each of us will tend to operate from one quadrant more than the others. As well, because the values underlying each quadrant are in conflict, individuals will have difficulty having a "natural" perspective from more than one quadrant. Individuals will tend to adopt one set of internally consistent values and find their views in conflict with or competing with those individuals with perspectives from other quadrants. The Competing Values Model is portrayed in Figure 3.6.

One of the strengths of Quinn's model is that it links organizational-level analysis with individual-level analysis. That is, we can examine an organization's processes and determine whether they are focused on external adaptation, internal adaptation, and so on. At the same time, Quinn suggests managerial skills that are needed for each quadrant. To increase the focus in a quadrant, one needs to have managers develop the competencies needed and design systems to reinforce those skill behaviors. Of specific interest to change leaders are those skills that help with change processes. (See Chapter 8 on change leaders for more on this.)

Every organization needs to attend to all four quadrants. It needs to know what is going on internally and also be aware of its external environment. It needs to control its operations and yet be flexible and adaptable. At the same time, too much emphasis on one dimension may be dysfunctional. That is, we need to be flexible, but too much flexibility can bring chaos. Conversely, too much control can bring rigidity and paralysis. In the end, organizations need to balance these in ways that are congruent with their external environmental realities.

Quinn labels the internal/flexibility quadrant as the Human Resources View of organizations. Similarly, the external/flexibility quadrant is the Open-Systems View, the external/control quadrant is the Rational Economic View, and the internal/control quadrant is the Internal Processes View. Each of these quadrants

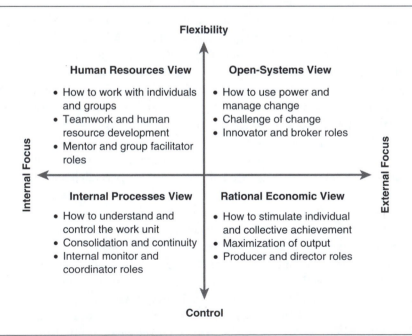

Figure 3.6   Quinn's Competing Values Model and Change

Adapted from Quinn, R. E., et al. (2003). *Becoming a master manager* (p. 13). New York: John Wiley & Sons.

may be associated with a particular way of thinking about the organization, with roles that managers need to play and with skill sets managers may learn that enable them to play these roles.[34]

Each quadrant provides a value orientation needed in organizations. At the same time, it suggests managerial roles and skills that will support those value orientations. For example, Quinn argues that innovator and broker roles are needed in the Open-Systems Quadrant. The innovator roles demand an understanding of change, an ability to think creatively to produce change, and the development of risk taking. The broker role involves the development and maintenance of a power and influence base, the ability to negotiate solutions to issues, and the skills of persuasion and coalition building.

Care must be taken not to be trapped into adopting one view and ignoring alternate perspectives. Too much focus on internal stability led IBM to miss the PC revolution for many years. Too much focus on the external world led many dotcoms to spin out of control in the technology boom of the early 2000s.

As managers, we tend to adopt a set of assumptions that causes us to isolate our focus on primarily one quadrant. Thus, Quinn argues, operations managers and management accountants tend to see the world from an internal control perspective. This view provides insight and understanding into how the organization was operating. At the same time, it limits understanding because the assumptions underlying this perspective minimize looking outside the organization and the need to adapt. Similarly, Quinn would argue that sales or marketing people tend to view the world externally and with an adaptation perspective. In essence, each perspective brings with it strengths and the risk of myopia concerning alternative perspectives.

We may use Quinn's model in several ways: to characterize an organization's dominant culture, to describe its dominant tasks, to portray the focus of its reward systems, and to describe a needed shift in task emphasis or in the types of people that it must recruit. To refer again to the McDonald's example, in 2003, franchisees were being encouraged to become more innovative, while at the same time, they had to focus increasingly on the internal control of service quality. Because these two value orientations are not joined easily, change leaders will know that the concurrent development of these two initiatives will require careful management. When Bennett was appointed as the new CEO of Intuit, he discovered that Intuit had an "employee-centric culture."[35] In his view (and using Quinn's model), their orientation or value set was too internal and too adaptable. He moved to increase the focus (i.e., increased control) on critical variables (based on his view of external realities). Thus, in Quinn's terms, he emphasized the rational, goal-achievement value set, and through this process, he shifted their focus.

Quinn's model provides both a framework that bridges individual and organizational levels of analysis and a framework to understand competing paradigms in organizations. While these perspectives are useful, they suggest a relatively static situation, not a dynamic one that we have argued for earlier in this chapter. In particular, Quinn's framework does not encourage us to consider possible changes that occur in organizations over time. As organizations grow from one-person, entrepreneurial ventures to larger functional entities to multidivisional, multinational entities, the nature of the organizations shifts because of size and complexity.

Greiner's model, described below, provides one framework for thinking of changes to organizations that occur over time.

How Do We Think of Organizational Change Over Time?

Greiner's Five Phases of Organizational Growth Model

The magnitude of organizational changes can vary markedly—from small, evolutionary changes to large, revolutionary ones.[*] The evolutionary shifts are, by definition, less traumatic for organization members and less disruptive to the organization. Since they typically involve small, incremental shifts in existing systems and behaviors, they are easier to plan and execute. However, they may not be what the organization needs in order to maintain health and vitality. As a change leader, you need to be very aware of the perceived magnitude of change. The dynamics and processes are very different. For incremental, evolutionary change, the challenge might be convincing people of the need and tweaking systems and processes to reinforce the desired outcomes. However, for disruptive, revolutionary change, the issue may well be keeping the organization operating while making significant alterations to how the organization views the world, its strategy, and how it goes about transforming inputs into outputs that its customers desire.

Many students of organizational change believe that organizations pass through periods of relative stability, punctuated periodically by the need for more radical transformations of current practices.[36] During the periods of relative stability, organizations tend to be in equilibrium and evolutionary approaches to change are adopted in order to incrementally improve practices. Eisenhart and others believe that organizations can force incremental change by "time pacing"—setting up targets and deadlines that require regular periodic change.[37] Greiner describes alternating periods of evolutionary and revolutionary change as natural as an organization grows over time. Figure 3.7 outlines Greiner's model.

Over time, these incremental changes in how we think about and how we operate the business become less effective, as they become increasingly less congruent with the internal and external realities that the organization must manage. This period of relative stability also decreases in length as the ambient rate of change in the environment increases. In Nadler and Tushman's terms, the organizational strategy and/or the transformational components (task, formal organization, informal organization, and people) becomes increasingly out of sync with the environment. Once the pressure builds sufficiently, it produces the need for more radical transformations of the organization. This relatively rapid and discontinuous change over most or all domains of organizational activity is referred to by Greiner as the revolutionary change period.[38]

As shown in Figure 3.7, Greiner outlines a model of typical stages of growth in an organization. He suggests that these patterns are progressive and logical as the organization grows. Greiner is prescriptive in that he claims that the organization

---

[*]The determination of the size of the change is of course dependent on organization level and perspective. An incremental change according to a CEO may well be viewed as transformational by the department head that is directly affected by the change.

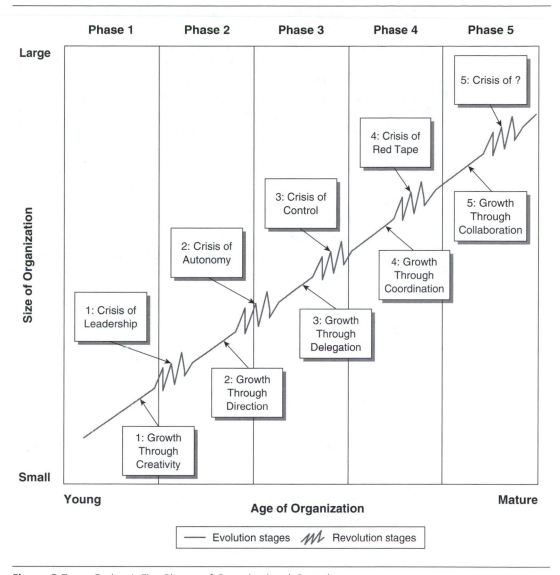

Figure 3.7   Greiner's Five Phases of Organizational Growth

Source: Reprinted with permission from "Evolution and Revolution as Organizations Grow," by Larry Greiner in *Harvard Business Review,* July-August, 1972. Copyright © 1972 by the Harvard Business School Publishing Corporation, all rights reserved.

must pass through these crises in order to grow and develop. The transitions are caused by a variety of issues: the death of the founder, the need for functional organization to develop needed specialties, the emergence of disruptive market forces and/or technology, the need to decentralize into divisions to keep closer to the customer, and, finally, the need to become more organic to enable the organization to use the potential of all employees.

This framework is appealing because of its logic and simplicity. However, in our view, the prescriptiveness of the model is too strong. Not all organizations follow the pattern suggested. In today's world, a small entrepreneurial venture may become a global competitor of reasonable size by using the Internet and collaborating with partners around the world. In other words, organizations need not develop as Greiner claims. Nevertheless, the framework is valuable in highlighting many of the crises faced by organizations and in relating those crises to the growth stage of the organization. The model reinforces the notion of the competing values that managers must keep in an appropriate state of dynamic tension. For example, as you move from the crisis of autonomy to growth through delegation, one can hypothesize a shift in values from control to flexibility.

In our McDonald's example, McDonald's has passed through most of the stages of growth and is now struggling with many of the tensions described by Greiner. While Greiner's model suggests that certain tensions predominate during different growth phases, such tensions don't vanish. As such, McDonald's continues to struggle with the generation of creative ideas under new leadership. The new management team is balancing the provision of direction and coordination to provide control but is also recognizing the essential autonomy of franchisees who will avoid red tape whenever possible. What things can be delegated, what things cannot, and which items need to be decided by collaboration will be continuing issues for McDonald's. For example, corporate cleanliness procedures and standards are essential for brand image. However, the enforcement of such standards is difficult given the ownership structure and the costs of enforcement.

While Greiner's model is prescriptive, it captures many of the issues faced by organizations both in growth and in dealing with the human side of organizational change. Too often, managers are trapped by their own perspectives. They fail to recognize that regardless of "who is right," others will see things differently and have different criteria to judge potential outcomes. An important key in identifying "what to change" is embracing multiple perspectives, recognizing that each comes with its own biases and orientation on what needs to be done. By developing a more balanced and comprehensive assessment, while being conscious of how your own biases and preferences tend to color your perspective, the change leader is likely to come to a more holistic understanding of what change is needed to produce the alignment needed for organizational success.

How Do We Capture the Complexity of Organizational Analysis?

Complexity Theory

Many models of organizational change rely on a "gap" analysis as the description of what needs to change.[39] Although this has the advantage of simplicity, change agents need to move beyond this to recognize the importance of interdependence and interrelationships.[40] We began this chapter by describing organizations as open systems, and we have developed this by presenting frameworks for analysis that can account for the dynamic, multilevel, time-dependant nature of organizations. As well, you've been encouraged to recognize that different situations require different levels of analysis, and the appropriate analytic tools will change dependent on that level. The importance of moving away from seeing change in primarily simple, rational, cause-and-effect terms should not be underestimated. Change leaders must learn how to cope with complexity and chaos as realities. This represents an important shift in our view of change.

Change agents need to extend their thinking from organizations as systems to organizations as complex, paradoxical entities that may not be amenable to control. One theory that develops our view of organizations is complexity theory. Stacey[41] identifies the following as the underlying propositions of complexity theory (adapted below):

- Organizations are webs of nonlinear feedback loops that are connected with other individuals and organizations by webs of nonlinear feedback loops.
- These feedback systems can operate in stable and unstable states of equilibrium, even to the point at which chaos ensues.
- Organizations are inherently paradoxes. On one hand, they are pulled toward stability by forces for integration and control, security, certainty, and environmental adaptation. On the other hand, they are pulled toward instability by forces for division, innovation, and even isolation from the environment.
- If organizations give in to the forces for stability, they become ossified and change impaired. If they succumb to the forces for instability, they will disintegrate. Success is when organizations exist between frozen stability and chaos.
- Short-run dynamics (or noise) are characterized by irregular cycles and discontinuous trends, but the long-term trends are identifiable.
- A successful organization faces an unknowable specific future because things can and do happen that were not predicted and that affect what is achieved and how it is achieved.
- Agents within the organization cannot control (through their actions, analytic processes, or systems and controls) the long-term future. They can act only in relation to the short term.
- Long-term development is a spontaneous self-organizing process that may give rise to new strategic directions. Spontaneous self-organization is the product of political interaction combined with learning in groups, and managers have to pursue reasoning through the use of analogy.
- It is through this process that managers create and come to know the environments and long-term futures of their organizations.[42]

Some complexity theorists would argue that the managed change perspective that underpins this book is fundamentally flawed. They would do so because it focuses on management of complexity and renewal through environmental analysis and programmatic initiatives that advance internal and external alignment, and through them the accomplishment of the goals of the change. Those who adopt a complexity perspective would view the change leader's job as one of creating conditions and ground rules that will allow for innovation and efficiency to emerge through the encouragement of the interactions and relationships of others.

Advocates believe that this approach can unleash energy and enthusiasm and allow naturally occurring solution patterns to emerge that would otherwise remain unseen (i.e., they self-organize into alignment). Vision and strategy are still valued by this approach because they can supply participants with a sense of the hoped-for direction. However, they are not viewed as useful when they attempt to specify the ultimate goal.

A close review of the complexity ideas, though, shows that this perspective is not really that far from the one advocated by this book. This book adopts an open-systems perspective and argues that the environment is characterized by uncertainty and complexity and that organizations are more likely to be successful over time if they develop adaptive (or, if you will, coevolutionary, in the language of complexity theory) capacities. This means that openness to new ideas and flexibility need to be valued and that organizations need to learn how to embrace the ideas, energy, and enthusiasm that can be generated from change initiatives that come from within the organization. This book recognizes the value that teams (including self-managed teams) can contribute to successful change, from needs assessment to the development of initial ideas and shared vision through to strategy development and implementation. Further, it acknowledges that too much standardization and reduction of variance will drive out innovation. Finally, it notes that greater uncertainty and ambiguity give rise to greater uncertainty over how things will ultimately unfold, thereby highlighting the importance of vision and strategy as directional beacons for change initiatives.

An important idea that comes from complexity theory is that small changes at key points early on can have huge downstream effects. But can one predict with any certainty where those changes and leverage points will be, or what downstream results will emerge as the result of actions we take today? Often the answer is no. Motorola likely had no clear idea where wireless technology would take the world when they began work on the cellular phone technology in the 1960s. Likewise, Monsanto probably had little sense of the magnitude of the marketplace resistance that would build for the genetically modified seeds when its research and development program was initiated in the 1980s.

We may not be able to predict precisely what will transpire over the longer term, but we can make complex and uncertain futures more understandable and predictable if we do our homework in an open-systems manner, look at data in nonlinear as well as more linear terms, engage different voices and perspectives in the discussion, and rigorously consider different scenarios and different approaches to envisioning what the future might look like.

When organizations do this, they are likely to get a better sense of what is possible from a vision, directional, and technological perspective. Further, through the engagement and involvement of others, change leaders are in a stronger position to initiate with a shared sense of purpose. They are also more likely to have identified critical actions and events that must occur and where some of the potentially important leverage and resistance points exist. As a result, they are more aware of how things may unfold and are in a stronger position to take corrective or alternative action as the result of their ongoing monitoring and management of the process.[43] As well, change agents will recognize the importance of contingency planning as unpredictable, unplanned events occur.

It may not be possible to predict absolute outcomes. However, it is possible to generally predict where an organization is likely to end up if it adopts a particular strategy and course of action. The identification of the direction and the initial steps allow us to begin the journey. Effective monitoring and management processes allow us to make adjustments as we move forward. The ability to do this with complex change comes about as the result of hard work, commitment, a suitable mind-set (e.g., openness and flexibility), skills and competencies, appropriate participation and involvement, access to sufficient resources, and control and signaling processes. In the end, the authors of this book subscribe to the belief that "luck is the intersection of opportunity and preparation."[44]

Summary

In this chapter, we explored models that will help managers develop a well-grounded sense of **what** needs to change in their organization. A solid analysis of an organization must be based on recognition of the organization's strategy, how it fits with the changing environment, and how the various components of the organization also fit with the strategy and environment. We described three models* that help managers categorize the complex organizational data that they must deal with. This book uses the Nadler and Tushman model as a framework. It focuses on achieving congruence between the organization's environment, strategy, and internal organizational components in order to achieve desired outcomes. In includes both the formal aspects of organizations and informal aspects. Finally, it fits neatly into a process approach to organizational change helping us to merge the **what** of change with the **how** of change. In the Beckhard and Harris model, this type of analysis will fit both at an initial organizational analysis stage and a gap analysis stage. Figure 3.1 identifies where this process of analysis rests within the Beckhard and Harris change management process that was described in Chapter 2. As such, it provides the foundation for much of what will follow in the remainder of this book.

While the book relies on both the Nadler and Tushman' framework and the Beckhard and Harris model, we argue that change leaders must be particularly sensitive to the dynamic nature of organizations, to the need for multiple levels of analysis, and to the shifts that organizations make over time. Sterman's, Quinn's, and Greiner's models are presented to reinforce these perspectives. As well, we discuss complexity theory. This theory challenges a simple goal-oriented approach that many change managers might take and encourages a much more emergent view of organizations.

Change leaders must recognize the assumptions and biases underlying their analysis and whether the assumptions they make limit their perspectives on needed change. Their diagnosis should recognize the stage of development of the organization and whether it is facing evolutionary, incremental change or, at the other end of the change continuum, more revolutionary, strategic change. By developing an in-depth and sophisticated understanding of the organization, change leaders will be better able to appreciate what has to be done to enhance the organization's effectiveness.

---

*These are the McKinsey 7-S model, the Burke-Litwin causal model, and the Nadler and Tushman congruence model.

Glossary of Terms

The How and What of Change

The How of change relates to the process one uses to bring about change.

The What of change relates to the assessment of what it is that needs to change—in other words, the content of the change.

Open-Systems View of Organizations

The Open-Systems View of Organizations considers the organization as a set of complex, interdependent parts that interact with the environment to obtain equilibrium.

Models of Organizations

McKinsey 7-S Model—The McKinsey 7-S model states that the key components of organizational analysis are strategy, structure, systems, style, staff, shared values, and skills. Understanding these variables will provide insight into the dynamics of an organization.

Burke-Litwin Causal Model—The Burke-Litwin causal model views organizations as composed of 12 key variables divided into two sets: transformational variables (external environment, leadership, mission and strategy, organizational culture, and individual and organizational performance) and transactional variables (management practices, structure, systems and policies, work unit climate, motivation, task requirements, individual needs and values, and individual and organizational performance).

Nadler and Tushman Organizational Congruence Model—The Nadler and Tushman model views organizations as composed of internal components (tasks, designed structures and systems, emergent structures, and systems and people). The model states that higher effectiveness occurs when the organization is congruent with its strategy and environment. This model forms the framework for this text.

Sterman's Systems Dynamics Model—Sterman's model describes organizations as interactive, dynamic, and nonlinear as opposed to the linear, static view that many individuals hold of organizations.

Quinn's Competing Values Model Framework—Quinn's model describes organizations as based on competing values: flexibility versus control and external versus internal. These two dimensions lead to four competing views of organizations: the human resource view, the open-systems view, the rational economic view, and the internal processes view.

Greiner's Five Phases of Organizational Growth Model—Greiner's model hypothesizes that organizations move through five phases of growth followed by five stages of crisis.

Complexity Theory—Complexity theory argues that organizations are webs of nonlinear feedback loops that connect individuals and organizations that can lead to self-organization and alignment between parts.

END-OF-CHAPTER EXERCISES

Toolkit Exercise 3.1 provides an exercise to practice thinking about the 7-S model.

TOOLKIT EXERCISE 3.1

Applying the 7-S Model and the Alignment Tool

1. Think of an organization that you are familiar with and analyze it using the 7-S model.

2. Now consider the changes that you believe would improve things. When you subject these changes to an analysis of alignment, do they solve the problems, or do they, in some cases, make the misalignment worse?

3. Use the process to refine your thinking about the nature of what needs to change.

TOOLKIT EXERCISE 3.2

Analyzing Your Organization Using Nadler and Tushman's Model

1. Use the congruence model to describe your organization or an organization you are familiar with. Categorize the key components of the environment, strategy, tasks, formal system, informal system, and key individuals. What outputs are desired? Are they achieved?

2. Is the strategy in line with the organization's environmental inputs? Are the transformation processes (the key tasks, the formal organization, the informal organization, and the key individuals) all aligned well with your organization's strategy? How do they interact to produce the outputs?

3. When you evaluate your organization's outputs at the organizational, group, and individual levels, do you see anything that might identify issues that your organization should address?

4. Are there some aspects of how your organization works that you have difficulty understanding? If so, identify the resources you can access to help with this analysis.

Notes

1. http://www.pbs.org/wnet/redgold/basics/bloodlettinghistory.html.

2. Magna reverses strategy, plans to take Parts subsidiaries private. (2004, October 26). *The Globe and Mail*, B1.

3. Bruch, H., & Gerber, P. (2005, March). Strategic change decisions: Doing the right change right. *Journal of Change Management*, (*5*)1, 99.

4. Op. cit., p. 98.

5. Adapted from Jang, B. (2005, March 2). Good enough for Celine—but maybe not for us. *The Globe and Mail*.

6. Stacey, R. D. (2003). *Strategic management of organisational dynamics: The challenge of complexity*. Englewood Cliffs, NJ: Prentice Hall.

7. See Holling, C. S. (1987). Simplifying the complex: The paradigms of ecological function and structure. *European Journal of Operations Research*, (*30*)2, 139–146; and Hurst, D. K. (1995). *Crisis and renewal: Meeting the challenge of organizational change*. Boston: Harvard Business Review Press.

8. Hegazy, Y. (2003). Value in troubled energy markets. *Energy Markets*, (*8*)7, 38–41.

9. See, for example, Bender, R., & Greenwald, R. (Eds.). (2003). *Sweatshop USA: The American sweatshop in historical perspective*. New York: Routledge; or Foo, L., & Fortunato, N. (2003, October). Free trade's looming threat to the world's garment workers. *Asian Labor Update*. http://www.amrc.org.hk/5201.htm.

10. Schumpeter, J. (1942). *Capitalism, socialism and democracy*. New York: Harper & Row.

11. Waterman, R., Jr., Peters, T., & Phillips, J. R. (1980, June). Structure is not organisation. *Business Horizons*, (*23*)3, 14–26; Pascale, R., & Athos, A. (1981). *The art of Japanese management*. London: Penguin Books; Peters, T., & Waterman, R. (1982). *In search of excellence*. New York, London: Harper & Row.

12. Effective change in higher education. http://www.effectingchange.luton.ac.uk/approaches_to_change/index.php?content=default.

13. Burke, W. W. (2002). *Organizational change: Theory and practice*. Thousand Oaks, CA: Sage.

14 Nadler, D. A., & Tushman, M. L. (1989). Organizational frame bending: Principles for managing reorientation. *Academy of Management Executive*, (*3*)3, 194–204.

15. Evans, J. R. (1997). Critical linkages in the Baldrige Award criteria: Research models and educational challenges. *Quality Management Journal*, (*5*)1, 13–30.

16. Collins, J. (2001). *Good to great: Why some companies make the leap . . . and others don't*. New York: HarperBusiness.

17. Webber, A. (2001, October). Good questions, great answers: An interview with Jim Collins. *Fast Company, 51*, 90.

18. Nadler, D. A., & Tushman, M. L. (1977). A diagnostic model for organizational behavior. In J. R. Hackman, E. E. Lawler, & L. W. Porter (Eds.), *Perspectives in behavior in organizations* (pp. 85–100). New York: McGraw-Hill.

19. Nadler, D. (1987). The effective management of organizational change. In Jay W. Lorsch (Ed.), *Handbook of organizational behavior* (pp. 358–369). Englewood Cliffs, NJ: Prentice Hall.

20. McManamy, R. (1995). Fourth quarterly cost report: South America—hyperinflation dying off. *ENR*, (*235*)26, 43–45.

21. Peters, T., & Waterman, R. H. (1982). *In search of excellence*. New York: Harper & Row.

22. Adapted from Gogoi, P., & Arndt, M. (2003, March 3). McDonald's hamburger hell. *Business Week.*

23. Big Mac's makeover. (2004, October 16). *The Economist, 63–65.*

24. Yetton, P. W., Johnson, K. D., & Craig, J. R. (1994). Computer-aided architects: A case study of IT and strategic change. *Sloan Management Review,* (*35*)4, 57–68.

25. Grant, R. M., Shani, R., & Krishnan, R. (1994). TQM's challenge to management theory and practice. *Sloan Management Review,* (*35*)2, 25–36.

26. Gates, R. (2003, September 3). How not to reform intelligence. *Wall Street Journal,* A16. See also Flynn, S., & Kirkpatrick, J. J. (2005, January 26). *The Department of Homeland Security: The way ahead after a rocky start.* Written testimony before a hearing of the Committee on Homeland Security and Governmental Affairs, U.S. Senate.

27. Burke, W. W. (2002). *Organization change: Theory and practice* (p. 191). Thousand Oaks, CA: Sage.

28. Sterman, J. (2001, Summer). Systems dynamic modeling. *California Management Review,* (*43*)4.

29. Argyris, C., & Schön, D. (1996). *Organizational learning II: Theory, method and practice.* Reading, MA: Addison-Wesley.

30. Senge, P. (1990). *The strategy.* London: Doubleday/Century Business.

31. Rao, A. R., Bergen, M. E., & Davis, S. (2000, March–April). How to fight a price war. *Harvard Business Review,* (*78*)2, 107–116.

32. Boosting productivity on the shop floor. (2003, September 12). *The Economist, 62.*

33. Quinn, R. E. (1991). *Beyond rational management.* San Francisco: Jossey-Bass.

34. See Quinn, R.E., et al. (1990). *Becoming a master manager.* New York: John Wiley & Sons.

35. Tischerler, L. Op. cit., p. 107.

36. For a detailed treatment of this topic, see Weick, K. (1999). Organizational change and development. In *Annual Review of Psychology;* Romanelli, E., & Tushman, M. L. (1994). Organizational transformation as punctuated equilibrium: An empirical test. *Academy of Management Journal,* 1141–1166; and Gersick, C. G. G. (1991). Revolutionary change theories: A multilevel exploration of the punctuated equilibrium. *Academy of Management Review, 16,* 10–36.

37. Brown, S., & Eisenhart, K. (1997). The art of continuous change: Linking complexity theory and time-paced evolution in relentlessly shifting organizations. *Administrative Science Quarterly,* (*42*)1, 1–34; or Eisenhardt, K., & Tabrizi, B. N. (1995). Accelerating adaptive processes: Product innovation in the global computer industry. *Administrative Science Quarterly,* (*40*)1, 84–110.

38. Greiner, L. (1972, July–August). Evolution and revolution as organizations grow. *Harvard Business Review.*

39. Beckhard, R., & Harris, R. T. (1987). *Organizational transitions: Managing complex change.* Reading, MA: Addison-Wesley.

40. Mitleton-Kelly, E. (2002). The principles of complexity and enabling infrastructures (ch. 2). In *Complex systems and evolutionary perspectives of organisations: The application of complexity theory to organisations.* London School of Economics Complexity & Organisational Learning Research Programme. London: Elsevier.

41. Stacey, R. D. (1996). *Strategic management and organizational dynamics* (2nd ed.). London: Pittman.

42.   Approaches to change (p. 41). (n.d.). In *Effecting change in higher education.* Luton, UK: University of Bedfordshire. www.effectingchange.luton.ac.uk/approaches_to_change/index.php?content=default.

43.   Noori, H., Deszca, G., Munro, H., & McWilliams, B. (1999). Developing the right breakthrough product/service: An application of the umbrella methodology (Parts A & B). *International Journal of Technology Management, 17,* 544–579.

44.   Letterman, E. Referenced in www.kaizen-training.com/free/our_favourite_quotes.html.

CHAPTER 4

Understanding and Building the Need for Change

Why should I change? I'm alright.

Chapter Overview

- This chapter asks the question "Why change?"
- It develops a framework for understanding the need for change based on making sense of external data, of perspectives of key stakeholders, of critical internal organizational data, and the change leaders' personal concerns and perspectives.
- The chapter describes what makes organizations ready for change and provides a questionnaire to rate an organization's readiness.
- It outlines how change leaders can create awareness for change.
- Finally, the chapter outlines the importance of the change vision and how change leaders can create a meaningful vision that energizes and focuses action.

Why do some people see the need for change and others don't? How is it that some can be galvanized to action while others refuse to see that what they are doing will no longer work?

You are in a theater, sitting there enjoying the film. Suddenly, someone yells "Fire." You leap to your feet and head to the exit.

This situation is obvious and straightforward. The need for change is clear and dramatic, and the required action is understood. There is a crisis that demands an immediate response. However, any move to action is less straightforward when no sense of crisis is evident and the question of what needs to be done is the subject of discussions by a management committee. If the issue is fire safety in general, an emergency doesn't exist. The need for change is less clear and open to argument. However, if the issue is that there is a fire **now**, everyone can see the need for an immediate response.

Often our past experience can cause us to discount warnings of an emergency. In our fire alarm example, if false fire alarms are regular occurrences in an office, people will often ignore the alarm, assuming this is nothing to be concerned about. If unionized employees are told that there is a crisis in their organization, their cynicism toward management may cause them to discount the warning. Several years ago, one of our fathers was in intensive care, hooked to a heart monitor. Shortly after arriving to visit him, the emergency alarm went off, but no one responded. We went looking for help but were told not to worry—the alarm goes off all the time—just hit the reset button. Needless to say, we were left feeling anything but secure concerning the quality of the system designed to monitor the need for change in a patient's treatment.

Demonstrating that the need for change is real and important is often a critical issue. Recently, General Motors (GM) has been struggling to convince employees and the United Auto Workers (UAW) that GM's healthcare costs and pension costs must be cut. Understandably, the UAW says that GM made a deal and should live up to it. GM has taken massive losses, and the threat of bankruptcy makes a strong argument for concessions to be granted. The union welcomed cuts to GM's dividend rate but resists further changes to their agreements. They state that "We have done our share," even while admitting that they had a shared fate with GM.[1]

This chapter helps you to understand the importance of need for change in directing the organization's attention to change and to galvanizing support for changes. It helps you think about how to unfreeze the organization by considering others' perspectives on a proposed change. The chapter will show you how to increase the awareness of the need for change. In particular, we focus on the use of a compelling, positive vision for change that people will respond to.

The importance of understanding if employees recognize the need for change was demonstrated at Yellow Freight Systems. Employees believed that their industry was regulated and that prices, time of delivery, and customer service were standard across companies. The reality was that competitors were competing on these variables, particularly delivery time. Employees would tell customers that their desired delivery times could not be met—and not think that this was a problem. These employee attitudes and resulting behaviors led to lower sales and profits and fewer customers. The change challenge at Yellow Freight was to motivate employees to behave in ways that reflected customer needs.[2]

Yellow Freight was able to overcome its inertia, but only after Bill Zollars, a new CEO, created an understanding of the need for change. Zollar took 18 months to travel the United States and personally persuade the 25,000 employees that change was needed. By 2000, Yellow Freight had reduced its customer defect rate from 40% to less than 5% and was more profitable than at any time previously.

The Yellow Freight change produced positive results. However, many well-intentioned change initiatives lose direction, bog down in conflict, and fail to stem employee disillusionment. The organization continues to deteriorate. Why don't such initiatives engender a determined drive for renewal and the positive results that they were designed to produce? Before Zollar arrived, management at Yellow Freight knew things were not going well. Why didn't Yellow Freight take positive action earlier? The external need was there but management seemed to do little.

Sustained confusion and disagreement over (a) the need for change and (b) what needs changing are fundamental reasons for the failure of many change management programs. The Sigmoid curve described earlier in Chapter 2 provides an explanation for the reluctance to take on new initiatives. Employees had standard ways of doing their work; changing those ways created immediate and tangible costs, while any benefits of the change were problematic and difficult to measure and might accrue only to the organization. This same phenomenon can hold for others in the organization—from their perspective, the immediate perceived costs outweigh the perceived benefits.

Ask organization members—from production workers to VPs—why their organization is floundering or is slow to adapt and you find that opinions abound. Even when those opinions are well informed, they are often fragmented and contradictory. Your perspective on the need for change depends on where you sit in the organization. The information about the environment that you have access to; performance measures and incentives; your training and experience; the reactions of your peers, supervisors, and subordinates; and personality factors all influence how you look at the world. When there has been no well-thought-out effort to develop a shared awareness concerning the need for change—instead, piecemeal, disparate, and conflicting assessments of the situation—its causes and solutions are likely to pervade the organization.[3]

People often see change as something that others need to embrace in order to address failings in their operations. One hears, "Why don't they understand . . ." or "Why can't they see what is happening" or "They must be doing this intentionally. . . ." But stupidity, blindness, and maliciousness are typically not the primary reasons for inappropriate or insufficient organizational change. Differences in perspective affect what we see. As the attributions of causation shift, so do our beliefs about whom or what is the cause and what should be done.[4]

This chapter asks change initiators, be they vice presidents or line operators, to seek multiple perspectives and to examine carefully the question of what is the need for change. There is typically no shortage of things that could be done with available resources. Change initiators must be able to make the case for why energy and resources need to be committed to address a particular need.

But recognizing the need is not sufficient. Many organizations are not ready for change. Change leaders need to mobilize interest in change by creating a compelling vision of the needed future direction. As a result, the chapter also explores the role of vision in creating a consensus concerning what the change needs to look like. It concludes by discussing some of the issues with "visions" in organizations today.

In terms of the change management process, the focus of this chapter is on the "why change" box contained in Figure 4.1. What is the compelling need to disrupt the status quo to change? Do we have a choice about changing? In many cases, it is not clear that change is needed. Companies can choose to try new paths or not. At the same time, individuals or groups may have a choice about changing. Even if management announces that change is needed, many employees may not be aware of this, may believe that it doesn't apply to them, or may think that the CEO or management doesn't have the power to force them to change. On the other hand, employees often do change because they understand the need and catch the vision

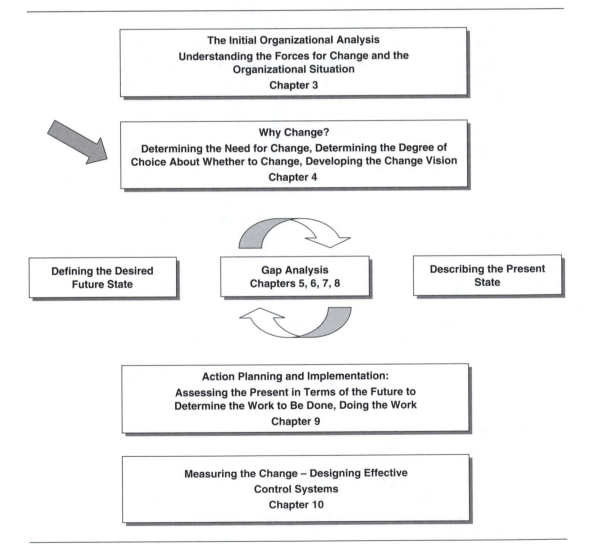

Figure 4.1   The Change Management Process

for change that is articulated. Thus, the final issue addressed in this chapter is, "What is our vision for change?"

Too often, those who should be responsible for leading change haven't done sufficient homework in determining why the organization should change—whether it has choices about change and what will create positive pressures for change. Change leaders need to understand and define the need for change. Even though there may be a general sense that things are amiss, the unfreezing needed to shift the organization has not been done. While change leaders may have amassed data on customers, production processes, suppliers, competitors, organization financials, and other factors relevant to the change, they may not have developed an integrated sense of what the information means. They may not have used that sense to persuade others that this specific change is critical. Change leaders need to answer the following questions:

- What do you as the change leader see as the need for change and the important dimensions and issues that underpin it? How much confidence do you have in your assessment, and why should others have confidence in that assessment? Is the appraisal of the need for change a function of a solid organizational and environmental assessment, or is it more a response to your personal needs?
- Have you as the change leader investigated fully the perspectives of others in the organization? Do you know who has a stake in the matter, and do you understand their perspectives? Or have you talked to only like-minded individuals?
- How does your view of the need for change compare with the perspective of other stakeholders? Are other stakeholders ready to change? That is, have they been "unfrozen" and see the need for change? Can different perspectives be integrated or consolidated in ways that embrace all the data and offer the possibility for a collaborative solution?
- Have you as change initiator framed a change vision that has the potential to move the organization to a higher state of readiness for and willingness to change? Or have your deliberations left change recipients feeling pressured and coerced into doing something they don't agree with, don't understand, or fear will come back to haunt them?

How Do We Develop Our Understanding of the Need for Change?

Change leaders need to develop their own views on the need for change and to understand how others see that need. Further, they need to know how to create awareness and legitimacy around the need for change when a shared awareness is lacking.

Change leaders, at times, exhibit split perceptions over the need for change. On the one hand, they may demonstrate extraordinary sensitivity to key data suggesting where the focus for change should be. On the other hand, once they become convinced of where the need for change lies, change leaders may exhibit frustration over the slowness and inability or unwillingness of others to see what is now obvious to them. In their desire to take action, they will want others to accept their judgment immediately and forget their own struggles and the time it took to reach their conclusions. Once their opinion has been formed, they may discount contradictory data and alternative interpretations as they move to action. In effect, they may forget that perceptions and judgments related to these same data will vary from person to person and that there is value in understanding these different perspectives.[5] While it is reassuring to reach a conclusion and exhibit confidence concerning the need for change, there is a risk of a flawed assessment. When they are doing their jobs effectively, change leaders will seek out and make sense of external data; they will identify and understand the perspectives of the stakeholders; they will assess what is happening inside the organization; and they will engage in self-reflection to understand their personal concerns and perspectives. Figure 4.2 outlines these factors.

Seek Out and Make Sense of External Data

Change leaders will scan the organization's external environment to understand and assess the need for change. Chris Argyris, Peter Senge, and others interested in organizational learning have pointed to the importance of exploring the external environment with blinders removed. We need to get "outside of the box" to avoid those blind spots that are created by "closed-loop learning" (learning that focuses on current practices and perspectives in ways that fail to develop a shared and meaningful exposure to external factors that have the potential to cause us to think about things differently).[6] Without exposure to such information, we may succeed in improving short-term efficiency but not necessarily increase our adaptation to the external environment or enhance long-term effectiveness. In studies of why previously successful organizations become unsuccessful, active inertia (doing

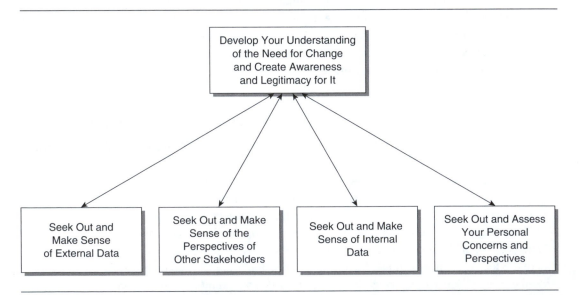

Figure 4.2 Developing Your Understanding of the Need for Change

more of the same), complacency, flawed environmental scanning and analysis (including environmental blind spots) and, under- or overreaction to risk are near the top of the list.[7] Executives tend to spend far too little time reflecting on the environment and its implications for the organization.[8]

If the organization is experiencing an externally driven crisis or transformational event that has created a sense of urgency and made the need for change obvious to all, then the change initiator's task will be easier in this area.[9] Such events can be used to galvanize action and unfreeze the system. In the absence of such events, many individuals and groups within the organization may not perceive a need for change. If they do see a need, they will not necessarily interpret it in the same way or grant it the same relevance. In the case of the fire safety example given earlier in the chapter, the absence of past concerns may raise questions over the need to spend time, energy, and money on this matter. This is where skilled change leaders add value.

The value of seeing organizations as systems open to their environment should not be underestimated in developing successful organizational change and adaptation. This analytic approach and the learning it promotes play an important role in the development of awareness and improved vision for the organization.[10] Working without it is the equivalent of driving with foggy windows and no maps and no mirrors, while relying on past experience to get you to your desired destination. It is much too easy to rely on past successes and fail to adapt to a changing environment.[11]

Seek Out and Make Sense of the Perspectives of Stakeholders

Change leaders need to be aware of the perspectives of key internal and external stakeholders and work to understand their predispositions and reasons for supporting or resisting change. If they do, they will be able to frame their approach and the content of the need for change in ways that demonstrate that they have done their homework. This increases the likelihood that they will not create unnecessary resisters and that these stakeholders will be more open to consider the arguments for the change.

At a macro level, these stakeholders may include suppliers, bankers, different levels and departments of government, customers, and alliance and network partners. At a more micro level, the internal stakeholders include those who are directly and indirectly affected by the change. If the change involves a reorganization of production processes, the internal stakeholders can include production supervisors and employees, human resources (recruitment and training implications), finance (budget and control processes), sales and marketing (customer service implications), IT (information implications), and engineering managers. In the General Motors example at the beginning of this chapter, the perspectives of the United Auto Workers and the employees are critical to management's being able to rescue General Motors from bankruptcy.

The point of view of the person championing the need for change will differ from the perspectives of other stakeholders who look at the matter from different vantage points and with unique backgrounds, experiences, and purposes or agendas. What is interesting and important to them will vary, and this will affect what data and people they pay attention to and what they do with the information. If the change leader hopes to enlist their support or, at minimum, mute the impact of their resistance, they need to capture and consider their perspectives and the underlying rationale.[12]

All this highlights the importance of doing preparatory analysis and having a purposeful discussion, if possible, with affected stakeholders and those who understand their perspectives and can potentially influence them. It will increase your awareness and sensitivity to the context, inform and strengthen your analysis, and alert you to blind spots and alternative explanations and paths.

A major telecommunications firm provides a good example of how to manage the development of a shared sense of the need for change. When it acquired a large high-technology equipment supplier, the CEO placed in charge of the acquisition was determined to have every employee understand the need for change, the new vision, and its implications. He arranged for a simultaneous telecast in which he described the changes and encouraged each employee to contact him if they had questions or concerns. He visited plants, key customers, and suppliers; held town-hall meetings; and set up a special Web site and phone line to answer questions in a timely and direct manner. Though staff fielded many of the inquiries, he stayed in close touch with what was going on and tried to personally answer as many of the concerns as he could. He responded to questions, listened, and made adjustments based on what he learned. This response tapped into the emotional needs of the "acquired" employees and gave them access to senior management. They believed that their views and concerns were being heard.[13] This CEO worked hard at communicating the need for change. Too many executives underestimate the need for communications. There is rarely too much top-level communications and support. A rule of thumb for managers is to talk up a change initiative at least three times more than you think is needed![14]

In another example, an executive vice president of a financial services firm was convinced that a new control system was needed at the independent sales agent level. Convincing the independent agents of the need for change was a difficult task. Key to this persuasion was to have the regional manager play a role. The vice president visited each regional manager, reviewed the analysis of the need for this change, explained how the new control system would address the matter, and asked the regional managers for their support. The analytic information in combination with the ability to openly ask questions without fear of sanction clarified the underlying rationale for the change. The personal contact by the CEO was a powerful demonstration of how important this change was and dramatically provided evidence to the sales agents and their regional managers of the commitment of senior management to the change. As a result, understanding and support were developed, performance was enhanced, and agent turnover was minimized.[15]

In both cases, change agents did their homework concerning the need for change, openly engaged stakeholders in dialogue, listened and responded with care and consideration, and then proceeded to the next stage in the change.

Seek Out and Make Sense of Internal Data

It comes as no surprise that change leaders need to pay careful attention to internal organizational data when developing their assessment of the need for change. It is very difficult to command internal respect and credibility if you don't appear to understand the fundamentals of what is going on within the firm and why. To address the need for change, you need to know what can be inferred from internal information and measures, how these are currently being interpreted by organizational members, and how they may be helping to lead the firm down the wrong path. Thought needs to be given to developing measures and information that will assist you in both assessing and building the case for change. Some of this will be in the form of so-called hard data—the sort that can be found in the formal information system and that is often numeric (e.g., customer retention and satisfaction, service profitability, cycle time, employee absenteeism). Other valuable information will be much softer and inferential and will often come from discussions with the various stakeholders. Consider how Thomas Tiller used such information and contacts to advance change at Polaris.

> Upon his arrival at Polaris as its new CEO, Thomas Tiller demonstrated the value of a committed, team-based approach that embraced internal and external perspectives. Polaris is a manufacturer of snowmobiles, ATVs, and other products. During the first 90 days on the job, he increased the likelihood of his acceptance and the future success of the firm by applying his considerable energy, interpersonal skills, and managerial and leadership talent to forging critical relationships and organizational perspectives. He engaged in one-on-one meetings, team-building initiatives, data assembly (internal and external), and meaningful discussions with managers concerning the data, their sense of the issues, the need for change, and the vision for the firm. This was an effort to promote frank and open discussion and debate; to build trust, learning, and mutual understanding; and to rapidly prepare the ground for the committed action that the emergent change vision would require.[16]

Tiller talked to many key people. At the same time, he relied on hard data to help create the need for change in the organization.

A second example comes from a successful marketing executive who joined an insurance brokerage firm from outside the industry. He understood sales and marketing but knew relatively little about insurance. Nevertheless, he believed that it was necessary for his brokers to begin developing expertise in specific industries rather than trying to service all potential clients. He took great care to respect his brokers' expertise by getting their perspectives and moving slowly in areas where they knew best. Over a 2-year period, he gained credibility and built an awareness of the need for change as he began grouping clients under industry experts.[17]

Seek Out and Assess Your Personal Concerns and Perspectives

"Know thyself" is a critical dictum in change leadership. It is vital to understand personal motivations and values, your strengths and weaknesses, and your preferences, prejudices, and blind spots. This is shown in the following example:

> Steve Miller's challenge as managing director of Royal Dutch/Shell was to change the face of leadership at Shell (one of the largest integrated oil businesses in the world). He believed that traditional leadership, top management driving change, was outdated. Solutions—how the company should change and by

which means—must come from the people closest to the action. The leader's role had changed from providing direction to providing necessary resources to front-line individuals. The leader had to become the coach or facilitator for employees when they ran into a challenge. When employees have the information to solve the problems, and are held accountable for solving them, they will quickly move to solve problems because they see them as "theirs."[18]

Miller had a clear sense of his priorities, mandate, and commitment. He was clear in his philosophy of leadership and was able to convey this to Shell employees. Such clarity is vital to clear, congruent communications. Self-awareness heightens the prospects that this will occur because it reduces the likelihood that mixed messages will be sent. Mixed messages are often the product of saying one thing but then behaving in an incongruent fashion. Managers are often unaware that they are doing this. For example, stating that the improvement of employee relations is a priority but then giving the matter minimal attention or support would send such a mixed message.

Whenever we deal with student groups who are attempting organizational change, we warn them not to assume that their perspectives are held by all. They fail to understand their own biases and needs and that others might not share them. In most cases, their rather fervent beliefs that they understand the situation and know what must be changed create significant barriers to their accomplishing anything. The strength of their concerns and their lack of self-awareness often cause them to block out dissenting perspectives. When they talk to stakeholders, they receive polite responses and assume that the modest oral agreement stated implies a commitment to action. Statements such as "That's an interesting approach" are taken as support rather than as a neutral comment. This failure to understand their own concerns and perspectives leads them astray.

Understanding the need for change and creating a vision for change are closely linked. Awareness of where you are now (the need for change) is a prerequisite for figuring out where you need to go. Beckhard and Harris argue that addressing the question "Why change?" is a necessary precondition to being able to define the desired future state (or the vision). If the question of "Why change?" is never meaningfully addressed, no one should expect the emergence of any shared sense of vision. The answer to "Why?" is a prerequisite to the "What?" and the "How?" of change.

Blind faith in management isn't enough for most of us. We want to understand why something needs doing—particularly when it means more work or sacrifice.[19] Appealing to organizational loyalty and trust about the need for change may help to sustain change agents when the going gets tough, if there is credibility and loyalty to begin with. However, such faith is limited and potentially delusional when it is not accompanied by the necessary preparation in the forms of data gathering, analysis, dialogue, and discussion. As was pointed out previously, sustainable change begins with a thorough analysis of what needs changing, a process that is often undertaken in conjunction with well-thought-out consensus seeking initiatives with other affected organization members.

Spector makes the point that while dissatisfaction with the status quo by top managers might be a **necessary** condition for change, it is unlikely to be a **sufficient** condition.[20] He argues that the creation of dissatisfaction in others is needed. This dissatisfaction can be developed by sharing competitive information, by challenging inappropriate behaviors, by developing a vision or model for the future, and by simply mandating dissatisfaction if one has the clout. The organization needs to be ready for change by being dissatisfied with the present. That readiness depends on previous organizational experiences, managerial support, the organization's openness to change, and the systems promoting or blocking change in the organization.

Is Your Organization Ready for Change?

Change initiators may understand the need for change but be in an organization that is not prepared to recognize that need. There are many examples of organizations that are not able to hear clear messages about their need to change. Their experiences, their management team, and their systems all make them relatively closed to change. As a result, those organizations can easily drift into difficulty.

> During the 1980s and early 1990s, Sears consistently lost money and market share. In response to record losses in 1992, it spun off noncore businesses that it had accumulated, but it still did not directly address the underlying causes. Finally, in 1995, under the leadership of its new CEO, Arthur Martinez, who had joined the firm to head up merchandizing in the fall of 1992, Sears moved in a committed and concerted fashion to address the underlying problems facing it. It redefined its value proposition and assessed its cultural capacity to deliver. It made hard choices on strategy, staffing, performance measurement, and organizational renewal and demonstrated its commitment to staying the course. Indicative of its earlier drift was its unwillingness to use credit cards other than the Sears credit card. All of its major competitors welcomed other cards, but Sears resisted, largely because its internal metrics showed that this was one of the few lines of business in the organization that was profitable. However, the policy of using only the Sears card was driving customers away and eroding its market share. The change in its credit card policy was an important indicator that it was now prepared to revisit past practices and performance indicators as part of its acceptance of the need for change.[21]

An organization's readiness for change will determine its ability to attend to environmental signals for change as well as its willingness to listen to internal voices saying that change is needed.[22]

An example of a situation where companies were not ready for change was the telephone industry prior to deregulation. Competition was controlled. Profits were regulated. The industry was dominated by large organizations that hadn't changed much in years. Employees had long employment service. They had developed deeply rooted patterns of behavior and ideas about how things "should be done." Major change in such an organization would be difficult. The forces against change would be numerous. Pressure for change would be trivial.

Deregulation of the industry transformed the environment and increased the pressures for change. Now change is rampant. New products and services are generated rapidly and are tested, tried, and dropped if they don't work out. New players have entered and redefined the industry. Voices regarding Internet protocols have begun to challenge the assumptions underlying the industry.

An organization's readiness for change is determined by the previous change experiences of its members; the openness, commitment, and involvement of leadership in preparing the organization for change; the openness to change; and the reward and measurement systems that influence where it focuses its attention.

Previous experiences will affect the receptiveness to future change. If the organization has experienced a successful change, it is likely that employees and managers will be more positive and ready to try something new. Conversely, if the change experience was negative, employees might become disillusioned and cynical.[23] Are they ready for change in the future, or are they likely to rest on their laurels once they finish consolidating their gains? Conversely, have they had exposure to an organization that has had a recent failure experience with change? Has its response been one of increased cynicism and resistance (i.e., we tried and it didn't work), or has it produced increased resolve concerning the need for change?

Have senior managers in the organization demonstrated awareness and support for the need for change? Writers regularly report that the development and maintenance of top management support is crucial to change success.[24] If senior managers are onboard, visibly support the change, and have their own success tied to the success of the initiative, then the organization is likely to be more receptive to change. However, it is not unusual to find differences of opinion concerning change at the senior management level, so a lack of unanimous support is a reality that many change leaders must navigate. Perhaps more troubling situations than the lack of visible support occur when senior management assures you of support but fails to provide it at crucial moments and engages in passive forms of resistance.

Organizations that have well-developed external scanning mechanisms are more likely to be aware of environmental changes. Structures and systems that encourage the collection of benchmark data will provide evidence to support change and will help make an organization ready for change.[25] If the culture supports such environmental scanning and encourages a focus on identifying and resolving problems rather than "turf protection," then organizations will be more open to change.

Steward used such questions to develop a rating system on an organization's willingness to change.[26] Holt extended this to develop a scale based on the beliefs among employees that they could implement a change, that the change is appropriate for the organization, that leaders are committed, and that the proposed change is needed.[27] Table 4.1 extends this work and provides a method of estimating readiness for change. To stimulate your thinking along these lines, think of an organization you know and rate its readiness for change using Table 4.1.

How Can We Make an Organization Ready for Change?

Creating Awareness of the Need for Change

How do change leaders spread the awareness that the status quo is inappropriate and that the organization must change its ways? Thinking individuals will want to critically assess the evidence concerning the need for change. The change leader

Table 4.1   Rate the Organization's Readiness for Change

Readiness Dimensions	Readiness Score
Previous Change Experiences	
Has the organization had positive experience with change?	Score +1
Has the organization had failure experience with change?	Score −1
What is the mood of the organization: upbeat and positive?	Score +1
What is the mood of the organization: negative and cynical?	Score −1
Does the organization appear to be resting on its laurels?	Score −1
Executive Support	
Are senior managers directly involved in sponsoring the change?	Score +1
Is there a clear picture of the future?	Score +1
Is executive success dependent on the change occurring? If yes,	Score +1
Has management ever demonstrated a lack of support?	Score −1
Openness to Change	
Does the organization have scanning mechanisms to monitor the environment?	Score +1
Is there a culture of scanning and paying attention to those scans?	Score +1
Does "turf" protection exist in the organization?	Score −1
Are the senior managers hidebound or locked into the use of past strategies, approaches, and solutions?	Score −1
Is conflict dealt with openly, with a focus on resolution?	Score +1
Or is it suppressed and smoothed over?	Score −1
Rewards for Change	
Does the reward system reward innovation and change?	Score +1
Does the reward system focus exclusively on short-term results?	Score −1
Are people censured for attempting change and failing?	Score −1
Measures for Change	
Does the organization have good metrics that can track changes and their need?	Score +1
Does the organization attend to these measures?	Score +1
Does the organization measure and evaluate customer satisfaction?	Score +1

The scores can range from −9 to +12.

The purpose of this tool is to raise awareness and questions concerning readiness for change.
   If the organization scores below 0, it is likely not ready for change and change will be very difficult. On the other hand, if the organization scores 7 or higher, the organization is likely much more ready for change—note that change is never "simple," but at least there are organizational factors in place to support the change if it is a good one.

The scores will point to factors that need attention in order to increase the organization's readiness for change. As such, they can be used to raise questions concerning what can be done to address them.

Source: Adapted from Stewart, T. A. (1994, February 7). Rate your "Readiness to Change" scale. *Fortune,* 106–110.

may experience blanket resistance and defensiveness or may experience more local-ized opposition. Individuals may recognize the need for change in other depart-ments and functions, but they may become increasingly resistant to recognizing the need for change as it gets closer to home.

Openness to change might be a desirable predisposition, but this is often not the reality that the change agents face. They must understand the attitudes and beliefs of different employee groups and other affected stakeholders regarding change. Individuals who see only the unraveling of what they've worked for and/or unpleas-ant alternatives ahead for them will be very reluctant to embrace change proposals.

Once change leaders understand the need for change, there are five approaches that can be taken to create a heightened awareness of this need in the organization. They may do the following:

1. Create a crisis or increase awareness that crisis conditions exist or are on the horizon.

2. Identify a transformational vision that creates dissatisfaction with the status quo in the organization.

3. Find a transformational leader who will build awareness of the need for change and provide the vision for change.

4. Focus on common or superordinate goals.

5. Create dissatisfaction with the status quo by providing education, informa-tion, and exposure to superior practices and processes, including those of both competitors and noncompetitors. This can include research or theory on effective organizations.

The first method involves either making the organization aware that it is in or near a crisis or creating a crisis that needs to be solved. Many of the dramatic turn-around stories that are reported are successful because the actions of people were galvanized and focused by the necessity for action. In the face of crisis, people find it difficult to deny the need to change and to change **now**. When the crisis is real, the issue will be one of showing employees a way out, which generally they will fol-low if they have any confidence in its viability, given that the alternatives are far from attractive.[28]

At times, managers will be tempted to generate a crisis, to create a sense of urgency to change and mobilize staff around a change initiative that may or may not be fully justified. Creating a sense of crisis when one does not really exist must be approached with care.[29] If mishandled, it may be viewed as manipulative and result in heightened cynicism and reduced commitment. The change leader's per-sonal credibility and trustworthiness are at stake. The reputation developed in and around change initiatives casts a long shadow (for better or worse). The currencies that change agents use are credibility and trustworthiness. These take a long time to develop and can be quickly squandered.[30]

An extension of the crisis is the "burn/sink your boats" approach. In this case, the change leader takes the process one step further and cuts off any avenue of retreat. That is, there is no going back. This approach is based on the belief that this will lead to increased commitment to the selected course of action. While it may aid in focusing attention, this approach can increase many of the risks outlined above. In particular, individuals may resent being forced into such a situation against their will. It may produce compliant behavior in the short term, due to the absence of available alternatives, but it can give rise to undesirable longer-term consequences if these actions come to be viewed as being unfair and inappropriate. Consequences may include elevated levels of mistrust, reduced commitment, and poorer performance.[31] An example of this approach may very well be the announcements by General Motors that they are closing plants and laying off thousands in order to regain competitiveness. Such public moves make it very difficult for senior managers to go back on such statements.[32]

A second approach to enhancing the need for change is by identifying a transformational vision based on higher-order values (such as the delivery of exceptional quality or superb service and responsiveness). Transformational visions or higher-order appeals tap into our needs to go beyond ourselves, to make a contribution, to do something worthwhile and meaningful, and to serve a greater good. These appeals can provide powerful mechanisms to unfreeze an organization and create conditions for change. In addition, transformational visions pull people toward an idealized future—a positive approach to needed change.

Cynics in the organization may reject these vision appeals for many reasons. They may see them as unrealistic, naive, Pollyannaish, and/or designed simply to serve the interests of those making the pronouncements. They may also dismiss the vision as inadequate or off target. If organization members have previously heard visionary pronouncements, only to see them ignored or discarded, they may believe the most recent iteration is simply the current "flavor of the week" approach to change.

Change agents need to ask themselves if they are really serious about following through on the values and action orientation that underlie their visionary appeals. If they are not, then they should stop, rather than contribute to the buildup of organizational cynicism and alienation that accompanies unmet expectations. Nevertheless, the power of truly transformational visions should not be underestimated.

A third approach to the enhancement of the need for change is through transformational leadership. Leadership, in general, and transformational leaders, in particular, continue to command attention in the change literature—not surprising, given its stature in Western culture and mythology.[33] From George Washington to Adolf Hitler, from Nelson Mandela to Mother Teresa to Saddam Hussein, we've elevated the positive exemplars and condemned the villains. The same is true for the corporate world. Lee Iacocca's rescue of Chrysler (with considerable U.S. federal help), Steven Jobs's resuscitation of Apple, Elizabeth Dole's stewardship of the American Red Cross, and Frank Stronach's development of Magna's auto parts empire provide examples of the work of successful transformational leaders. The appeal of charismatic and transformational individuals is powerful. They seem to have the capacity to create strong, positive responses and a willingness to change in followers that often overrides the followers' personal concerns. Richard Branson (Virgin Airlines), Earl Graves (Black Enterprise Magazine), Jack Welch (GE), and

Oprah Winfrey are individuals who are often held up as positive, charismatic exemplars. However, recent corporate scandals (e.g., Bernie Ebbers of WorldCom and Ken Lay of Enron) remind us of some of the risks of idolizing CEO exemplars. Even Jack Welch's image took a beating with the published reports of the size and nature of his retirement package.[34]

Caution is needed if you are relying on charisma to induce followers to change. First of all, do you have the necessary skills? Many of us lack the capacities needed to create a charismatic response in others, and we may lack access to someone who supports the change and possesses those skills. More important, is this the best approach to mobilizing people around a vision of change? There are good reasons for people to be suspicious of charismatic appeals because history demonstrates that personal magnetism is not always directed toward desirable outcomes. In summary, enlisting charismatic leaders can prove valuable when attempting to overcome the reluctance of organization members to join in a change initiative. However, it's important to note that many leaders are very effective change agents without being particularly charismatic. Some of those who have proven to be most influential in nurturing long-term organizational success have been much quieter in their approach.[35] Such a list would include Meg Whitman (eBay), Darwin Smith (Kimberly-Clark), and Lou Gerstner (IBM).

A fourth way of stimulating awareness of a need for change is by taking the time to identify common or shared goals and working out ways to achieve them. Finding common areas of agreement is a very useful way to avoid and/or surmount resistance to change. Instead of focusing on what might be lost, an examination of what will be gained can create momentum for change. This is often achieved by having people seriously consider their longer-term interests (rather than their immediate positions) and the higher-order and longer-term goals that they would like to see pursued. If the change leader can focus on the needs of resisting individuals or groups, new and interesting perspectives on change can emerge. A shared interest in and a commitment to higher-order or superordinate goals can provide a powerful stimulus for commitment and mobilization.

Fifth, information and education can also raise awareness of the need for change. Reluctance to change may be a result of lack of information or awareness of its implications. This can be overcome with a well-organized communications campaign that provides employees with the needed information (e.g., data about the practices and approaches of others).[36] Research and theories on effective organizations can provide a contrast effect to the current mode of operation that can stimulate interest in change. We know a great deal about high-performance organizations. Using that knowledge to stimulate interest and discussion can facilitate change.

Once again, the change agent's personal credibility is crucial here. If employees are suspicious of the motives of the change agent or the accuracy of the information, or if there has been a history of difficult relationships, one should not expect the information to be accepted without serious reservations. Once information has been accepted, the ground is much more fertile for the development of a shared sense of the need for change and the vision for that change.

Robert Frey's experience with turning around the Cin-Made Corporation provides a graphic example of the dilemmas senior managers face when they must change and adapt their vision over time. Frey had purchased an organization with a paternalistic and low-achieving culture. His initial attempts to bring the organization to profitability involved a confrontational, combative style that was viewed as mean and aggressive by many employees. Unhappy with the results of confrontation—it obtained compliance and suspicion and little else—Frey decided to alter his vision for the organization (and his style) to one of information sharing and empowerment. Since Frey's credibility was minimal because of his previous autocratic management style, he had to create a paradoxical situation where through autocratic and demanding means he was able to move the organization to an empowered and involved environment. When an employee refused to engage in problem solving because it "wasn't his job," Frey threw a fit (his terminology). Only when confronted with these demands and with major changes to the reward system did his employees change their mode of operation. As the changes began to take root and demonstrate their value to employees, the improvement initiatives developed a reinforcing momentum of their own that nurtured and sustained future changes.[37]

What Are the Factors That Block People From Recognizing the Need for Change?

The need for change can create the dissatisfaction necessary for employees to know that change must occur. However, the future directions are not always obvious. An organization's past success, existing culture, and current vision can sometimes prove to be among the strongest impediments to creating awareness of the need for change.

For example, it took Continental Airlines a long time to wake up to the fact that attempting to rectify matters by doing existing things faster or more cost-effectively had become an unsuccessful downward cycle. Changing this could require more than a shift in strategy. It could require realignment of underlying systems and processes and, in more extreme situations, realignment of the corporate culture.

Newly elected chief executive officer (CEO) Gordon Bethune, and his newly appointed chief operating officer (COO) Greg Brenneman, carried out one of the most successful corporate turnarounds ever when they transformed Continental Airlines from a perennial loser into a profit maker. In less than six months, they inspired Continental's demoralized employees to move the firm from the worst of the 11 major U.S. airlines on the Department of Transportation's (DOT) on-time ratings to the fourth. Continental went from a loss of $200 million in 1994 to a pretax profit of $556 million in 1996. Bethune and Brenneman have continued this transformation, and the airline usually places in the top five in airline performance categories. Only the September 11 disaster that compounded already weak earnings potentials for the industry has marred their success story.

Bethune and Brenneman used a business strategy of superior customer service to achieve competitiveness for Continental. They achieved superior service by investing in and valuing the employees who had to supply that service. These leaders provided employees with a sense of purpose, rewards for success, and an improved climate within which to work. They showered them with praise, empowered them to solve problems, and built relationships with employees that other top managers had shunned. An important part of that schema is found in their management of culture and cultural artifacts.* As all good strategic managers would, they aligned major strategy-execution factors such as organizational structure and systems and processes with the new strategy. A key ingredient was aligning relevant parts of the organization's culture, its value systems and norms, with the new strategy.[38]

All too often strategists will introduce a new strategy, or even seek to change organizational culture to some degree, without attending to the question of the impact of the cultural artifacts on the desired change.[39] The artifacts are important because they help to define and operationalize the culture. Managers who retain cultural artifacts that reinforce elements of the old culture they want to change are leaving in barriers to their success. One of the major reasons that Bethune and Brenneman were so successful in implementing Continental's turnaround was their introduction of new cultural artifacts that reinforced service as a key value and replaced previous artifacts that had reinforced poor levels of service.

For example, a reward system was put into place (at Continental) for improved service. Performance-reward systems themselves are not necessarily cultural artifacts, but this reward system was tied directly to corporate performance, and the financial rewards were paid in a separate check to employees to draw attention to the relationship between performance and rewards. This reward system not only reinforced a new value at Continental, but it also became a symbol to employees of the importance of high levels of performance in the new Continental, as opposed to the acceptance of poor performance in the old Continental. In addition, stories were told throughout Continental about how the new CEO told jokes to employees, answered questions honestly, and was an all-around good guy to work for. These and numerous additional artifacts replaced old ones that had reinforced bureaucracy and the acceptability of poor performance, and that had led to unbelievably low employee morale.[40]

Scull argues that organizations trapped in their past successes often exhibit lots of activity, but the outcome is active inertia because they remain essentially unchanged.[41] He believes this occurs because of the following reasons:

- Strategic frames, those mental models or sets of assumptions of how the world works, become blinders to the changes that have occurred in the environment.
- Processes harden into routines and habits that are very difficult to change—they become ends in themselves rather than means to an end.
- Relationships with employees, customers, suppliers, distributors, and shareholders become shackles that limit the degrees of freedom available to respond to the changed environment.

---

*Cultural artifacts are those sets of attributes that give rise to attitudes, beliefs, and behaviors that help to differentiate one organization from another. There are at least five primary types of cultural artifacts: (1) key values and norms; (2) myths and sagas; (3) language systems and metaphors; (4) symbols, rituals, and ceremonies; and (5) the use of physical surroundings including interior design and equipment.

- Values, those deeply held beliefs that determine corporate culture, harden into dogmas in the form of rigid rules and regulations that have legitimacy, due to their previous existence and due to the fact that questioning them is seen as tantamount to heresy.

During periods of decline, senior management teams may become more polarized in their positions and may isolate themselves from data they need and thus incorrectly assess the need for change. Self-censorship, conflict avoidance, and other protective barriers used by senior management teams (e.g., unwillingness to solicit independent assessments) prevent concerns and critical information from being tabled as they attempt to preserve cohesion and commitment to a course of action. These are conditions that lead to groupthink* and can result in disastrous decisions that flow from the flawed analysis.[42] Change agents need to be vigilant and take action to ensure that such groupthink does not cloud their capacity to assess the need for change or impair the judgment of the teams with which they are working. If they are dealing with a cohesive team exhibiting the characteristics of groupthink, they need to take such action with care, considering how best to make them aware of the factors that may be clouding their judgment. Individuals who attempt to alert such teams to these realities are often dealt with harshly, since "shooting the messenger" is a speedy way for teams to protect themselves from difficult data. Strategies for avoiding groupthink include the following:

- Have the leader play an impartial role, soliciting information and input before expressing an opinion.
- Actively seek dissenting views. Have group members play the role of devil's advocate, challenging the majority's opinion.
- Actively pursue the discussion and analysis of the costs, benefits, and risks of diverse alternatives.
- Establish a methodical decision-making process at the beginning.
- Ensure an open climate for discussion and decision making and solicit input from informed outsiders and experts.
- Allow time for reflection and do not mistake silence for consent.[43]

Additional factors that obstruct managerial judgment over the need for change and the inability to develop constructive visions for future action have been highlighted in both the business and academic press. Ram Charan and Jerry Useem summarize such factors in their *Fortune* magazine article on organizational failure:

- They have been softened by past success.
- They see no evil (internal and external blindness).
- They fear the CEO and his/her biases more than competitors.
- They overdose on risk and play too close to the edge.
- Their acquisition lust clouds their judgment.

---

*Groupthink is "a mode of thinking that people engage in when they are deeply involved in a cohesive in-group, when the members' striving for unanimity overrides their motivation to realistically appraise alternative courses of action" (Janis, 1972). wps.prenhall.com/wps/media/objects/213/218150/glossary.html

- They listen to Wall Street more than employees and others who have valuable insights they should be attending to.
- They employ the "strategy du jour"—the quick-fix flavor of the day.
- They possess a dangerous corporate culture—one that invites high-risk actions.
- They find themselves locked in a new-economy death spiral—one that is sustained and accelerating.
- They have a dysfunctional board that fails in its duties around governance.[44]

Developing a well-grounded awareness of the need for change is a critical first step for change leaders when helping organizations overcome inertia, rein in high-risk propensities, address internal and external blind spots, and otherwise view their environment in ways it needs to be seen.

So far, this chapter has asked you to appreciate the variety of perspectives that will exist regarding the need for change. It emphasizes that your perspective may not be held by others and that often you need to develop or strengthen the need for change before trying to make specific changes. (A Checklist for Change is shown in Appendix 1 of this chapter.) In Lewin's terms, you need to unfreeze the organizational system. In Beckhard's terms, you need to create the need for change. One of the ways to enhance the perceived need for change and begin to create focused momentum for action is to contrast it with a clear statement concerning the vision for change.

How Do You Create a Powerful Vision for Change?

Change leaders must both recognize the need for change and create a change vision that captures the hearts of those involved. This change vision is best when it lines up with the organizational vision rather than working against it.

Recognizing the need for change begins a process of mobilizing others to act, but this potential must be focused if it is to have impact. The creation of a vision for change facilitates this by clarifying the road ahead for others to help them to see the purpose and what is expected of them. Better yet, if they (or their agents) help develop this vision, there is a greater chance that they will personally identify with the vision and will in turn become more actively engaged in bringing the change to fruition. As noted in an old English church inscription, "Vision without task is but a dream. Task without vision is drudgery. A vision and a task is the hope of the world."[45]

Vision can be used to embrace and strengthen the existing culture, or it can be used to transform the existing culture. At a micro level, it is used to focus awareness, energy, and initiative around local issues, processes, and opportunities. At their best, change visions provide well-grounded, challenging reasons for hope and optimism. At their worst, they are trite bromides that accelerate organizational cynicism, hallucinations that are confusing or misguided, or specific directions that are simply inappropriate or counterproductive.

As change leaders, we use change visions to create and advance the mental picture we have of the future and to provide directional guidance for others that we need to enlist in the enterprise. In Beckhard's terms, creating the vision is a key part of defining the future state and is central to any gap analysis done by a change leader.

Before addressing how to develop a vision for change, let's understand where organizational vision comes from. In an ideal world, it stems from the mission of the organization (its fundamental purpose or reason for existence) and is reflective of the core philosophy and values of the institution (what we believe about how we should do business). Vision identifies the desired ideal future. From this should flow the strategies, goals, and objectives.[46] If the process has been fully developed, the strategies, goals, and objectives will address the organizational level (What business are we in?), business level (Who is our target customer and what is our value proposition?), and operational level (How will we deliver on our value proposition?) of the enterprise.

The change agent's vision for change either flows from the overall mission and vision of the firm or it represents an undertaking to bring about change to the existing vision. Change agents create "subvisions" in order to generate emotional energy, commitment, and directional perspective for the organizational change as it proceeds from planning through to implementation and completion. If FedEx's overriding commitment to its customers for its express service is "absolutely, positively overnight," then a change leader's vision concerning a logistics support initiative might deal with enhancing accuracy in package tracking to reduce error rates.

Beech states that "vision is an agenda of goals . . . vision is a dream about how the ideal future might be . . . it gives rise to and dictates the shape of plans . . . vision infuses the plan with energy because it gives it direction and defines objectives. Even the most unassuming vision constitutes a challenge to become something stronger, better, different."[47] Approached properly, it can mobilize and motivate people[48] and have a positive impact on performance and attitudes.[49]

Jick outlines three methods of creating vision: leader developed, leader–senior team developed, and bottom-up visioning.[50] While bottom-up visioning may be time consuming and difficult, it can be valuable in facilitating the alignment of each organization member's vision with the overall vision. This appears to be particularly important when cultural changes are involved.[51] If organization members are aligned with you, you may be able to galvanize action by capturing in the vision the deep emotions felt by employees. If employees are diverse and have mixed feelings, this will take more time. If you do it successfully, you have the organization with you. Some refer to this as an employee-centric approach. If they both "get it" (i.e., the vision) and "want to get it," subsequent support for change will prove much easier to develop, leverage, and put into operation.

When thinking about vision, consider the following slogans that have been used to capture the essence of the message:

- We try harder. (Avis)
- Like a rock. (GM trucks)
- Everyday low prices. (Wal-Mart)
- We bring good things to life. (GE)
- Intel Inside.

These slogans are tied to mission and vision. They are recognizable to many of us and provide messages that are clear to employees and customers alike. They are meant to show initiative, durability, value, innovation, and quality.

The slogan "Quality is job 1" was used by Ford to symbolize its determination to improve quality in the 1980s. In the aftermath of quality and safety concerns that buffeted Ford, the automaker successfully used these words, with an accompanying concerted program of action, to refocus employee and public perceptions of the importance of quality to Ford and, ultimately, the excellence of their products. This major initiative spanned several years and was ultimately successful in taking root in the minds of employees and the public. More recently, the Ford Explorer/Firestone controversy[52] concerning vehicle stability in emergency situations reopened public questions of Ford's commitment to quality and safety and put extreme internal and external pressure on Ford and Bridgestone (Firestone's parent organization) to restore the public trust. The important lesson to draw from Ford's experience is that an image built on a vision that took years to develop can be shattered quickly.

Johnson and Johnson's response to the Tylenol tampering scare[53] and Procter & Gamble's[54] response to inappropriate competitive intelligence activities related to hair care products provide two examples of how clear vision can help organizations respond effectively to potentially damaging events. In the case of Tylenol, this best-selling brand was quickly pulled from store shelves until the company was confident it had effectively addressed the risk of product tampering, at the cost of tens of millions of dollars. In the Procter & Gamble situation, when the president of the company found out, he fired those involved, informed their competitor that they had been spied on, took appropriate action with respect to knowledge that had been inappropriately gained, and negotiated a multimillion-dollar civil damage payment to the aggrieved competitor. The actions of these two firms demonstrated their commitment to their respective visions and reinforced public and employee confidence in the firms and what they stood for.

According to Todd Jick, good change visions are[55]

- Clear, concise, easily understood
- Memorable
- Exciting and inspiring
- Challenging
- Excellence centered
- Stable, but flexible
- Implementable and tangible

The power of visions is exemplified by the vision of Opportunities 2000, a social service organization: "eliminating poverty in organizations."[56] This vision led a specific change campaign to persuade organizations to identify those people working for them who were living below the poverty line. The social service organization then undertook to work with these employees to help them move themselves out of poverty. The link between the transformational values and concrete action was fully developed by the social service organization. Does this vision statement meet the criteria that Jick specifies? Could it be improved? How?

The process of creating a vision statement encourages us to dream large, but sometimes we lose sight of what we really need to do. When visions become too grand and abstract, they can cease to have much impact. Alternatively, they may provide guidance that energizes and mobilizes individuals to undertake initiatives that unintentionally work at cross-purposes to other initiatives that have been embarked upon, or that may even have the potential to put the organization at risk.[57]

Lipton adopts a pragmatic view of what makes for an effective vision statement. He argues that it needs to convey three key messages: "the mission or purpose, the strategy for achieving the mission, and the elements of the organizational culture that seemed necessary to achieving the mission and supporting the strategy."[58] In turn, he believes visions will be more likely to fail when they lack certain qualities:

- Actions of senior managers are incongruent with the vision. They fail to walk the talk.
- It ignores the needs of those who will be putting it into practice.
- Unrealistic expectations develop around it that can't possibly be met.
- It is little more than limited strategies, lacking in a broader sense of what is possible.
- It lacks grounding in the reality of the present that can be reconciled.
- It is either too abstract or too concrete. It needs to stimulate and inspire, but there also needs to be the sense that it is achievable.
- It is not forged through an appropriately messy, iterative, creative process requiring a combination of "synthesis and imagination."
- It lacks sufficient participation and involvement of others to build a consensus concerning its appropriateness.
- Its implementation lacks "a sense of urgency . . . and measurable milestones."[59]

Visions can come in many forms. At the organizational level, they can take the form of statements, slogans, and stories that characterize what things will be like in the future. They can be explicit and written or implicit and understood. Effective visions are paradoxical. They need to tap into our highest values and lift our perspective to new horizons. Faith and hope create the energy to pursue the dreams captured in vision statements. At the same time, change visions need to be rooted in reality. Visions that are not connected to the current organization or fail to create a believable image and bridge to what is possible are ignored or rejected. To quote one change leader, you need to differentiate vision from hallucination and mirage! Obviously, both the quality of the message and the messenger are very influential to success or failure in this area.

Visions need to paint pictures that challenge the imagination and enrich the soul. Too many vision statements are insipid and dull. Too often they represent generic "pap"—right sounding words but ones devoid of real meaning because they were designed for plaques and outside consumption and are not rooted in the heart of the organization. Such visions focus on the lowest common denominator, something politically neutral that no one could object to. By trying to say everything or appeal to everyone, they say nothing and appeal to no one![60]

Table 4.2 contains the "Handy-Dandy Vision Crafter," a cynical view of organizational visions statements and how they are developed. While many statements may end up containing words similar to those in the model, the "Handy-Dandy Vision Crafter" ignores the hard work and the difficult creative process and activities that

Table 4.2   The Handy-Dandy Vision Crafter

Just fill in the blanks with the words that best suit your needs!

We strive to be the _____

(premier, leading, preeminent, world-class, dominant, best-of-class)

organization in our industry. We provide the best in _____

(committed, caring, innovative, expert, environmentally friendly, reliable, cost-effective, focused, diversified, high-quality, on-time, ethical, high value-added) (products, services, products and services, business solutions, customer solutions)

to _____

(serve our global marketplace; create customer, employee, and shareholder value; fulfill our covenants to our stakeholders; serve our customers' needs; delight our customers)

through _____ **employees**

(committed, caring, continuously developed, knowledgeable, customer-focused)

in the rapidly changing and dynamic _____ .

(industry, society, world)

Source: Unknown (adapted).

organizations go through to develop a vision statement that works for them. In many ways, the process of getting the vision is as important as the vision itself. Too many vision statements read as if the "Vision Crafter" had been used to create them.

Vision statements need punch, and that punch can be used to point the direction for the organization. By inference, they can have significant impact on which areas of the organization will grow and which ones will shrink. Great visions exude emotion; you can taste the appeal of the direction they indicate.

As noted earlier, companies can be trapped by the existing vision of their organization.[61] Goss, Pascale, and Athos argue that narrow definitions of what the company is about, failure to challenge the accepted boundaries and assumptions of the company, and an inability to understand the context lead to inadequate or mediocre visions. They show the problems that can occur when a vision is achieved—now what? Once the vision is achieved, motivation is lost. It is a bit like a team whose vision was to "make it to the Superbowl"—it is at a distinct disadvantage when playing against a team whose vision is to "win the Superbowl."

Once the vision is clear, the issue becomes one of acceptance by employees. Wheatley addresses this by saying that one must "get the vision off the walls and into the halls!"[62] She claims that we are often trapped by a mechanical view of vision, one that is limited to only a directional component of vision (vision as a vector). She argues that we need to view vision as a field that touches every employee differently, is filled with eddies and flux and shifting patterns. This view emphasizes the need to understand how each individual "sees" or "feels" the vision. As Beach says, "Each member (of the organization) has his or her own vision."[63] Somehow these individual visions need to be combined into an overall sense of purpose for the organization.

What Is the Difference Between an Organizational Vision and a Change Vision?

While the rules for crafting a vision remain the same, the focus of the vision can shift depending on the level and position of the change leader. For example, The Home Depot identifies at least four "subvisions" within an overall company framework. (See Table 4.3.)

Change leaders need to recognize the tensions that exist within organizations and then craft specific visions for the change initiatives they are creating. Their goals are advanced when they develop compelling messages that appeal to the particular groups of people critical to their change initiative. Ideally, this vision will fit neatly into the overall corporate mission and vision. In practice, there will be tensions between the changes proposed and what other parts of the organization might want.

When change leaders develop their vision for change, they are challenged with the question of where to set the margins. A narrower, tighter focus will make it easier to meet the test of Jick's characteristics of effective vision for a specific target audience, but it may also reduce the prospects for building alliances and a broader base of support for change. As the need for change extends to the strategic and cultural areas of a firm, this issue of building a larger constituency for the change becomes increasingly important. The first of two questions that must be answered is, where, if anywhere, do the common interests lie? Second, can the vision for change be framed in terms of the common interest without diverting its purpose or watering it down to the point where it no longer delivers a vision that will excite, inspire, and challenge?

This was a challenge that Dr. Martin Luther King, Jr. met superbly during his famous "I Have a Dream" speech in front of the Lincoln Memorial in 1963, on the 100th anniversary of the publishing of the Emancipation Proclamation by President Lincoln. This was at a critical point in the civil rights movement, and Dr. King succeeded in seizing that moment by enunciating a compelling vision that embraced a larger coalition. Attention to the coalition is apparent in his words: "The marvelous new militancy which has engulfed the Negro community must not lead us to distrust of all white people, for many of our white brothers, as evidenced by their presence here today, have come to realize that their destiny is tied up with our destiny and their freedom is inextricably bound to our freedom. We cannot walk alone." Dr. King then went on to set out a vision in language all would understand: "I have a dream that one day this nation will rise up and live out the true meaning of its creed: We hold these truths to be self-evident: that all men are created equal."[64]

The broader the appeal is of the vision, the more people that will be pulled by it and included. The risk is that the general appeal can break down when the vision

Table 4.3   The Home Depot "Subvision" Statements

The Home Depot strives to be the best corporate partner possible in our communities. We make positive contributions as a neighbor, an employer, a retailer, and a profitable investment opportunity through successful and strategic operations of our company.

The Home Depot helps people fulfill their dreams by helping them:

To live in a clean, safe, and caring community

To be part of a challenging, diverse, and inclusive workplace

To build and live in the house of their dreams

To create wealth and financial security

What does it mean to be the Neighbor of Choice?

For The Home Depot, being a partner to our cities and towns is of paramount importance. Our business creates jobs and opportunities for other businesses in the community. We strive to purchase locally, therefore keeping local dollars in the community. We're committed to bettering our community through local and area volunteer projects. And by offering home solutions in your neighborhood, we help consumers you to fulfill their dreams of turning a house into a home.

What does it mean to be the Employer of Choice?

To be the Employer of Choice means creating an inclusive and associate-centered culture. At The Home Depot, that means providing meaningful and challenging work for our associates that creates opportunity for growth and development. We also strive to provide economic opportunities through competitive wages and exceptional benefits packages to all associates. We recognize the contributions of our associates and reward their achievements, hard work, and dedication.

What does it mean to be the Retailer of Choice?

The Home Depot provides our customers with excellent service every time they come into our stores. We offer the right products, the right selection, the right prices, and a team of associates passionate about your needs. We build lasting relationships by helping customers realize their dreams and growing their trust through our products and services.

What does it mean to be the Investment of Choice?

Being an Investment of Choice means increasing economic growth through strategic marketing in stores and of products. It also means making decisions that reflect our policies surrounding social responsibility and considering the impact on our community. Being an Investment of Choice means continuing to gain on comparable store sales through innovative initiatives and growing adjacencies to meet the needs of the public to increase our economic bottom line and our corporate reputation.

Source: http://corporate.homedepot.com/wps/portal/!ut/p/.cmd/cs/.ce/7_0_A/.s/7_0_111/_s.7_0_A/7_0_111.

gets translated into actions. For example, the National Campaign to Prevent Teen Pregnancy was able to appeal to a very broad range of groups, from Catholics who opposed abortion to Planned Parenthood who accepted abortion.[65] Regardless of their positions in general, all groups wanted to prevent teen pregnancy. However, each of these groups had very different ideas about the strategies for prevention.

The coalitions that can be developed around a common vision can sometimes be surprising. For example, the ability for environmentalists and conservative Republicans to forge a common cause around the reduction of fossil-fuel consumption is not something many expected but one that now exists. Though their perceptions of the underlying rationale for the need for change are very different, they have been able to identify a common vision for change:

Environmentalists aren't the only ones applauding the sales tumble of big SUVs and pickups in the face of high gas prices.

Groups of conservative Republicans see an opportunity to step up a campaign to promote alternative-fuel vehicles and wean the nation from dependence on foreign oil. While skeptical about links between autos and global warming, the conservatives have concluded that cutting gasoline consumption is a matter of national security.

A who's who of right-leaning military hawks—including former CIA director R. James Woolsey and Iraq war advocate Frank J. Gaffney, Jr.—has joined with environmental advocates such as the Natural Resources Defense Council to lobby Congress to spend $12 billion to cut oil use in half by 2025. The alliance highlights how popular sentiment is turning against the no-worries gas-guzzling culture of the past decade and how alternative technologies such as gas-electric hybrids are finding increasingly widespread support.

"I think there are a number of things converging," said Gary L. Bauer, a former Republican presidential candidate and former head of the Family Research Council, who has signed on to a strange-bedfellows coalition of conservatives and environmentalists called Set America Free. "I just think reasonable people are more inclined right now to start thinking about ways our country's future isn't dependent on . . . oil from a region where there are a lot of very bad actors."[66]

In the past, visions have generally been viewed as organization-level statements. However, change programs can benefit from the clear sense of direction and purpose that vision statements provide. The most powerful visions tap into our need to be part of something better; they appeal to our emotions and move us beyond where we are. More mundane (but important) change programs involving restructuring or profit-focused issues need clear, concise targets.

---

*We use the following definitions. Mission means the overall purpose of the organization. Vision means the ultimate or ideal goal pursued. Thus, for a social service agency, the mission might be to look after the homeless. The vision would be to have no more homeless. An accounting firm's mission might be to provide excellent service in the provision and interpretation of financial information, while its vision might be to become the largest provider of such information in America.

Visions form the starting point for the chain of vision and mission—> objectives—> goals—> activities.* Change agents need to specify measurable goals for their change efforts. The research on goal setting has been quite clear on the benefits of **SMART** (specific, measurable, attainable, relevant, and time-bound) goals.[67] The provision of direction with measurable results for feedback galvanizes many people to pursue desired aims. This is easy to say, but defining the right measurable goals is not always straightforward. Perhaps a critical task is to persuade a key stakeholder to view the change positively. How does one assess when such attitudes are beginning to change? Identifying interim goals for a change project that demonstrate progress toward the end goals is often a difficult task.

Summary

In summary, change occurs when there is an understanding of the need for change, the vision of where the organization should go, and a commitment to action. Change leaders need to address the question "Why change?" and develop both a sound rationale for the change and a compelling vision of a possible future.

The rationale for change emerges from a sound understanding of the situation: (a) the external and internal data that point to a need for change, (b) an understanding of the perspectives of critical stakeholders in the organization, (c) internal data in the organization that affect any change and (d) the personal needs and abilities of the change leader. Critical in this is an understanding of the organization's readiness for change and the awareness of the need for change throughout the organization. Finally, the chapter discusses the creation of powerful visions and how to develop a specific change vision for a change project.

In addition to creating appealing visions of the future and demonstrating a compelling need for change, change agents need to understand the particular contexts of the major individuals in the change events. These stakeholders, or key players, will have an impact on the change situation, so their motives and interests need to be analyzed. The next chapter explores that topic.

Glossary of Terms

Need for Change—The need for change is the pressure for change in the situation. This need can be viewed as a "real" need, that demonstrated by data and facts, and a "perceived" need, that seen by participants in the change.

Perspective of the Stakeholder—The perspective of the stakeholder is the unique point of view of important participants in the change process. Understanding this perspective is critical to recognizing why this stakeholder supports or resists change.

Readiness for Change, Individual—Individual readiness for change is the degree to which the individual perceives the need for change and accepts it.

Readiness for Change, Organizational—Organizational readiness for change is the degree to which the organization as a whole perceives the need for change and accepts it.

Strategic Frame—A strategic frame is the mental model or set of assumptions held by change participants about how the world works.

Change Vision—The change vision is the idealized view of the future that will be realized after the change occurs.

APPENDIX 1: A CHECKLIST FOR CHANGE

Creating the Readiness for Change

1. What is the "objective" need for change? That is, what are the consequences to the organization of changing or not changing? Are people aware of these risks?

2. Are organization members aware of the need for change? Do they feel the need for change, or do they deny its need? Can they be informed?

3. Remember that individuals are motivated toward change only when they perceive the benefits as outweighing the costs. Do they see the benefits as outweighing the costs?

4. If individuals believe the benefits outweigh the costs, do they also believe that the probability of success is great enough to warrant the risk taking, including the investment of time and energy that the change will require?

5. Are there other change alternatives that they are more predisposed to? What is it about their costs, benefits, and risks that make them more attractive? How should these alternatives be addressed by the change leader?

EXAMPLE VISION AND MISSION STATEMENTS

Google

Google's mission is to organize the world's information and make it universally accessible and useful.

Bank of America

Bank of America helps build strong communities by helping people achieve their dreams. We reach for higher standards every day, in everything we do—for our customers, our shareholders, our associates, and our communities, upon which the future prosperity of our company rests.

The Home Depot

The Home Depot strives to be the best corporate partner possible in our communities. We make positive contributions as a neighbor, an employer, a retailer, and as a profitable investment opportunity through successful and strategic operations of our company.

The Home Depot helps people fulfill their dreams by helping them:

To live in a clean, safe, and caring community

To be part of a challenging, diverse, and inclusive workplace

To build and live in the house of their dreams

To create wealth and financial security

Wal-Mart

> "The secret of successful retailing is to give your customers what they want. And really, if you think about it from your point of view as a customer, you want everything: a wide assortment of good-quality merchandise; the lowest possible prices; guaranteed satisfaction with what you buy; friendly, knowledgeable service; convenient hours; free parking; a pleasant shopping experience." —Sam Walton (1918–1992)

General Motors

Diversity—Many People, One GM, Now

At GM, we are striving to create and maintain an environment that naturally enables the people of General Motors, its unions, suppliers, and dealers to fully contribute and achieve personal fulfillment in the pursuit of total customer enthusiasm.

General Electric

We are GE: For 124 years, what has remained constant is our dedication to change and progress. And it's what will keep us growing over the next 100 years. From jet engines to power generation, from financial services to plastics, from television to medical imaging, GE people worldwide are dedicated to turning good ideas into products and services that make the world a better place.

Harvard Business School

We educate leaders who make a difference in the world.

In this time of extraordinary change throughout the world, our clarity of purpose gives the School unmatched strength and influence. Our commitment to general management education focuses on building a deep understanding of business, teaching with skill and passion, and communicating ideas that have power in practice. Our dedication to field-based, problem-focused research and to the case method of instruction remains as meaningful today as it was at the beginning of this century.

But much about the School is changing as we embrace a rapidly changing world. We are educating students and building knowledge for a global community that is increasingly entrepreneurial and ever more reliant on technology—and therefore more dependent on its shifts. These times demand creative leadership.

As we prepare for the future, we will rely on our cornerstones to ensure that our fundamental values and focus endure.

We could not achieve this delicate and remarkable balance without a remarkable community of people—faculty, students, staff, and alumni—who work together to make this unique learning environment possible.

Johnson & Johnson—Our Credo

We believe our first responsibility is to the doctors, nurses and patients, to mothers and fathers and all others who use our products and services. In meeting their needs everything we do must be of high quality. We must constantly strive to reduce our costs in order to maintain reasonable prices. Customers' orders must be serviced promptly and accurately. Our suppliers and distributors must have an opportunity to make a fair profit.

We are responsible to our employees, the men and women who work with us throughout the world. Everyone must be considered as an individual. We must respect their dignity and recognize their merit. They must have a sense of security in their jobs. Compensation must be fair and adequate, and working conditions clean, orderly, and safe. We must be mindful of ways to help our employees fulfill their family responsibilities. Employees must feel free to make suggestions and complaints. There must be equal opportunity for employment, development, and advancement for those qualified. We must provide competent management, and their actions must be just and ethical.

We are responsible to the communities in which we live and work and to the world community as well. We must be good citizens—support good works and charities and bear our fair share of taxes. We must encourage civic improvements and better health and education. We must maintain in good order the property we are privileged to use, protecting the environment and natural resources.

Our final responsibility is to our stockholders. Business must make a sound profit. We must experiment with new ideas. Research must be carried on, innovative programs developed, and mistakes paid for. New equipment must be purchased, new facilities provided, and new products launched. Reserves must be created to provide for adverse times. When we operate according to these principles, the stockholders should realize a fair return.

Walgreen's Mission Statement

Walgreen's mission is to offer customers the best drugstore service in America. We are guided by a century-old tradition of fairness, trust, and honesty as we continue to expand our store base and offer career opportunities to a fast-growing and diverse group of men and women. Our goal is to develop people who treat customers—and each other—with respect and dignity. We will support these efforts with the most innovative retail thinking, services and technology. The success we achieve will allow us to reinvest in our future and build long-term financial security for our employees and our shareholders.

The Hospital for Sick Children (Toronto)

Mission

The Hospital for Sick Children is a healthcare community dedicated to improving the health of children. Our mission is to provide the best in family-centered, compassionate care, to lead in scientific and clinical advancement, and to prepare the next generation of leaders in child health.

Our Vision

The Hospital for Sick Children will create, evaluate, apply, and disseminate knowledge to improve the health of children. We will lead in providing exemplary family-centered care, innovation, and discovery, focusing on those areas in which we can make the greatest contribution. Collaborating with others, we will become the best pediatric academic health science centre in the world.

Our Values

- Family-centered

We believe that children should be provided with the highest-quality care and with the opportunity for continuing improvement of their health. Our patient care, prevention, and health promotion activities are compassionate, responsive, family-centered, and recognized as a responsibility of all staff. We strive to be sensitive to the physical, spiritual, and emotional needs of the multicultural community we serve.

- Leadership and accountability

We are each accountable for our contribution to HSC's mission of improving care and the health of children. Individually and as team members, we are responsible for identifying opportunities, initiating self-learning, and persevering to improve child health. Leadership at all levels will be supported throughout HSC.

- Critical inquiry and innovation

We seek answers to the unanswered questions and challenge the boundaries of patient care, research, and education. Our learning leads to discoveries and break-throughs and we seek to disseminate the new knowledge broadly and rapidly. We foster an environment of inquiry and innovation, and provide the tools to support individuals and teams in accomplishing their goals. We promote a learning organization that continually expands our capacity to create our own preferred future.

- Collaboration, teamwork, and citizenship

Individuals and the institution are partners for the greater whole. We recognize that all of our advances have been produced through the work and passion of many. We respect and value each individual's unique contributions and recognize and harness the power of teams. We give back to HSC in our efforts both to improve child health and to make this a great place in which to work. We value our partnership with the University of Toronto and our collaborations with other organizations. We are committed to sharing with others in the development of research, patient care, and education programs in facilities beyond HSC.

- Quality, integrity, and advocacy

We conduct all of our endeavors—patient care, education, research, and the management of our organization—to the highest quality and with the greatest personal and professional integrity. We are dedicated to using our special expertise to advocate on behalf of children.

- Efficient use of resources

Increased financial independence and a stable funding base are essential to the fulfillment of our mission. We deploy our resources effectively and efficiently at all levels in the organization. We are committed to further developing and maintaining the fiscal strength of The Hospital for Sick Children.

END-OF-CHAPTER EXERCISES

TOOLKIT EXERCISE 4.1

Developing the Background to Understand the Need for Change

As suggested earlier in this book, a careful diagnosis is essential for successful organizational change. Much of this diagnosis is needed to understand the need for change that the organization faces and then to engage and persuade organization members concerning the need for change.

1. Consider an example of an organizational change that you are familiar with. What data could help you understand the need for change?
   Have you:
   a. Understood and made sense of external data? What else would you like to know?

   b. Understood and made sense of the perspectives of other stakeholders? What else would you like to know?

   c. Understood and assessed your personal concerns and perspectives and how they may be affecting your perspective on the situation?

   d. Understood and made sense of internal data? What else would you like to know?

2. What does your analysis suggest to you about the need for change?

TOOLKIT EXERCISE 4.2

Writing a Vision Statement[68]

Think of an organization you are familiar with that is in need of change. If you were the change leader, what would be your vision statement for change?

1. Write your vision statement for the change you are striving for.

2. Check out this vision with others in the course. What is their response to it? Do they see it as:
   - Clear, concise, and easily understood?
   - Memorable?
   - Exciting and inspiring?
   - Challenging?
   - Excellence centered?
   - Stable and yet flexible?
   - Implementable and tangible?

3. Does the vision promote change and a sense of direction?

4. Does the vision provide the basis from which you can develop the implementation strategy and plan?

5. Does the vision provide focus and direction to those who must make ongoing decisions?

6. Does the vision embrace the critical performance factors that organization members should be concerned about?

7. Does the vision engage and energize, as well as clarify? What is the emotional impact of the vision?

8. Does the vision promote commitment? Are individuals likely to be opposed to the vision, passive (let it happen), moderately supportive (help it happen), or actively supportive (make it happen)?

TOOLKIT EXERCISE 4.3

Developing the Need for Change

For any change to be successful, the need for change must be real and must be perceived as real. If the organization does not accept the need for change, the chances of anything substantive happening are negligible. Thus, developing the need for change is vital.

Understanding the **gap** between what is and what is desired is important in order to accurately describe the need for change.

Think of an organization that you are familiar with that is in need of change.

1. What is the **gap** between the present state and the desired future state?

2. How strong is the need for change?

3. What is the source of this need? Is it external to the organization?

4. Is there tangible evidence of the need for change in that there is concrete evidence of the need or a crisis situation that demonstrates the need for change?

5. If the change does not occur, what will be the impact on the organization in the next 2 to 6 years?

6. What is the objective, long-range need to change?

People can be motivated by higher-order purposes, things that relate to fundamental values. Change visions can be crucial in capturing support for change and in explaining the nature of change to others. Creating such a change vision is tricky. If one aims too high, it taps into higher values but often fails to link with the specific change project or program. If one aims too low, the vision fails to tap into values that motivate us above and beyond the ordinary. Such a vision looks like and feels like an objective.

7. Write a vision statement for a change project that this organization needs to undertake. It should capture a sense of higher-order purpose or values that underpin the change and communicate what the project is about.

8. Explain how the vision links the need for change.

Notes

1. More pain, waiting for the gain. (2006, February 11). *The Economist,* 58.

2. Salter, C. (2002, February 4). Fresh start 2002: On the road again. *Fast Company.* http://www.fastcompany.com/online/54/yellow.html.

3. Lanes, W. J., III, & Logan, J. W. (2004, November). A technique for assessing an orga-nization's ability to change. *IEEE Transactions in Engineering Management,* (*51*)4, 483.

4. Keeton, K. B., & Mengistu, B. (1992, Winter). The perception of organizational cul-ture by management level: Implications for training and development. *Public Productivity & Management Review,* (*16*)2, 205–213.

5. Skinner, D. (2004). Evaluation and change management: Rhetoric and reality. *Human Resource Management Journal,* (*14*)3, 5–19.

6. Senge, P. M. (1994). *The fifth discipline: The art and practice of the learning organiza-tion.* New York: Currency Doubleday.

7. Sull, D N. (1999, July-August). Why good companies go bad. *Harvard Business Review,* 42–52; Charan, R., & Useem, J. (2002, May 27). Why companies fail. *Fortune,* (*145*)11, 50–62; Schreiber, E. (2002, March). Why do many otherwise smart CEO's misman-age the reputation asset of their company. *Journal of Communication Management,* (*6*)3, 209–219.

8. Hamel, G. (2002). *Leading the revolution.* New York: Penguin Group.

9. Kotter, J. P. (2002). *The heart of change.* Boston: Harvard Business School Press.

10. Mintzberg, H., & Westley, F. (1992). Cycles of organizational change. *Strategic Management Journal,* 13, 39–59.

11. Sull, D. N. (1999, July). Why good companies go bad. *Harvard Business Review,* 42–52.

12. Weisbord, M., & Janoff, S. (2005). Faster, shorter, cheaper may be simple; it's never easy. *The Journal of Applied Behavioral Science,* (*41*)1, 70–82.

13. Personal experience of the authors.

14. Sirkin, H., Keenan, P., & Jackson, A. (2005, October). The hard side of change man-agement. *Harvard Business Review,* 4.

15. Personal experience of the authors.

16. Barnett, C. K., & Tichy, N. M. (2000). Rapid-cycle CEO development: How new leaders learn to take charge. *Organizational Dynamics,* (*29*)1, 16–32. Reprinted with permis-sion from Elsevier.

17. Personal experience of the authors.

18. Pascale, R. (1998, April). Grassroots leadership—Royal Dutch/Shell. Retrieved on February 23, 2002, from Fast Company.com, http://www.fastcompany.com/online/14/grass roots/html.

19. Decker, D. C., & Belohlay, J. A. (1997). Managing transitions. *Quality Progress,* (*30*)4, 93–97.

20. Spector, B. (1993). From bogged down to fired up. In T. D. Jick (Ed.), *Managing change: Cases and concepts* (pp. 121–128). Boston: Irwin/McGraw-Hill.

21. Rucci, A. J., Kirn, S. P., & Quinn, R. T. (1998, January-February). The employee-customer profit chain at Sears. *Harvard Business Review,* 83–97.

22. Trahant, B., & Burke, W. W. (1996). Creating a change reaction: How understanding organizational dynamics can ease reengineering. *National Productivity Review,* (*15*)4, 37–46; Lannes, W. J., III, & Logan, J. W. (2004). A technique for assessing an organization's ability to change. *IEEE Transactions in Engineering Management,* (*51*)4, 483.

23. Ratterty, A., & Simons, R. (2002). The influence of attitudes to change on adoption of an integrated IT system. *Organization Development Abstracts.* Academy of Management

Proceedings; and Mitchell, N., et al. (2002). Program commitment in the implementation of strategic change. *Organization Development Abstracts.* Academy of Management Proceedings.

24. Hyde, A., & Paterson, J. (2002). Leadership development as a vehicle for change during merger. *Journal of Change Management, (2)*3, 266–271.

25. Nevis, E. C., DiBella, A. J., & Gould, J. M. (1995, Winter). Understanding organizations as learning systems. *Sloan Management Review, (36)*2, 73–85.

26. Stewart, T. A. (1994, February 7). Rate your readiness to change. *Fortune,* 106–110.

27. Holt, D. (2002). Readiness for change: The development of a scale. *Organization Development Abstracts.* Academy of Management Proceedings.

28. Havman, H. A. (1992). Between a rock and a hard place: Organizational change and performance under conditions of fundamental environmental transformation. *Administrative Science Quarterly, (37)*1, 48–75.

29. Barnett, C. K., & Pratt, M. G. (2000). From threat-rigidity to flexibility: Toward a learning model of autogenic crisis in organizations. *Journal of Organizational Change Management, (13)*1, 74–88.

30. Simons, T. L. (1999). Behavioral integrity as a critical ingredient for transformational leadership. *Journal of Organizational Change Management, (12)*2, 89.

31. Hosmer, L. T., & Kiewitz, C. (2005). Organizational justice: A behavioral science concept with critical implications for business ethics and stakeholder theory. *Business Ethics Quarterly, (15)*1, 67.

32. Op. cit., More pain, waiting for the gain. *The Economist.*

33. Tucker, B. A., & Russell, R. F. (2004). The influence of the transformational leader. *Journal of Leadership and Organizational Studies, (10)*4, 103–111.

34. Naughton, K. (2002, September 30). The perk wars. *Newsweek, (140)*14, 44.

35. Mintzberg, H., Simons, R., & Basu, K. (2002, Fall). Beyond selfishness. *Sloan Management Review,* 67–74; Collins J. (2001). *From good to great: Why some companies make the leap . . . and others don't.* New York: HarperBusiness; De Geus, A. (1997). The living company. *Harvard Business Review, (75)*2, 51–59.

36. Wall, S. J. (2005). The protean organization: Learning to love change. *Organizational Dynamics, (34)*1, 37.

37. Frey, R. (1993, September-October). Empowerment or else. *Harvard Business Review,* 80–94.

38. Bethune, G., & Huler, S. (1998). *From worst to first: Behind the scenes of Continental's remarkable comeback.* New York: John Wiley & Sons; and Brenneman, G. (1998, September October). Right away and all at once: How we saved Continental. *Harvard Business Review,* 162–173.

39. Higgins, J. M., & McAllaster, C. (2004). If you want strategic change, don't forget to change your culture artifacts. *Journal of Change Management, (4)*1.

40. Higgins & McAllaster, op. cit., pp. 63–73.

41. Scull, D. N. (1999, July-August). Why good companies go bad. *Harvard Business Review,* 42–52.

42. Eaton, J. (2001). Management communication: The threat of groupthink. *Corporate Communications, (6)*4, 183–192.

43. Whyte, G. (1989). Groupthink reconsidered. *Academy of Management Review,* 14, 40–56; Neck, C. P., & Moorhead, G. (1992). Jury deliberations in the trial of U.S. v. John DeLorean: A case analysis of groupthink avoidance and enhanced framework. *Human Relations, (45)*10, 1077–1091.

44. Charan, R., & Useem, J. (2002, May 22). Why companies fail. *Fortune,* 50-62.

45. Simons, G. F., et al. (1998). Inscription on an 18th-century church in England. In S. Komives, J. Lucas, & T. R. McMahon, *Exploring leadership* (p. 54). San Francisco: Jossey-Bass.

46. Thornberry, N. (1997). A view about vision. *European Management Journal,* (*15*)1, 28–34.

47. Beach, L. R. (1993). *Making the right decision.* Englewood Cliffs, NJ: Prentice Hall.

48. Nanus, B. (1992). *Visionary leadership.* San Francisco: Jossey-Bass; Kirkpatrick, S. A., & Locke, E. A. (1996). Direct and indirect effects of three core charismatic leadership components on performance and attitudes. *Journal of Applied Psychology,* 81, 36–51.

49. Baum, I. R., Locke, E. A., & Kirkpatrick, S. A. (1998). A longitudinal study of the relation of vision and vision communication to venture growth in entrepreneurial firms. *Journal of Applied Psychology,* 83, 43–54.

50. Jick, op. cit., pp. 145–147.

51. Higgins, J. M., & McAllaster, C. (2004). If you want strategic change, don't forget to change your cultural artifacts. *Journal of Change Management,* (*4*)1, 63–73.

52. Kalogeridis, C. (2005, January). The Ford/Firestone fiasco: Coming to blows. *Radnor,* (185)1, 22–24.

53. The National Business Hall of Fame. (1990, March 12). *Fortune,* (*121*)6, 42.

54. Serwer, A. (2001, September 17). P&G's covert operation. *Fortune,* (*144*)5, 42.

55. Jick, T. (1993). The vision thing (A). In T. Jick, *Managing change* (pp. 142–148). Homewood, IL: Richard D. Irwin.

56. Personal experience of the authors.

57. Langeler, G. H. (1992, March-April). The vision trap. *Harvard Business Review,* 46–55.

58. Lipton, M. (1996, Summer). Demystifying the development of an organizational vision. *Sloan Management Review,* 83–92.

59. Lipton, op. cit., p. 86.

60. Levin, I. M. (2000). Vision revisited. *Journal of Applied Behavioral Science,* (*36*)1, 91–107.

61. Goss, T., Pascale, R., & Athos, A. (1993, November-December). The reinvention roller coaster: Risking the present for a powerful future. *Harvard Business Review,* 97–108.

62. Wheatley, M. (1994). *Leadership and the new sciences* (ch. 3). San Francisco: Berrett-Koehler.

63. Beach, op. cit., p. 58.

64. Dr. Martin Luther King Jr.'s I Have a Dream Speech. The Martin Luther King Jr. Papers Project at Stanford University, www.stanford.edu/group/King/publications/speeches/address_at_march_on_washington.pdf.

65. National campaign to prevent teen pregnancy. (2000, March). *Harvard Business School Case Study,* 9–300–105.

66. Schneider, G. (2005, March 31). An unlikely meeting of the minds. *Washington Post,* E1 Copyright © *The Washington Post.* Reprinted with permission.

67. Latham, G. P., & Locke, E. P. (1987). How to set goals. In R. W. Beatty (Ed.), *The performance management sourcebook.* Amherst, MA: Human Resource Development Press.

68. Drawn from Jick, T. (1993, Summer). The vision thing (A). In T. Jick, *Managing change.* Homewood, IL: Richard D. Irwin; Lipton, M. (1996, Summer). Demystifying the development of an organizational vision. *Sloan Management Review,* 83–92.

Northwell Inc.[1]

Case Study 1

When Northwell's senior management and board first gave Claudia Leung the leadership role in the development of a virtual medical product and service mall with Medichek, a year and a half ago, she was delighted. She and Nathan Daniels (VP Marketing) had uncovered the opportunity, Medichek was an excellent organization, and it had been clear that this was a venture well worth embracing. Claudia Leung, CFO of Northwell, had an excellent working relationship with senior management at Medichek. Since Northwell's major contribution in the shorter term would be cash ($7.5 million as of now), she was the ideal candidate for the assignment. The development of this initiative would increase her entrepreneurial skill set and profile and looked to be a manageable addition to her portfolio of responsibilities.

Claudia was beginning to wonder if this dream assignment was about to become a nightmare. The project had run into technical problems, was 4 to 5 months behind schedule, and the board and senior management at Northwell were frustrated and putting pressure on Claudia to get things moving. Executives at Medichek were pushing back, in response to their own frustration, stating that Claudia's interventions were hindering progress. In addition, she'd been hearing growing rumblings of concern and unhappiness in the sales and marketing areas, evidenced in the recent resignation of three staff members and the loss of a good distributor from the U.S. Midwest.

Northwell's senior management and board chair had asked Claudia to recommend a course of action that would rectify problems with this undertaking. They were expecting this advice to be tabled within the next two weeks.

History of the Firm

Northwell Medical was founded 25 years ago, as the result of a merger between a Canadian and U.S. firm. Northern Medical, the Canadian partner, had specialized in durable hospital/medical products, while Wellness Medical had focused on consumable hospital products. Both had distributed their products in Canada and the United States for a decade prior to the merger and had shared marketing and distribution services for 5 years.

The actual merger announcement was anticipated and welcomed by most shareholders and managers. There were some initial difficulties as structures, systems, processes, roles, and reporting

---

[1]This case was prepared by Professor Anthony Atkinson of the University of Waterloo and Professor Gene Deszca of Wilfrid Laurier University. Copyright© G. Deszca and A. Atkinson.

relationships were sorted out during the first year. By year three, the merger was viewed by both insiders and outsiders as a success. Market penetration and sales accelerated while average costs declined (after accounting for onetime restructuring costs). Growth rates averaged 20% (discounting for inflation) throughout the next 15 years in what was a fairly mature market. Northwell made aggressive investments in technology and product development during this period. Profitability grew at rates 10% above industry norms, with the return on equity averaging 18% during this period. This growth was partially stimulated by the addition of new and/or improved products, but it was largely due to Northwell's spreading reputation for value, service, and support. They won market share from competitors, even though their price structure was typically 2% to 10% higher.

As consolidation occurred in the hospital and nursing care delivery systems, it was clear that Northwell was well positioned to solidify its position as a preferred supplier among purchasing agents, administrators, and hospital user groups. In U.S. industry surveys of hospital suppliers, Northwell regularly placed in the top five for quality, service, support, and overall customer satisfaction during the two decades that followed.

Northwell Medical produced a wide range of medical products for institutional usage. Products ranged from consumable patient supplies such as wound dressings, bandages, and disposable surgical supplies to more durable products (e.g., IV units, walkers, canes). In addition to the products it produced, Northwell used their sales network to distribute high-quality, higher-margin products, sourced largely from European and smaller North American specialty manufacturers. Ten years ago, these accounted for 10% of the products listed, 15% of sales, and 6% of the profits, and by the most recent year end, they represented 10% of products listed, 15% of sales, and 25% of profits. These products included hospital beds, wheelchairs, and orthopedic supports (braces for limbs and neck). The intent was to provide purchasing agents and their therapeutic committees with one-stop shopping for their medical product needs in particular product categories.

Northwell's production facilities were located in the United States, Canada, and Mexico. The Canadian plant specialized in products that involve metal fabrication (approximately 20% of total manufactured products, 25% of sales, and 30% of profits in the most recent year end), while the two U.S. plants manufactured both plastic and fabric related products (40% of manufactured products, 30% of sales, and 15% of profits). The Mexican plant also produced plastic and fabric related products (20% of manufactured products listed, 15% of sales, and 10% of profits). In addition, Northwell outsourced manufacturing services for some of their products in the Asia-Pacific area (10% of manufactured products listed, 10% of sales, and 15% of profits).

In North America, Northwell marketed and sold their products primarily through their own sales force. In addition, a number of medical-product distribution companies carried some or all of the Northwell line. They were prequalified by Northwell and tended to service smaller hospitals and nursing homes, medical and dental offices, and regional medical-product retail supply outlets. The prequalification checks included financial stability, reputation, and service quality. Those selected committed to agreed-to minimum sales volumes. Distributors were not given exclusive territories, but over the years, they had sorted themselves out in ways that meant that most American markets were well serviced. These independent distributors accounted for 25% of sales and approximately 30% of the profits. Wholesale prices allowed for dealer margins that varied from 15% to 30%, depending on the type of product and the complexity involved in selling and servicing the product (e.g., in-service hospital staff training in product use).

Over the years, certain managers and board members had expressed interest in extending their activities into foreign markets (Europe and Japan were the ones most frequently mentioned).

However, Northwell had shied away from these opportunities, due to concerns over their ability to compete and the belief that there were more profitable growth opportunities available in North America. Throughout the years, at the request of specific European firms they trusted, Northwell had engaged in the export of a limited range of relatively unique products. For the most recent year end, these accounted for approximately 5% of sales and 5% of the profits.

Growth and profitability slowed at Northwell 9 years ago and flattened thereafter. A year ago, sales growth was 4%, profitability had fallen to 6% of sales, and the return on equity was 6.5%. Their reputation as a benchmark to be emulated in the medical-products sector was now a memory.

Two notable new-product failures about a decade ago had resulted in staff changes and a new director of New Product Development. Since Sales and Marketing were seen as the primary clients of New Product Development, funding responsibility for R&D shifted to Sales and Marketing 8 years ago. The changes succeeded in reducing costs in this area by 33% through more careful screening and approval processes and tighter budget controls. However, within 2 years of the change, most of the output from New Product Development was in the form of incremental product improvements, and there was limited work under way in the area of significant product innovations. In an effort to increase their productivity, New Product Development personnel restricted their direct field involvement with Sales personnel and clients. The problem/opportunity-finding role was delegated to Marketing and Sales personnel, who were expected to forward project and product suggestions to the Product Development Approval Team. The director of New Product Development chaired this committee, with representation from Sales, Marketing, and Finance/Accounting.

The percentage of sales coming from products introduced in the previous 4 years declined from 25% a decade ago to 8% a year ago. Finger pointing had become the order of the day, as frustration surfaced over the slow pace of innovation. New Product Development staff complained about a lack of resources, equipment, and bureaucracy, while Sales and Marketing personnel grumbled that Northwell's reputation as a problem solver and innovator was being eroded due to the inability of R&D to deliver the right products at the right time and price.

Profitability was negatively affected during the past 8 years by competitive pressures on price and customer servicing costs. Northwell was still a preferred supplier, but the emergence of healthcare cost-containment pressures and powerful buying groups had reduced Northwell's capacity to command a price premium. More importantly, key competitors caught up with Northwell in the areas of sales, support, and solutions and were able to do so in innovative ways that reduced their sales costs (e.g., call centers, logistical streamlining, and electronically distributed training support). Sales and servicing costs at Northwell were now approximately 15% higher than their key competitors. However, customers did not perceive significant differences in the levels of support and responsiveness.

Exhibit 1 summarizes the financial results and performance over the last 4 years.

The Medichek Opportunity

Two years ago, Northwell's senior management team received clear feedback that stockholders were very dissatisfied with cost-containment and market-expansion activities. At that time, the board replaced the vice presidents of Sales and Manufacturing (the president was replaced a year earlier). All three appointments were from outside the organization—something unheard of in the past. In addition, the board instituted performance contracts with members of the senior management team. These performance contracts required the following improvements to be achieved within a 4-year period: sales growth of 30% over levels in the most recent year; a return on equity of 18%; a return to gross profitability levels that exceeded industry averages by 10%;

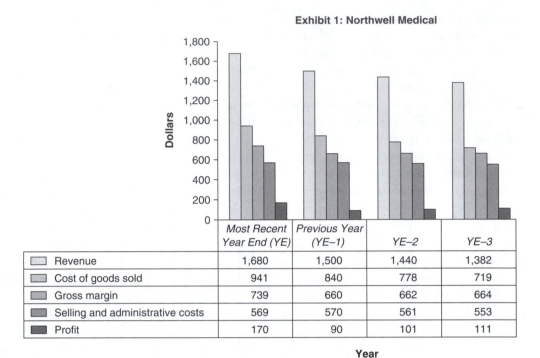

Exhibit 1: Northwell Medical

	Most Recent Year End (YE)	Previous Year (YE–1)	YE–2	YE–3
Revenue	1,680	1,500	1,440	1,382
Cost of goods sold	941	840	778	719
Gross margin	739	660	662	664
Selling and administrative costs	569	570	561	553
Profit	170	90	101	111

Year

15% of sales coming from products introduced in the previous 4 years; and a return of customer satisfaction levels to those achieved a decade earlier.

Nathan Daniels, the vice president of Marketing, and Claudia Leung, the CFO, had grown up at Northwell, and both had the trust and respect of the new CEO and the board chair. Both were appointed to their senior roles 3 years ago, following the early retirement of their predecessors. Approximately 2 years ago, the CEO gave them joint responsibility for identifying growth opportunities. Nathan and Claudia had bumped heads in the past over the value of marketing expenditures, but they recognized the assignment's importance and decided to set aside past difficulties. Both possessed a strong interest in emerging information technologies, and this quickly led them to investigate Web-based marketing, distribution, and e-commerce opportunities for Northwell.

Research conducted 3 years ago told Northwell that their primary customers were either currently able to order and receive information over the Internet or soon would be Internet-enabled. Sales personnel reported that an increasing amount of their customer communications was being conducted over the Internet and that Northwell's capacities in this area were lagging behind their key competitors, as they were in other areas of technology-enabled customer support. Further, many of these primary customers seemed quite interested in exploiting this technology to enhance efficiency, speed, communications, and the efficacy of training and development. These interests seemed to fit well with the ideas that Nathan and Claudia were pursuing.

Shortly after being assigned responsibility for identifying growth opportunities, Nathan and Claudia decided to meet with the senior management of Medichek. Medichek was an emerging Net-based U.S. firm, specializing in health care. They had been founded 8 years ago, were located in Dallas, were growing very quickly (200+% per year), and had 275 employees.

Medichek's primary business was the design and management of Web sites for a number of leading healthcare organizations (hospitals, nursing homes, pharmaceutical manufacturers and distributors, medical-product manufacturers), including Northwell's (as of approximately 2 years ago). In addition, 3 years ago, Medichek launched a subscription service that provided online access to medical information to healthcare professionals and researchers. This was an expensive service to develop and maintain, but subscriber growth over the first 18 months exceeded Medichek's expectations by a factor of 2. Medichek had a reputation for innovation, honesty, responsiveness, quality, candidness, and trustworthiness. They were very selective in terms of whom they chose to do business with. It was said that Medichek picked their clients and those who were selected were the lucky ones.

Medichek was 75% owned by the five individuals who had founded the company (all were in their 30s and directly involved in the business). They had resisted takeover and IPO opportunities, preferring to develop and control their own organization. Nathan first met Medichek's owners 3 years ago, when he was looking for a Web site designer for Northwell. True to form, it was Medichek who, after careful deliberation, selected Northwell as a client. While initially "put off" by Medichek's approach, Nathan and Claudia quickly became fans, and this enthusiasm extended to other members of senior management. Their work was fairly priced by industry standards, but more importantly, their strategic approach to site design and management resulted in customer accolades and industry awards in recent years. Sales and marketing personnel responded favorably to Northwell's new Web site when it went live, reporting positive customer reactions to its layout, content, and functionality. Though they still felt that technology-enabled customer support was lagging (e.g., electronic access to technical training support materials), they viewed this as an important step in the right direction.

Medichek's owners and employees often commented about how comfortable they felt working with Northwell. They particularly appreciated Northwell's commitment to dealing with their clients in ways that emphasized customer knowledge, value, and informed decision making. Medichek officials complained that Northwell's decision making sometimes took too long, that Northwell overattended to cost rather than value, and that Northwell had difficulty keeping their "fingers out of the pot" once decisions were made. However, they discounted these frustrations, chalking them up to Northwell's concern for quality and competitiveness.

During the development of Northwell's Web site, it became apparent to Claudia and Nathan that there might be good reason to get closer to Medichek concerning another venture they were pursuing. Medichek had been exploring the development of a virtual health-service mall for use by the healthcare industry. The idea was that professional end users (hospitals, nursing homes, physicians, pharmacists) could access this site in order to electronically shop for the products they needed. Products and services supplying firms would be carefully screened to ensure that they met quality, value, and customer service standards. Quotes could be solicited, orders placed, and payments received electronically. Further, the mall would serve as a primary source of product information, product warnings and recalls, educational online healthcare forums, and healthcare news and would distribute Web-based training in healthcare matters (e.g., product use education).

From the initial meeting on the virtual mall approximately 2 years ago, Medichek was clear that they wanted to partner with Northwell in the development of this undertaking. They proposed that the mall be established as an independent business unit and that Northwell and Medichek own it equally. Northwell would commit to becoming a prime occupant in the mall and would supply the needed development funds (estimated at $5 to $10 million). Medichek would develop the necessary technology platforms, structure the services and pricing arrangements with mall occupants, structure the entry criteria, and market the mall service. Medichek's reputation would prove very helpful here. They estimated that it would take a year to make this project a reality.

Nathan and Claudia were excited by this opportunity. It had the potential to significantly reduce costs for both customers and suppliers and provide Northwell with the opportunity to dramatically extend their reach into foreign markets. Though quality competitor products would also be listed at the mall, these were already readily available in the marketplace. More importantly, the mall would be selective concerning who was allowed to be listed and exhibit. When combined with the quality of the information, news, and other services available, it was anticipated that there would be a very positive halo cast on firms allowed to market their goods and services at the site.

When Nathan and Claudia talked to Northwell's IT group and the CEO about this opportunity, interest and excitement spread. Sales and marketing personnel also expressed interest, but they were concerned with the implications on existing channels of distribution and customer contact. This was a company that had built their reputation on their personal relationships with their distributors and customers (i.e., responsiveness and support), and they were concerned with how things would be affected by this new venture. Nathan and Claudia asked them to relax and give the new venture time to develop. They told staff that the new venture would increase the exposure and reach of Northwell, thereby opening up new opportunities. Channels would not change overnight, and staff was advised that Northwell would monitor things closely and help employees adapt and transition into new roles, as needed. They were told that this was new territory for everyone, so the keys were to be patient and open-minded, communicating information, questions, and concerns in a timely fashion.

Claudia worked with Medichek's CFO to develop the business plan, projections, and a Letter of Understanding during April a year ago.

Northwell's board was first informed of the possible opportunity in January a year ago. In May, Northwell's senior management team recommended the partnership (as set out in the Letter of Understanding) to its board. Medichek and Northwell jointly signed the Letter of Understanding in June a year ago, with the first $2 million installment of development support issued in June. Northwell's managers were shocked (pleasantly) by the speed of the approval process. Primary responsibility for managing the relationship with Medichek was assigned to Claudia.

During the latter half of the previous year, Medichek hired additional staff and proceeded with the development work. By February of the current year, Northwell had advanced $4.5 million in development support. During this period, Northwell had focused on shoring up their internal operations and improving their profitability. By December of the previous year, products introduced within the past 4 years had grown to 9% of sales, and growth had increased 12% over the previous year. Profitability had improved to 10% of sales and an 8% return on equity, and customer satisfaction results had improved marginally. Both the board and the senior management team were pleased to see progress but felt there was still a long way to go. Discussion among these groups clearly indicated that they saw the virtual mall as the initiative with the greatest potential, as well as the greatest risks.

Personnel in sales and marketing expressed increasing concern over how their functions and roles would be affected by the new venture and what would be the impact on their customers. Nathan continued to tell them to relax while they were waiting to see how roles and functions would need to adapt in the wake of the virtual mall. Though he couldn't guarantee there would be no job losses, he truly believed this new venture would open up significant new opportunities and more meaningful customer relationships for many. In spite of these words of reassurance, the number of voluntary resignations in these areas rose by 15%, and there were rumors that others were looking as well. Many of these resignations involved individuals viewed as high performers. In addition, some distributors were also expressing concern and looking for alternative lines of business to represent, in the event that they became redundant to Northwell.

Human resources advised the executives to slow their recruiting initiatives for departing personnel until the effects of the new venture were better understood. Nathan and other senior managers in sales and marketing saw the wisdom in this advice, but they were also concerned about sending the wrong message to staff, customers, and distributors. As a result, recruitment was slowed, positions were left unfilled for longer than in the past (150 days on average vs. 60), and contract employees were brought in to help, where needed. The consideration of a new call center was also put on the back burner until the ramifications for Nothwell of the virtual mall were better understood.

By April, the senior management team was placing increasing pressure on Claudia to get the mall up and running. Marketing of the mall was going extremely well. Product and service suppliers had been solicited and screened, and a critical mass of these organizations was signed and ready to go (i.e., their initial product information, visual material, and related systems and supports were developed). The news and related information services and site features had been developed, staffed, and beta-tested by those who would be using the mall. Primary customers were anxiously awaiting access to the new service. However, Medichek reported that the development of the technological platform and related supports (in particular, the e-commerce and security components) were proving more difficult than originally anticipated and that the complete mall's formal launch was about 4 months behind schedule.

Claudia began to spend more time monitoring the pace of developments at Medichek. Monthly visits became weekly. In May, she requested biweekly reports on progress achieved,

funds expended, and the time allocations of the various project teams. These were very similar to the reporting Northwell required from their own operations.

Relations with Medichek chilled in response to the increased frequency of site visits and the request for more detailed reporting. At first they resisted complying with the reporting request, but after a month of mounting pressure, they acquiesced. Medichek's senior management wrote that such information would be furnished under duress, because it would serve no useful purpose, be expensive and time-consuming to develop, and divert attention from where it was most needed.

The resignation of three more capable staff members from the sales and marketing area and the loss of a valued distributor from the U.S. Midwest in the late spring elevated Nathan's anxiety over progress, and he wanted to know just how much longer it would be before "Virtual Northwell" would be fully operational. Nathan continued to believe that it would be unwise to make major changes in sales and marketing until they really knew how customers would react to the new channel. He felt that it was difficult to predict, with any degree of certainty, what the ideal approach to sales and marketing should be, and he preferred to adopt an approach that reacted to what evolved as a result of the new channel. However, he was also aware of the need to address employee and distributor uncertainty as quickly as possible, recognizing that the "be patient until we have a better understanding" strategy was not working well. Since Claudia was in charge of the new venture and since there would be organizational design, budget, and control implications, he wanted Claudia's advice on how best to handle the matter.

When Medichek reported continuing development problems in July, senior management at Northwell voiced increasing dissatisfaction with the progress to date and asked Claudia to recommend a course of action that would rectify matters.

Case Study 1

Questions for Class Discussion

1. Claudia has asked for your help. What are the management and strategic issues that Northwell faces? What is your analysis of the need for change? Use relevant tools from the chapters to assist you in this.

2. Develop a vision statement for the change initiative that you believe Claudia needs to lead.

3. What would you recommend that Claudia do, and how should she implement your recommendations?

CHAPTER 5

Organizational Structures and Systems and Change

If you're going to sin, sin against God, not the bureaucracy; God will forgive you but the bureaucracy won't.

—H. G. Rickover, U.S. Admiral,
quoted in the New York Times, Nov. 3, 1986

Chapter Overview

- This chapter examines how the formal structure and systems can foster or impair change initiatives.
- It outlines how change leaders can develop an understanding of existing systems and structures.
- It discusses the basics of organizational design (differentiation and integration), organic and mechanistic structures, and the impact of organizational uncertainty.
- It considers the role of systems and structures in gaining approval for change initiatives. Formal, coalition-building, and renegade approaches are dealt with.
- The role of systems and structures in facilitating the acceptance of change initiatives is reviewed.
- Finally, it reviews the ways to develop more adaptive systems and structures to increase the acceptance of change.

An organization's formal structure is defined by how tasks are formally divided, grouped, and coordinated.[1] Careful attention needs to be paid to systems and structures because of the impact they have on what gets done, how it gets done, and the outcomes that ensue. Sometimes they represent what needs to change, but they can also play an important part in decisions about how to change.

Formal structures and systems are designed to enhance order, efficiency, effectiveness, and accountability. They serve as guides and controls on decision making. They coordinate and integrate operations, provide direction to internal governance, and attempt to promote desired behavior and organizational outcomes.[2] The organization chart is the most common view of organizational structure. The formal systems include all planned routines and processes such as strategic planning, accounting and control systems, performance management, pay and reward systems, and the information system.

Organizations vary in their need for structure and systems (i.e., bureaucracy), but all require some degree of formalization to function effectively and efficiently. If you are AT&T, Wal-Mart, or Sealinks (a global supplier of cargo containers for ships), your business model requires sophisticated systems and structures that you can rely on. Without them, containers are lost, calls disappear into cyberspace, and the supply chain delivering products to outlets breaks down. If you are the corner grocer, you need simple systems for such things as accounting, staffing, pricing, inventory control, supplier management, and customer service.

Formal systems and structures significantly influence where, how, and why decisions are made and what action ensues. They play important coordination, communication, and control roles.

Change leaders need to develop a deep understanding of how existing structures and systems are currently influencing outcomes plus how they are likely to facilitate or impede the proposed changes. Once that understanding is developed, change leaders need to put that system and structure awareness to use to promote and enact change. To advance this agenda, the chapter is divided into five sections:

1. Understanding existing systems and structures

2. Understanding the fit of different structures and systems

3. Understanding how structures and systems influence the approval process of a change initiative

4. Understanding how structures and systems facilitate or hinder the acceptance of change

5. Understanding how to develop more adaptive structures and systems so that future change is enhanced or made easier

The purpose of this chapter is to describe the roles that systems and structures play in advancing change. It also helps to identify the gap between the existing structures and systems and what is needed after the change. Figure 5.1 outlines where this chapter fits in the change management process. This chapter is the first of four that detail how change leaders can develop a sophisticated gap analysis. This chapter deals with formal systems and structures. Chapter 6 deals with the informal

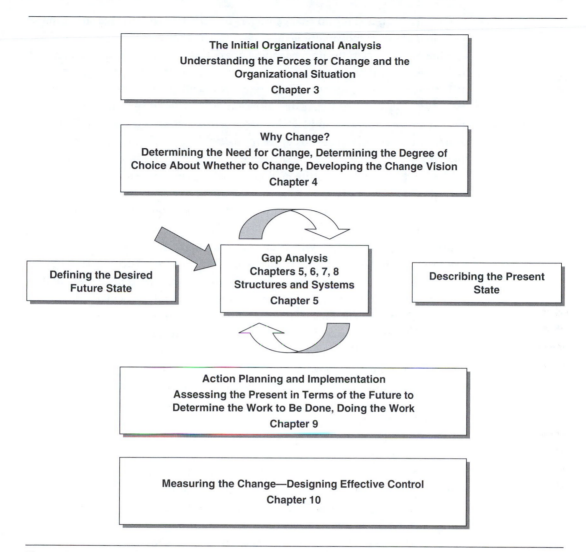

The Initial Organizational Analysis
Understanding the Forces for Change and the
Organizational Situation
Chapter 3

Why Change?
Determining the Need for Change, Determining the Degree of
Choice About Whether to Change, Developing the Change Vision
Chapter 4

Defining the Desired
Future State

Gap Analysis
Chapters 5, 6, 7, 8
Structures and Systems
Chapter 5

Describing the Present
State

Action Planning and Implementation
Assessing the Present in Terms of the Future to
Determine the Work to Be Done, Doing the Work
Chapter 9

Measuring the Change—Designing Effective Control
Chapter 10

Figure 5.1   Structures and Systems in the Change Management Process

and emergent aspects of organizations. Chapter 7 deals with change recipients, and Chapter 8 deals with change leaders themselves.

How Can We Document Existing Structures and Systems?

In Chapter 3, the Nadler and Tushman model was introduced and with it a discussion of the importance of organizational systems and structures to the outcomes that organizations achieve. Knowledge of these components contributes to the change leader's understanding of why the organization performs as it does. It permits the assessment of where structural or system impediments to change may exist and where structures and systems might be used to facilitate strategic alignment and change. Further, it can help change leaders identify ways to leverage structures so that their efforts can be multiplied.

One place to begin the understanding of existing systems and structures is with the paper trail. Review organizational documents that show the organizational structure, outline organizational processes, or document systems and procedures. How have they evolved? Where does decision making and formal authority lie with respect to the structures and systems described? What are the decision limits and zones of discretion available to decision makers (e.g., spending limits, approvals, time frames, etc.)? Exploring these formal systems and structures provides a basic understanding of where legitimate power and authority are supposed to exist. As well, they provide guidance as to what is supposed to occur.

Second, talk to long service employees and interview individuals who have experience with the structures and systems. This will help you develop a more complete understanding of how the systems and structures actually work (versus how they are formally supposed to work). How and where are the structures and systems interconnected, and how do they influence one another? Who is involved with their use? What are the power and influence patterns around particular systems and structures? Such discussions will increase your understanding of the stated versus emergent purpose or intent of the systems and where the points of leverage for change are likely to reside. As well, your understanding of what is required to use the structures and systems will be enhanced. This would include (a) where and how to access the systems, (b) what information is required, (c) what lead times and time frames to keep in mind, (d) whose support is needed, and (e) what flexibility exists in how the structures and systems are applied.

Third, develop a process map that tracks the change idea from start to finish in terms of the systems and structures. Which of these systems and structures directly influence the success of the change? Which indirectly influence success? Where in the change process do these systems and structures come into play and how should they be managed? Who has direct and indirect influence on how relevant systems and structures are applied?

The goal is to fully understand the systemic and structural pieces that you must work with, since they represent an important part of the context that must be managed. This will allow you to develop a more informed change plan for how, when, and where to proceed.

Consider the role that formal systems and structures have played in initiating and inhibiting change in the airline industry. At United, American, Air Canada, British Airways, and other traditionally organized air carriers, air routes were organized in what is called a "hub-and-spoke" design. That is, passengers were collected at many points and delivered to a central hub where they changed planes and were sent out on a different spoke to their final destination. For many years, this strategy delivered cost savings to the airlines and served them well. Recently, discount airlines, such as Southwest, have structured their air routes to provide "point-to-point" service. That is, they fly passengers directly to their destination at a lower price. As a result, the hub-and-spoke route structure that was designed to facilitate coordination, efficiency, and service effectiveness has become a problem for traditional air carriers and contributes to their recent profit problems.

Table 5.1   Sizing Up the Formal Systems and Structures

---

1. What does the paper trail have to say about which formal structures and systems have to be considered when leading the change?

2. What are the key points in the process that we need to be conscious of (e.g., timing of meetings, getting on the agenda, cycle time, types of decision made and where decisions are made)?

   a. How are the relevant systems and structures interconnected? How do they influence one another?

3. Develop a process map that tracks the change idea from start to finish.

   a. Where does formal authority and decision making lie?
   b. What are the decision parameters that are normally applied, and are there zones of discretion available to decision makers?
   c. What are the power and influence patterns around particular systems and structures? Who has direct and indirect influence on how the systems and structures are applied?
   d. How should these systems and structures be managed in order to reduce resistance? Are there ways that they can be managed that will create leverage that will advance the change?

These new structures and processes adopted by the competition have led to growing demands for major improvements from banks, shareholders, pension funds, and other stakeholders. Structural and system realignment have been key targets of change. Those who sought to resist the changes, such as the airline staff labor unions, have attempted to leverage existing structures and systems to advance their interests. The following example provides a fascinating but different look at the role that existing structures can play in organizational change.

UAL's Use of the Courts to Promote Internal Change

In order to implement its restructuring plans, UAL Corp.'s United Airlines asked the U.S. Bankruptcy Court to let the airline void current labor contracts with its five unions. With this permission, United would be able to rewrite its labor contracts, which would sharply lower the company's expenses. The carrier would gain more flexibility to outsource work and move to create a separate low-cost airline.

"To seek to wipe out this contract by the stroke of a judge's pen is disheartening," said Capt. Paul Whitford, chairman of the Air Line Pilots Association branch at United. "We believe United's proposal (on labor concessions for the pilots) is an overreach." According to the Association of Flight Attendants, "the cuts United is proposing would put thousands of flight attendants at an income level qualifying them for welfare and other government-aid programs." Nevertheless, both groups said it is in their best interest to reach negotiated settlements and avoid a court order.[3]

The above request to the courts enabled UAL to force internal change in a highly resistant situation. One of the ways that the board at United Airlines responded to the competitive realities and the disastrous financial results was to use formal processes to replace a number of key executives[4] and charge senior management with responsibility for turning things around. Staffing arrangements, work rules, and labor costs were among the many areas that attracted the attention of senior management tasked with effecting change. Management analyzed and then used existing systems and structures (including formal judicial components) to advance and legitimize changes to their collective agreements and, by extension, changes to staffing levels, the organization of work, and related terms and conditions of work. In response, employee groups enlisted formal (as well as informal) systems and structures to protect their interests—actions that airline executives saw as resisting needed changes. UAL's use of existing structures and systems to effect change was viewed by employee groups as adversarial, generating serious resentment in what was obviously a very difficult context.

The use of existing structures and systems to advance change does not always have to produce adversarial consequences. Rather, their application is often undertaken in a manner that facilitates understanding, builds support (or lessens the resistance), and legitimizes change among those who have serious reservations. For example, Agilent downsized in 2002 and laid off 8,000 employees.[5] Management was generally seen by its employees to have acted responsibly and humanely. Those exiting reported that they had been treated with respect and dignity, while those remaining were left with hope for the future of the firm and confidence in the leadership. Part of this had to do with the fair and open way in which appropriate systems and structures were applied by executives to the restructuring challenge. To go through this level of downsizing and still be ranked number 31 on *Fortune*'s "100 Best Companies to Work For" in the following period is no small accomplishment.

From a change perspective, awareness and understanding of existing structures and systems is a necessary, but not sufficient, step in the right direction. It sets the stage for success by increasing the likelihood that the existing systems and structures will be managed in ways that will avoid unnecessary roadblocks and, where possible, build support for change. Interestingly enough, this includes changes focused on the realignment and renewal of the existing systems and structures themselves.

How Can We Make Sense of Organizational Structures and Systems?

This chapter is not intended to be a primer in formal organizational structures and systems. However, an overview of certain concepts that are helpful to change leaders is provided.* This section will briefly explore the impact of uncertainty and complexity on the fit of different structures and systems. Mechanistic and organic approaches to organizing will be addressed as will different structural design variables and the information-processing view of organizations.

---

*For a detailed treatment of the topic, see Daft, R. L. (2006). *Organization theory and design* (9th ed.). Cincinnati, OH: South-Western College Publishing.

There are a number of perspectives that can be applied when assessing an existing set of structures or designing new ones. Traditional design variables that change leaders may want to consider include the following:[6]

a. **To what degree are tasks subdivided into separate jobs? (Differentiation[†])**— the question of who does what, when, how, and where; the degree to which jobs are specialized and differentiated from one another horizontally, vertically, and spatially.

b. **What is the basis for grouping jobs together? (Departmentalization or Integration)**—the extent to which activities are integrated and the processes by which the organization attempts to integrate its efforts.

c. **What is the reporting structure? (Chain of Command)**—to whom do individuals and groups report?

d. **How many individuals report to one manager? (Span of Control)**—how flat or tall is the organization? That is, how are effectiveness and efficiency affected by the number of individuals reporting at each level?

e. **How is decision making distributed in the structure? (Centralization)**—is decision making centralized at the top of the organization or delegated to lower-level employees?

f. **How many rules and regulations exist, and what are the expectations that these will be followed? (Formalization)**—to what extent are the structures and processes of the organization formalized (set down in writing) and expected to be adhered to?

Researchers have examined the structural dimensions above and have classified organizations into two types: (1) those that are more formal, more differentiated, more centralized, and more standardized and (2) those that are less formal, less differentiated, more decentralized, and less standardized. The terms that are applied to this organizational typology are *mechanistic* and *organic*. Table 5.2 outlines the characteristics of mechanistic and organic organizational forms as opposite ends of a continuum.[7]

Mechanistic organizations rely on formal hierarchies with centralized decision making and a clear division of labor. Rules and procedures are clearly defined and employees are expected to follow them. Work is specialized and routine. Organic organizations are much more flexible. They have fewer rules and procedures, and there is less reliance on the hierarchy of authority for centralized decision making. The structure is flexible and not as well defined. Jobs are less specialized. Communication is more informal and lateral communications more accepted. While it may appear that one structural form is more appealing than the other, both can be effective depending on the organization's particular fit with its environment.

The application of the above design variables will provide change leaders with multiple dimensions through which to consider structure. This can prove helpful when assessing the internal consistency of structures and systems and their congruence or alignment with the strategy, vision, culture, and environment. When cost

---

[†]In many texts, the process of breaking tasks into subtasks is referred to as specialization.

Table 5.2   Mechanistic and Organic Organization Forms

More Mechanistic	More Organic
Tasks are broken down into separate parts and rigidly defined and assigned	Flexible tasks that are adjusted and redefined through teamwork and participation
High degree of formalization, strict hierarchy of authority and control, many rules	Relatively little formalization, less reliance on a hierarchy of authority and control, few rules, greater participation and decentralization
Narrow span of control with reliance on hierarchies of people in specialized roles	Wide span of control
Knowledge and control of tasks are centralized at the top of the organization, limited decision making at lower levels	Knowledge and control of tasks are decentralized and located throughout the organization; highly decentralized decision making
Communication is vertical	Communication is horizontal and free flowing, with many integrating roles
Simple, straightforward planning processes	Sophisticated environmental scanning, planning, and forecasting, including the use of scenarios and contingency thinking

Source: Adapted from Daft, R. L. (2007). *Organization theory and design* (9th ed.). Mason, OH: Thomson South-Western.

strategies in a traditional manufacturing context are critical, a more mechanistic approach is seen as more appropriate. When innovation is the key strategic variable, organic approaches provide a better fit.[8]

Robert Duncan provides us with a way of thinking about the environment and organizational structure. He suggests two dimensions of uncertainty: (1) the number and similarity of factors that influence that environment (degree of complexity) and (2) the rate of change of those factors over time (degree of dynamism).[9] He uses these two dimensions to identify four environments and suggests which structures are most appropriate for those environments:

1. Simple and static—an environment with few, simple factors having an impact and where those factors are relatively unchanging. Duncan's example of such an environment is the soft drink industry.

2. Simple and dynamic—an environment with relatively few factors, where those factors change rapidly. An example of such an environment would be that of movie theaters or the fashion industry.

3. Complex and static—an environment with a larger number of relatively unchanging, stable factors that determine the situation. Bureaucracies such as universities fit into this category.

4. Complex and dynamic—an environment with many factors having an impact and where those factors change rapidly. Common examples would be the computer industry and biotechnology firms.

Organizations operating in static, simple environments are often viewed as requiring more mechanistic structural and systemic approaches to the handling of their information-processing needs. Organizations in more uncertain and changing environments would require more organic approaches where the ability to adapt quickly to those changing conditions is needed.

When complexity is added to the picture, systems and structures need to adapt to the added challenges they bring with them. Under conditions of low uncertainty but high complexity, more mechanistic approaches to organizing still make sense, but they need to adapt to handle the more complex information-processing and decision-making context. Environments characterized by high uncertainty and complexity represent an even greater organizing challenge, because the organic approach that provides needed flexibility and adaptiveness needs to be coupled with integrating processes that assist the organization in maintaining its focus and integrity (see Table 5.3).

In other words, organizations need to align their structures with their environments. In Nadler and Tushman's terminology, there needs to be congruence between the environment and the structure.

By understanding the nature of the organization's environment, a change leader can gain insights into the types of structures and systems that are appropriate.

Change leaders also need to be aware that even in a fairly mechanistic organization, different departments and divisions may face very different information-processing needs and will therefore need to be structured and managed differently. For example, a firm's R&D group's environment may very well be much more dynamic and complex than that faced by a production department, characterized by well-developed, standardized processes. Likewise, those involved with the launch of a new product or expansion into a new market will have to deal with higher levels of uncertainty than those responsible for mature products and markets, where concerns for structures and systems that enhance efficiency are likely the norm.

Another way of thinking about the impact of systems and structures on how and why firms operate is to assess how they formally manage information. One of the primary purposes of formal structures and systems is to place the right information into the hands of appropriate individuals in a timely fashion. Information technology has been instrumental in allowing us to develop structures and systems that are more robust, dynamic, and flexible. For example, it has allowed organizations such as Dell to move from mass-production models to mass customization, with little productivity loss.[10] By extension, technology has also allowed us to think differently about the structures and systems when planning and managing organizational change.

Galbraith referred to this as the information-processing view of organizations.[11] If the organization is to perform effectively, there needs to be a fit between the organization's information-processing requirements and its capacity to process information through its structural design choices. The better the fit between them, the

Table 5.3   Impact of Environmental Uncertainty and Complexity on Structure and System Alignment

Rate of Change	Degree of Environmental Complexity	
	Simple	Complex
Static Environment	• Centralized, simple mechanistic structure • Use of rules, policies, procedures, and hierarchy • Few departments • Low need for integrating roles • Efficiency & stability focused, little imitation	• Centralized, mechanistic structure, more sophisticated information and control systems • Use of rules and policies, procedures and hierarchy, but adapted to the complexity • Many departments, some boundary spanning • Modest need for integrating roles and systems • Some environmental scanning, imitation, and planning activity
Dynamic Environment	• Decentralized, organic structure, participative and team focused • Fewer rules, policies, procedures • Few departments, much boundary spanning • Few integrating roles • Much environmental scanning, imitation, and a strong planning orientation	• Decentralized, organic structure, participative and team focused, very sophisticated information and control systems • Fewer rules, policies, and procedures • Many differentiated departments, much boundary spanning • Many integrating roles • Extensive environmental scanning, imitation, and sophisticated planning and forecasting systems

Source: Adapted from Daft, R. L. (2007). *Organization theory and design* (9th ed., p. 146). Mason, OH: Thomson South-Western.

more effective the organization will be. As uncertainty increases, the amount of information that must be processed between decision makers during the transformation process increases. The organization must either increase its capacity to handle that information or restructure itself to reduce the need for information handling. Figure 5.2 outlines Galbraith's work.

As uncertainty increases, the traditional methods of uncertainty reduction will prove insufficient, and the organization will require methods that either reduce the need for information processing or increase the capacity of the organization to process information.[12] Organizations can reduce the need to process information by adding slack resources to act as buffers (e.g., extra people and inventory) and by creating self-contained tasks (e.g., divisions organized around product categories,

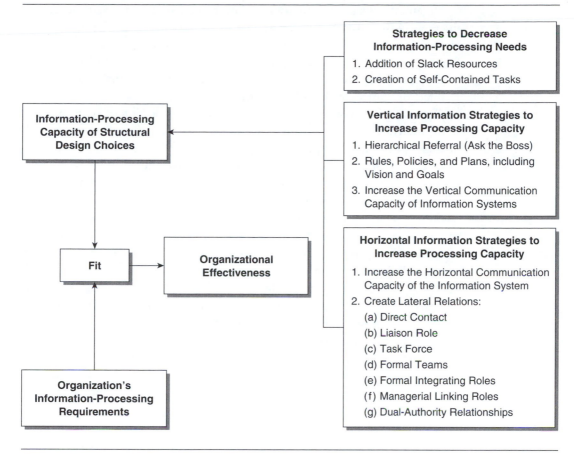

Figure 5.2   An Information-Processing View of Organizational Structure

Adapted from Galbraith, J. R. (1997). *Organization design. Reading,* MA: Addison-Wesley; and Daft, R. L. (2003). *Organization theory and design* (8th ed.). Cincinnati, OH: South-Western.

geography, or customers). For example, extra inventory means that increased variation in demand for a product will be handled by drawing down or increasing inventory levels. Similarly, separating an organization into divisions operating as profit centers means that the divisions may not need to coordinate their activities as much. This reduces the information-processing requirements.

Initially, organizations attempt to increase their information-processing capacity by using the hierarchy. That is, if you are uncertain what to do, ask your boss. If the situation repeats itself, create a decision rule to guide the decision. If the subordinate knows more about the situation than the boss, they can agree on a set of objectives or goals or focus on the organizational vision that allows the subordinate to act independently and handle the uncertainty. These represent what Galbraith calls vertical information strategies.

A further vertical information strategy is when organizations increase their capacity to process information by investing in vertical information systems (e.g., computer-generated performance reports, decision support systems).

Organizations also can improve their information-processing ability by increasing their horizontal communication capacity (e.g., e-mail systems, intranets, and electronic bulletin boards). Finally, they can increase the capacity to process information horizontally by creating lateral relationships that vary in complexity from something as simple as direct, informal contact to complex, formal structures that facilitate the horizontal flow of information.

The role of the information systems is to develop needed information and get it to the individuals who most need it. Interdepartmental and interdivisional boundaries and jurisdictional disputes can impede the flow of information (see the investigation of the 9/11 tragedy as an example of this[13]). Galbraith identified seven types of lateral relations that will help overcome such boundaries. These include (1) direct contact between affected individuals (e.g., a product designer and a manufacturing engineer), (2) use of individuals in liaison roles to bridge groups, (3) multidepartment task forces, (4) formal teams, (5) integrating roles such as a product managers with cross-department authority, (6) managerial linking roles (similar to the integrating roles but with more formal decision authority, and (7) structures with dual-authority relationships such as those found in a matrix organization. If the organization is to perform effectively, this model points to the importance of congruence or fit between the firm's information-processing requirements (e.g., market and competitive information, operational information) and the information-processing capacity that the firm's design choices have given rise to.

Change leaders need to be aware of the impact of vertical and horizontal information strategies on information flows and organizational performance when assessing what needs to change. Further, sensitivity to these issues needs to extend to the actual management of the change process. This is because even well-managed change will increase uncertainty in at least the short term and major changes will significantly increase it for longer periods of time. This will give rise to information-processing needs that change leaders will need to manage. Otherwise, the lack of fit may impair the effectiveness of the change initiative. Often multiple strategies are needed—extra resources to increase the capacity to process information, a focus on understanding the goals and purposes, and a significant increase in lateral relations.

An Example of Structural Changes Made to Handle Increased Uncertainty

From a structural perspective, the quest for enhanced organizational effectiveness often starts by looking at what needs to change in the organization and deciding how best to break things down and allocate the work. These differentiation approaches include aspects such as division of labor and departmentalization. If this has already been done, the challenge usually shifts to a discussion of how to integrate the components together so that they can accomplish the intended results. The vertical and horizontal information linkage strategies identified by Galbraith in Figure 5.2 are examples of such integrating approaches.

Boeing's redesigned approach to the development and manufacturing of its aircraft provides an excellent example of the application of structural changes in a very complex business. The aircraft manufacturer realized that they had to change their approach to compete with Airbus and they did so in their approach to the development of the 787:

> Before the 787, Boeing did all the engineering design work itself. The main reason to change, says Mike Bair, head of the 787 development team, was that the company realized it had to trawl the world and find the best suppliers in order to compete with its main rival in the market for commercial aircraft, the increasingly successful Airbus.
>
> Airbus, a joint European venture involving French, German, British and Spanish partners, started from scratch. Almost by accident it stumbled on an organisational architecture that, along with generous subsidies, helped it over-take the giant of the business in less than two decades.
>
> These days, Boeing is organising itself more like Airbus. It scoured the globe for new partners and found some in Europe, some in Japan and some not far from its home base in the United States. Whereas with the 777 aircraft the company worked with 500–700 suppliers, for the 787 it has chosen just under 100 "partners."
>
> The difference is not just in the numbers, but in the relationship. Suppliers provide what they are asked for; partners share responsibility for a project. For over six months in 2005, teams of people from the various 787 partners met at Boeing's base in Everett, north of Seattle, to work together on the configura-tion of the plane—something that until then Boeing had always done by itself. Now the partners are back at their own bases, responsible for all aspects of their piece of the puzzle. The partners are building their own production facil-ities for their bits of the aircraft. The first flight is scheduled for 2007, and the 787 is due to come into service in 2008. As Mr. Bair says, "it puts a high pre-mium on the choice of partners in the first place."
>
> It also puts a high premium on the management of that network of part-ners. Boeing holds a partners' "council meeting" every six weeks, and has set up a network to facilitate global collaboration which makes it possible for designers all over the world to work on the same up-to-the-minute database.
>
> The company is also putting great faith in videoconferencing and has set up high-bandwidth facilities that are in constant use. People come into their offices in the middle of the night to have virtual meetings with colleagues in different time zones. Technically, the 787 will be an American plane; but in reality it will be a global one.[14] (From *The Economist*, January 21, 2006.)

Boeing provides a graphic illustration of how structural approaches are chang-ing in response to increasing turbulence and ambiguity. In the aircraft maker's case, this included a radical reappraisal of where and how aircraft design and manufac-turing should be undertaken, the role of suppliers and Boeing in the process, the treatment of intellectual property, and how the process should be managed. They recognized that their current approach was making them uncompetitive, and they have worked to break down silos and bring their suppliers into the design process as part of a dynamic network. This has necessitated a cultural shift toward treating their carefully selected suppliers as trusted contributing partners to the design and manufacturing challenges, and it has required the use of information-processing strategies to link it all together.

Boeing has demonstrated a willingness to tackle fundamental questions of how best to deal with the structural challenges of differentiation and integration in order to enhance their performance. Wetzel and Buch[15] argue that organizations are more comfortable with increasing both differentiation and integrating mechanisms. Organizations tend to overuse these strategies. For example, a need for specialized response leads to a more structurally differentiated organization. This in turn leads to a need to coordinate or integrate more. An alternate strategy would be to decrease the need to differentiate, easing information-processing needs in Galbraith's terms. Wetzel and Buch believe that it is useful to consider the benefits of such a reduction in the amount of structural differentiation in the organization, through such mechanisms as flattened structures, multiskilled workers, automated processes, and self-managed teams. By reducing their reliance on differentiating structural solutions, organizations can reduce their need for integrating mechanisms and increase the likelihood of developing congruent interventions. From an information-processing perspective, this falls into the category of strategies to ease information-processing linkage needs (see Figure 5.2).

Boeing provides an example of this approach at the enterprise level. At a more micro level, this approach was used by a medical regulatory body. By automating the certification checking process and having physicians directly enter their professional certification data, the need for both differentiation and integrating mechanisms were reduced by the regulatory body, and efficiency and effectiveness were significantly enhanced, without a loss of control.[16]

Toolkit Exercise 5.1 asks you to examine the impact of structures and systems on an organizational change with which you are familiar.

How Do We Use Systems and Structures in Obtaining Approval of a Change Project?

Change is made easier if you understand when and how to access and use existing systems to advance your cause.

In larger organizations, the formal approval processes for major initiatives are often well defined. For example, in universities, significant academic decisions usually require the approvals of department councils, faculty councils, and university senates in the form of formal motions and votes. The change agent's task is to engage in tactics and initiatives that will increase the likelihood of a positive vote for the proposed change.

In business organizations, formal processes also exist. For example, any significant change will likely cost money and will have to fit into the budget cycle of the firm. In these situations, the budget process needs to be understood and support for the proposed change must be nurtured with the departments and individuals who approve the financial support. The likelihood of approval in the short term is less if the organization is in the middle of the budget cycle and available funds have already been allocated. Timing is obviously important. Efforts to build interest and support need to begin well in advance of when significant funds are needed, building to coincide with key decision dates.

Earlier in this book, two dimensions of change were considered: the magnitude or size of the change and the proactive-reactive initiation dimension. Change projects that are more incremental will normally require fewer and lower levels of organization approval, with some noted exceptions (for example, those with safety or regulatory compliance implications). As the change increases in magnitude and strategic importance, change leaders will find that they will need to pay greater attention to the formal approval processes. Reactive strategic changes tend to attract the greatest attention because of the risk, visibility, and criticality of such changes to the future of the organization.[17]

When senior decision makers believe that the change initiative has significant strategic and/or financial implications and risks, the change may require the formal approval of the organization's senior executive team or its board of directors. As a change initiator, you need to know the approval levels and hurdles associated with different types of changes—that is, at what level does this become a board matter, a senior executive matter, or a matter that can be dealt with at a local level? What will they be looking for in the way of analysis and support? No two organizations will be the same. For example, organizations in which there are significant negative consequences of failure (e.g., a nuclear power plant or a pharmaceutical manufacturer) may require senior levels of approval for what appear to be relatively modest undertakings. Likewise, the hurdle levels are likely to be more rigorous in organizations with senior managers and/or a culture that has a low tolerance for ambiguity.

How Do We Position the Change Projects to Enhance Approval Prospects?

Change leaders have a variety of factors they need to consider concerning the use of systems to increase the likelihood of approval.

First, they need to ask themselves if formal approval is required or if the change decision already rests within their span of control. If no approval is required, they may choose to make people aware of their intent and engage them in discussion, in order to increase downstream acceptance. However, why initiate activities that trigger unnecessary formal approval systems and processes when they are not required? Figure 5.3 outlines the various considerations regarding positioning the approval of a change proposal.

In all cases:

a. When there is a decision maker, identify his attitudes to the change and attempt to work with him.
b. Demonstrate how the change project relates to the strategy or vision of the organization.
c. Use good process to legitimize the change proposal.

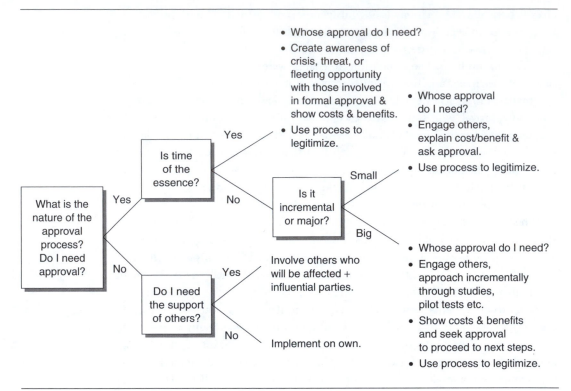

Figure 5.3   Positioning the Change for Formal Approval

If formal approval is required, change leaders need to be able to demonstrate that the change is aligned with the vision and strategy of the organization, advances the organization's agenda, and has benefits that exceed the costs. If the needed changes modify the vision or strategy or the elements that make up the organization, the change leader will need to demonstrate how such changes will enhance organizational health and have downstream benefits that exceed the costs and risks associated with these more significant organizational changes. Included in such a calculation should be the costs and risks of doing nothing.

If changes are more extreme and if there is sufficient time, the change leaders can frame and introduce the change in ways that increase management familiarity and comfort with the proposed change. They can do this through incremental approaches that make use of such vehicles as preliminary studies, task force reviews, consultant reports, and pilot projects prior to the request for formal approval. This, in turn, reduces perceived risks, enhances a sense of the benefits, and essentially conditions the organization to embrace (or at least not resist) more fundamental changes to the alignment systems.

If time is of the essence due to a crisis or emerging threats, the change leader can act with urgency and use the danger to focus attention, facilitate approval and acceptance of the change, and generate motivation to proceed. Formal approval processes often have expedited processes available for dealing with eminent threats and emergencies.

When formal approval is required, a change leader will need to know whose agreement is needed. However, if broader acceptance is important before gaining formal approval, then those involved in approval discussions will need to be expanded accordingly. Approval and acceptance are generally enhanced when people are involved in the discussion and feel that they have been heard. It is also enhanced when there is the perception that the analysis and discussion around the alignment systems (e.g., vision, strategy, goals, balance scorecards, and strategy maps) have been broadly based and thorough.[18]

Acceptance is sometimes increased among the uncommitted and resistant when they believe that there has been a rigorous review process in place for the assessment of a change. That is, the procedures are thorough and complete. Further, when there is active involvement of those individuals or their representatives in the planning and approval processes, their understanding and acceptance of the change tend to rise, though some resistors may see this as a co-option strategy.

Approval systems, when used in the manner outlined above, can increase the perception that a change has been assessed, has been tested, is legitimate, and is therefore worthy of support. However, you need to be mindful of the fact that those who are opposed to the change may be tempted to apply approval systems in ways that intentionally act as barriers to an initiative. That is, change suggestions are forced into approval processes that are bureaucratic and sap the energy of the change leaders. Their motives in doing this may be unsullied (the desire for due diligence, due process, and careful review), but sometimes their motives are clearly to obstruct. Assess their motives first, because your response will likely need to be tempered by the purposes under-lying why they've used the systems as they have. For example, if a review and approval committee is stacked and managed in order to generate a "no vote," your response is likely to be quite different than if a rigorous assessment was the real motive.

How Can We Use the Formal Approval Process?

Howell and Higgins[19] identified three different ways of approaching the formal approval process. The first involves the straightforward rational approach. Proposals are typically developed and brought forward for consideration and they are reviewed for inclusion on the agenda. Once the proposal is presented and dis-cussed, it is approved, rejected, or sent back for further study or rework. The like-lihood of gaining approval is increased when:

- You have a well-placed sponsor.
- You know your audience and their preferences.
- You understand the power and influence patterns and the implications of the project for the firm and for those involved in the approval process.
- You do your homework with respect to your detailed knowledge of the change project, its scope and objectives, its costs and benefits, and risk areas.
- You obtain needed approval and support in advance.

- You have the change project effectively presented by an appropriate individual.
- You have a good sense of timing concerning when best to bring it forward.[20]

The systems associated with obtaining formal approval for planned changes vary greatly. In organic or entrepreneurial organizations, the process may be loose and idiosyncratic. As organizations mature, even very entrepreneurial firms tend to systematize and formalize the approval processes in order to increase control.

The decision making associated with formal approval processes take many forms (e.g., formal voting by an executive committee, consensus mechanisms, and go/no go decisions controlled by individual executives). While the exact approval process will be unique to the firm, the level of rigorousness and formality used to assess proposed changes usually varies with the magnitude of the change, the levels of perceived risk and uncertainty, the preferences of those involved with the decision, and the power dynamics at work in the organization.

There is much advice in the literature concerning how the formal approval process should be designed and managed (e.g., involve individuals with diverse perspectives, ensure that decision making is data based and objective, be strategically as well as operationally focused). However, the creation of an ideal approval process (if there were such a thing) is not our purpose here. Our goal is to ensure that change leaders give thought to the nature of the approval processes they must deal with, so that they can better manage them.

When the proposed change lies in an area in which much is known, decision makers tend to focus on concrete information (e.g., benchmark data, industry patterns, and performance data). They then use this to help them to come to a decision.[21] When the changes reside in areas that are inherently more ambiguous, attention tends to turn to an assessment of the quality of the analysis and logic of the advocate of the change. In essence, the decision makers need to decide whether or not they trust the judgment of the change leader and the skills and abilities of the change team.[22]

As organizations mature, they often adopt a staged approval approach for changes that are viewed as strategically significant, expensive, wide-reaching in their impact, and potentially disruptive. A staged approach attempts to establish decision approval stages in ways that ensure that they do not prematurely dismiss ideas worthy of further exploration while controlling the increasing commitment of time and resources that would be required if the change were to progress to the next stage.[23] The goal is to provide focus to what is undertaken (through vision and strategy alignment), allow proposed initiatives to be explored and assessed in a rational manner, avoid unpleasant surprises, manage risk, and keep an eye on the portfolio of change initiatives to ensure that the organization does not become overwhelmed with change.

As one proceeds through the approval stages, the assessment process becomes increasingly rigorous and the hurdles that must be met before proceeding to the next stage arise. When the process is working well, it should stimulate innovative thinking and initiatives, enhance the quality of assessment, reduce the cycle time from ideation to implementation, and reduce the likelihood of dysfunctional political behavior.

The formal approval process does more than ensure that the decision making concerning change is thorough and reasoned. If the process is viewed as legitimate by others in the organization, its decisions will lend legitimacy to what changes are pursued and enhance acceptance. When an incremental or staged approval process has been adopted to gain approval (e.g., commencing with concept and initial plan approval, followed by a field experiment or a pilot test, a departmental trial, and a final review prior to large-scale adoption), then the outcomes achieved and reactions to the results (e.g., the credibility of the data and the reaction of opinion leaders) will play an important part in building support for approval and downstream acceptance by others.

In addition to addressing the traditional hierarchical approach, Howell and Higgins identified two other ways to use system awareness to advance change: strategies based on creeping commitment and coalition building, and strategies involving simply forging ahead without formal approval.

How Can We Use Creeping Commitment and Coalition Building?

As an alternative to directly pursuing or relying on the formal approval approach, change leaders can employ a strategy of creeping commitment (the foot-in-the-door approach[24]) and coalition building. Initiatives such as customer and employee surveys, benchmark data, pilot programs, and other incremental system-based approaches can be used to acclimatize organization members to the change ideas. Such initiatives can be used systematically to clarify the need for change, refine the initiative, address concerns, reduce resistance, and increase comfort levels. As well, it can create opportunities for direct involvement that will build interest and support for the change within key groups. This, in turn, will reduce resistance and increase the prospects for support if and when formal approval is sought. Howell and Higgins have noted the importance of the coalition-building aspect of this approach because of the roles such coalitions might play later, during the formal approval process.

In the next chapter, we examine the process of stakeholder analysis. Change leaders need to use their understanding of the key players to develop influential coalitions that will support the changes that are to be proposed. Often in systems or technological changes, if key user groups want to adopt new software or systems, management may be more willing to accept the innovation (just ensure that the new systems can interact with others and do not create more problems than they solve!). In other situations, developing the coalition provides the political clout to move the decision in a favorable manner.

The intent of this approach is to create the momentum needed to reach a tipping point[25] that significantly enhances the likelihood of approval. When formal approval is required, the support from key coalition members and stakeholders should make the process more manageable. If the change has been accepted by a sufficient number of key stakeholders, it may make the approval process all but automatic.

Developing coalitions for change often makes a great deal of sense when seeking formal approval. However, coalition building is not without its risks. This approach takes time and adds complexity (more fingers are in the pie) that may impede the approval process. It can also become political and divisive. Avoid getting trapped in tactics that seriously harm relationships, diminish your integrity, and/or compromise your longer-term objectives.

How Can We Bypass the Formal Approval Process?

The need to seek formal approval can sometimes be bypassed entirely. An example of this involved Peter Grant, a banker who was responsible for major changes in the employee demographics of his employer. No formal permission was ever sought. Grant understood the systems in his organization and used this awareness to quietly advance a change agenda over a 30-year period. Through this approach he dramatically altered the nature of his organization. He would appear to have followed the classic change dictum, "Don't ask, just do it."

Peter Grant* understood his bank's existing structures and systems:

> Peter Grant was a black manager, one of few in the firm when he joined. Over his career he pursued his personal goal of bringing more women and minorities into the firm. Each time he had the opportunity, he hired a qualified minority. And he encouraged others to do the same. Over his career, he was instrumental in hiring the 3,500 talented minority and female members who had joined the organization.[26]

Peter Grant's understanding of the existing structures and systems enabled him to make significant change with minimum disruption.

When the scope of the change is manageable, defensible, and arguably within their scope of authority, change leaders should seriously consider proceeding on their own without waiting for formal approval. Just ensure that key people such as supervisors are kept sufficiently in the loop so that they are not unpleasantly surprised or left with the belief that someone acted in an underhanded fashion.

When the "just do it" strategy is effectively applied, the dynamics can be powerful. Those who might otherwise be predisposed to oppose the change may not notice it or be lulled into acquiescence as the change proceeds in a lower-key fashion during the initial phases (e.g., data gathering, preliminary experimentation). This approach allows for change refinement, the generation of supportive data, and the building of momentum for change that is difficult to stop.

Howell and Higgins refer to this as the renegade process.[27] It grows out of the premise that it is often easier to gain forgiveness than permission to do something in organizations. This tactic can prove helpful in the early stages of product innovation, but Frost and Egri[28] argue that securing permission is an important contributor to success when social innovations are involved. When using a renegade process, one must be careful not to create enemies unnecessarily or engage in tactics that create long-term damage to your reputation and credibility or the reputation of the firm.

The renegade method does not mean the chaotic introduction of disturbances merely to shake things up. Most organizations are already experiencing enough turbulence. Nor does it mean acting in organizationally naïve ways. Rather, this approach begins with a careful assessment of organizational and environmental factors, including the needs and preferences of key individuals who have the potential

---

* Peter Grant's name is disguised in the article (cited above) that reports on his actions.

to harm or assist the change and the change leader. Finally, it asks change leaders to recognize the power and influence that they have to get things done through launching the initiative on their own and when the situation is appropriate, to "just do it!"

How Can We Use Alignment to Aid the Approval Process?

Gaining approval for change becomes less daunting when you are able to show how the change aligns with the organization's mission, vision, and strategy. When change plans are being developed, questions of their relationship to these dimensions and their alignment with other existing systems need to be addressed.

If the case can be made that the change initiative adds considerable value over other alternatives and fits within the context of the mission, vision, and strategy and significant downstream systems (e.g., information and reward systems, organization structure), the likelihood of acceptance and adoption of the change is enhanced. If the resources required for the change seem relatively minor relative to the benefits, approval is also more likely. For example, consider a proposed change in the level of customer service offered by call center personnel that has high potential to increase customer satisfaction and significantly reduce the need for callbacks. The likelihood of approval and acceptance is higher if the only required actions are an additional half day of training, the development of needed support materials, the modification of a couple of decision support screens, the presence of supervisory support, and the modification of performance metrics to reinforce the desired change. In effect, the change leader will have demonstrated that there is little to fear because the change is incremental, not particularly disruptive in nature, and contains benefits that outweigh the costs.

Change leaders often find it is useful to frame changes in ways that reduce the sense of incongruence with existing structures and systems. In general, this approach makes it easier to gain approval because it reduces the sense of disruption and risk that the change will entail. For example, if the end state of a change were to move from mass marketing to relationship-focused, one-to-one marketing, this would be a huge change. The perceived risk can be reduced by breaking the change down into a number of smaller, manageable stages that begin with exploratory research and evaluation, followed by a pilot project, assessment of learning and system alignment challenges, extension to a customer group that was particularly well suited to the approach, and so on. By starting small and minimizing the incongruence with existing systems, the change leader can move in a systematic fashion in the desired direction, learning and modifying systems and structures in ways that look incremental in the short term but have significant long-term effects.

As momentum and the critical mass of support build for a revolutionary change that is positioned as incremental, the change may take on a life of its own. When those smaller change elements are added together over time, the cumulative changes will look far more significant in retrospect than they did at any point along the way. The term "morphing" captures the sense of this approach to change because it depicts a slow and steady transformation of the organization over time.[29]

Abrahamson refers to this as the "change without pain" approach, though not all recipients would share this sentiment.[30] The lesson is that approval can often be advanced by avoiding the depiction of the change as a marked departure of heroic proportions. An evolving series of 10 5% changes, over the course of 3 years, produces a total change of 50% in organizational performance, and that does not include the compounding effects!

The Interaction of Structures and Systems With Change

Structures and systems not only have an impact on a change leader's ability to gain acceptance for a change project, they may have a significant impact on the change success. The transformation at MASkargo, a state-of-the-art Malaysian air cargo facility, provides an example of system-enabled changes. Changes involving tens of millions had been invested in systems and technology in order to produce a premier air cargo–handling center. However, performance fell far short of expectations. Rather than panic, MASkargo opted for a change path that began by working with and assessing existing systems and structures. They then used the learning from that assessment to modify and extend those systems and structures to improve existing services and develop new initiatives.

MASkargo's Advanced Cargo Center Delivers on Its Promise

Malaysia's state-of-the-art one-stop air cargo handling facility had, in its first two years of operation, been plagued by system failures, bottlenecks, and misplaced shipments that proved extremely costly. However, MASkargo was able to correct these issues by ensuring employees knew how to use the new structures and systems. Cargo-handling glitches were identified and rectified. Workers became more familiar with the fully automated operational process and results were improved. MASkargo recorded a RM52 million profit in the 2002/03 third quarter to sharply turn around from an RM242.86 million loss for the whole of 2001/02.

In the process, MASkargo has been nominated as Best Air Cargo Carrier (Asia), Best Air Cargo Terminal Operator (Asia), and Best Cargo Airport. "Our selling points are reliability and efficiency. All the sophisticated equipment will come to naught if we cannot deliver," says Mohd Yunus Idris (General Manager of Operations).

Amongst other things, they have established performance benchmarks for their key operations (e.g., cargo is processed in just 90 minutes for uploading to connecting aircraft to 100 destinations across six continents). More importantly they take action when benchmarks aren't achieved. "If a process takes longer than specified, agents may immediately lodge a complaint and we will take action," says Yunus. Rising tonnage, their ability to handle very diverse cargo effectively and efficiently (from day-old chicks to elephants and Formula 1 cars), profitability, and high levels of customer satisfaction suggest their improvement changes are working.[31]

The change task at MASkargo was made easier by the fact that the facility was new, systems were well documented, and participants understood that refinement and improvement initiatives were to be expected and embraced. MASkargo recognized the value of aligning systems and structures with the vision and strategy and used this to promote the needed changes. Further, they avoided getting bogged down in finger-pointing and other defensive tactics when things didn't pan out initially. Such actions can derail progress in even what appears to be a relatively straightforward problem.

As mentioned earlier in this chapter, awareness of the nature and impact of existing structures and systems puts change leaders in a better position to identify when and where these may present challenges that will need to be managed, and where they can be used to facilitate change. This awareness can also be used to promote the awareness of future risk points to which leaders in the organization need to pay attention. The MASkargo and the Peter Grant change examples involved approaches that refined and exploited existing systems in support of the desired changes.

All too often, though, change leaders fail to pay attention to important systemic factors and their influence on desired outcomes. Toolkit Exercise 5.2 asks you to engage in an assessment of the role that existing structures and systems are likely to play in an organizational change and how they might be managed and used to increase the likelihood of success.

Toolkit Exercise 5.3 asks you to relate a change project to how you might gain approval.

In summary, change agents need to understand the approval processes for their particular project. They need to know the key players and how formal the process is. Does it require a vote? Will the "go ahead" be authorized at a management or executive meeting? Alternatively, can the change agent act to develop a coalition first or just act, using his or her own resources and power base? In the next section, we will explore the role of systems in change approval, change acceptance, and change implementation.

How Can We Use Structures and Systems to Facilitate the Acceptance of Change?

Change agents may be tempted to breathe a sigh of relief and relax once a change project is approved. However, gaining formal approval is not the same as gaining generalized acceptance of the change. Too often, the anticipated chorus of excitement fails to materialize, and in its stead change agents experience begrudging cooperation or covert or overt resistance. The assumption that approval will automatically lead to acceptance is a dangerous one.

Success rates in getting change acceptance are sometimes low. For example:

Complex implementations, failure to yield desired results, escalating maintenance costs have all marred the reputation of Customer Relationship Management programs. . . . 50% of CRM projects generally fail . . . and almost 42% of CRM software licences bought end up unused. . . . While some fault lies with the vendors, sometimes it is, unfortunately, the business that gets itself in a rut.[32]

Despite their best intentions, change leaders often have less than stellar success in bringing approved change to fruition in their organizations. Lack of acceptance often plays a role in this. Systemic factors in an organization can be used to ease the legitimization and acceptance of a change initiative. However, they can also derail progress. The inappropriate delegation of sponsorship and the misapplication of systems are two of the most commonly cited mistakes made by top management in change initiatives.[33]

Paul Tsaparis of Hewlett-Packard did not make the mistake of underestimating the role that systems and structures can play:

> In May of 2002, Paul Tsaparis, 42, president of Hewlett-Packard (Canada) Ltd., began managing the massive integration of Hewlett-Packard and Compaq in Canada. The new 6,800 person organization had annual revenues in excess of $3 billion (Canadian). As is often the case with organizational integration, staff reductions were involved.
>
> Tsaparis approached the integration challenge by getting out and putting a human face on the challenges and changes. He needed to communicate the vision and corporate strategy, and let people know what was happening to their employment situation as soon as possible. He needed to reassure other key stakeholders (customers, suppliers) that they would not be lost in the shuffle. Tsaparis knew he needed to develop organizational structures, systems, and processes that would support HP's strategy, reinforce the integration change initiative, and increase the likelihood of longer term organizational success. He created a team of individuals to facilitate the organizational changes. This, in turn, required structures, systems, and processes that would support the change team in the pursuit of their objectives.[34]

Tsaparis faced significant structural and systemic challenges to change. Each organization, HP and Compaq, had its own way of doing things. And many of those systems and structures would have explicit as well as implicit implications—ways of doing things that might not even be written down but were firmly embedded in the habits of organization members. As a result, the conscious development of structures and systems that would support HP's strategy represented an important step in the building of an infrastructure that would support change and promote acceptance. Conflicting and misaligned structures and systems needed to be identified and addressed so that the resulting web of structures and systems was aligned.

Change agents need to understand the effects of structures and systems from the perspective of the person who is on the receiving end of the change—the actual person who will be asked to behave differently. If people do not accept the change (whether they like it or not), they are unlikely to modify their behavior in the desired direction, no matter how excellent the change project is.

Interestingly, acceptance or compliance does not necessarily mean attitude change. That is, attitude change need not come first. It may well evolve after the needed behavior is obtained. That is, if systems can be used to promote the desired behavior in individuals (e.g., through having them live with new structural or systemic arrangements), their attitudes toward what they are doing may adjust over time in the desired direction as they live with the new context.[35]

The effective use of the formal communication, performance management, and reward systems can play a useful role in gaining acceptance and commitment. Clarity of purpose and direction, combined with employee involvement and rewards for desired behavior, can all be used to advance the engagement and involvement of employees in change-related initiatives. A top-down directive that orders change can lead to less information sharing, reduced risk taking, less acceptance of change, and greater employee turnover.[36] Unless the employees buy into the legitimate authority of executives and the legitimacy of the change, they may not accept it and engage in actions that may slow, disrupt, or sabotage progress.

Much of the change champion's difficulty in thinking through the impact of structure on acceptance flows from their assumptions. They see clearly the need for change and the rationale underlying the change—to them, the change is immensely logical. From that position, it is much too easy to assume that others will see, and accept, the logic of the change agent! But the logic falls flat for organization members facing a reward system that works against the change, or an organizational structure that emphasizes characteristics contrary to the desired change (e.g., cost controls rather than customer focus).

When Sears undertook major renewal in the 1990s, its approach was anchored in an understanding of the use of systems and structures to advance change.[37] Because time was of the essence, change leaders leveraged the urgency to gain acceptance and adopted a ready-fire-aim approach. Certain structural changes were announced and enacted unilaterally (e.g., the closure of the catalogue), and these were used to reinforce the urgency and commitment of those leading the change to take action, produce some quick improvements, and build momentum and hope. Later, participative systems and processes were utilized as the changes moved closer to matters involving cultural adjustment, and these were reinforced by changes to the reward system.

Changes of this magnitude required leadership commitment that can sustain the change over time (in the case of Sears, years). Accepted systems (with modifications) were used to approve the commencement of large-scale change. In combination with temporary systems and structures (e.g., task forces), they protected people that built and tested the changes. This set the stage for the development and installation of systems and processes that were very different from those they replaced. Though the changes were revolutionary in nature, change leaders leveraged accepted systems and processes to facilitate the design, testing, and implementation of needed changes and to build legitimacy and commitment.

The three strategies proposed earlier by Howell and Higgins will have different impacts on downstream acceptance. Proceeding through the formal approval channel may enhance the legitimacy of the change and reduce second-guessing. A coalition-building strategy will tend to involve others in the decision process, and involvement increases the likelihood of understanding and acceptance by coalition members and their associates. Finally, a renegade approach often carries with it certain characteristics that can influence acceptance levels. Organization members who are predisposed to the change and value individual initiative may be secretly (if not overtly) cheering the initiative. Those who place their trust in hierarchy and/or fear a loss of power, influence, or control could very well develop negative attitudes to the change.

The passage of time can influence the acceptance of change. When a change initiative has been the subject of discussion for an extended period, this gestation period can allow the idea to become more acceptable. Initiatives that are shocking at first may appear less threatening after a period of reflection. Alternatively, if approval has been granted and there seems to be little activity or visible progress, acceptability and support may diminish.

In summary, systems and structures, properly deployed, can play an important role in the speed and rate of acceptance of change. People don't resist all change. Lots of things have the potential to be seen as worth doing, and people tend to respond positively to change initiatives that they understand and believe are worth the effort and risk. The way that systems and processes are deployed will influence the perception of the change.[38]

How Can We Develop More Adaptive Systems and Structures?

The ability of organizations to adapt to change is aided by their ability to learn. Nevis suggests that organizations can be viewed as learning systems that acquire knowledge, disseminate it through the organization, and use that knowledge to accomplish their missions.[39] Learning is facilitated when organizations do the following:

1. Systematically and deliberately scan their external environment.

2. Have a shared perception of the gap between the current and desired level of performance.

3. Have a concern for measurement of performance.

4. Develop an experimental mind-set where they try new things.

5. Create an organizational climate of openness and accessibility.

6. Engage in continuous education at all organizational levels.

7. Use a variety of methods, appreciate diversity, and take a pluralistic view of competencies.

8. Have multiple individuals who act as advocates for new ideas and methods.

9. Have an involved, engaged leadership.

10. Recognize the interdependence of units and have a systems perspective.

Many of these learning actions are influenced by organizational structures and systems. The presence of early-warning systems and opportunity-finding systems advance the scanning capacity of the organization. The presence of a formal strategy and environmental review process, complete with performance metrics, will increase the likelihood that firms will systematically review where they are and where they want to go. Systems that reward innovation and information sharing will increase the prospects for openness and exploration. Systems that fund and reinforce development will open people to continuous education. Likewise, appropriately designed systems and processes can be used to advance diversity and the exploration of new ideas. Finally, systems can be used to increase the prospects that interdependencies are recognized and that a systems perspective is brought to problem solving.

Organizations that are more flexible and adaptive have an easier time adjusting to incremental changes and more upending changes.[40] Change leaders find that more flexible systems and structures are, by their nature, somewhat easier to work with. As the complexity and turbulence of organizational environments increase, more flexible, adaptive systems will be required (this was discussed earlier in the chapter).

To cope with turbulence and complexity, firms are being designed in unconventional ways that include the use of formal and informal networks with external organizations. For example, designer, supplier, producer, and distributor capabilities are being brought together in ways that increase flexibility and adaptability. Thus, a product might be designed in Italy, built in Korea from Brazilian materials, and distributed in the United States by a Scandinavian firm. Think "IKEA" for this type of network.[41] The network partners are held together by market mechanisms such as contracts, just-in-time logistics, shared market intelligence and production systems, and customers' demands rather than by organizational charts and controls.[42]

One of the roles of the change agent is to help organizations learn from the past and evolve systems and structures that are more likely to help them succeed in the future. Focusing on how organizations acquire knowledge and spread it throughout the organization can be a valuable diagnostic tool in this regard. By facilitating the development of more adaptive systems and processes (keeping in mind the competitive realities and the need for congruence with the environment), change agents will succeed in enhancing the capacity of the organization to adjust to change in the future.

Summary

In Chapter 5, we have investigated the role of formal systems and structures from the perspectives of how they influence change and how they can be worked with in order to advance the change leaders' initiatives. We began by addressing the importance of understanding them, how they operate, and how they influence the change process. We used this knowledge to explore the systems and structures related to the approval process so that change leaders would have a better understanding of how to work with, through, and around them in order to increase the prospects of the change being adopted. Next we turned to how formal systems and structures can be used to advance acceptance of the change in the organization. And finally, we addressed the desirability of adaptiveness in formal systems and structures.

In Chapter 6, our focus will shift to the emergent or informal structures and systems in organizations and their influence on the change process.

Glossary of Terms

Organization Structure and Systems—The organizational structure and systems is how the organization formally organizes itself to accomplish its mission. Structure is how the organization's tasks are formally divided, grouped, and coordinated. The structure would include the organizational hierarchy, the structure of any manufacturing operation, and any formal procedures such as the performance appraisal system as well as other structures. Systems are the formal processes of coordination within the organization.

Change Approval Process—The change approval process is the formal procedure that change agents must follow for organizational approval of a change project.

Acceptance of Change—The acceptance of change is the degree to which change participants accept or "buy into" the change that has been implemented.

Mechanistic Organization and Organic Organization—Organizations can be viewed metaphorically as machines or as organisms. A mechanistic organization is one that exhibits machinelike qualities. An organic organization is one that exhibits organism-like qualities.

Environmental Uncertainty—Environmental uncertainty measures the degree of variability of the environment. Duncan suggests two dimensions of uncertainty: degree of complexity of the environment and degree of dynamism.

Information-Processing View of Organizations—The information-processing view of organizations considers organizations as information-processing mechanisms. This view argues that the better the fit between the information-processing capabilities of the organization and its environment, the more effective the organization.

The Formal Approval Process—This is the traditional approach in which a person or persons develop a proposal and bring it forward for assessment and formal approval by the appropriate organization members.

Creeping Commitment—Creeping commitment is the gradual increase in commitment by change participants toward the change project. Such an increase is often obtained by involving participants in decision making.

Coalition Building—Coalition building is the forming of partnerships to increase pressures for or against change.

Renegade Approach—Change is initiated without having first obtained formal approval. This is often done in conjunction with creeping commitment and coalition-building tactics. The intent of the approach is that the change is advanced to the point that it cannot easily be reversed by those with formal authority.

Adaptive Systems and Structures—Adaptive systems and structures are those that are relatively ready for change compared to others.

END-OF-CHAPTER EXERCISES

TOOLKIT EXERCISE 5.1

Impact of Existing Structures and Systems on the Change

Think of a change situation you are familiar with.

1. How did the organization use structures and systems to deal with uncertainty and complexity in its environment? Was this an appropriate response?

2. How did existing structures and systems affect the ability of the change leader to bring about desired change?
   a. What systems and structures were involved?

   b. How did these systems and structures influence what happened? Was this related to how they were formally designed? Or was this related to how they actually came to be used in practice?

3. Who influenced how the systems and structures were used, and how did this affect the outcomes that ensued?

TOOLKIT EXERCISE 5.2

Gaining Approval for the Change Project

1. Consider a change project in an organization with which you are familiar. What is the approval process for more minor change initiatives? For more major change initiatives? Can you describe the processes involved?

   a. If a project requires capital approval, are there existing capital budgeting processes?

   b. If the project needs dedicated staff allocated to it, or if it will lead to additions to staff complement, what are the processes for adding people permanently and selecting and developing staff?

   c. Does the project alter the way work is organized and performed? What are the systems and processes used for defining jobs and assessing performance?

   d. Can the project be approved by an individual? Who is that person? What approval power does he or she have?

2. Are there ways that the perceived risks of the change could have been reduced by the way the change leader staged the project and managed the approval process?

TOOLKIT EXERCISE 5.3

Using Existing Structures and Systems to Promote the Change

1. Look back at the questions raised in Toolkit Exercise 5.1. How could the existing structures and systems have been approached and used differently to advance the desired change?

2. What role could incremental strategies that were nested within existing systems and structures have played? Would they have really moved the process forward or simply avoided the real changes that needed to be addressed?

3. What role could more revolutionary strategies have played? Would they produce issues related to their alignment with existing systems and structures? How would you manage the challenges created by this?

Notes

1. Robbins, S., & Langton, N. (2003). *Organization behaviour* (p. 531). Toronto: Pearson Education.

2. Daft, R. L. (2003). *Organization theory and design* (8th ed.). Cincinnati, OH: South-Western College Publishing.

3. Carey, S. (2003, March 18). Leading the news: Two airlines press workers for deeper cost cuts—UAL's United Airlines seeks court permission to void labor pacts with unions. *Wall Street Journal.*

4. Former ChevronTexaco executive tapped in special Labor Day board meeting, money.cnn.com/2002/09/02/news/companies/ual/index.htm, September 3, 2002.

5. Roth, D. (2002, February 4). How to cut pay, lay off 8,000 people and still have workers who love you? It's easy: Just follow the Agilent way. *Fortune.*

6. Robbins, S. P., & Langton, N. (2003). *Organizational behaviour: Concepts, controversies, applications* (3rd Canadian ed., p. 456). Englewood Cliffs, NJ: Prentice Hall.

7. Daft, R. L. (1998). *Organization theory and design* (6th ed., p. 95). Cincinnati, OH: South-Western College Publishing.

8. Robbins, S., & Langton. N. (2003). *Organization behaviour* (p. 477). Toronto: Pearson Education.

9. Duncan, R. (1979, Winter). What is the right organization structure? *Organizational Dynamics.*

10. Tu, Q., Vonderembse, M. A., Ragu-Nathan, T. S., & Ragu-Nathan, B. (2004). Measuring modularity-based manufacturing practices and their impact on mass customization capability: A customer-driven perspective. *Decision Sciences, (35)*2, 147–168.

11. Galbraith, J. R. (1977). *Organization design.* Reading, MA: Addison-Wesley.

12. Daft, R. L. (2003). *Organization theory and design* (6th ed., pp. 204–211). Cincinnati, OH: South-Western College Publishing.

13. The 9–11 Commission. (2004). *9/11 Commission Report: Final Report of the National Commission on Terrorist Attacks upon the United States.* Washington, DC: Government Printing Office.

14. Survey: Partners in wealth. (2006, January 21). *The Economist, (378)*8461, 18. Copyright (c) 2006 The Economist Newspaper, Ltd. All rights reserved. Reprinted with permission. Further reproduction prohibited. www.economist.com.

15. Wetzel, D. K., & Buch, K. (2000, Winter). Using a structural model to diagnose organizations and develop congruent interventions. *Organization Development Journal, (18)*4, 9–19.

16. Hill, D. (2004). The case for standards. *Health Management Technology, (25)*10, 48–50.

17. Nadler, D., Shaw, R. B., Walton, A. E., & Associates, (1994). *Discontinuous change: Leading organizational transformation.* San Francisco: Jossey-Bass.

18. Simons, R. (1995, March–April). Control in the age of empowerment. *Harvard Business Review,* 80–88; Simons, R. (1999, May–June). How risky is your company? *Harvard Business Review,* 85–94.

19. Howell, J., & Higgins, C. (1990). Champions of change: Identifying, understanding and supporting champions of technological innovations. *Organizational Dynamics, (19)*1, 40–55.

20. Tight, G. (1998, January). From experience: Securing sponsors and funding for new product development projects—the human side of enterprise. *The Journal of Product Innovation Management, (15)*1, 75–81; Harrold, D. (1999). How to get control & automation projects approved. *Control Engineering, (46)*8, 34–37.

21. Harrold, D. (1999). How to get control & automation projects approved. *Control Engineering,* (*46*)8, 34–37.

22. Drew, S. A. W. (1996). Accelerating change: Financial industry experiences with BPR. *The International Journal of Bank Marketing,* (*14*)6, 23–35.

23. Noori, H., Deszca, G., & Munro, H. (1997). Managing the P/SDI process: Best-in-class principles and leading practices. *International Journal of Technology Management,* 245–268.

24. Dillard, J., Hunter, J., & Burgoon, M. (1984). Sequential request persuasive strategies: Meta-analysis of foot-in-the-door and door-in-the-face. *Human Communication Research, 10,* 461–488.

25. Gladwell, M. (2000). *The tipping point: How little things can make a big difference.* New York: Little, Brown.

26. This example is drawn from Meyerson, D. E. (2001, October). Radical change, the quiet way. *Harvard Business Review,* 94–95.

27. Howell, J., & Higgins, C. (1990). Champions of change: Identifying, understanding and supporting champions of technological innovations. *Organizational Dynamics,* (*19*)1, 40–55.

28. Frost, P. J., & Egri, C. P. (1990). Influence of political action on innovation: Part II. *Leadership and Organizational Development Journal,* (*11*)2, 4–12.

29. Marshak, R. J. (2004). Morphing: The leading edge of organizational change in the twenty-first century. *Organizational Development Journal,* (*22*)3, 8–21.

30. Abrahamson, E. (2000, July–August). Change without pain. *Harvard Business Review,* 75–79.

31. Abdullah, M. (2003, March). *Business Times* (Kuala Lumpur).

32. Choy, J. (2003, March 17). The cold truth about CRM. *Asia Computer Weekly.*

33. Prosci Benchmarking Report. (2000). *Best Practices in Change Management,* 2.

34. Drawn from Pitts, G. (2002, September 30). *Globe and Mail,* B3.

35. Waldersee, R., & Griffiths, A. (2004). Implementing change: Matching implementation methods and change type. *Leadership and Development Journal,* (*25*)5, 424–434.

36. Mishra, K. E., Spreitzer, G. M., & Mishra, A. K. (1998, Winter). Preserving employee morale during downsizing. *Sloan Management Review,* 83–95.

37. Rucci, A. J., Kirn, S. P., & Quinn, R. T. (1998, January–February). The employee-customer-profit chain at Sears. *Harvard Business Review,* 83–97.

38. Mishra, K. E., Spreitzer, G. M., & Mishra, A. K. (1998, Winter). Preserving employee morale during downsizing. *Sloan Management Review,* 83–95.

39. Nevis, E. C., DiBella, A. J., & Gould, J. M. (1995, Winter). Understanding organizations as learning systems. *Sloan Management Review,* (*36*)2, 73–85.

40. Beatty, R. W., & Ulrich, D. O. (1991, Summer). Re-energizing the mature organization. *Organizational Dynamics*; Beer, M., & Nohria, N. (2000). Cracking the code of change. *Harvard Business Review.*

41. Margonelli, L. (2002, October). How IKEA designs its sexy price tags. *Business 2.0.*

42. Miles, R. E., & Snow, C. C. (1992, Summer). Causes of failure in network organizations. *California Management Review,* (*34*)4, 53–72.

CHAPTER 6

The Emergent or Informal Organization

Resistance to Change,
Force Field Analysis,
and Stakeholder Analysis

People don't resist change; people resist being changed.

Chapter Overview

- Change leaders recognize the importance of understanding the sources of support for and resistance to change.
- Understanding the power dynamics in an organization is important in successful change.
- Force field analysis and stakeholder analysis are two key tools in understanding the informal organizational system and how to change it.

As a change leader, you have done the analysis. You recognize both the real and perceived need for change, and you understand the ins and outs of your organization. You have crafted a powerful, transforming vision. And still people don't seem to fall over themselves trying to follow your lead and implement the change. Why not? What is needed, and why, seem so obvious to you!

This chapter examines the emergent or informal side of the organization. The chapter challenges the commonly held view that resistance to change is somehow negative. Instead, it suggests that the change leader's task is to examine both the key forces at play in the organization and the important stakeholders in the change situation. The sources of power are described to enable change leaders to understand how to gain better leverage in their organizations. Force field analysis and stakeholder analysis are described as tools to be used by change leaders in understanding the organization. Figure 6.1 places the chapter in Beckhard and Harris's change model. Our understanding of both the present state and the desired future state depends on our analysis of the organization. Chapter 5 looked at the formal structural and systems aspects of that understanding. Chapters 7 and 8 examine the impact of key individuals in the organization. This chapter provides the background on the informal and emergent aspects to organizations.

How Can We Understand Resistance to Change?

When managers talk about organizational change, they often view resistance to change in terms of how "those people won't get with the program." Managers often see people as stuck with their opinions and who simply "don't understand the situation." People are viewed as blockers, obstructionists, old'guard, complacent, apathetic, naïve, and so on. They are viewed in negative terms and that framing won't help the situation! Paradoxically, so-called "resistors" often use similar words: change agents who don't understand how things really work; change initiators who are fixated on a program (including a formula approach) that doesn't fit and who are trying to force their opinions on others; or change agents who are arrogant or naïve in what they are trying to do. Before long, each may come to view the other as the enemy, escalating an already unhealthy situation.[1]

The reality is that many people seek variety, embrace novelty, and want change. Often, we cannot see this in people. We just see them as opposing change. Why is it that we often see resistance in others when we act as change agents or change initiators?

Much of what is called "resistance" in others is based on different information, different perceptions, different needs, different beliefs, and the impact of informal systems and processes. Too often, change agents fail to understand the dynamics of the situation and the positions of key people and groups in the organization. They tend to frame the situation in ways that make the misunderstandings and so-called resistance worse. Sometimes polarization is inevitable, but these cases are the exception, not the general rule.[2] When change agents fail to recognize this, they do so at their own peril.

The use of language frequently moves people into we-they oppositional camps. By framing the situation into "good guys" (change initiators who support change) and "bad guys" (change resistors who prevent change), change agents create the very situation they need to avoid. Instead of nurturing the support of those they need to adopt the change, change agents alienate them and increase their opposition. To control resistance, they often use "top-down" approaches to change that reflect a rational, hierarchical model. This classic bureaucratic paradigm, with its emphasis

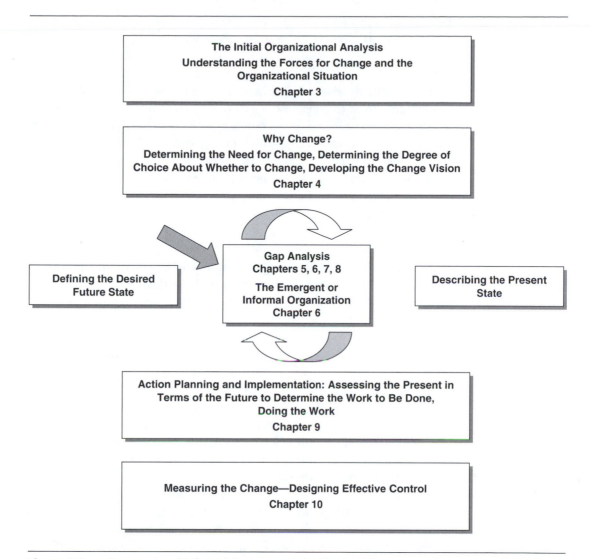

Figure 6.1   Emergent and Informal Systems and the Change Management Process

on command and control, doesn't reach out to the minds and hearts of many change recipients. This management approach attempts to superimpose the change agent's logic onto the situation and assumes that their perspective is complete and logical. From this perspective, the views of others appear irrational and illogical to the change leader. When change agents assume that they possess legitimacy, they may come to view those who oppose them as illegitimate.

Resistance to change is real. At times, people do oppose change. There is no magic bullet that will shift people miraculously to the change leader's perspective. Just because you have taken the time to listen, understood the resistor's point of view, and tried to incorporate that view into the change program does not mean that a resistor will somehow just fall in line. What is important for change leaders is that they understand the reasons for the resistance. Then they can plan an appropriate response.

One metaphor that is helpful is to view change as a process of persuasion and the change recipient as a potential consumer of our change. Change agents need to understand the recipient's position and what is important to them before they can persuade them. Of course, the process is reciprocal. Skilled change agents listen carefully, are informed by what they hear, and make refinements to the design of the change and its implementation. Just as a customer is introduced to a new product or service and is gradually shifted to a purchase position, so too can a change recipient be persuaded to adopt a change. This is more successful when change recipients believe that their concerns and insights have been understood and responded to.

We seem to be able to do this in the marketing world. Consider the following example from Play Lab where designers assess the perceptions and actions of potential customers and put them to use in the design and delivery of more effective products:

> At the Play Lab, engineers and designers test toys by giving them the ultimate test—they let kids play with them, bend them, throw them, smash them, stab them, or do anything they wish. They do this to ensure that the product is safe and sound and attractive to kids.

> "Kids are pretty humbling," says Don Stucke, a sweet-natured View-Master product designer. "You can have what you think is a great idea and they shoot it down in minutes." This approach works both for older kids and for infants. Babies react immediately to something they don't like by pushing or throwing it away.[3]

Why is it that change leaders intuitively understand that the best plans and designs need reality testing with various types of customers and users (in the above example, the kids), but in organizational change, they sometimes assume that the plans and designs, generated in relative isolation, are ripe and ready for application? They may fail to adequately assess the assumptions underpinning the change or see the need to field-test the approach. If they do test, they may select supportive environments or contexts that are not reflective of the realities they will face in the field, in order to generate supportive data. Further, they may assume that one size fits all and that what they made work in one locale will work everywhere.

Contrast two cases of significant organizational change: (1) the merger of Daimler and Chrysler a few years ago and (2) the changes to 3M brought about by McNerney as their new CEO.

The Daimler-Chrysler merger of several years ago provides a classic example of the impact of informal systems. This merger was hailed as having potential for great synergy. The need for change was relatively clear as far as the market was concerned, and the merger made good business sense. However, the ability to implement that change floundered on the different cultures of the two companies and the needs of the executives.

> When Daimler Benz and Chrysler Corp. announced their $36 billion "merger of equals" in 1998, it was hailed as a marriage made in heaven. At the time, Chrysler was the world's most profitable and cost-efficient carmaker, while Daimler was renowned as the planet's premier luxury carmaker. DaimlerChrysler became

the new model for a global automotive powerhouse and its stock soared into triple digits, forcing rival automakers into mergers of their own. But in remarkably short order the mass/class union has hit the skids, undermined by a transatlantic culture clash and a damaging exodus of talent. Virtually the entire "dream team" of Chrysler executives that built the hot models and big profits of the 1990s has departed, leaving behind a chaotic American operation where costs are spinning out of control.[4]

As a Merrill Lynch auto analyst said, "The problem is not the concept of the partnership but the execution. . . . This is a partnership where the two companies haven't partnered."[5] The need for change as conceived and perceived by the executives was not enough to carry the day with the legion of individuals who were the recipients of change and keys to effective implementation. These individuals saw things differently, were confused or misinterpreted what was being asked of them, and acted accordingly! A partnership that had significant potential became bogged down because of the inability of management to communicate a compelling vision, engage and elicit timely feedback and support, and anticipate and cope with the predictable responses by others.

In contrast, the arrival of McNerney at 3M was very different. Here, the CEO was able to work with those around him:

McNerney of 3M's style has let employees feel that they, not McNerney, are driving the changes. He was able to introduce data-driven change without forcing his ideas from General Electric onto the organization.

McNerney was able to rely on existing 3M management rather than importing other GE executives. "I think the story here is rejuvenation of a talented group of people rather than replacement of a mediocre group of people," he says. As part of his change plan, he avoids giving orders and reinforces the 3M culture whenever he can. "This is a fundamentally strong company. The inventiveness of the people here is in contrast with any other place I've seen. Everybody wakes up in the morning trying to figure out how to grow. They really do." The diplomacy has generally played well with the 3M faithful. "He's delivered a very consistent message," says Althea Rupert, outgoing chair of Technical Forum, an internal society for all 3M technical people. "There's a sense of speed and a sense of urgency."[6]

In the 3M case, there is clear understanding shown of the players, their perspectives, and their needs, which made the implementation much easier to accomplish. Perhaps McNerney had no choice. But he did act in ways that involved people, focused their attention and interest, and brought them along, rather than attempting to impose a set of views.

While these two situations are different, they demonstrate the impact of the informal system. How change leaders deal with these systems will affect the amount and nature of the resistance to change that occurs in a change project.

In the vast majority of change situations, initial and continuing resistance and concern in various forms and amounts are normal. At the inception of a new change initiative, there are typically, at most, a handful of individuals who understand

and support it (often those who have been directly involved in its design and development) and an overwhelming majority who don't understand. For many, the proposal will appear new and will seem to be disruptive and negative in its impact.

Resistance is normal and can be positive if change leaders know how to respond to it. At minimum, they need to know why people are resisting. Kotter described four reasons why people might passively or actively oppose change:[7]

1. **Parochial self-interest**. The proposed change will lead to a loss of something valuable and as a result individuals resist. They may not have time to make the change, or they believe the change to be harmful to themselves or the organization.

2. **Misunderstanding and lack of trust**. Often employees may not understand the implications of what is proposed. If the history of the organization or the culture is such that trust levels are not high, suspicion results and may lead to resistance.

3. **Different assessments of the consequences**. Employees will have a different perspective on the change—frequently they are closer to things than senior management. They may be aware of details that make the proposals unworkable.

4. **Low tolerance for change**. Some employees are not ready for change. They may not have the skills, or they may have personalities that seek stability. The organization may have had too much change—change that did not work out and thus the tolerance for change is low.

Managers of change find it too easy to interpret alternative viewpoints and concerns as self-serving nay-saying, ignorance, pig-headedness, or subversive. Such discounting reduces the need to seriously consider them and acts as a defensive shield. Managerial expectations of the negative impact of resistance can also become self-fulfilling and lead to opposition that may be unnecessary. Davidson argues that "resistance has come to include anything and everything that workers do which managers do not want them to do, and that workers do not do that managers wish them to do."[8]

In the DaimlerChrysler example above, the "resistance" of the Chrysler executives led to an escalating negative cycle that resulted in valuable employees exiting. Perhaps this was inevitable. However, it would seem that the outcomes of resistance could have been much more positive if the turnover risk had been anticipated and managed to greater advantage.

When assessing resistance, change managers need to recognize the impact that history can have. Employees may have had significant experience with change that leads them to be wary. They have also worked with the existing approaches and have their own perspectives on what is needed, so ambivalence and concern are natural—particularly in individuals who have demonstrated commitment to the organization and the quality of the outcomes achieved.[9] Many change projects that employees have been part of are downsizings in disguise, and yet change leaders somehow expect employees to welcome such initiatives with open arms. Surely, such optimism is naïve! Friedman tells the story of an Israeli taxi driver talking about the *intifada* and how Israel should respond. The driver said, "You know what we should do? We should take our clubs and hit them over the head, and **hit them** and **hit them** and **hit them**, until they finally stop hating us."[10] Somehow some managers think similar tactics of repetition and escalation will succeed in generating acceptance!

In summary, change agents should not be surprised to find that there is ambivalence toward, concern with, and resistance to change. It often seems inevitable. Change facilitators should encourage the voicing of concerns in an organized manner. Once they are public, they can be addressed. Resistance that has gone underground is much more difficult to deal with. Toolkit Exercise 6.1 will help you to think about resistance to change in your organization.

What Are the Power Dynamics in Organizations?

You think you have power and influence? Well, try and give orders to another person's dog![11]

It is clear that if you have enough power, you can get your way—on the surface at least. People respond to power and authority. Although employees can reconcile themselves because of the power situation, unintended consequences often make the use of power riskier than managers think. (As an unknown author cynically stated, "Reconciliation is where one side gets enough power and the other side gets reconciled.") The other parties often have options that you are either unaware of or only vaguely aware of, and these can have a profound impact on the outcomes achieved. Ill-considered applications of power to influence outcomes can unnecessarily cause loyalty to be replaced with passive resistance, active opposition, sabotage, or with exit from the firm. As mentioned, in the DaimlerChrysler example, key senior executives left.* Such exits may in some cases be desirable, because of interpersonal conflict or fit with the organizational change. However, the unnecessary loss of important skills is never desirable.

When individuals express their reservations more actively, they use their voices to raise concerns. Such attempts are often political in nature, as they attempt to build support for their perspective and influence decision makers concerning the change.[12] Change agents often object strongly to those who resist overtly. They view concerns and dissent as personal and obstructive and take direct action to counter challenges to their authority. In the end, one side loses while the other wins and opportunities for mutual gain are lost. In knowledge-intensive firms, in particular, this sense of loss by employees can lead to the withdrawal and exit of those workers that the firm most needs.[13] However, a more insidious and difficult response is that of passive resistance.[14] Those persons who oppose quietly and persistently are difficult to identify and respond to. For many managers, you talk things over, believe you have agreement, and then go away. Weeks later, you discover nothing positive has

---

*A useful way of thinking about this is given in Rusbult and Lowery's classic work, When bureaucrats get the blues. *Journal of Applied Social Psychology, (15)*1, 83, where they classify the responses as active and constructive (Voice), passive and constructive (Loyalty), active and destructive (Exit), and passive and destructive (Neglect).

been done and that forces of resistance have been rallied and solidified—what you thought was agreement was really passive resistance and/or subterfuge! In a study of resistance to change in Italian middle managers, researchers found that the failure to actively promote the change was more common than open and active opposition.[15]

The power to do things in organizations is critical to achieving change It is a critical resource used by change agents to influence the reactions and actions of others. Exactly how much power do you have, and what are its sources? Do you know what formal power you have as a result of your position? For example, what authority does your signature have—what is the limit of expenditure you have? Can you hire someone based on your signature, or do you need others' approval?

Our beliefs about what power we have and the reality often vary. What counts, of course, are the beliefs that others have about our power. Clearly, power can be real—you can influence people because of your knowledge, persuade due to the strength of your personality and integrity, or use your ability to reward and punish; you can sign for things based on formal authority, and so on. But the perception of power is just as important, if not more important. If people don't believe you have the support to influence others or know what you are talking about, the fact that you do will have little influence until those perceptions are changed. Alternatively, if people believe you possess the needed expertise or have the "ear of the CEO," it is less likely that someone will challenge you concerning such matters. Often the assumption that you have the power needed to do something is all you need. Having the trust of the CEO also means that you want to maintain that trust and are not likely to use inappropriate influence tactics on your boss.[16]

Recently, the mediator between Air Canada (Canada's largest national and international airline) and its unions demonstrated the impact of perception.[17] Clearly, he had significant real power—he was appointed as a go-between and had the authority to demand serious negotiations. However, he ordered the senior executives of Air Canada to cancel their appointments for one evening and fly to Toronto to meet with union representatives (whom he had ordered to come). As a mediator, he would not have the formal authority to demand this in the way a judge would have, but he took a position, exercised moral suasion, and once the executives and union representatives agreed to comply, he did, in fact, have the power. Similarly, in the classic change case at AT&T Dallas, the change team often resorted to "if you don't like it, check with the general manager," and other managers (not wanting to bother the boss) went along with the proposed changes![18]

Power, regardless of its tainted image, is essential to make things happen. Robbins and Langton define power as the capacity to influence others to accept one's ideas or plans.[19] There is nothing inherently good or bad about power. Rather, it is the application and purposeful use of power and its consequences that will determine whether it is "good" or "bad." The mediator, in the example above, created power and used it to construct a labor settlement under very difficult conditions.

What gives people and organizations power? Individuals have power because of the position they hold, who they are (character and reputation), and who and what they know. These individual sources of power can be classified in the following ways:[20]

Position Power—This is power that resides in the legitimate authority of the position. In today's egalitarian world of flattened hierarchies and virtual organizations, this type of power is lessening in effectiveness as people demand to know the "why" of things. This is most true in cultures where deference to positional power is lower.[21]Nevertheless, the formal right to make decisions often comes with position, and this is a major source of power.* As well, a position often endows the incumbent with the ability to reward and punish. This access to resources provides influence over individuals and activities.

Knowledge Power—Knowledge power can be **expert** power, **information** power, or **connection** power. Expert power is the possession of a body of knowledge essential to the organization. An example would be the insights and expertise gained by MBAs or individuals in other professional programs. As they complete their programs, they develop skills and knowledge that assist them in achieving results. Credentials and even grades provide independent certification of expertise and increase one's ability to influence. Information power is power gained through the flow of information: by creating, framing, redirecting, or distorting information and by controlling who receives the information. Connection power arises because the network of connections of individuals permits them to access and pass on information.

Personality Power—Charisma, the ability to inspire trust and enthusiasm in others, provides many leaders with significant individual power. Reputation, which comes from reports of success (or failure), influences personal power.

In addition to personal or individual sources of power, departments within an organization have different levels of power depending on the centrality of the work the department does, the availability of others to accomplish that task, and the ability of the department to handle the organization's environment. These can be categorized as follows:

Ability to Cope With Environmental Uncertainty—Departments and individuals gain power if they are seen to make the environment appear more certain. Thus, marketing and sales departments gain power by bringing in future orders, diminishing the impact of competitors' actions, and providing greater certainty about the organization's future vitality in the marketplace. During times of economic turbulence, finance gains power by its ability to help the firm navigate its way. Likewise, other departments and functions either enhance or diminish their power, based on their ability to absorb uncertainty and make the world more predictable and manageable for the organization.

Low Substitutability—Whenever a function is essential and no one else can do it, the individual or department has power. Think, for example, of the power of human resources departments when no one else can authorize replacement positions, or the power of data-processing departments prior to the advent of the personal computer.

---

*Another way of looking at power is in terms of "yea-saying" or "nay-saying" power. Yea-saying means that a person can make it happen. For example, they could decide who would be hired. Nay-saying power means that a person could prevent something happening. Thus, nay-saying power would mean that they could prevent a particular person from being hired but they could not decide who would be hired.

Centrality—Power flows to those departments whose activities are central to the survival and strategy of the organization or when other departments depend on that department for the completion of work. In most white-collar organizations, systems people have power because of our dependence on the computer and the information derived from it. Close the system and you shut down the organization. Strong systems anchor the success of Federal Express, Dell, Wal-Mart, Statistics Canada, The Bank of Montreal, Scotland Yard, and BMW.

Cynthia Hardy added to our understanding of the sources of power with her classification.[22] She described three dimensions of power:

1. **Resource Power**—the access to valued resources in an organization. These include rewards, sanctions, coercion, authority, credibility, charisma, expertise, information, political affiliations, and group power. Resource power is very similar to the individual power listed above.

2. **Process Power**—the control over formal decision-making arenas and agendas. Examples of process power would be the power to include or exclude an item on a discussion agenda, and to determine who gets to sit on committees to make decisions (usually determined by nominating committees).

3. **Meaning Power**—the ability to define the meaning of things. Thus, the meaning of symbols and rituals and the use of language provide meaning power. For example, a shift from "reserved parking" and large corner offices for executives to "first-come parking" and common office space can symbolize a significant move away from the reliance on hierarchical power.

Hardy's introduction of process and meaning power adds significantly to our understanding of how we might influence a change situation. Anyone who has tried to get an item added to a busy agenda will understand the frustration of not having process power. And when you are told "we don't do things that way," you have run into meaning power!

Too often, middle managers feel powerless—trapped in the middle. Top management pressures them from above, putting demands for performance onto ever more chaotic work conditions.[23] Meanwhile, lower-level employees may resist going along due to their desire for work–life balance, concerns about job security, the belief that the decision is fundamentally wrong, the desire to protect the power of their group or bargaining unit, or just simply the availability of exit options. Regardless of the reality, the perception of power or lack of it is the critical issue. Interestingly enough, middle managers potentially have access to far more power than they think they have, but we will deal with this later.

While many sources of power exist, the type of power used by managers can have different effects. As well, some types of power or influence are used more frequently than others. One research study found that managers used different influence tactics depending on whether they were attempting to influence superiors or subordinates. Table 6.1 outlines the usage of these tactics. It shows that managers claim they use rational methods in persuading others. The use of overt power, either by referring something to higher authority or by applying sanctions, is not a popular tactic.

Table 6.1   Usage Frequency of Different Power Tactics[i]

	When Managers Influenced Superiors	When Managers Influenced Subordinates
Most Popular Tactic	Using and giving reasons	Using and giving reasons
	Developing coalitions	Being assertive
	Friendliness	Friendliness
	Bargaining	Developing coalitions
	Being assertive	Bargaining
	Referring to higher authority	Referring to higher authority
Least Popular Tactic		Applying sanctions

Using power is often, by definition, political in nature and can involve the development of coalitions, the building and using of alliances, dealing with the personality of the decision maker, and using contacts to obtain vital information. Don't underestimate the power of "will," the determination to make something happen. Resistance sometimes crumbles because people don't have the time or don't want to take the time to oppose—they don't care enough, and if you do care enough, you might get them to step aside or comply with the change. Of course, a better strategy, when it is possible, is to manage the situation so that key stakeholders see that it is in their best interest to participate in the proposed change.[24] Often, involvement in the proposed change can be positive for both sides. For example, Giangheco and Peccei, in their study of Italian managers, found that perceptions of the costs and benefits of the change and the extent of the managers' participation in the change had a significant impact on the resistance to the change.[25]

What sources of power are you comfortable with, and which ones do you have access to? Your personal style and comfort zone will affect your choice of tactics.

Increasingly the reliance on positional power to effect change is becoming more limited in our organizations.[26] Although it is important to know exactly the sources and limits to your power, it is more important to understand the key players, structures, and systems in a change situation. Who are the informal influencers who can pave the way for the change you are making? What structures and systems exist that can either facilitate your change or block it completely?

How Can We Change Organizations, One Person at a Time?

Each individual chooses to consider and adopt a proposed organizational change— or chooses not to. Sometimes they do this willingly and other times they choose reluctantly, feeling either forced or mixed about their decision. This perspective is valuable when thinking about increasing the success of organizational change, for it is at the individual level that people choose—or don't choose. Their choice depends on their view of the situation and how it impacts their lives.

In the recent past, many change programs have been focused on cost cutting, including the downsizing of the number of employees in the organization. People are bright. They understand what is happening. And if a program will cost them their job, why would you expect them to be enthusiastic and positive? Such resistance demonstrates the point that individuals will choose to cooperate or not, depending on their personal circumstances. Individuals will adopt or accept change only when they think that their perceived personal benefits are greater than the perceived costs of change. This can be summarized as follows:

Change Occurs When:
Perceived Benefits of Change > Perceived Cost of Change

This simple formula highlights several things. First, change agents have to deal with both the reality of change and its perceptions. Again, perception counts as much as reality. Second, in many situations, the costs of change are much more evident than the benefits of change. In most change situations, first the costs are incurred and then the benefits follow. The perceived benefits of change depend on whether people think the benefits are likely—that is, the probability of the change being successful. As well, the benefits of change depend on the state of "happiness" or dissatisfaction with the status quo. Interestingly, people also tend to focus on the consequences of the change, rather than the consequences of not changing and remaining the same. The more dissatisfied people are, the more they as individuals will be willing to change. The formula can be modified to capture this as follows:

Change Occurs When:
Perception of Dissatisfaction With the Status Quo
  × Perception of the Benefits of Change
    × Perception of the Probability of Success
      > Perceived Cost of Change

Thus, as change agents, we need to increase the dissatisfaction with the status quo by providing data that demonstrate that other options are better and that the overall benefits are worth the effort of the change and show that the change effort is likely to succeed. Early successes become part of the change agent's toolkit.

It is important to differentiate what the costs and benefits to the organization are from the costs and benefits to the individual. Too often, change leaders focus on the organizational benefits and miss the impact at the individual level. The earlier example highlighted this. If an individual sees that the change will increase profits and result in job loss, why would a manager expect support? It takes a very secure person who feels that they have alternatives and are being equitably treated to be positive under these circumstances even if they believe the change is needed.

Table 6.2 captures this. It contrasts the impact on individuals and the impact on the organization to predict the resulting support for a change initiative.

The purpose of Table 6.2 is not to suggest definitive predictions but rather to encourage you to avoid the trap of assuming that positive organizational outcomes will automatically be supported. In addition to considering the direct impact of a change on them, individuals will also think about and be influenced by the effects of the change on their coworkers and teammates. The strength of interpersonal bonds (e.g., the shared values, goals, and norms) can have a significant impact on attitudes and actions, but more will be said about this in Chapter 7.

Change agents need to think of the impact on individuals—particularly critical people. Toolkit Exercise 6.3 helps you to think through the perceived impact of change in an organization. Table 6.2 also helps us to focus on the people who actually have to change. A general manager may decide that new systems are needed,

Table 6.2   Organizational and Individual Consequences and the Support for Change

Perceived Impact of the Change on the Organization	Perceived Impact of the Change on the Individual	Direction of Support of the Change
Positive consequences for the organization	Positive outcome for the individual (e.g., less work, better work)	Strong support for change
Positive consequences for the organization	Negative outcome for the individual (e.g., more work, worse work)	Indeterminate support for change but very possibly resistance
Neutral consequences for the organization	Positive outcome for the individual (e.g., less work, better work)	Positive support for change
Neutral consequences for the organization	Negative outcome for the individual (e.g., more work, worse work)	Resistance to change
Negative consequences for the organization	Positive outcome for the individual (e.g., less work, better work)	Indeterminate support for change
Negative consequences for the organization	Negative outcome for the individual (e.g., more work, worse work)	Resistance to change

but it is the individual who will be operating the systems who will have to learn how to work with them and change their behavior.

How Can We View the Organization as a System in Balance?

In the second and third chapters, we described several models or ways of thinking about your organization and how it can be changed. Each of these models assumed that organizations consist of people, systems, and structures that interact according to the forces at play. In organizational change, the key is to understand these forces and how they respond to shifts in pressure. In system terms, the technical phrase is "homeostasis," meaning a system in dynamic but relatively stable balance that tends to return to its original conditions. Organizations are as they are because the forces involved are in balance. If you change one force, it could affect many things and may be resisted. Alternatively, it may give rise to unanticipated support for the change.

Two tools are particularly useful in helping change managers to understand such forces and why the organization changes (or doesn't).

1. **Force field analysis**—a process of identifying and analyzing the "force field" in your organization and then of altering those forces to accomplish your change.

2. **Stakeholder analysis**—a process of identifying the key individuals or groups in the organization who can influence or who are impacted by the proposed change, and then of working with those individuals or groups to make them more positive to notions of change.

Once these tools have been deployed, it is relatively easy to integrate them. Stakeholders will show up in the force field analysis as forces that need to be considered. An in-depth assessment of those stakeholders will put the change agent in a stronger position to manage those forces in ways that will advance the change.

Force Field Analysis[27]

Many change agents use force field analysis, an analytic tool to understand the dynamics of change. In force field analysis, the forces for and against change are identified. In situations that are stable or in equilibrium, the forces for change (driving forces) and the forces opposing change (restraining forces) are balanced. To create change, the balance must be upset by (a) adding new pressures for change, (b) increasing the strength of some or all the pressures for change, (c) reducing or eliminating the pressures against change, or (d) converting a restraining force into a driving force. Figure 6.2 depicts a force field analysis chart.

Pressures for change are often external. They may be market forces resulting in deceased profits in private-sector firms, or they may be increased cost and

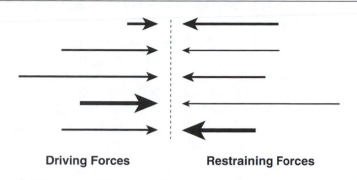

Driving Forces   **Restraining Forces**

Figure 6.2   Force Field Analysis

performance pressure and declining revenue allocations in the public sector. Alternatively, external factors may involve opportunities for future growth. Pressures for change could also come from internal factors, such as the vision of a champion or leader. These visionary pressures for change might be strengthened by reward systems that promote innovation or a culture that encourages change.

Resisting those forces for change would be the organizational systems that reward efficiency, running at lowest cost and minimizing experimentation or variance from standard. Changes that are seen as threats to individuals will lead to resistance. Habits or patterns of behavior may make it difficult to change, even when individuals are supportive. The longer those habits have been in place, the more difficulty individuals will have in extricating themselves from those patterns. (Arguably, organizations that utilize continuous improvement approaches tend to have less difficulty with change because organization members develop greater flexibility and adaptiveness.) Existing reward systems also play an important role. Often, managers or leaders espouse risk taking and change, but the organizational reward systems punish those who do experiment and reward those who do not.

To do a force field analysis, the forces acting in a situation need to be identified and their strength needs to be estimated. Both immediate and longer-term forces need to be considered. Once this is accomplished, the change agent needs to understand how to alter these forces and how to create maximum leverage with minimum effort on the change agent's part. Finally, agents need to look beyond the immediate impact of their strategy for increasing support and reducing resistance and consider unanticipated consequences that may result. For example, you may be able to reduce resistance by throwing financial rewards at individuals, but in doing so, you may inadvertently promote unethical behavior, reduce organizational commitment, and destroy your compensation system.

In the 3M example mentioned earlier, the appointment of McNerney created a new force in the organization. The system he introduced from GE (Six Sigma) was data based and thus appealed to the values of 3M employees. At the same time, he reduced defensiveness as a force by praising the 3M culture and showed how the employees could achieve more by focusing on the data and explicit goals. All of these things added to forces for change and reduced or eliminated forces against change. As positive outcomes began to ensue from these initiatives, the process provided sustaining reinforcement.

Strebel suggests that we look at this graphically, that is, to consider the forces for and against change separately—not necessarily opposing each other directly but operating orthogonally (at right angles).[28] Figure 6.3 shows this.

Strebel's view of the change arena allows us to plot where forces for and against change are in balance. The change arena helps us to identify four areas with which many change agents are familiar: (1) areas of constant change, (2) areas of high resistance, (3) areas of "breakpoint" change, and (4) areas of "sporadic" or "flip-flop" change. In areas of "breakpoint" change, pressures are significant and the resistance will be strong. Under these circumstances, resistance will prevent change until the driving forces strengthen to the point that the system snaps to a new configuration. For example, World War II was seen by many Americans to be someone else's battle until the attack on Pearl Harbor dramatically altered the status quo. When breakpoint change occurs, it will be radical and will create significant upheaval because of the strength of the changes involved. The situation faced by General Motors and the UAW in 2006 is a classic breakpoint situation. The market pressures on General Motors are very strong. The UAW faces equally strong resistance forces from its membership who wish to protect their health benefits and their pension plans.[29] In "flip-flop" change, forces are weak—change events are not very important and the situation could change only to reverse itself easily. Flip-flop changes tend to occur when participants have shifting preferences or are ambivalent concerning matters that are of only modest importance to them.

Force field analysis can be very useful for the change agent. It requires careful thinking about the dynamics of the situation and how people, structures, and systems

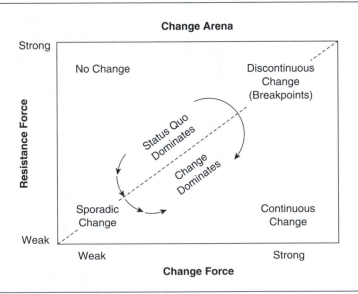

Figure 6.3   Forces for and Against Change

Source: From "Choosing the Right Change Path," by Strebel. Copyright © 1994 by the Regents of the University of California. Reprinted from *California Management Review, 36*(2) by permission of The Regents.

affect what is going on. How will these factors assist or prevent change? Toolkit Exercise 6.4 will help change agents to do a force field analysis.

Such analysis does lead us to think in relatively linear ways—forces are either for or against change. Their influence is linear and direct. Wheatly describes organizations in much more dynamic ways.[30] She contrasts seeing organizations in classical physics terms versus seeing them in quantum physics terms. Using a classical physics metaphor, forces in organizations are vectors and can be viewed as linear. An organizational or change vision, for example, would be viewed as a vector, and the size and direction of the vector would indicate the force in the organization and what it was pushing toward. In contrast, quantum physics would suggest viewing organizations in field terms. Here, forces parallel electromagnetic fields where there are eddies of nonlinear forces swirling through the organization. Vision, using this metaphor, would be viewed as a series of eddies, affecting different parts of the organization differently and having different impact on different parts of the organization.

All of this is to suggest that force field analysis moves us to a classical physics metaphor of organizations. Clearly, Newtonian physics is helpful—and using force field analysis is as well.

However, a different, more nonlinear perspective is sometimes needed. A tool called stakeholder analysis is valuable in gaining insights into a more nonlinear interactive view of organizations.

Stakeholder Analysis

Stakeholder analysis is the identification of those who can effect the change or those who are affected by the change. Included in this is the analysis of the positions, the motives, and the power of all key stakeholders. Stakeholder management is the explicit influencing of critical participants in the change process. It is the identification of the "entanglements" in the organization, the formal and informal connections between people, structures, and systems.

In doing a stakeholder analysis, the first step is to identify those people we need to concentrate on:

- Who has the authority to say "yes" or "no" to the change?
- Which areas or departments will be impacted by the change? Who leads and has influence in those departments?
- Who has to change their behavior or act differently for the change to be successful? This is a key question—the change ultimately rests on having these people doing things differently.
- Who has the potential to particularly ease the path to change, and who has the potential to be particularly disruptive?

The Stakeholder Map

Change agents need to know who the key participants are, what motivates these participants, and what the relationships are between them. Creating a visual picture of the key participants and their interrelationships can be helpful to understanding the dynamics of the situation. A stakeholder map lays out the positions of people pictorially and allows the change agent to quickly see the interdependencies. In drawing stakeholder maps, some add complexity to the picture:

a. Members of the same groups can be encircled.
b. Different thickness of lines can be used to signify the strength of the relationship.
c. Different colors can be used to signify different things (e.g., level of support or resistance).
d. Arrows can be used to point to influence patterns, with their thickness often used to characterize the strength of the relationship.

The only constraint on the construction of a stakeholder map is one's ability to translate data into a meaningful visual depiction of the key stakeholders and their interrelationships. Some of the factors it is useful to depict are (a) their wants and needs, (b) their likely responses to the change, (c) how they are linked, (d) sources of power, (e) level of power and influence, and (f) the actual influence patterns. Figure 6.4 shows a hypothetical stakeholder map.

Cross and Prusak classify organization members as follows:

- Central connectors—people who link most employees with one another. For example, Stakeholder 4 links Stakeholders 2, 3, and 6.
- Boundary spanners—people who cross organizational boundaries and connect the formal and/or informal networks to other parts of the organization. In the map, the change agent and Stakeholder 4 are both serving as boundary spanners.
- Information brokers—people who link various subgroups transmitting key information across those subgroups. In Figure 6.4, the change agent has the potential to play that role.
- Peripheral specialists—people who have specialized expertise valuable to network members but who can work apart from most in the network.[31]

Once the stakeholder map is developed, the change agent can visually see groupings and influence patterns, levels of support and resistance, and the strength of existing groupings and relationships. They can use this map to assess their assumptions concerning the stakeholders by soliciting input and feedback from others. Action plans can be reviewed relative to the map to see if the strategies and tactics are likely to produce stakeholder responses that will contribute to the desired results. These are just a few of the ways these maps can be applied.

It is important to recognize that Cross and Prusak focus on organization members. Often key stakeholders reside outside the immediate organization.

Understanding the position of key players or stakeholders is essential if a change agent is to alter the forces that resist change and strengthen those that promote change. In many ways, the process of dealing with stakeholders is similar to a marketing problem where one is attempting to have the stakeholder "buy into," not just buy! One can think about moving each stakeholder on a change continuum from an **awareness** of the issues, to **interest,** to a **desire for action,** to **taking action** or

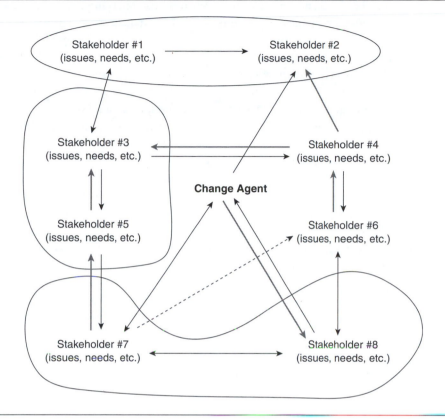

Figure 6.4   Stakeholder Map

supporting action on the change. One also wants to guard against unnecessarily driving them to actively resist the change.

Classifying stakeholders according to this continuum is useful because it can guide what change tools you should use. For example, in the initial stages of a change process, the issue may be one of creating awareness of the need for change. Here, publicity counts. Articles in an internal organizational newspaper can educate people. Forums or open sessions discussing the issues can play a role. Addresses by senior executives would not only inform but perhaps generate interest in a topic.

However, we would not expect newspaper articles to persuade many people to buy into a change situation or to try something out. Other tactics would be necessary. Thus, benchmark data may convince skeptics that change was necessary. Or a special budgetary allocation or a pilot project may pave the way for people to try out a change program.

As a general rule, change leaders should shift from low-intensity forms of communication to higher-intensity forms as individuals shift from becoming aware to needing to be persuaded. Impersonal but educational messages might inform, but persuasion often takes direct one-on-one action. For example, in one organization, the CEO wanted independent sales agents to adopt a new and relatively expensive software program. Persuasion efforts about the costs and benefits had limited success.

Finally, the change agent identified two things: First, the key influencers were the managers of the sales agents, and second, these managers could be classed as supportive, neutral, or negative. The change agent had the CEO phone each manager directly, emphasize the strategic importance of the adoption of the software, query them about concerns they might have, and then directly ask them for their support. Clearly, this was a very powerful and persuasive technique, using all the power and prestige of the president along with his considerable interpersonal skills.[32]

Stakeholders will vary not only in their readiness to change but also in their attitude toward or predisposition to change. Some individuals tend to be inherently keener about change and fall into the categories of **innovators** and **early adopters.** Others will wait until the first results of the change are in—they follow the initial two groups of adopters and form the **early majority.** The **late majority** wait longer before adopting. They want more definitive data concerning the change and the reactions of others before they are prepared to commit. Finally, some will, by their nature, resist change until late in the process and can be classified as **laggards** or **late adopters** and **nonadopters.**

In most organizations, we tend to know the innovators. They are constantly trying something new, including new products and services. Risk and novelty seem to provide the adrenalin needed to get through the day. Change comes easily and is sought. In contrast, we also know those who tend to be uncomfortable with new things. These individuals have a strong preference for order and routine. Change is to be avoided, and when it must happen, it happens only after most others have shown the way and the status quo is no longer viable.

Change agents need to identify and work first with innovators and early adopters. There is no sense trying to shift someone whose personality resists change until others have adopted the change. It may be useful to keep certain stakeholders informed of your activities, even though they are typically later adopters, so as to avoid unnecessary backlash. However, the simple act of keeping people informed is not the same as working closely with innovators and early adopters to advance the initiative. Early in any change program, change agents must anticipate that they will lack support. Few people will know about the change let alone support it. The process of adoption will often be gradual until a critical mass of support exists. This will be explored in greater detail in Chapter 9 when the topic of the "tipping point" is introduced.

Although the willingness to change can be viewed as a personality variable, it is also dependent on the degree to which someone understands the change and their commitment toward the change. Floyd and Wooldridge differentiated between understanding and commitment.[33] In their view, someone could have high or low understanding of the change and have high or low commitment to the change.* This provides a matrix of possibilities that helps us to think about stakeholders and their positions. Change agents need to consider those who actively oppose the change as well as those who are positive in their commitments. Being neutral or skeptical due to ambivalent feelings about the change is not the same as being an informed opponent of the change. See Table 6.3.

---

*Another way of looking at commitment is to categorize people as "make it happen," "help it happen," and "let it happen."

Table 6.3   Stakeholder's Understanding and Commitment

	High Understanding of the Change	Low Understanding of the Change
High, Positive Commitment to the Change	Strong consensus	Blind devotion
Low, Positive Commitment to the Change	Informed skeptics	Weak consensus
Negative Commitment to the Change	Informed opponents	Fanatical opponents

Adapted from Floyd, S., & Wooldridge, B. (1992). Managing the strategic consensus: The foundation of effective implementation. *Academy of Management Executive*, (6)4, 29.

Floyd and Wooldridge make the point that we, as change agents, need to understand where people are in terms of their perspective on the change and that there is no one "right" position. Often we assume that it is best to have people who both understand the change and are committed to it. This is the strong consensus cell shown in Table 6.3. Floyd and Wooldridge argue that at different times, blind devotion, informed skeptics, or a weak consensus is desirable. That is, at times we may need people to be blind devotees—if the change is a strategic secret, we want people to accept the change and be committed to act and not ask questions because we are not in a position to be able to answer them. On the other hand, when we are beginning a project and testing out ideas for action, we may want informed skeptics—people who understand the situation well and who are not too committed. These people may give us valuable advice regarding change tactics and strategies and the actual design of the change.

Table 6.4 provides a grid that allows each stakeholder's position and degree of resistance and awareness to be plotted. This form should help in a systematic analysis of stakeholders. In the second column, each stakeholder's predisposition toward change can be noted. Are they typically an innovator or an early adopter, or do they wait and see how others are reacting? If they wait, are they normally a part of the early majority of adopters, the late majority group, or do they tend to lag further (i.e., the laggard and nonadopters)?

The second column can also be used to assess their current commitment profile. Are they currently resistant to the change, ambivalent, neutral, somewhat predisposed and supportive, or are they already committed to the initiative? The change agent can then consider power and influence patterns and develop strategies and tactics that will move the individual stakeholders along the adoption continuum (aware, interested, wanting the change, and desiring and committed to the change). The movement of the stakeholders can be plotted in the appropriate columns, with attention given to learning (e.g., what was the impact of the action undertaken?) and the refining of strategies and tactics in the future. In the end, the objective is to

Table 6.4   Analysis of Stakeholder's Readiness to Take Action

Stakeholder's Name	**Predisposition to Change:** *(innovator, early adopter, early majority, late majority, laggard)* **Current Commitment Profile:** *(resistant, ambivalent, neutral, supportive or committed)*	*Aware*	*Interested*	*Wanting Change*	*Desiring Action*
Jones					
Smith					
Douglas					

Adapted from Kipnis, D., et al. (1984, Winter). Patterns of managerial influence: Shotgun managers, tacticians and bystanders. *Organizational Dynamics.*

move key stakeholders along the adoption continuum or, at minimum, prevent them from becoming significant obstacles to the success of the change initiative.

How Do We Manage Stakeholders?

The purpose of stakeholder analysis is to develop a clear understanding of the key individuals who can influence the outcome of a change and thus be in a better position to appreciate their positions and recognize how best to manage them and the context of the change. A useful starting point is to think carefully about who has to change their behavior in order for the change to be successful. An obvious but often overlooked point is exactly that—someone or some people must change their behavior![*]

Once the key person or persons are identified, change leaders must focus on who influences those people and who has the resources or power to make the change happen or to prevent it from happening.

Savage developed a model that plotted stakeholders on two dimensions: their potential for threat and their potential for cooperation.[34] If a stakeholder has high

---

[*]We are reminded of the old definition of insanity-"Doing the same things over and over, but expecting a different result!"

potential for both threat and cooperation, Savage suggests that a collaborative approach should be developed. In this way, the stakeholder is brought onboard and his or her support is obtained. If the stakeholder is "supportive," that is, has high potential for cooperation and low potential for threat, Savage argues for a strategy of involvement where the change agent maximizes support from the stakeholder. A stakeholder who is "nonsupportive," that is, has limited potential for cooperation but high potential for threat, should be defended against. Finally, a "marginal" stakeholder, one with limited potential for either cooperation or threat, should be monitored to ensure that the assessment is correct.

Once these vested interests are mapped, the change leader can examine the effects of organizational systems and structures. Only with this deep understanding can change be managed well. Toolkit Exercise 6.5 provides a checklist for doing a stakeholder analysis.

Summary

Change agents need to understand the power structures and people in their organization. They must recognize that resistance to change is highly likely and that there is potential to use resistance in a positive way. People resist for good reasons and change agents need to know those reasons.

Two powerful tools to help us think through the organizational situation are force field analysis and stakeholder analysis. Force field analysis helps change agents to plot the major structural, system, and people forces at work in the situation and to anticipate ways to alter these forces. Stakeholder analysis helps us to understand the interactions between key individuals and the relationships that form the web of interactions between individuals.

Glossary of Terms

Resistance to Change—The desire to *not* pursue the change. Resistance can stem from a variety of sources, including differences in information, perceptions, needs, and beliefs. In addition, existing informal and formal systems and processes have the potential to act as impediments to change.

Informal Structures and Systems—The structures, systems, and processes that emerge spontaneously from the interaction of people within the formal systems and structures that define the organizational context. They include informal leadership, communication, and influence patterns; norms and informal roles; and, at a macro level, the culture of the organization that emerges and influences behavior.

Power—The capacity to influence others to accept one's ideas or plans.[35] This chapter set out a number of sources from which power can be derived.

Power Tactics—Strategies and tactics deployed to influence others to accept one's ideas or plans.

The Change Equation—Change occurs when the perception of dissatisfaction with the status quo × the perceived benefits of the change × the perceived probability of success > the perceived cost of the change.

Force Field Analysis—A process of identifying and analyzing the force field in an organization and then altering those forces to accomplish your change. The force field is made up of driving and restraining forces.

Stakeholder Analysis—The identification and assessment of those who can effect the change or who are affected by the change. Included in this are the analysis of the positions, the motives, and the power of all key stakeholders. It is the identification of the relationships in the organization, the formal and informal connections between people, structures, and systems. Stakeholder management is the explicit influencing of critical participants in the change process. As such, it is common to see stakeholders also reflected in the force field analysis.

Breakpoint Change—Change that occurs in a context defined by strong forces for change and strong sources of resistance. When things occur that heighten the change forces and/or weaken the resistance forces, the system is snapped into a new configuration.

Sporadic or Flip-Flop Change—Change that occurs within a context of weak change forces and resistance forces. Within this context, the change is not viewed as particularly important, and as a result, change may occur, only to be easily reversed.

Continuous Change—Change occurs continuously because the forces for change are strong and the resistance forces are weak.

Stakeholder Map—A visual representation of the key stakeholders; their interrelationships and influence patterns; their wants, needs, and issues; and their predisposition toward the change.

Readiness to Change—A person's predisposition toward change in general. Is the individual generally an innovator, an early adopter, a member of the early majority, a member of the late majority, or a laggard?

Commitment Profile—A person's orientation toward the specific change in question. Is the individual resistant, ambivalent, neutral, supportive, or committed to the change?

END-OF-CHAPTER EXERCISES

TOOLKIT EXERCISE 6.1

Reconsidering Resistance to Change

1. What is the history of concerns with respect to change and resistance to change in your organization? How are they viewed by management?

2. Does your organization take a "hit them over the head until they like us" view of change? Or does the organization seek to understand why people are concerned and resist?

3. Do people welcome change? Which ones? Why?

4. If there are serious concerns and resistance, what is causing them?

    a. Parochial self-interest?

    b. A misunderstanding of the consequences?

    c. Lack of trust?

    d. Differences in the assessment of organizational consequences?

    e. Low tolerance for change in individuals?

    f. Something else?

5. Too often behavior is attributed to individual factors such as personality rather than to systemic causes that may be promoting such behavior. Are there system or structural issues that promote resistance behavior?

TOOLKIT EXERCISE 6.2

Where Does the Power Lie in Your Organization?

1. Pick an organization you are quite familiar with. What were the perceptions around power in the organization? In particular, what factors led to the assumption of power? Which departments carried more weight and influence? What behaviors were associated with having power?

2. Think of a change situation in the organization. What types of power were at play? Who had position, knowledge, and personality power? What individuals and departments handled uncertainty, were central, and were not very substitutable?

3. In Hardy's terms, who controlled resources? Who had process power—that is, set the agendas, managed the nomination or appointment process to key committees, and so on? Who had meaning power and was key in defining what things meant and how important they were.

4. Who had "yea-saying" power? On what issues? Who had "nay-saying" power? On what issues?

5. If you examine Table 6.1, what types of power were used most often? What types are you most comfortable using when you are attempting to influence others? Where and how would you use them and why did you select them?

TOOLKIT EXERCISE 6.3

Perceived Impact of Change

1. Consider the impact of a change on an organization you are familiar with and then consider the impact on the individuals concerned. Were these impacts both positive? Are you certain they were perceived that way?

2. What were the perceived costs of change? Who perceived these? Were the perceptions accurate? How could they be influenced?

3. What were the perceived benefits of change? Were the perceptions accurate? What was the probability of achieving these benefits? Were the employees and managers dissatisfied with the present state? Why? What were the costs of not changing?

4. Did the organization incur the costs of change prior to the benefits? If so, why did the organization agree to this risk (i.e., incurring rather definite costs but indefinite benefits)?

TOOLKIT EXERCISE 6.4

Understanding the Forces for and Against Change: The Force Field Analysis

Consider an organizational change situation you are familiar with.

1. What are the forces for change? Include external forces as well as a consideration of key individuals or groups. Who is championing the change? How strong and committed are these forces? (Who will let it happen? Who will help it happen? Who will make it happen?)

2. How could these forces be augmented or increased? What forces could be added to those that exist?

3. What are the forces that oppose change? Include structural forces such as reward systems or formal processes in the organization. Consider as well the effect of informal processes, groups, or the culture of the organization.

4. How could these forces be weakened or removed? What things might create major resentment in these forces?

TOOLKIT EXERCISE 6.5

Stakeholder Analysis Checklist

Who are the key stakeholders in this decision or change effort?

1. Is there a formal decision maker with the formal authority to authorize or deny the change project? Who is that person (or persons)? What are his or her attitudes to the project?

2. What is the commitment profile of stakeholders? Are they against the change, neutral (let it happen), supportive (help it happen), or committed champions of the change (make it happen)? Do a commitment analysis for each stakeholder.

3. Are they typically initiators, early adopters, early majority, late majority, or laggards when it comes to change?

4. Why do stakeholders respond as they do? Does the reward system drive them to support or oppose your proposal? What consequences does your change have on each stakeholder? Do the stakeholders perceive these as positive, neutral, or negative?

5. What would change the stakeholders' views? Can the reward system be altered? Would information or education help?

6. Who influences the stakeholders? Can you influence the influencers? How may this help?

7. Which coalitions could be formed among stakeholders? Which alliances could you form? Which ones could form to prevent the change you wish?

8. By altering your position, can you keep the essentials of your change and yet satisfy some of the needs of those opposing change?

9. Can you appeal to higher-order values and/or goals that will make others view their opposition to the change as petty or selfish?

Notes

1. Waddell, D., & Sohal, A. (1998). Resistance: A constructive tool for change management. *Management Decision,* (*36*)8, 543–548; and Dent, E., & Goldberg, S. (1999, March). Resistance to change: A limiting perspective. *Journal of Applied Behavioral Science,* 45–47.

2. Piderit, S. K. (2000). Rethinking resistance and recognizing ambivalence: A multidimensional view of attitudes toward an organizational change. *Academy of Management Review,* (*25*)4, 783–794.

3. McGray, D. (2002, December). Babes in an R&D toyland: Inside Fisher-Price's Play Lab, where the ultimate compliment is a baby's drool. *Fast Company, 65,* 46.

4. Naughton, K. (2000, December 11). A mess of a merger. *Newsweek.*

5. Eisenstein, P. (2000, December 13). Signs of discontent. *Professional Engineering.*

6. Useem, J. (2002, July 21). 3M + GE = ?: Jim McNerney thinks he can turn 3M from a good company into a great one—with a little help from his former employer, General Electric. *Fortune.*

7. Kotter, J., & Schlesinger, L. (1982). Choosing strategies for change In *Managing organizations: Readings and cases.* Boston: Little, Brown.

8. Davidson, J., as reported in Piderit, S. (2000). Rethinking resistance and recognizing ambivalence: A multidimensional view of attitudes toward an organizational change. *Academy of Management Journal,* (*25*)4, 785.

9. Piderit, op. cit.

10. Friedman, T. L. (1995). *From Beirut to Jerusalem* (p. 391). New York: Anchor Books.

11. Source unknown.

12. Carnall, C. A. (1986). Toward a theory for the evaluation of organizational change. *Human Relations,* (*39*)8, 745–766.

13. Robertson, M., & Swan, J. (2004). Going public: The emergence and effects of soft bureaucracy within a knowledge-intensive firm. *Organization,* (*11*)1, 123–148.

14. Marakas, G. M., & Hornik, S. (1996). Passive resistance misuse: Overt support and covert recalcitrance in IS implementation. *European Journal of Information Systems,* (*5*)3, 208–219; Hultman, K. E. (1995). Scaling the wall of resistance. *Training and Development,* (*49*)10, 15–18.

15. Giangheco. A., & Peccei, R. (2005). The nature and antecedents of middle manager resistance to change: Evidence from the Italian context. *The International Journal of Human Resource Management,* (*16*)10, 1812.

16. Ringer, R. C., & Boss, R. M. (2000). Hospital professionals' use of upward tactics. *Journal of Management Issues,* (*12*)1, 92–108.

17. *Globe and Mail,* June 2, 2003.

18. Jick, T. (1993). AT&T: The Dallas works (B). In *Managing change.* Homewood, IL: Irwin.

19. Robbins, S., & Langton, N. (2003). *Organizational behaviour* (p. 356). Toronto: Prentice Hall.

20. Treatment of these power-related concepts can be found in Whetten, D. A., & Cameron, K. S. (1995). *Developing management skills* (3rd ed., ch. 5, pp. 290–355). New York: HarperCollins College Publishers.

21. Hofstede identified and referred to this cultural variable as power distance. See Hofstede, G. (1993, February). Cultural constraints in management theories. *Academy of Management Executive,* 81–94.

22. Hardy, C. (1994, Winter). Power and organizational development: A framework for organizational change. *Journal of General Management,* (*20*)2.

23.   Oshry, B. (1993). Converting middle powerlessness to middle power: A systems approach. In T. Jick, *Managing change* (p. 401). Homewood, IL: Irwin.

24.   Barnsley, J., Lemieux-Charles, L., & McKinney, M. M. (1998). Integrating learning into integrated delivery systems. *Health Care Management Review,* (*23*)1, 18–28; Floyd, S. W., & Wooldridge, B. (1992). Managing strategic consensus: The foundation of effective implementation. *The Executive,* (*6*)4, 27–39.

25.   Giangheco & Peccei, op. cit.

26.   Stewart, T. A. (1997). Get with the new power game. *Fortune,* (*135*)1, 58 (5 pages).

27.   Lewin, K. (1951). *Field theory in social science.* New York: Harper & Row; Thomas, J. (1985). Force field analysis: A new way to evaluate your strategy. *Long Range Planning,* (*18*)6, 54–59.

28.   Strebel, P. (1994, Winter). Choosing the right change path. *California Management Review,* 29–51.

29.   More pain, waiting for the gain. (2006, February 11). *The Economist,* 58.

30.   Wheatley, M. (1994). *Leadership and the new science.* San Francisco: Berrett-Koehler.

31.   Cross, R., & Prusak, L. (2002, June). The people who make organizations go—or stop. *Harvard Business Review,* 5–12.

32.   P. Luksha, personal communication to T. Cawsey.

33.   Floyd, S., & Wooldridge, B. (1992). Managing the strategic consensus: The foundation of effective implementation. *Academy of Management Executive,* (*6*)4.

34.   Savage, G. T., et al. (1991). Strategies for assessing and managing organizational stakeholders. *Academy of Management Executive,* (*5*)2.

35.   Robbins, S., & Langton, N. (2003). *Organizational behaviour* (p. 356). Toronto: Prentice Hall.

CHAPTER 7

The Recipients of Change

Those on the Receiving End

Progress is great, but it has gone on far too long.

—Ogden Nash

Chapter Overview

- People respond to change in many ways. Some react positively to change. Others are ambivalent. Some view change negatively. Change leaders need to understand why people react to change as they do.
- When people are ambivalent to change, change leaders can use that period of mixed feelings to influence those individuals to see the positive aspects of the change.
- Change leaders need to rethink their assumptions about resistance to change. Employees may have good reasons for resisting the change leaders' proposals, and these reasons need to be understood.
- Change leaders need to be aware of the psychological contract between the organization and the employees and to recognize that changes to the psychological contract need to be handled carefully.
- When disruptive change occurs, recipients often go through a predictable series of reactions to change. The impact of change can occur both prior to the change and after the change as well as during the change. Prechange anxiety, shock, defensiveness, bargaining, depression and alienation, acknowledgment of the change, and finally adaptation and acceptance can all be reactions to change.

> • Recipients' views of change are influenced by their personalities, their prior experience with change, the attitudes and opinions of their peers, and by the change leaders themselves.
> • Change leaders need to consider how to minimize the negative effects of change, in part by making change the norm and by encouraging recipients to become change leaders or change implementers themselves.

The focus of this book to this point has been on you as an agent of change. The models of change and the analysis that is suggested are from the perspective of the manager who is making change happen. However, the reality of our lives is that we're probably more often on the receiving end—the recipients of change. This chapter develops the understanding of how recipients of the change will react and how change agents can incorporate this understanding to improve their change plans.

The chapter deals with the reality of those who find themselves on the receiving end of change. It will consider different reactions to change: support or enthusiasm for the change, mixed feelings or ambivalence toward the change, and resistance or opposition to the change. Although positive responses toward change are fairly common (depending on the nature of the change and how it is introduced), the chapter focuses on recipients who are mixed or negative toward the change. The chapter helps you as a recipient of change to cope, by describing the stages many go through when facing change. As well, the chapter considers the factors that influence how recipients respond to change: their personality, their coworkers or teammates, and their leaders or managers. Finally, Chapter 7 looks at how change leaders can reduce the negative effects of change initiatives.

Chapter 7 continues the discussion of organizational factors affecting our ability to manage change. Our understanding of the gap between the organization's desired state and the existing one was begun with Chapter 5, Organizational Structures and Systems and Change, and with Chapter 6, The Emergent or Informal Organization. It will conclude with Chapter 8, Change Agent Types and Effectiveness. Figure 7.1 positions this chapter in the change management process.

How Do People Respond to Change Initiatives?

Many managers assume that resistance is inevitable in change situations.[*] It is time to dispel this myth. Recipients do not always react negatively, and in many situations, they will react quite positively. Will they raise questions and experience a sense of uncertainty or ambivalence when change is introduced? Of course they will. They are thinking individuals, trying to make sense out of the change and its

---

[*]Our tendency to focus on resistance is suggested by a Google search that recorded 788,000 hits for "resistance to change," but only 85,300 hits for "support for change" and 166,000 hits for "embracing change" (March 2006).

Figure 7.1   Recipients of Change and the Change Management Process

impact. This questioning often is perceived as resistance, but it is not necessarily the same. Often if resistance arises, it does so after recipients resolve their mixed feelings. If they conclude that the benefits to them clearly outweigh the costs and consequences, have high personal relevance, and are consistent with their attitudes and values, support is highly likely.[1] As was noted in Chapter 6, negative reactions to change increase in frequency and intensity when people believe that the potential costs and consequences to them and the things they value outweigh the benefits.

Some researchers have suggested that "resistance to change" is a term that has lost its usefulness, because it oversimplifies the matter and becomes a self-fulfilling prophecy. That is, if change leaders assume that resistance will occur, it becomes more likely. Change leaders should focus on trying to understand why people react to the change as they do and how those reactions are likely to evolve over time.[2]

When changes are introduced, recipients often find themselves pulled in different directions. Conflicting messages are often delivered by friends, relatives, coworkers, subordinates, and managers and so are influential in opinion formation. If things become polarized around the change, people who have come to a decision may view those who are of a different opinion with suspicion and disapproval. All of these pressures can lead to ambivalence.

The mixed feelings that many feel can be magnified by concerns about the impact of the change on (a) their relationships with others, (b) their ability to do what is being asked of them, (c) the fit with their needs and values, and (d) their future prospects. These concerns are further enhanced when they lack confidence that matters can be resolved positively or produce the intended results. When recipients see themselves as relatively powerless, a variety of undesirable coping responses, including alienation, passivity, sabotage, absenteeism, and turnover, may result.[3]

The perceptions of costs and benefits of change depend on what people are concerned about, what they have experienced in the past, and what they think they know. Sometimes relatively small changes will produce strong responses in one group due to the perceived consequences, whereas much more significant changes will produce mild reactions in another group due to perceptions that the impact on them will not be significant.[4]

Consider the likely reactions of employees of the Bank of Japan to the following announcement:

The Bank of Japan (BoJ) announced plans to overhaul its organizational structure and salary system to speed up decision-making and meet rapid changes in financial technology.

BoJ Governor Toshihiko Fukui instructed his staff to begin work on the overhaul on Monday (Sept. 1, 2003). It will be the first time the central bank has conducted such a major change since April 1998.

Specifically, the BoJ will scrap divisions set under the departments of its head office and instead create cross-department task forces to tackle various problems. The BoJ will also examine adopting an annual salary structure based on performance, instead of the current automatic pay raise system, for employees in administrative posts, (BoJ officials said).

The BoJ plans to adopt the changes gradually from the next fiscal year, beginning in April 2004, the official said.[5]

What did such an announcement mean for thousands of Bank of Japan employees? Obviously, they will be in a new structure. Their jobs may be redesigned. They may have new bosses—or perhaps multiple bosses if cross-departmental or matrix-like arrangements emerge. If they were in supervisory or senior management roles, they may discover that their previous positions no longer exist or have been altered substantially. Further, future pay increases may be shifted to a performance-based method—increasing perceptions of risk and ambiguity for employees.

Senior management assured employees that all of this will be done gradually. Although a gradual approach to change is often desirable because it provides time to adjust and modify approaches, sometimes it is viewed as just extending the pain over a longer period—particularly if all it really does is draw out the period of uncertainty and unpleasantness!

In the Bank of Japan example, employees who assume that the status quo will continue are likely to be proven wrong. The announcement notes that significant changes can no longer be avoided and that the bank's internal world of work will be altered in significant ways. Many bank employees will experience uncertainty and varying degrees of distress. Some will feel pressure to pursue a more active role in the change process, and some will be genuinely excited by the prospects of change. Many will feel ambivalent about the change and its implications; some will resist and some will come to feel victimized, believing that they are about to become road kill on the path to change.

How they perceive the changes will depend on their assessment of the situation. If they see themselves and the organization benefiting from the change, they are more likely to embrace the change. If they see themselves as involved and partici- pating in the initiative, they are more likely to be supportive.[6] If the outcomes are viewed as likely to be negative for the organization and the individuals, they will be unsupportive of the change. If their views are mixed, they will experience ambiva- lence concerning the change.[7] Why would you expect otherwise? When the change is viewed as positive for the organization but mixed or negative for the individuals (or vice versa), the emergence of mixed feelings means that predictions concerning support for the change become more complicated.

In our Bank of Japan example, a twenty-seven-year-old highly educated employee with needed skills may see this restructuring as both a competitive neces- sity and an opportunity to expand his or her skills. His or her response to the announcement would be positive. However, if an employee had fewer educational qualifications and had spent several years in the same functional position, the per- sonal risks and costs of change may be viewed as high and the employee would view the change more negatively. Some recipients may be conflicted about aspects of the change because they are concerned that the decision may have a negative impact on factors they consider to be important to the bank's health (e.g., client management and customer service). The range of possible perceptions is complex, as recipients assess the change against their interests, attitudes, and values.

By understanding the variety of possible responses, a change leader's compre- hension of the change at the Bank of Japan will be enriched, and adjustments and revisions to change plans can be considered. This is particularly valuable at the beginning of a change process, where such discussion and dialogue can be used to help shape the initiative. These discussions can advance the development of a shared understanding (sensemaking) of the change and create informed support. Recipient understanding and responses to the change will evolve over time, as the change unfolds. As a result, the approaches used by change leaders will need to vary over the course of the change process. Whereas factual information delivered in a speech or a consultant's report may be useful when dealing with beliefs and developing initial awareness, informal discussions and support may be much more useful when ambivalence is stemming from conflicting emotions.[8] If downsizing or relocation is required, it will take more than the rational presentation of data or delivery of equi- table relocation packages or early retirement provisions to alleviate distress.

If resistance occurs, it may stem from those in middle and/or more senior roles, since they often have the most to lose. They may be seeking to maintain power and influence, sustain their capacity to perform, and avoid what they perceive to be a worsening of their position.[9] Change leaders need to be aware of this. Finally, attribution errors may cause change leaders to fixate on individual resistance rather than probe more deeply for causal factors. For example, behavior that is being categorized as individual resistance may be due to misaligned structures and systems rather than individual opposition.[10] As well, many managers are predisposed to expect resistance in subordinates. Care needs to be taken that a self-fulfilling prophecy is not created.

What Are the Consequences of Positive Feelings in Recipients?

As mentioned above in the Bank of Japan example, many individuals may welcome change. To these people, change could represent a chance for personal growth or promotion. Some may enjoy variety and seek novelty. Others may want the challenge of new situations.

This chapter focuses on those with ambivalent or negative feelings toward change. It is important, however, to anticipate some of the risks of positive feelings in recipients. Change managers will welcome enthusiastic, positive support of their change initiatives. They will have to channel that energy in positive ways, not letting the enthusiasm for change overwhelm legitimate concerns. Blind acceptance may lead to a lack of reflection and risk groupthink. Strong positive support of organizational initiatives may cause others to censor their doubts, and the risks of this rise with the level of cohesion. This potential tyranny of the majority may lead to a stereotyping of those ambivalent or opposing the change as "the enemy." This could lead to infighting rather than thoughtful analysis and the productive pursuit of organizational benefits.

Clearly, change leaders need and want strong support for change initiatives. Without wide support, any change project is at significant risk. Nevertheless, untrammeled enthusiasm for a change project has its own risks that need to be considered.

How Do Ambivalent Feelings Affect Recipients' Responses?[11]

It comes as no surprise that recipients are likely to have mixed feelings about change, as change often gives rise to perceptions of increased complexity, uncertainty, and risk. Recipients' beliefs about a change and its potential impact can be both positive and negative and can vary in intensity. To illustrate this, consider the example of an industrial paint manufacturer that changed how it handled its major customers by moving key technical service representatives from head office to the customers' plants. The change provided staff with desired opportunities for increased responsibility, autonomy, and pay, but it required their relocation to a new workplace and the disruption of their cohesive work group. Naturally, their feelings were mixed. Some were excited; some, anxious about their new responsibilities. Some were sad about leaving close friends behind. Those who had acted in ways that were inconsistent with existing attitudes experienced ambivalence.[12] For example, the new duties required service representatives to play a much more active client management role. These were activities that customer service representatives had viewed as belonging to sales personnel.

When ambivalence is prevalent, change leaders should expect to hear people voice concerns, particularly if the environment welcomes feedback. Piderit states that recipients are more likely to speak up when the ambivalence stems from conflicting beliefs. When conflicting emotions are involved, though, she notes that individuals often have more difficulty giving voice to negative emotional responses. She hypothesizes that "they would be more likely to wrestle with their ambivalence alone or to avoid the subject entirely."[13]

Ambivalence generates discomfort for recipients that they seek to resolve. Once this resolution occurs, subsequent changes to attitudes become more difficult. In Lewin's terms of unfreeze—change—refreeze, the creation of ambivalence unfreezes the recipient. Once attitudes solidify, the recipient is refreezing and becomes locked into the new attitude set. We protect our attitudes by employing a variety of strategies. We turn to habits and approaches that have served us well in the past,[14] and engage in selective perception (actively seeking out confirming information and avoiding disconfirming data),[15] selective recall (we are more likely to remember attitude-consistent rather than inconsistent data),[16] and denial in the form of counterarguments geared to support and strengthen one's position.[17] More extreme defensive responses can include sarcasm, anger, aggression, and withdrawal. Since attitudes become much more difficult to change once they solidify, there is all the more reason to invest the time needed at the front end of the change, to effectively process people's reactions to change. To quote an old advertisement, "You can pay me now, or pay me (a lot more) later."

Rather than interpreting mixed feelings as resistance, change leaders are better served by focusing on helping recipients make sense of the proposed changes, constructively reconcile their ambivalence, and sort out what actions are now needed. If negative attitudes have already solidified, change leaders can explore whether or not matters can be dealt with in ways that will give rise to renewed ambivalence that can be constructively processed—that is, unfreeze the situation again. It is almost always in the best interests of change agents to actively engage recipients in meaningful discussions early in the change process. Recipients' input can prove invaluable in identifying potential problems and risk points.[18] Their engagement and involvement can allow concerns to be addressed.[19] Meaningful engagement can increase the likelihood of the formation of supportive attitudes toward the change, as they attempt to make sense of what they are being asked to do.[20]

Balogun and Johnson note that once the blueprint for more complex changes is set out, it is brought to life through the interpretations and responses of the recipients. As a result, these authors argue that "managing change is less about directing and controlling and more about facilitating recipient sense-making processes to achieve an alignment of interpretation."[21] As this evolves, so too does the change that subsequently unfolds.

Why Do Negative Reactions to Change Occur?

Change leaders undertake an initiative because they believe the benefits will outweigh the costs. However, recipients of change, those on the receiving end, may have a very different perspective. They may feel imposed upon and unprepared, or see themselves and their coworkers as negatively affected by the changes. They may perceive risks to the organization, see problems or shortcomings with the initiative that do not seem to have been thought through, be confused about the implications of the change, or mistrust the change leader. Table 7.1 outlines the causes of negative reactions to change.

Table 7.1   Causes of Negative Reactions to Change

1. Negative consequences clearly outweigh the benefits.

2. The communication process is flawed, leading to confusion and doubt.

3. There is concern that the change has been ill conceived, insufficiently tested, or may have adverse consequences that are not anticipated.

4. The recipients lack experience with change and its implications, or have habituated approaches that they rely on and remain committed to.

5. The recipients have had prior negative experience with a similar change.

6. The recipients have had prior negative experience with those advocating the change.

7. The negative reactions of peers, subordinates, and/or supervisors whom you trust and respect and with whom you will have to work in the future influence your views.

8. The change process is seen to be lacking procedural justice and/or distributive justice.

Concerns and negative reactions toward change develop for a variety of reasons. First, the perception concerning the negative consequences of the change may simply be true. The change may be fundamentally incongruent with things the recipients deeply value about their job (e.g., autonomy, significance, feedback, identity, and variety)[22] or the workplace (e.g., pay, job security). The loss of work is likely the most extreme form of this. When significant job losses are involved, such as when the major employer in a town decides their plant needs to be closed for the good of the corporation, the costs are all too real for the recipients. In such situations, it is difficult, if not impossible, for recipients to see positive consequences ensuing from the change.[23] The closing of the Fishery Products International plant provides an example of employment loss.

The closing of the Fishery Products International processing plant in Harbour Breton, Newfoundland, is "devastating," says Earle McCurdy, president of the Fish, Food and Allied Workers Union. "This closing has put 350 people out of work in a community of 2,100. You don't have to be a Ph.D. to determine the size of the impact," he says. "And it's not only Harbour Breton; it's the entire peninsula."

FPI officials blame the closing on an independent report that claims that "the plant has major structural problems and is no longer safe for occupancy." However, FPI spokesman Russ Carrigan released a statement saying, "The entry of' China into the market for headed and gutted cod has driven the commodity price up dramatically—well beyond the point of our commercial viability."[24]

In this example, recipients would have difficulty accepting the corporate perspective.

Second, communication processes may be flawed and recipients may be left feeling ill informed or misled.[25] Support is less likely when people feel that they lack the information they need to make an informed judgment. The prospects for support diminish further and faster when they feel that information has been intentionally and arbitrarily withheld or manipulated. In our FPI example, there appears to be confusion over the reasons for the closure. Is it the structural problems or the entry of Chinese competition into the marketplace?

Third, the recipients may have serious doubts about the impact and effectiveness of the change. They may be concerned that the change initiative has not been sufficiently studied and tested, or they may believe that the change will have adverse consequences that have not been thought through.[26] For example, a move by head office to consolidate warehouse operations and trim inventory levels may be seen as a surefire way to increase efficiency, but this could cause serious concerns in sales and marketing about the firm's ability to effectively service its customers.

Fourth, recipients may react negatively because they lack experience with change and are unsure about its implications or their capacity to adjust. When conditions in an organization have been stable for long periods, even modest changes can seem threatening. Our Bank of Japan example earlier in the chapter is a situation where employees are facing a shift from a stable to a more dynamic environment. Related to this is the impact of well-ingrained habits. Habituated approaches represent strategies that we believe have served us well in the past and that we are often not even conscious of. They become more entrenched during extended periods of stability, and the patterned behavior can result in negative reactions to change.

Fifth, recipients may have had negative experiences with change initiatives or approaches that seem similar to the one being advocated. To use an old adage, once burned, twice shy. If recipients have learned that change initiatives lead to layoffs or that the initiatives begin with great fanfare but are never completed, recipients will be more negative. They have learned that they should be skeptical about change and its consequences.[27]

Sixth, they may have had a negative experience with those advocating the change. They may mistrust the judgment of those promoting the change, their ability to deliver on promises, their access to resources, their implementation skills, or their integrity.

Seventh, recipients may be influenced by the negative reactions of peers, subordinates, or supervisors whom they trust and respect and/or whom they have to work with in the future. These opinion leaders can have a significant impact.

Last but not least, there may be justice-related concerns. Recipients may see the process as lacking in procedural justice; that is, was the process fair? Did people have an opportunity to question change leaders, voice opinions, and suggest options? An absence of participation and involvement may leave recipients feeling ignored and relatively powerless.[28] They may also believe that distributive justice was lacking (i.e., the final decision was fundamentally unfair).[29] For example, people may believe that FPI's decision was unfair and could call for government intervention as a result.

When things do not unfold as planned, resistance is often flagged as the cause. Rather than assess the situation carefully and objectively, managers responsible for change are quick to lay the blame at the feet of those thought to be acting as obstacles.[30] The dynamics of this likely increases resistance, as each blames the other and tensions rise. When managers and employees point fingers at each other as the cause of change difficulties, the focus is not on advancing the agenda for change. The key question is not "who is to blame?" but rather, what is happening, why is it happening, and what does this tell us about what we should do now?

Kotter notes that impediments to change are much more likely to come from problems related to the misalignment of structures and systems than from individuals engaged in resistance.[31] For example, if existing systems continue to reward competitive behavior, why would you expect change recipients to begin to behave in a more cooperative manner?[32] Likewise, if critical information or resources are not available, how can individuals implement the change program? Change leaders need to be aware of the tendency to focus on individuals and not systems or processes.

In summary, resistance is one of the responses to a change initiative. If the resistance is based on differing views of the consequences, the reasons need to be understood and change plans modified if appropriate. Toolkit Exercise 7.1 asks you to explore your experiences as a change recipient.

How Does Change Affect the Psychological Contract?

As mentioned earlier, organizational context plays a role in determining reactions of recipients to change. The **psychological contract** that people have with the organization can be a critical contextual variable.[33] The psychological contract represents the sum of the implicit and explicit agreements we believe we have with our organization. It defines our perceptions of the terms of our employment relationship and includes our expectations for ourselves and for the organization, including organizational norms, rights, rewards, and obligations.

Much of the psychological contract is implicit. Because of this, change initiators may be unaware of it when they alter existing arrangements. In effect, they don't recognize the impact such changes may have on the psychological contract. Often they fail to realize that change recipients may have a very different view than they do of what constitutes their employment contract: what they have a right to expect, and what is fair and equitable. The perceptions of sudden and arbitrary changes to the psychological contract of employees lead to change trouble. While most of us recognize that our psychological contracts will have to adapt to changing conditions, we don't react well to surprises and unilateral actions that fail to consider our input (or those of our representatives). Changes that threaten our sense of security and control will produce a loss of trust, fear, resentment, and/or anger.[34] As recipients, we will need to devote time and effort to absorb the change and its implications, plus make sense of our reaction to it. Even unilateral changes that have a positive impact on employees may be resisted because of factors such as suspicion over the "real agenda" and concerns about a reduced sense of control.

Toolkit Exercise 7.2 asks you to reflect on the psychological contract and consider what happens when an organization change causes key terms to be altered.

Are There Predictable Stages in the Reaction to Change?

Change is Inevitable—Growth is Optional (from a bumper sticker)

Change can be thought of as occurring in three phases: before the change, during the change, and after the change. These parallel Lewin's three-phase change model discussed in Chapter 2. Reaction to change typically begins in advance of the actual change as individuals worry about what will happen and their personal consequences. The reaction can continue until long after the change initiative has been completed as people work through the feelings created by the change. When experiencing more traumatic changes and transitions, recipients tend to go through a predictable sequence of stages similar to those outlined by Elizabeth Kübler-Ross in her work on grieving.[35] The model suggests that people will work through issues until they accept the change. This may not be the case, as individuals can be frozen in an alienated, resisting position. Table 7.2 integrates her insights with those of Fink,[36] Jick,[37] and Perlman and Takacs.[38]

People who are anticipating significant change experience **prechange anxiety**. At this stage, people think something is in the wind but they don't know exactly what it is or how it will show itself. Uncertainty escalates and people often find themselves agonizing over the impact it could have on them, as well as its impact on others. For many, the anticipation phase can be debilitating. In their desire to reduce uncertainty and anxiety, many will search for signs of what might be on the horizon. Rumors may abound. Others will deny the signs and signals of change, finding it too threatening to think about. During this phase, the organizational rumor mill often moves into high gear and increases anxiety levels. The confusion and uncertainty created often continues long after the change has been announced, and it may be coupled with fear, anger, alienation, defensiveness, and a variety of other responses that have strong attitudinal and performance implications. Ambivalent feelings described earlier are often generated at this point and are evident in comments and actions. As noted earlier in this chapter, recipients are more likely to speak up when the mixed emotions stem from conflicting beliefs. When conflicting emotions are involved, though, individuals often have more difficulty giving voice to negative emotional responses.[39]

Once change is announced, **shock** often sets in. Individuals at this stage may feel overwhelmed by events to the point of immobilization. During the next stage, **defensive retreat**, people strive to hold on to the past and they experience anger

Table 7.2   Stages of Reactions to Change

Before the Change	During the Change	After the Change
Anticipation and Anxiety Phase	Shock, Denial, and Retreat Phase	Acceptance Phase
Issues: Coping with uncertainty and rumors about what may or may not happen.	Issues: Coping with the change announcement and associated fallout, coping with uncertainty and rumors, reacting to the new "reality."	Issues: Putting residual traumatic effects of change behind you, acknowledging the change, achieving closure, and moving on to new beginnings—adaptation and change.
1. Prechange Anxiety— Worrying about what might happen, confusion, and perhaps significant denial of what change is needed or likely.	**2. Shock**—Perceived threat, immobilization, no risk taking. **3. Defensive Retreat**—Anger, rejection and denial, compliance; sense of loss, risk taking unsafe. **4. Bargaining** **5. Depression and Guilt, Alienation**	**6. Acknowledgment**— Resignation, mourning, letting go, energy for risk taking begins to build. **7. Adaptation & Change**— Comfort with change, greater openness and readiness; growing potential for risk taking.

over the changes. Insecurity and a sense of loss and unfairness are common reactions. People will often try to avoid dealing with the real issues and try to reduce their risk taking by lowering their exposure and relying on habituated responses that have worked in the past. The sense of betrayal will be strongest for those who place the greatest trust in the firm and who feel their contract with the organization has been most clearly violated. Their trust in the leadership will typically decline. Some individuals may agree outwardly, announcing their willingness to cooperate ("We're behind you all the way!"), only to act in a noncompliant manner when they are out of sight of those advocating the change. This behavior can sometimes extend to sabotage. The **bargaining** stage is involved with negotiations aimed at trying to make the change go away or at least minimize its negative impact. **Depression and guilt,** stress and fatigue, and reduced risk taking and motivation have been regularly reported to follow such unsuccessful attempts to reverse the tide. **Alienation** can result.

Finally, people begin to accept the change and **acknowledge** what they have lost. They begin to let go of the past and start to behave in more constructive ways. At this point, they can again take risks—not those associated with getting even, but rather those associated with liberation from the past and moving on. As risks are rewarded with success, confidence builds in the change. Finally, during the

adaptation and change stage, people become more comfortable or acceptant of the change, internalize it, and move on.

These stages were originally derived from observing the reactions of those who have experienced severe personal trauma, including job loss, serious illness, divorce, or the death of a loved one.[40] As such, it is important to recognize a key assumption. The models assume that we cannot move on to adaptation and change unless we have worked our way successfully through the previous phases. Failure to do so will result in the individual's continuing to be mired in an earlier, unresolved phase. Some recipients have demonstrated their capacity to hold on to the past tenaciously and continue to work for its return long after any prospects for this have faded. Others carry emotional baggage from the change with them that will get played and replayed until they have finally worked their way through it and moved on. Thankfully, in the end, most of us manage to adapt to significant change at work, although not without some pain.

Even when recipients recognize the need for difficult decisions, they often have difficulty emotionally accepting and adapting to consequences of change decisions.[41] This emotional distress can be true regardless of the consequences. For example, even those who are retained after organizational downsizing will be upset. The *survivor syndrome* is a term that refers to the reaction of those who survive a poorly handled, traumatic change such as a downsizing.[42] Survivor syndrome effects include lower levels of job satisfaction, motivation, and organizational loyalty, greater stress, greater ambiguity and vulnerability about one's future position, a sense of entrapment in a negative situation, and guilt about being retained while others have been let go.[*]

William Bridges offers a second framework, the **Transition Stages Perspective,** for examining change transitions.[43] It includes an ending phase, a neutral phase, and a new beginnings phase. During the **ending phase,** individuals need to let go of their former situation. This period is characterized by fear, confusion, and anger, as employees disengage from the old, experience a loss of identity, and feel deceived and betrayed. The **neutral phase** is the stage in which people feel lost and confused. The confusion stems from the fact that people are leaving behind the former reality, but they don't fully understand the new one. This is disorienting, but it is also where one begins to find the energy needed to carry on. Finally, the **new beginnings phase** occurs when employees begin to explore new possibilities and start to align their actions with a new vision.

As Jick points out, the above provides a prescriptive, optimistic, and simplistic view of how individuals adjust to disruptive change.[44] Some will move through the stages quickly, others will move more slowly, some will get stuck, and some will move more quickly than they should, taking unresolved issues with them. As an example, consider the actions of a senior executive who was released as the result of a merger. During the eight months it took him to find a new position, he focused on maintaining a very positive attitude. Friends marveled at his resilience, though some questioned whether he was living in denial. Upon joining a new firm as a vice president, he became increasingly critical and bitter about his new employer. His hostility had little to do with the organization he had joined or his new position. It was

---

[*]For a detailed treatment of dealing with the survivor syndrome, see Noer, D. M. (1993). *Healing the wounds.* San Francisco: Jossey-Bass.

unresolved anger and other baggage related to his earlier dismissal. His inability to recognize and deal with this hostility ultimately cost him the new position.[45] When individuals get "stuck" in the early and middle stages, extricating themselves can prove very difficult.

Individual reactions to organizational change will be related to perceptions of the potential outcomes, and most changes will not be as severe and disruptive as those envisioned above. In the next section, the chapter explores three specific factors that have an influence on how people adapt to change:

1. Our personality and our experience with the rate of change

2. The reactions of our coworkers and teammates

3. Our experience with and trust in our leaders

How Does Personality Influence the Reactions of Recipients?

As noted in Chapter 6, when stakeholder analysis was discussed, some individuals are generally more predisposed to change (innovators, early adopters, early majority). Others tend to more carefully review the experience of others and commit later in the process (the late majority and late adopters). Finally, there are those who resist adopting change until the bitter end. These predispositions are influenced by individual difference factors such as susceptibility to the social influence of others, tolerance for risk and ambiguity, and self-image (e.g., innovator versus cautious adopter).

Our perception of the change experience and the risk of change will be influenced by our personality.[46] Recipients of change who have a low tolerance for turbulence and uncertainty tend to be more comfortable in more stable environments. As the rate of change accelerates, they will experience increased stress as they attempt to cope and adjust. At low to moderate levels, though, this increased stress may also lead to increased job satisfaction if people experience success with change. However, as change becomes more radical, the resulting stress and strain will tend to produce elevated levels of anxiety and fear, defensiveness, fatigue, alienation, and resignation. Elevated levels of absenteeism and turnover, errors and accidents, and depressed levels of work satisfaction are commonly observed.[47]

Recipients of change who have a higher tolerance for turbulence and uncertainty will find stable and unchanging environments less satisfying after a period of time. Their need for novelty leads to boredom, and higher rates of absenteeism and turnover often result.[48] This is seen in the positive relationship between satisfaction and the desire for new challenges and role ambiguity in managers who are experiencing frustration with plateauing careers.[49] As the rate of change begins to increase to moderate levels, so will their levels of satisfaction and interest (particularly if they become directly engaged with the change). As the rate of change becomes more extreme, effects similar to those observed in low-tolerance individuals are observed, though these effects occur later at higher rates of change.

Take a few moments to revisit the question of how you react to change and reflect on your experience (see Toolkit Exercise 7.3). How do you typically react? Do you seek out change? Embrace it? Wait to see what others do before deciding how to respond? Avoid it until it is clear it is viable? Argue against it?

What Is the Effect of Prior Experience With Change?

Previous experience with change will affect a recipient's views. Long periods of stability and minimal change will lead to people's seeing change as more unsettling and risky than those with more frequent encounters with change.[50] Even those who are thinking "thank goodness, we're finally doing something!" may feel the risk because of exposure to moderate levels of change.

A sustained period of continued success can cause individuals and organizations to be trapped by those strategies and tactics that have served them well. The tendency to rely on competencies and strategies that have worked in the past is referred to as a competency or a complacency trap.[51] Faced with the need for change, they rely on those approaches that have worked well in the past, even though the old strategies are not effective. To use the language of Chapter 3, the organization is incongruent with its environment. Breaking out of these traps is not easy.

If organizations are used to moderate levels of change or if employees have adapted successfully, then the employees are likely to be more open and flexible. The organizational change "muscles" have been used and are ready for more change exercise. Those who have regular, ongoing exposure to moderate amounts of positive change (e.g., through continuous improvement) tend to find change to be less unsettling and hence less risky because they become accustomed to believing that tomorrow will likely be different from today and that this is not something that needs to be avoided.[52]

However, when organizations and employees live in an environment with extended periods of major upheavals and uncertainty, the sense of personal risk escalates and remains high. Under these conditions, employees may become exhausted and feel increasingly vulnerable to the next wave of change. They become jaded and alienated, if earlier promises and hopes for improvement have gone unmet. Those who have not exited the firm may resign themselves to adopt a strategy of keeping their heads down to avoid personal risk. Under these extreme conditions, the perceived risk attached to a particular change initiative may actually diminish. Like those in danger of being swept overboard in a storm, individuals may be prepared to grasp at any plausible change initiative that looks like it could serve as a lifeline, unless their alienation is such that they have effectively given up.

Figure 7.2 depicts a hypothetical connection between past rate of change experienced by recipients and the degree of perceived risk with the anticipated change. If recipients have experienced long periods of minimal change, they will likely perceive higher risks with the proposed change. This risk perception of the proposed change declines when people's ongoing experience with change in general increases to a moderate level. In essence, past experience has normalized change for these individuals and enhanced their comfort level with it. As the normal rate of change increases in intensity, the perception of risk associated with the new change begins to rise again until the recipient is ready to grasp at anything with the potential of offering a way out. This pattern can be seen when participants recognize that the organization is in a crisis state—they become unfrozen and ready to change. In a crisis situation, one can expect initial defensiveness, followed by openness to change.[53]

As has been discussed, both personality and experience with change affect how recipients of change view proposed changes. Table 7.3 outlines the hypothesized interactions between an individual's need for change, tolerance for ambiguity, and the frequency and magnitude of the change experience.

Reflect on Figure 7.2 and Table 7.3. Does this match your experience? Where are you in terms of the frequency of change that you have faced? That is, have you dealt with change often? Have you had to cope with prolonged periods of serious upheaval or periods of extreme turbulence? Have these experiences affected your acceptance of change? Toolkit Exercise 7.4 asks you to consider your tolerance for change.

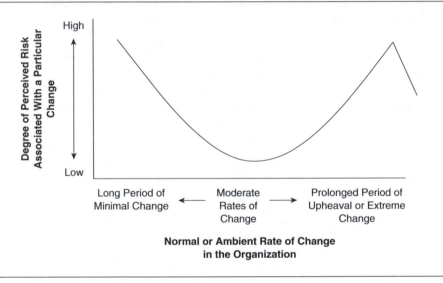

Figure 7.2   The Past Rate of Change and the Perceived Risk of the New Change

Source: C. Gene Deszca, 2005.

What Influence Do Coworkers and Teammates Have on Change Recipients?

Our views are influenced by the comments and actions of those around us—particularly by those whose opinions and relationships are valued (see Table 7.4). Trusted mentors, managers, and friends can be particularly influential. If those we

Table 7.3   The Interaction of Personality With the Experience of Change

Individual Difference	Change Experience			
	Low	Some	Frequent	Chaotic
	No change experience for an extended period, a belief that this job will last indefinitely.	Some change experience that demonstrates both the difficulties and survivability of change.	Frequent change experience, nothing static, major upheavals and uncertainty.	Chaotic environment, characterized by temporary systems, fluid environments, and constant change.
Individuals who have higher tolerance for ambiguity, novelty, and change.	Restlessness; boredom, attempts to create change or to disrupt routines.	Grappling with change issues; feelings of invigoration and new meaning in the job, expectation of improvement.	Stress showing, coping strategies being developed; energy still present but fatigue starting; voicing of concerns; the desire to exit increases.	Stress effects, fear and fatigue as they attempt to cope; voicing of concerns exists, but the likelihood of resignation, alienation rises, and/or a willingness to grasp at a plausible course of action as a way to reduce the chaos.
Individuals who have a lower tolerance for ambiguity, novelty, and change	Acceptance of the situation, buy into the steady state, no preparation or anticipation of change.	Stress effects present, concerns voiced, but a willingness to adjust to moderate amount of change present.	Significant coping difficulties; stress effects including fear, fatigue, and alienation often present. Increased willingness to grasp at a plausible course of action to reduce the chaos.	Severe coping difficulties and resultant stress and strain; alienation, resignation, and/or exit at high levels and/or elevated willingness to grasp at plausible courses of action to reduce the chaos.

trust are positively predisposed toward change, we may be influenced in that direction. Similarly, if they are experiencing serious concerns about the change or are opposed to it, they will influence us to consider factors that may move us in the opposite direction.[54]

Coworkers and work groups play a particularly critical role in how recipients sort out their own reactions to change, because these individuals live in a very similar organizational world, and their relationships are bound together by norms, roles, and shared obligations and experiences. When coworkers are more mixed on the desirability of a particular change, one can expect to see more ambivalence in the individual as they attempt to sort out their own feelings about the matter. The importance of coworker reactions increases as the strength of their relationship rises. The more coworkers see themselves as part of a cohesive team, the greater will be their influence.[55] Even groups that seem to be in conflict will often become very cohesive and turn on the "outsider" who is seen to be threatening group members. Change leaders who ignore cohesion, norms, and ambient levels of ambivalence do so at their own peril.

Table 7.4   Impact of Trusted Peers on Recipients

Opinions of Those Trusted by Recipients	Recipients' Initial Attitude to the Change	Possible Implication
Positive Toward the Change	Positive Toward the Change	Very motivated to support and predisposed to get involved.
	Negative Toward the Change	Opposed to the change but potentially open to other perspectives because of new information and peer pressure.
Negative Toward the Change	Positive Toward the Change	Support of the change may become more tempered due to information and the perspectives offered by trusted peers. Will often experience pressure to reconsider their support or perhaps be silenced by peer pressure.
	Negative Toward the Change	Opposed to the change and reinforced in those views by trusted peers and the peer group.

What Impact Do Change Leaders Have on Recipients' Reactions to Change?

As noted earlier, how recipients view and react to change is influenced by their perception of the change leaders. If they have had good experiences with their leaders, if they believe they recognize their perspective and interests, and if the recipients have learned to trust them, they are likely to respond more positively to their suggestions of change.

When change leaders talk about significant change, they often focus on the rationale, including the costs and benefits of changing. Some attention may be paid to the costs of not changing, but usually little focus is given to the benefits of the status quo. Recipients, on the other hand, assessing change at a personal level, will often reflect on the benefits of not changing and discount the costs of staying with the status quo. They may prefer the devil they know to the unknown one that is being proposed. They can estimate (and sometimes inflate) the costs of changing but may feel far less certain about the benefits. As a result, change leader and recipient estimates of the benefits and costs related to change can differ dramatically. If change leaders recognize this and deal with the matter factually, constructively, and sensitively, recipients' concerns can be brought to the surface and addressed. From a procedural justice and a personal efficacy point of view, people want their voices to be heard, even if it doesn't result in a change in the decision. The president of Continental Airways did that when he had to tell employees that he was closing their operations in an airport, and his candor (combined with his positive reputation as a leader) resulted in much higher acceptance of the change.

> I met with the employees and their families—about 600 people in all. Along with explaining the details of the closing and relocation plans (the company had doubled the financial aspects of the relocation package over what was required by the contract), I also shared with them my vision for Continental and how far we had come. I then opened the floor to questions and answers.
>
> For about five minutes, employees expressed appreciation that I had personally come to give them the news and had developed a financial package to meet their needs. But then the pilots walked in—in full uniform—with their families. They surrounded the room and refused to sit down. A pilot came to the microphone to express how incompetent he felt management was and how Continental was once again making the wrong decision. The rest of the pilots applauded.
>
> Do you know what happened? The rest of the employees, led by a baggage handler who was also being relocated, stood up and defended me, one after another, for 20 minutes. They told the pilots that they should feel lucky that Continental finally had a senior management team that treated them with enough respect to deliver the bad news—as well as the good relocation package—in person. I left to a standing ovation.[56]

How change leaders handle the perceptions and the alterations to the psychological contract will matter to recipients. The president of Continental was more successful in managing the shift in the psychological contract with the employees than with the pilots. This was influenced by the employees' view that they were being treated reasonably under the circumstances—procedural and distributive justice was upheld.[57]

As recipients of change, developing our adaptive skills to constructively work our way through our reactions to significant change will serve us well both professionally and in terms of personal well-being. Likewise, as change leaders, we need to think through initiatives and actions we can undertake that help recipients to successfully adapt. Some of these have already been highlighted in this chapter, such as managerial responses to the disruption of the psychological contract. Additional advice will be offered in the subsequent section and in Chapter 8.

Dealing With Skepticism and Cynicism

Prior experience can lead some of us to believe our leaders when they promise us a better future or when they tell us we have no alternative except what is offered. However, others of us are more skeptical—often for good reasons. We may believe the promises are suspect, particularly if the leader is relatively unknown or untested. If we have heard such promises before and found them to be false, we will be skeptical. Change recipients sometimes report that change leaders have said the right things but acted in ways that advanced their self-interest, ignoring not only what was good for most employees but also what was best for the organization. No wonder many of us have learned to question the vision and commitments made by individuals leading change.

Such skepticism can shift to cynicism (a real loss of faith) and heightened pessimism when others whose opinions we value share a similar negative belief.[58] The price of such cynicism includes reduced satisfaction, less organizational commitment, less motivation to work hard, more accidents and errors, less willingness to engage in future change initiatives, and less leader credibility. As Reichers, Wanous, and Austin say, "People do not deliberately become cynical, pessimistic and blaming. Rather these attitudes result from experience, and are sustained because they serve useful purposes. Cynicism persists because it is selectively validated by the organization's mixed record of successful change, and by other people in the organization who hold and express similar views."[59]

The perceived trustworthiness and integrity of the change leader play an important role in the judgments made by the recipients. When change leaders are viewed as credible and trustworthy, their vision of the future can reduce the sense of uncertainty and risk in recipients, as the recipients put their faith in the leader's judgment. From the power literature, we know that recipients often turn to credible leaders and colleagues to help them absorb uncertainty and make sense of the confusion.[60]

Periods of transition represent a time when the ethical and reputation risks for leaders are particularly high. The "best course of action" often is far from clear. Offering hope and direction without misleading or seriously overstating the case is the narrow path that change leaders must navigate. As one CEO recently noted, the difference between a visionary leader and a huckster is the thin edge that is integrity.[61]

Table 7.5 outlines ways in which change leaders can minimize cynicism about change and eliminate many of the negative aspects resulting from such cynicism.

Table 7.5   Ways to Manage and Minimize Cynicism About Change

1. Keep people involved in making decisions that affect them.

2. Emphasize and reward supervisors who foster two-way communications, good working relationships, and show consideration and respect for employees.

3. Keep people informed about ongoing change: when, why, and how; and include honest appraisals of risks, costs, benefits, and consequences.

4. Keep surprises to a minimum through regular communications about changes, anticipating questions and concerns.

5. Enhance credibility by

   a. Using credible spokespersons who are liked and trusted.
   b. Using positive messages that appeal to logic and consistency.
   c. Using multiple channels and repetition.

6. Acknowledge mistakes, accept responsibility, apologize, and make amends.

7. Publicize successful changes and progress.

8. Use two-way communications in order to see change from the employees' perspective, and use this awareness to help with planning and future communications related to change.

9. Provide opportunities for employees to express feelings and to receive validation and reassurance. Ensure you address the concerns raised.

Source: Adapted from Reichers, A. E., et al. (1997). Understanding and managing cynicism about organizational change. *Academy of Management Executive, 11*(1), 53.

Avoiding Coercion as a Change Strategy if at All Possible

Change leaders may find that they have to resort to the use of coercion. Kramer argues that under certain circumstances (high technology, entertainment, and politics), intimidating leaders apply their political intelligence to creatively push followers to higher levels of performance than would otherwise have been achieved.[62] It is important to note that he specifically makes the point that while such individuals are tough and demanding, they are not simply bullies. The initial coercion is to unfreeze the situation and achieve initial shifts in position. However, leaders who rely primarily on the application of fear and force to gain commitment to change are taking significant risks. While it may be true that "if you have them by their throats, their hearts and minds will follow,"[63] we suspect that any release of the throat would lead to predictable revolts and resistance.

At times, employees respond to leaders out of fear of what will happen if they don't comply. While fear can motivate, leaders who rely primarily on fear or coercion are following a risky path—both ethically and pragmatically (i.e., will the support still be there when the stick or threat is no longer present?).[64] In his book *From Good to Great*, Collins refers to this "doom loop" as the enemy of effective leadership.[65]

Leaders, frustrated by a lack of progress, are attracted to the use of punishment and fear because these tools are available, immediate in their short-term effects, and carry the illusion of control through obedience and compliant behavior.[66] However, we do *not* recommend the use of such strategies in most situations. Years ago, Deming noted that the move to total quality could not be achieved through fear, and evidence in the intervening years continues to demonstrate the lack of effectiveness of fear.[67] While activity controls like fear may produce compliance in the short run, they have proven to be ineffective over the intermediate to longer term.[68] Further, such techniques can create undesirable side effects (e.g., frustration, withdrawal in the form of absenteeism and turnover, aggression and sabotage).

A much more desirable and less risky course of action is through the positive engagement of recipients of change through initiatives that enhance the recipients' capabilities to deal effectively with the change.[69]

Creating Consistent Signals from Systems and Processes

While the leader's words and deeds are important, so are other parts of the organizational context. As has been mentioned in Chapters 3 and 5, leader credibility will either be enhanced or diminished by the extent to which organizational systems and processes are seen to send a consistent message, or are themselves the focus of changes that will bring them into alignment with the change vision.

Credibility and trust are diminished when the leader's words say one thing (e.g., quality is critical) but the systems and processes signal something else (e.g., ship now, fix later). In *Built to Last*, Collins and Porras noted that firms with staying power possess resilient cultures that have the capacity to adjust and realign their systems and processes in response to changing conditions. This resilience was made functional by the underlying value set and supportive systems and processes that were installed by leaders.[70] As such, they provided continuity for organization members, while at the same time contributing to the adaptability and change of existing systems and processes. In essence, this reflects an interesting and important paradox for the change leader. The successful management of change is enhanced by giving voice to factors that enhance the sense of continuity, the connection between the past and the future, as well as by giving voice to the need for and nature of the change.[71]

Toolkit Exercise 7.5 asks you to examine how your leadership has affected your views of change.

What Specific Steps Can Be Taken to Minimize the Negative Effects of Change?

Those who have been involved in significant changes know from firsthand experience that how recipients view the change will have a profound impact on the ultimate success or failure of a change initiative.[72] The change recipients need to become willing change implementers. Therefore, the effects on the recipients of change need to be approached with care during the initial planning phases and throughout the change, including the postchange period.

Trust is increased and rumors are reduced when you share information about what you are considering, what you know and don't know, what your process will be, and how you will keep recipients informed of progress, conclusions, action plans, and time lines. When coupled with the personal involvement of engaged leaders and executives and a meaningful degree of employee involvement in decisions that affect them (at minimum, the ability to ask questions, voice concerns, and receive answers that reduce uncertainty), individual adaptation and acceptance are advanced.[73] Recipients want to know where things are going, why, and what the implications are on the organization, their parts of the operation, and on them personally. When change leaders don't know the answers to questions that are raised, recipients need to know when they can expect to hear the answers.

Recipients also want to be able to vent their concerns and frustrations and, at times, grieve what has been lost. No one benefits when recipients first hear about change on the evening news or in the local coffee shop. When this begins to happen, the information needs to be quickly and credibly dealt with through internal communication channels—otherwise, the rumor mill will shift into overdrive, as recipients attempt to make sense of new and potentially conflicting information.[74]

A variety of communication channels are available to change leaders and multiple channels are best. Redundancy is clearly preferable to gaps. Communicating through executive staff briefings, teams, task forces, recipient representatives, advisory groups, video, newsletters, hotlines, and the creative use of the intranet (including bulletin boards and e-mail to monitor concerns and expedite the delivery of answers)—all have a role to play in helping recipients adapt to change. When coupled with transparency, authenticity, and minimal levels of executive defensiveness, these communication approaches advance recipient engagement and adaptation to change.

Change communications are far from unidirectional. Change leaders can learn as much or more from such exchanges as the recipients. Exposure to recipient feedback and reactions allows change leaders to adapt strategies and approaches in a far more informed and sensitive manner, making it possible to enhance further the prospects for successful recipient adaptation. For example, tracking themes from e-mails and postings on bulletin boards can provide insights into how recipients are interpreting and responding to the change. The importance of such feedback proves the adage that leaders who think they know it all have a fool as their advisor. To quote the movie director Blake Edwards, "Every time I think I know 'where it's at,' it's usually somewhere else."

Jick and Peiperl have identified a number of strategies that can assist both the recipients of change and their managers in coping with different stages of the change. Recipients of change need to understand how they can shift from accepting their feelings and managing the stress to exercising their responsibilities in achieving successful change. Change leaders need to aid recipients by rethinking resistance and helping recipients as they adapt. As well, change leaders need to understand how to build the organization's capability for change. These are outlined in Table 7.6.

As a change recipient, if we know the stages of change, we can develop support networks that facilitate our letting go and moving on. As a change leader, if we

Table 7.6   Strategies for Coping With Change

Recipients	Change Leaders
Accepting Feelings as Natural	*Rethinking Resistance*
• Self-permission to feel and mourn • Taking time to work through feelings • Tolerating ambiguity	• As natural as self-protection • As a positive step toward change • As energy to work with • As information critical to the change process
Managing Stress	*Giving First Aid*
• Maintaining physical well-being • Seeking information about the change • Limiting extraneous stressors • Taking regular breaks • Seeking support	• Accepting emotions • Listening • Providing safety • Marking endings • Providing resources and support
Exercising Responsibility	*Creating Capability for Change*
• Identifying options and gains • Learning from losses • Participating in the change • Inventorying strengths • Learning new skills • Diversifying emotional investing	• Making organizational support of risks clear • Providing a continuing safety net • Emphasizing continuities, gains of change • Helping employees explore risks, options • Suspending judgment • Involving people in decision making • Teamwork • Providing opportunities for individual growth

Source: Adapted from Jick, T., & Peiperl, M. A. (2003). *Managing change, cases and concepts* (2nd ed., p. 307). New York: McGraw-Hill.

understand the dynamics around change, we will recognize that we need to work through the change management process in a systemic and supportive fashion.

Often the understanding of change recipients may lag behind that of change leaders. By definition, those leading change will already have worked their way through the need for change, mourned the loss of the old, understood and embraced the new vision, and moved to action. Change recipients need to work through the same process—but are lagging their leaders and lack their direct involvement. As change leaders, we need to give them time to adapt and catch up!

The approaches that change leaders can adopt to ease the negative impact on recipients represent the application of classic transformational leadership skills.[75] First, through the communication of shared meaning and clarification of direction and impact, they reduce uncertainty and ambiguity. Even when the news is bad, knowing is easier to cope with than guessing.[76] When uncertainty is rampant, people magnify the sense of risk and loss and act in ways that magnify the risks. When leaders listen and help recipients to frame the effects in less odious terms, recipients are less stressed. The ability to adapt and behave with integrity inspires confidence.[77]

Toolkit Exercise 7.6 asks you to think about strategies for coping with change from the perspective of recipients.

Can We Reduce the Intensity of Change by Making Change the Norm?

One way that organizations can reduce the perceived threat of changes is through adopting a managerial approach that causes employees to regularly question the status quo and seek to improve existing approaches to work as part of their ongoing activities. If organization members have not been used to questioning and initiating changes in how things are done, even minor shifts can be seen as major and threatening events. By working to create an organizational climate in which incremental changes are sought out and embraced, you generate an atmosphere in which change is seen to be a naturally occurring condition. The fact that tomorrow is unlikely to be exactly the same as today becomes the expected norm as opposed to an unexpected shock.[78]

One benefit of approaches such as continuous quality and organizational improvement lies in the fact that these approaches legitimize and promote the healthiness of ongoing change in ways that provide continuity with the past. Rather than spend all your time searching for the silver bullet that will produce the cure for current organizational evils, these approaches seek to advance less heroic, ongoing initiatives that will enhance organizational health in more incremental ways.[79] In so doing, these approaches also make more revolutionary changes appear less threatening because the perceived magnitude of the change is reduced. After all, the perception of revolutionary change lies in the eye of the beholder.

If the organizational culture promotes an ongoing and constructive embrace of change, perceptions of the threat related to change are bound to be reduced. Abrahamson refers to this as dynamic stability and points to firms like GE as exemplars of the approach.[80] The experience tells organization members that changes are normal and tend to work out for the best.

Even when the news is bad, an approach of ongoing employee engagement with change can lead to lower levels of uncertainty, quicker response times (people know what they are facing), improved outcomes (e.g., less undesirable employee turnover), and higher levels of satisfaction than likely would otherwise have occurred. If recipients (or their representatives) have participated in the analysis, planning, and/or implementation efforts, this tends to further reduce the fear and uncertainty.[81]

A final approach to reducing the perceived threat of change is to use approaches that do not cause people to believe they have to "bet the farm." One can do this through encouraging the use of experimentation and pilot programs and through ensuring that the perceived rewards and punishments associated with success and failure are not excessive. Again, experience has demonstrated that a series of smaller, interrelated changes by dedicated change agents over time can produce substantial, even revolutionary changes in the organization—sometimes without the organization even knowing they were under way.[82]

Become a Change Agent Yourself and Avoid the Recipient Trap

It is clear from this chapter that being a change recipient is not as energizing or exciting as being a change agent! Change agents are active and involved. Change recipients find themselves on the receiving end and may experience a lack of power and control. So one way to reduce the negative effects of change is to take the risk, get more involved, and become a change agent. Get out of the receiving role and make things happen!

When recipients engage in attempts to influence the events swirling about them, they are, in effect, acting as their own change agents. Since they are often in subordinate roles and dependent, to varying degrees, on the actions of others, skilled recipients manage the influence process by recognizing whom they are dependent on[83] and engaging in appropriate stakeholder analysis.

By taking action, presenting ideas, and attempting to make a difference, potential change recipients can gain power in real or perceived terms. And they will be viewed differently in the organization.

So, if you are at risk of becoming an unwilling change recipient, create a change target, go back to the beginning of this book, begin the process, and proceed with your eyes open, cognizant of the risks you need to manage!

Summary

This chapter has dealt with how recipients of change react and why they respond positively, negatively, or with ambivalence. It suggests that change leaders use feelings of ambivalence as an opportunity to influence recipients. As well, change leaders need to understand resistance to change and use such resistance to understand the change environment better.

The chapter outlines the prescriptive model of change phases that change recipients are seen to go through when more disruptive changes are involved. Although the evidence on this model is mixed, knowing the model provides us with useful insight as to how we could act. The chapter deals with the factors that affect how recipients view change: their personalities, their experience with change, their coworkers, the organization, and the change leaders themselves. Finally, the chapter ended by considering what change recipients and change leaders can do to manage the process and minimize the negative impacts of change.

A concluding toolkit exercise is provided to help you think about recipient readiness for change (see Toolkit Exercise 7.7). Implicit in the scoring is advice for change leaders concerning things they can do to increase recipients' receptiveness to change.

Glossary of Terms

Recipients of Change—Those individuals who find themselves on the receiving end of a change initiative.

Resistance to Change—Actions that are intended to slow or prevent change from happening. Resistance arises when an individual comes to believe that the costs outweigh the benefits and that opposition is warranted. Actions can vary from the expression of concern and "go slow" responses, through to more active forms of resistance, including coalition building, formal protests, and even sabotage.

Ambivalence to Change—The mixed emotions that a change can often trigger. Ambivalence arises from uncertainty and occurs when we are asked to act in ways that are inconsistent with our existing attitudes. These mixed emotions generate discomfort that we seek to resolve. There is evidence that suggests we have an easier time giving voice to mixed feelings involving conflicting beliefs than we do when negative emotional responses are involved. Once the individual has resolved their ambivalence, subsequent changes to those attitudes become much more difficult, until a new sense of ambivalence arises.

Psychological Contract—The psychological contract represents the sum of the implicit and explicit agreements we believe we have with key individuals and the organization concerning our employment relationship. These ground our expectations concerning ourselves and the organization, concerning terms and conditions, norms, rights, rewards, and obligations.

Stages in the Reaction to Change—The three primary stages that individuals typically must progress through when coping with a more traumatic change are the **anticipation and anxiety phase**; the **shock, denial, and retreat phase**; and the **adaptation and acceptance phase**.

Transition Stages Perspective—The transition stages perspective begins with the **ending phase**, which involves letting go of your former situation, and is often characterized by fear, confusion, and anger. The **neutral phase** is the stage in which individuals feel lost and confused. The **new beginnings phase** occurs when individuals begin to explore new possibilities and start to align their actions with a new vision.

Tolerance for Turbulence and Ambiguity—Tolerance for turbulence and ambiguity involves our comfort level with these conditions. Individuals who have higher tolerance levels generally will be more comfortable and open to change, while those who have lower tolerance levels will prefer more stable and predictable environments.

Predisposition to Change—Relates to our general inclination toward change. Are we typically innovators, early adopters, members of the early majority of adopters, members of the late majority, or in the group of individuals who are very late adopters or nonadopters?

Skepticism and Cynicism Toward Change—**Skepticism** relates to doubts and concerns we may have concerning the capacity of the change to deliver the promised results. These may be rooted in the change itself, the adoption process, concerns about the change leadership, or unease about the organization's and other key stakeholders' responses to the change.

Cynicism occurs when we fundamentally lose faith in the change, the adoption process, the key individuals involved, or the organization.

END-OF-CHAPTER EXERCISES

TOOLKIT EXERCISE 7.1

Personal Reactions to Change

1. Think through your organizational experiences at school and at work when you have been a recipient of change. How have you typically responded to these changes? What were the factors that led to those responses?

   To help you think about these questions, ask yourself the following concerning three to four such changes:

   a. What was the change and how was it introduced?
   b. What was the impact on you?
   c. What was your initial reaction? Enthusiasm? "Wait and see" attitude? Ambivalence, due to conflicting reactions? Cynicism?
   c. Did your attitudes change over time? Why or why not?

2. Was there a pattern to your response?

   a. Under what circumstances did you support the change? When did you resist? What can you generalize from these experiences?
   b. If you experienced ambivalence, how did you resolve it and what happened to your attitudes toward the change once the ambivalent feelings were resolved?

3. Overall, have your earlier experiences with change been largely positive, largely negative, or mixed? Have these experiences colored your expectations and feelings toward change in the future?

TOOLKIT EXERCISE 7.2

Disruption of the Psychological Contract

Think about a change initiative that you are aware of. What happened or will likely happen to the psychological contracts of recipients?

1. What is the existing psychological contract? (If this is in the past, what was the contract?)

2. In what ways did the change disrupt the existing psychological contract? To what extent was this perception real? (If this is in the past, in what ways did the change actually disrupt the psychological contract?)

3. Given the individuals and the context, what reactions to these disruptions to the psychological contract do you anticipate? (If this is in the past, what were the reactions?)

4. Are there steps that could be taken to reduce the negative effects stemming from the disruption? (If this is in the past, could anything have been done?)

5. How should a new psychological contract be developed with affected individuals? (If this is in the past, how could this have been done?)

6. If you are the recipient of change, what steps could you take to better manage your way through the development of a new contract? (If this is in the past, what could you have done?)

TOOLKIT EXERCISE 7.3

Your Normal Reaction to Innovation and Change

When you find yourself dealing with matters of innovation and change, how do you typically react?

1. Do you find that you fall into the category of innovator or early adopter, readily considering and often adopting new approaches well in advance of most people?

2. Or do you generally fall into the category of the early majority? If the initial responses and experiences of the early adopters are generally positive, you are willing to take the risk and adopt the new approach.

3. Or are you generally in the category of the late majority? You wait until the innovation or new approach has been tried and tested by many people before you commit to adopt.

4. Or are you a person who typically does not adopt the innovation or new approach until the vast majority of people have done so? In other words, are you a late adopter or even a nonadopter until forced to do so?

TOOLKIT EXERCISE 7.4

Your Tolerance for Change

1. What is your tolerance for change? What level of turbulence and ambiguity in a work situation do you find most stimulating and satisfying?

2. How do you react when the rate of change is quite low and is likely to remain there?

3. How do you react when the rate of change is at a moderate level? What constitutes a moderate level for you? Are your tolerance levels lower or higher than others you know?

4. What price do you find that you pay personally when the rate of turbulence and ambiguity exceed what you are comfortable with? When it is either too low or too high?

5. Have you had to cope with prolonged periods of serious upheaval or periods of extreme turbulence? Have these experiences affected your acceptance of change?

TOOLKIT EXERCISE 7.5

Leadership and Change Recipients

Think more specifically about an example of change leadership that you know:

1. What was the nature of that leadership?

2. Was the leader trusted?

3. Did he or she deserve the trust given?

4. What kind of power did the leader use?

5. How were the messages about the change conveyed? Were they believable messages?

6. Did organizational systems and processes support or, at minimum, not impair the change leader's messages?

7. Was there a sense of continuity between the past and the anticipated future? How was that sense of continuity developed and communicated? What was the impact?

8. What can you learn about the impact of the leader on recipients of change as a result of your responses to the above questions?

9. What can you learn about the impact of organizational systems and processes on the recipients of change?

10. Talk to others about their experiences. Can you generalize? In what way? What cannot be generalized?

TOOLKIT EXERCISE 7.6

Working Through the Phases of Change

1. Consider a significant and disruptive change situation that you know about (or talk to a friend or relative about such a change situation). Can you identify the different phases of change? What phases are you aware of?

2. Can you identify strategies that recipients used or could have used to help them work their way through the different phases?

3. Can you identify strategies that change leaders used or could have used to help recipients work their way through the different phases?

	Awareness Yes/No	Strategies recipients can use to help them work through stage	Strategies change leaders can use to help recipients work through stage
Prechange Anxiety			
Shock			
Defensive Retreat			
Bargaining			
Depression, Guilt, and Alienation			
Acknowledgment			
Adaptation and Change			

Does the model hold? Why or why not?

What other consequences of change can you identify?

TOOLKIT EXERCISE 7.7

Assessing Recipients' Openness to Change

In the previous sections, we have discussed the impact of the recipients' personality, their sense of their psychological contract, and their coworkers, supervisors, and leaders on their reaction to change. Toolkit Exercise 7.7 will provide you with a general sense of the openness of the recipients of change to a specific undertaking.* Likewise, it can be used to evaluate your own openness to the change. If your scores are in the +50 or greater range, you will likely be quite open to change and ready to cope. Negative scores would suggest the opposite, while scores in the middle range (+50 to −50) point to increasing ambivalence. What do the scores tell you about what might be done to increase the openness of the recipient to the change?

Think about a change situation you know of or are involved with. How are the recipients of change likely to rate the following factors?	Score
1. Past experience with change, particularly changes similar to that advocated	Very Negative −10 −5 0 +5 +10 Very Positive ___
2. Normal rate of change that has been experienced by the organization	Very Low −10 −5 0 +5 +10 Moderate to High ___
3. Recipients' general predisposition to change as reflected in their personality	Late Adopter −10 −5 0 +5 +10 Early Adopter ___
4. Recipients believe they understand the nature of the proposed change and the reasons for it (i.e., the need for change)	Low −10 −5 0 +5 +10 +10 High ___
5. Recipient's personal belief about the need for this particular change	Very Negative −10 −5 0 +5 +10 Very Positive ___
6a. Reactions of coworkers to the change	Very Negative −10 −5 0 +5 +10 Very Positive ___
	multiply by
6b. Strength of coworker relations (norms)	Weak 0.1 0.3 0.5 0.7 1.0 Strong
7. Leader credibility	Low −10 −5 0 +5 +10 High ___
8. Leader gains compliance through fear versus gains commitment through understanding and empathy	Fear −10 −5 0 +5 +10 Support ___
9. Organizational credibility (i.e., will it follow through on commitments related to change?)	Low −10 −5 0 +5 +10 High ___
10. Congruence of systems and processes with the proposed change (or confidence that they will be brought into congruence)	Very Incongruent −10 −5 0 +5 +10 Very Congruent ___
Predisposition to Change Index: Scores can range from −100 to +100	Overall Score ___

*This index is not the product of empirical testing. It was created to provide you with food for thought concerning openness to change and what may be facilitating and impairing the receptiveness that you are experiencing.

Notes

1. Frijda, N. H., & Mesquita, B. (2000). Beliefs through emotions. In N. H. Frijda, A. S. R. Manstead, & S. Bem (Eds.), *Emotions and beliefs: How feelings influence thoughts* (pp. 43–54). Paris: Oxford University Press.

2. Dent, E. B., & Goldberg, S. G. (1999). Challenging "resistance to change." *Journal of Applied Behavioral Science, (35)*1, 25–41.

3. Withey, M. J., & Cooper, W. H. (1989). Predicting exit, voice, loyalty, and neglect. *Administrative Science Quarterly, 34,* 521–539.

4. Lines, R. (2004). Influence of participation in strategic change: Resistance, organizational commitment and change goal achievement. *Journal of Change Management, (4)*3, 193–215.

5. Jiji Press America, September 1, 2003.

6. Lines, op. cit.

7. Piderit, S. K. (2000). Rethinking resistance and recognizing ambivalence: A multidimensional view of attitudes toward an organizational change. *Academy of Management Review, (25)*4, 783–794.

8. Piderit, op. cit.

9. Smith, K. K. (1982). *Groups in conflict: Prisons in disguise.* Dubuque, IA: Kendall/Hunt; Spreitzer, G. M., & Quinn, R. E. (1996). Empowering middle managers to be transformational leaders. *Journal of Applied Behavioral Science, (32)*3, 237–261.

10. Piderit, op. cit.

11. Much of the material on ambivalence and change management is drawn from two excellent articles: Lines, R. (2005). The structure and function of attitudes toward organizational change. *Human Resource Development Review, (4)*1, 8–32; and Piderit, S. K. (2000). Rethinking resistance and recognizing ambivalence: A multidimensional view of attitudes toward an organizational change. *Academy of Management Review, (25)*4, 783–794.

12. Lines, op. cit., 2005.

13. Piderit, op. cit., p. 789.

14. Sull, D.N. (1999, July–August). Why good companies go bad. *Harvard Business Review,* 42–52.

15. Festinger, L. (1957). *A theory of cognitive dissonance.* Stanford, CA: Stanford University Press.

16. Hymes, R. W. (1986). Political attitudes as social categories: A new look at selective memory. *Journal of Personality and Social Psychology, 51,* 233–241.

17. Lines, op. cit., 2005.

18. Barr, P. S., Stimpert, J. L., & Huff, A. S. (1992). Cognitive change, strategic action, and organizational renewal. *Strategic Management Journal, 13,* 15–36; Floyd, S. W., & Wooldridge, B. (1996). *The strategic middle manager.* San Francisco: Jossey-Bass.

19. Lines, op. cit., 2004.

20. Giora, D. A., & Thomas, J. B. (1996). Identity, image, and issue interpretation: Sensemaking during strategic change in academia. *Administrative Science Quarterly, 41,* 370–403; Labianca, G., Gray, B., & Brass, D. J. (2000). A grounded model of organizational schema change during empowerment. *Organizational Science, (11)*2, 235–257; Lines, op. cit., 2004; and Sagie, A., & Koslowsky, M. (1994). Organizational attitudes and behaviors as a function of participation in strategic and tactical decisions: An application of path-goal theory. *Journal of Organizational Behavior, (15)*1, 37–47.

21. Balogun, J., & Johnson, G. (2005). From intended strategies to unintended outcomes: The impact of change recipient sensemaking. *Organizational Studies, (26)*11, 1596.

22. Hackman, J. R., & Oldham, G. R. (1980). *Work redesign.* Reading, MA: Addison-Wesley.

23. Gustafson, B. (2005). Plant closure "devastates" Newfoundland community. *National Fisherman, (85)*10, 11–12.

24. Gustafson, op. cit.

25. Gopinath, C., & Becker, T. E. (2000). Communication, procedural justice, and employee attitudes: Relationships under conditions of divestiture. *Journal of Management, 26*, 63–83.

26. Piderit, op. cit.

27. Reicher, A. E., Wanous, J. P., & Austin, J. T. (1997). Understanding and managing cynicism about organizational change. *The Academy of Management Executive, (11)*1, 48–60.

28. Lines, op. cit., 2004.

29. Kickul, J., Lester, S. W., & Finkl, J. (2002). Promise breaking during organizational change: Do justice interventions make a difference? *Journal of Organizational Behavior, 23*, 469–488.

30. Watson, T. J. (1982). Group ideologies and organizational change. *Journal of Management Studies, 19*, 259–275.

31. Kotter, J. P. (1995). Leading change: Why transformation efforts fail. *Harvard Business Review, (73)*2, 59–67.

32. Kerr, S. (1995). On the folly of rewarding A, while hoping for B. *Academy of Management Executive, (9)*1, 7–14.

33. Turnley, W. H., & Feldman, D. C. (1999). The impact of psychological contract violations on exit, voice, loyalty, and neglect. *Human Relations, (52)*7, 895–922; Rousseau, D. M. (1995). *Promises in action: Psychological contracts in organizations.* Thousand Oaks, CA: Sage.

34. Deery, S. J., Iverson, R. D., & Walsh, J. T. (2006). Toward a better understanding of psychological contract breach: A study of customer service employees. *Journal of Applied Psychology, (91)*1, 13; Suazo, M. M., Turnley, W. H., & Mai-Dalton, R. R. (2005). The role of perceived violation in determining employees' reactions to psychological contract breach. *Journal of Leadership and Organizational Studies, (12)*1, 24–36.

35. Kübler-Ross, E. (1969). *On death and dying.* New York: Macmillan.

36. Fink, S. L. (1967). Crisis and motivation: A theoretical model. *Archives of Physical Medicine and Rehabilitation.*

37. Jick, T. (1990). The recipients of change. *Harvard Business School* #N9–491039. In T. Jick & M. A. Peiperl, *Managing change, cases and concepts* (2nd ed.). New York: McGraw-Hill Higher Education.

38. Perlman, D., & Takacs, G. J. (1990). The ten stages of change. *Nursing Management, (21)*4, 33–38.

39. Piderit, op. cit.

40. Noer, D. M. (1993). *Healing the wounds: Overcoming the trauma of layoffs and revitalizing downsized organizations.* San Francisco: Jossey-Bass; Kübler-Ross, E., & Warshal, M. (1987). *Working it through.* New York: Macmillan.

41. Doherty, N., Banks, J., & Vinnicombe, S. (1996). Managing survivors: The experience of survivors in British Telecom and the British Financial Services sector. *Journal of Managerial Psychology, (11)*7, 51–60.

42. Bedeian, A. G., & Armenakis, A. A. (1998, February). The cesspool syndrome: How dreck floats to the top of declining organizations. *Academy of Management Executive*, 58–67; Mishra, K. E., Spreitzer, G. M., & Mishra, A. K. (1998). Preserving employee morale during downsizing. *Sloan Management Review, (39)*2, 83–95.

43. Bridges, W. (1986, Summer). Managing organizational transitions. *Organizational Dynamics*, 24–33.

44. Jick & Peiperl, op. cit., p. 326.

45. Personal conversation with the author.

46. Deckop, J. R., Merriman, K. K., & Blau, G. (2004). Impact of variable risk preferences on the effectiveness of control of pay. *Journal of Occupational and Organizational Psychology*, (*77*)1, 63–80.

47. Probst, T. M. (2003). Exploring employee outcomes of organizational restructuring: A Solomon Four-Group Study. *Group & Organization Management*, (*28*)3, 416–439.

58. Kass, S. J., Vodanovich, S. J., & Callender, A. (2001). State-trait boredom: Relationship to absenteeism, tenure, and job satisfaction. *Journal of Business and Psychology*, (*16*)2, 317–326.

49. Tremblay, M., & Roger, A. (2004). Career plateauing reactions: The moderating role of job scope, role ambiguity and participation among Canadian managers. *The International Journal of Human Resource Management*, (*15*)6, 996–1017.

50. Park, D., & Krishnan, H. A. (2003). Understanding the stability-change paradox: Insights for the evolutionary, adaptation, and institutional perspectives. *International Journal of Management*, (*20*)3, 265–270.

51. Barnett, W. P., & Sorenson, O. (2002). The red queen in organizational creation. *Industrial and Corporate Change*, (*11*)2, 289–325.

52. Kelly, P., & Amburgey, T. (1991). Organizational inertia and momentum: A dynamic model of strategic change. *Academy of Management Journal, 34*, 591–612; Huff, J., Huff, J., & Thomas, H. (1992). Strategic renewal and the interaction of cumulative stress and inertia. *Strategic Management Journal, 13*, 55–75.

53. Kovoor-Misra, S., & Nathan, M. (2000). Timing is everything: The optimal time to learn from crises. *Review of Business*, (*21*)3–4, 31–36.

54. Geller, E. S. (2002). Leadership to overcome resistance to change: It takes more than consequence control. *Journal of Organizational Behavior Management*, (*22*)3, 29; and Brown, J., & Quarter, J. Resistance to change: The influence of social networks on the conversion of a privately-owned unionized business to a worker cooperative. *Economic and Industrial Democracy*, (*15*)2, 259–283.

55. Bettenhausen, K. L. (1991). Five years of groups research: What we have learned and what needs to be addressed. *Journal of Management*, (*17*)2, 345–381.

56. Brenneman, G. (1998). Right away and all at once: How we saved Continental. *Harvard Business Review*, (*76*)5, 162–173.

57. Tyler, T. R., & De Cremer, D. (2005). Process-based leadership: Fair procedures and reactions to organizational change. *Leadership Quarterly*, (*16*)4, 529–545.

58. Reichers, A. E., Wanous, J. P., & Austin, J. T. (1997). Understanding and managing cynicism about organizational change. *Academy of Management Executive*, (*11*)1, 48–60.

59. Reichers, Wanous, & Austin, op. cit., pp. 50–51.

60. Munduate, L., & Bennebroek Gravenhorst, K. M. (2003). Power dynamics and organisational change: An introduction. *Applied Psychology: An International Review*, (*52*)1, 1–13; Weick, K. E., & Quinn, R. E. (1999). Organizational change and development. *Annual Review of Psychology, 50*, 361–386.

61. Personal communication, 2004.

62. Kramer, R. M. (2006). The great intimidators. *Harvard Business Review*, (*84*)2, 88–96.

63. Source unknown.

64. Stimson, W. A. (2005). A Deming inspired management code of ethics. *Quality Progress*, (*38*)2, 67–75; Farson, R., & Keyes, R. (2002). The failure-tolerant leader. *Harvard Business Review*, (*80*)8, 64; Casio, J. (2002). Scare tactics. *Incentive*, (*176*)9, 56–62.

65. Collins, J. C. (2001). *From good to great: Why some companies make the leap . . . and others don't.* New York: Harper Business.

66. Werther, W. B., Jr. (2000). Loyalty: Cross-organizational comparisons and patterns. *Leadership and Organization Development Journal, (8)*2, 3–6.

67. Deming, W. E. (1986). *Drastic changes for Western management.* Madison, WI: Center for Quality and Productivity Improvement.

68. Challagalla, G. N., & Shervgani, T. A. (1996). Dimensions and types of supervisory control: Effects on salesperson performance and satisfaction. *Journal of Marketing, 60,* 89–105.

69. Appelbaum, S. H., Bregman, M., & Moroz, P. (1998). Fear as a strategy: Effects and impact within the organization. *Journal of European Industrial Training, (22)*3, 113–127.

70. Collins, J. C., & Porras, J. I. (1994). *Built to last: Successful habits of visionary companies.* New York: HarperCollins.

71. Kolb, D. G. (2002). Continuity, not change: The next organizational challenge. *The University of Auckland Business Review, (4)*2, 1–11.

72. Balogun, J., & Johnson, G. (2005). From intended strategies to unintended outcomes: The impact of change recipient sensemaking. *Organizational Studies, (26)*11, 1573–1601.

73. Evans, C., Hammersley, G. O., & Robertson, M. (2001). Assessing the role and efficacy of communication strategies in times of crisis. *Journal of European Industrial Training, (25)*6, 297–309; Ashkenas, R. N., DeMonaco, L. J., & Francis, S. C. (1998). Making the deal real: How GE capital integrates acquisitions. *Harvard Business Review, (76)*1, 165–176.

74. Difonzo, N., & Bordia, P. (1998). A tale of two corporations: Managing uncertainty during organizational change. *Human Resource Management, (37)*3–4, 295–304.

75. Dionne, S. D., Yammarino, F. J., Atwater, L. E., & Spangler, W. D. (2004). Transformational leadership and team performance. *Journal of Organizational Change Management, (17)*2, 177–193.

76. Mishra, K. E., Spreitzer, G. M., & Mishra, A. K. (1998). Preserving employee morale during downsizing. *Sloan Management Review, (39)*2, 83–95.

77. Kellerman, B. (2004, January). Leadership—"warts and all." *Harvard Business Review,* 40–45.

78. Tersine, R., Harvey, M., & Buckley, M. (1997). Shifting organizational paradigms: Transitional management. *European Management Journal, (15)*1, 45–57.

79. Schneider, B., Brief, A. P., & Guzzo, R. A. (1996). Creating a climate and culture for sustainable organizational change. *Organizational Dynamics, (24)*4, 6–18.

80. Abrahamson, E. (2000, July–August). Change without pain. *Harvard Business Review,* 75–79.

81. Burke, R. J. (2002). The ripple effect. *Nursing Management, (33)*2, 41–43; Weakland, J. H. (2001). Human resources hollistic approach to healing downsizing survivors. *Organizational Development Journal, (19)*2, 59–69; Mishra, Spreitzer, & Mishra, op. cit.

82. Meyerson, D. E. (2001, October). Radical change, the quiet way. *Harvard Business Review,* 92–100.

83. Cohen, A. R., & Bradford, D. L. (1990). *Influence without authority.* New York: John Wiley & Sons; Keys, B., & Case, T. (1990). How to become an influential manager. *Academy of Management Executive, 4,* 38–49.

CHAPTER 8

Change Agent Types and Effectiveness

In the middle of change, everything can look like a failure.

—Rosabeth Moss Kanter

Chapter Overview

- The success of a change agent involves the person, a vision, and the situation.
- Successful change agents appear to have a set of characteristics: interpersonal skills, communication skills, emotional resilience, tolerance for ambiguity, tolerance for ethical conflict, political skills, persistence, pragmatism, dissatisfaction with the status quo, openness to information, flexibility, and adaptiveness. They act in a manner likely to build trust. Change agents develop their skills with experience in change situations.
- This chapter describes four change agent types: the emotional champion, the intuitive adapter, the developmental strategist, and the continuous improver.
- This chapter considers two situational factors related to being a change agent: whether you are an internal or external change agent and the nature of your change team.

Change agents are key to the entire change process, from initial diagnoses to implementation. They are sources of energy and intellect that help organization members recognize the need for change, see what the future can look like, build support, mobilize to close the gap, create alignment, and then assess where to proceed next.

This chapter examines what makes a change agent. It looks at individual characteristics and how they interact with the situation given a powerful vision. The chapter contrasts change managers with change leaders and examines how change leaders develop through stages to become more effective. Four types of change leadership are identified: the emotional champion, the intuitive adapter, the continuous improver, and the developmental strategist. The skills of an internal change agent are examined, and the usefulness of change teams is highlighted. The chapter ends with "rules of thumb" for change agents gleaned from the wisdom of organizational development and change agent experts. Figure 8.1 highlights where this chapter is in our change management process. The change leader is shown as embedded in the organization and as a critical part of the gap analysis. In Nadler's model (from Chapter 3), change leaders are key individuals in the organization.

Taking on the role of change agent is not without career hazards, frustration, and the risk of failure. It can also prove energizing, exciting, educational, and enriching. As a change agent, you are likely to improve your understanding of the organization, develop special skills, and increase your network of contacts and visibility in the organization.[1] On the other hand, those who choose not to respond to the challenge of being a change agent will avoid the ego and career-related risks of failure but run the risk of becoming increasingly less central and relevant to the operation of the organization. When changes fail, there is often the sense that the change agent's career is likely at an end. However, this is not necessarily the case. Failure experiences are painful, but change agents tend to be resilient. For example, when Jac Nasser left Ford in 2001, many thought he was a spent force. However, about a year after leaving Ford, he took over as chairman of Polaroid after it was acquired by One Equity in a bankruptcy auction. In two and a half years, Nasser turned it around, and its resale resulted in a $250 million gain for One Equity.[2]

Many individuals find it confusing to identify where they fit into the change process. They find it difficult to believe that they can initiate change given their experiences. Years of responding to autocratic or risk-averse bosses and organizational cultures make it difficult to believe that this time the organization needs (and possibly even wants) change or innovation. Critics of our education system have suggested that schools encourage dependent, rather than change agent, thinking. If teachers and professors see the students' role as absorbing and applying within prescribed boundaries, rather than raising troubling questions, independent thought and innovative thinking will not be advanced.[3]

Regardless of the above, individuals may find themselves either initiating or responding to factors that cast them into the role of change initiator, implementer, facilitator, and/or task force team member. The exact role may vary over time and will depend on a variety of factors, such as (a) the context in which the change is based; (b) the skills and abilities needed to advance the change; (c) the change agent's skills, abilities, power, and influence; and (d) the characteristics of others who are involved.

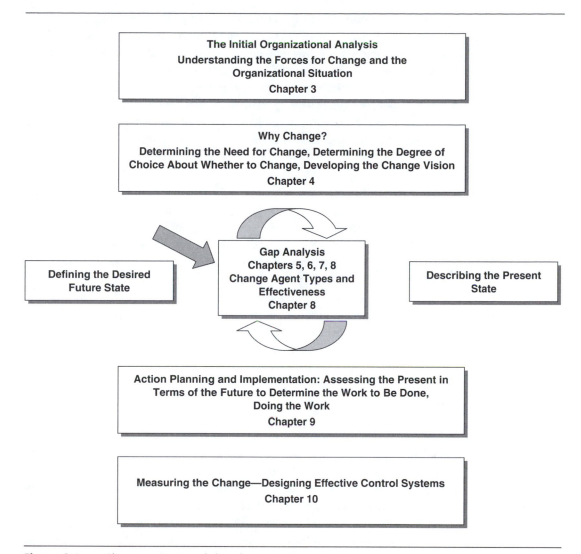

Figure 8.1 Change Agents and the Change Management Process

When adopting a more active change role, it is important to consider what is best for the organization and for you over the intermediate and longer term.

Moving to more active roles is important, because simply providing information or offering armchair solutions seldom produces meaningful change. If either of these approaches did produce change, our organizations would run like well-oiled machines, we would all be psychologically and physically fit, and successful organizational adaptation and renewal would be the norm. To disrupt inertia and drift, change management requires that at least some individuals move from the passive to the active. Those who wish to add value to the organization and make a difference will want to challenge themselves to take on a more active role.

For many, their implicit model of change assumes that they must have the involvement and support of the CEO or some other senior sponsor in an organization before they can create meaningful change. There is no question that if a change initiative has the support, budget, and commitment of a senior change champion, the job is immeasurably easier. However, for many individuals acting from subordinate organizational roles (e.g., technical professionals, first-line and middle managers, frontline staff), the changes they want require them to challenge existing systems and processes, with little in the way of visible support when they begin. To quote Margaret Mead, "Never doubt that a small group of thoughtful, committed individuals can change the world. Indeed, it's the only thing that ever has."[4] The following story describes an influential teacher and shows how a person can make a difference in an unusual way:

> *Reflections on a Teacher:* The teacher that influenced me the most was concerned with our learning and not with the power and influence of the administration. For example, when *Catcher in the Rye* was deemed unfit for our youthful eyes, he informed the class that this book was classed as unsuitable. This teacher reported that the book by J. D. Salinger should be avoided and while it was recognizable because of its red cover with yellow print and found in most bookstores, libraries and magazine stores, we should not seek it out. Later, the same teacher was instructed to black out certain risqué phrases from one of the assigned books for class. Of course, he marched in to the class, described that the phrases on p. 138 lines 7 and 8 were to be blacked out and that he was enlisting the class's help to do the work for him. (Anonymous caller, CBC Radio, January 2004.)

Hamel, in his book *Leading the Revolution,* claims that every "company needs a band of insurrectionists." The revolutionists challenge the rules, break the rules, and take the risks—much as our teacher above. Challenging orthodoxies becomes critical in the drive to keep pace with environmental demands.[5] This example points out that who the champion of change is lies in the eyes of the beholder. The individuals wanting to remove student exposure to the perceived immorality in the books likely thought they were change agents as well.

With the rise in concern for intrapreneurship, innovation, and change in organizations, there has been a shift in valuing change management as an essential part of every good manager's skill set.[6] Change agentry has shifted from "lone ranger," top-down notions of heroic leadership to ones involving leaders who create enabling conditions in which change teams and empowered workers envision change and make it happen[7] and, as Jick points out, "implementing their own changes as well as others."[8] While we might think that change is led from the top, Jick and others dispute this. "Most well-known change initiatives (*that are*) perceived as being "top-down" or led by a senior executive or the CEO, probably started at the bottom or the middle, years earlier."[9]

As Rosabeth Moss Kanter states, real change is the long haul. It "requires people to adjust their behavior and that behavior is often beyond the direct control of top management."[10] Bold strokes easily taken by top management likely do not build the long-term capabilities of the organization, unless they are buttressed by a concerted commitment to an underlying vision. Bold strokes can reduce, reorganize, and merge organizations, but each of these takes a toll on the organization. Unfortunately, the long-term benefits can prove to be illusory if the initiative fails to sustainably embrace the hearts as well as the heads of organization members in ways that generate internal and external environmental congruence.

What Factors Influence Change Agent Success?

The Role of Personal Attributes, Vision, and Situation

Our images of organizational change agents often revolve around personalities that appear to be bigger than life. We think of Jack Welch, formerly of GE, Bill Gates of Microsoft, and Charlotte Beers of eBay. These mythical images also tend to fade quickly when things don't work out—think of Carly Fiorina (H-P) or Paul Tellier (Bombardier). If such grand standards are the benchmarks employed to assess personal qualities and potential as a change agent, most will inevitably fall far short of the mark.

However, history shows us that successful change and being a change agent is more than just the person. In the 1930s, Winston Churchill was a politician in decline. World War II propelled him to greatness as prime minister of Great Britain. When the war began, suddenly his skills and personality matched what was needed, and the British public believed he was uniquely qualified. Similarly, before September 11, 2001, George W. Bush and his presidency appeared to be in trouble. After the terrorist attack, Bush became exceptionally popular with Americans through his strong antiterrorist stands and actions. Neither Churchill nor Bush changed who they were, but the situations they found themselves in permitted them to take actions that changed history and their reputations. This match of person and situation is further highlighted by the fact that Churchill experienced electoral defeat in the postwar environment, despite his enormous popularity during the war. Similarly, George W. Bush's popularity plummeted in the years following the American invasion of Iraq.

In each of these cases, it was the person that mattered, but it was more than the person. It was also the situation, the vision that person had, and the actions they took to build support. Rather than focus solely on the individual, a more robust model for change considers the interaction between personality, vision, and situation. Michael J. Fox provides us with an example of a person who became a change agent supreme in the fight against Parkinson's disease:

> Most people get Parkinson's disease late in life. Michael J. Fox, a television/ movie star, contracted it when he was 30. Before his disease, Fox was focused on his career. Within a year, Fox had created the Fox Foundation that had become an exceptionally effective organization in fund raising and in shaping the research agenda for Parkinson's disease.[11]

Fox's basic personality didn't change with the onset of Parkinson's. But suddenly he was faced with a situation that generated a sense of purpose and vision that both transcended self-interest and captured the attention and emotions of others. This powerful vision was crucial, of course, to Fox's transformation from movie star to change agent. He deployed his energy, interpersonal skills, creativity, and analytic and decision-making skills to pursue this vision. His contacts, profile, and reputation gave him access to an influential board of directors. In record time, he recruited a key executive director and created a foundation that became a funding force. Most important, he chose to act.

The same process of engagement, vision, and action can be seen with Paul Newman. He and a close colleague, A. E. Hotcher, took a salad dressing he liked and made it into "Newman's Own Natural Salad Dressings." This turned into a business that has generated well in excess of $150 million for charity.[12]

In both the above cases, the interaction of the person and the situation, combined with a powerful vision, resulted in that person's becoming a change agent. This can be summarized as

$$\text{Being a Change Agent} = \text{Person} \times \text{Vision} \times \text{Situation}$$

The situation plays a critical role in how you as change agent react. Some situations invigorate and energize the change agent. Enthusiasm builds as coalitions form, and the proposed change gains momentum and seems likely to succeed. Other situations suck energy out of the change agent and seem to lead to a never-ending series of meetings, obstacles, and issues that prevent any sense of progress. Roger Dickout calls the former situations **exothermic** change situations. Here energy is liberated by actions.[13] Conversely, the latter situations he calls **endothermic**. Here the change program consumes energy and arouses opposition, which in turn requires more energy from you, the change agent. Change agents need situations that "liberate the energy to drive the change."[14]

Change agents typically experience both exothermic and endothermic periods in a change process. Initial excitement and discovery are followed by snail-paced progress, setbacks, dead ends, and then perhaps a small victory. . . . The question is, do the agents have the staying power and the ability to manage their energy flows and reserves during this ultra-marathon? Do they have a team to help replenish their energy and keep them going? Or do they run out of energy and give up? Colleagues who serve as close confidants can play an important role in sustaining energy. They help to keep things in perspective and grounded so that the change leader doesn't lose sight of the challenges and pitfalls ahead. While action taking is the defining visible characteristic of change, discussion and reflection play important and often undervalued roles in the development and maintenance of change leaders.[15]

What Are the Characteristics
of Successful Change Leaders?

Are Change Leaders Different
From Change Managers?

While personality and individual skills will not make you a successful change agent, they do matter. This isn't to say that certain skills are sufficient to lead and create change. Rather, the attributes discussed below increase the chances of change happening. Raelin argues that everyone can serve as a leader and that we should dismiss any distinction between managers and leaders.[16] Katzenbach disputes this, claiming that real change leaders are significantly different in their orientation than traditional managers.[17] Critical to Katzenbach's view is a basic mind-set of a "real change leader" who does it, fixes it, tries it, changes it, and does it again—a trial-and-error approach rather than an attempt to optimize and get it perfect the first time.

Doyle talks about potential change agents who lack the level of sophistication in interpersonal and communication skills to be effective.[18] He describes change agents as requiring emotional resilience and tolerance for ethical conflicts and ambiguities. As well, political skills of a high order are essential for success. This political awareness about what needs to be done, political intelligence, according to Kramer, may lead to abrasive, confronting, intimidating behavior.[19] Such challenging behavior may be what is needed to "unfreeze" a complacent organization.

Change agents need a dogged determination to succeed in the face of significant odds. In particular, as Kanter's quote at the beginning of this chapter highlighted, agents need to persist when it looks like things have gone wrong and success appears unlikely.

Change agents also need to focus on the practical—getting it done. They must be ready to modify their plans to pursue new options or divert their energies to different avenues as the change landscape shifts—sometimes because of their actions and sometimes because of others' responses to change pressures. Doggedness is balanced by flexibility and adaptiveness. Time for dialogue and reflection on the change process is needed to give perspective and make informed judgments.[20]

The characteristics of a change agent also include restlessness, dissatisfaction with the status quo, and a willingness to take informed risks to make change happen. It is therefore not surprising to find that openness to experience is an attribute common to many change agents. These individuals embrace change rather than denying it and seeing it as "the enemy." They are constantly scanning the environment, picking up clues and cues that allow them to develop a rich understanding of their organization's situation and the need for change. As the situation shifts, they are aware of those shifts and respond appropriately to them. They make this easier for themselves by ensuring that they are part of networks that will tell them what they need to hear, not what they want to hear. They build these networks through their trustworthiness, credibility, and interpersonal skills (after all, networks don't work for long if others don't feel they are getting value from them). And they are wise enough to remember to never be seen as shooting the messenger. They may dislike the information and disagree with the conclusions, but if messengers believe that the act of communicating will put them at risk, they will alter their behavior accordingly.[21]

Intelligence is a characteristic of change agents.[22] It is needed to engage in needed analysis, to assess possible courses of action, and to create confidence in a proposed plan. In general, one has more confidence in a proposal developed by a bright individual than one brought forward by a dullard. Interpersonal and communications skills are needed to frame proposals effectively. This social dimension is likely why emotional intelligence has also been included in discussions of change agent characteristics.[23]

Caldwell differentiates the attributes of change leaders from those of change managers.[24] Table 8.1 (see p. 251), outlines his view of the differences. His use of the term *change manager* is similar to the differentiation made earlier in this book between change leaders and change implementers or facilitators. Caldwell emphasizes the motivational aspects of vision and risk taking in change leadership. Adaptability and openness are critical aspects of the leader. Change managers, on the other hand, are more concerned about working with others, dealing with resistance, and problem solving. Caldwell argues that "change leaders and managers perform complementary roles . . . the two roles may often be indistinguishable, because the attributes required to lead and manage change are simply inseparable aspects of managerial work in organisations . . . ."[25] Of course, all these attributes may be found in one person. The ones that are crucial depend on the situation.

Toolkit Exercise 8.2 asks you to reflect on your personal attributes.

Many of the behaviors shown in Table 8.1 could be classified into categories of change behaviors: framing behaviors, capacity-creating behaviors, and shaping behaviors.[26] That is, change can be viewed first as framing behaviors: changing the sense of the situation, establishing starting points for change, designing the change journey, and communicating principles. Second, it involves creating the capacity for change by increasing individual and organizational capabilities and creating and communicating connections in the organization. Finally, it can involve shaping what people do by acting as a role model, holding others accountable, thinking about change, and focusing on individuals in the change process. Higgs and Rowland examined such behaviors in a recent study and discovered that "framing change and building capacity are more successful than . . . shaping behavior."[27] They suggest that a shift from a leader-centric, directive approach to a more facilitating, enabling style is appropriate in today's organizations.

How Do We Become a Change Agent?

Developmental Stages

Inexperienced change leaders often believe that their change perspective is "correct" and that somehow those who oppose their change simply do not understand or do not recognize its benefits. To change others' minds, all they need to do is to "explain things better." These change agents lack the insight that multiple perspectives and differing objectives are not only possible but likely. A rational model of the world, while useful, is limiting and incomplete. Experienced change agents, on the other hand, recognize the diverse, pluralistic world they live in and respond accordingly.

While formal study and education are of value in heightening the awareness and skills of would-be change agents, experience is particularly valuable. Bennis describes four rules that he believes change leaders should accept to enhance their self-development:

1. You are your own best teacher.

2. You accept responsibility and blame no one.

Table 8.1   Attributes of Change Leaders and Change Managers

Attributes of Change Leaders	Score out of 100
Inspiring vision	92
Entrepreneurship	87
Integrity and honesty	76
Learning from others	72
Openness to new ideas	66
Risk taking	56
Adaptability and flexibility	49
Creativity	42
Experimentation	38
Using power	29
Attributes of Change Managers	Score out of 100
Empowering others	88
Team building	82
Learning from others	79
Adaptability and flexibility	69
Openness to new ideas	64
Managing resistance	58
Conflict resolution	53
Networking	52
Knowledge of the business	37
Problem solving	29

Source: Caldwell asked experts to rank these attributes according to whether they are attributes of change leaders or change managers. See Caldwell, R. (2003). Change leaders and change managers: Different or complementary? *Leadership and Organization Development Journal,* (*24*)5, 285–293.

3. You can learn anything you want to learn.

4. True understanding comes from reflection on your experience.[28]

The fundamental message from Bennis rests in the importance of taking responsibility for your own learning and development as a change leader. Take risks, try, accept responsibility, and then take the time to reflect carefully on the experience. The assumption made by inexperienced change agents, "that my logic is the right logic," can result from a lack of reflection on their experiences.

David Miller argues that change leadership skills can be developed. Individuals progress through stages of beliefs about change, increasing in their complexity and sophistication.[29] See Table 8.2 (p. 253) for an outline of his belief stages. He believes that movement from Stage 1 (Novice) to Stage 2 (Junior) or 3 (Experienced) might be learned vicariously—by observing others or by studying change—but movement to Stage 4 (Expert) requires living with a change project and suffering the frustrations, surprises, and resistance that come with the territory. Stage 1, or novice, change managers assume a rational model. They believe that if things are explained better, everyone will then understand and agree. At Stage 2, managers think that recipients of change need to be convinced of the change. Thus, they believe that powerful communications will influence recipients and lead to the desired change. By Stage 3, change managers recognize the differing perspectives of others and then devise plans to deal with those differences. However, they do not recognize that they may need to modify their beliefs to achieve the buy-in of others. Finally, at Stage 4, expert change managers understand the complexity of change situations and work with others to achieve fundamental change—change that is likely different from the original plan because it incorporates others' views.

Discussions with change agents confirm the premise of Miller's stages. People new to change (particularly those trained in areas where they expect right and wrong answers to objective data such as engineering and the sciences) seem to believe that they need only to explain rationally their ideas to others, and those others will be struck by a flash of insight and convert immediately. Seldom does it work that way! More often, change is a complex, shifting kaleidoscope of perceptions and events. Skilled change agents tap into these patterns and recognize how to use them to facilitate change and to involve others in those change initiatives. There is evidence that these change agent skills and competencies can be acquired through the systematic use of developmental assignments in this area.[30] Toolkit Exercise 8.3 will help you assess your maturity level as a change agent.

What Types of Change Leaders Exist?

Regardless of the change agents' skills, their ability to sense and interpret significant environmental shifts is of particular importance. Part of such ability comes from the deep study of a field or industry. As well, some might have the intuition to understand significant changes in the environment by their ability to detect and interpret underlying patterns.[31]

For example, Glegg Water Treatment Services was an entrepreneurial organization that grew at a compound growth rate of 20%–25 % per year for more than 15 years. The executives of this organization had developed a clear and strong vision for their organization ("pure water for the world"). They used this vision to pull the organization in the direction they wanted. At the same time, they were tough, realistic analyzers of their situation. They used whatever data they could find to provide a sophisticated understanding of the organization's situation. They used this analysis to convince others and push them into accepting the needed changes. They were truly committed to growing their company. Also striking were the alternative periods of continuous growth and change and strategic leaps into new areas. Three times in their history, the

Table 8.2   Miller's Stages of Change Beliefs

Stage	Description
Stage	*Description*
Stage 1 Novice	Beliefs: People will change once they understand the logic of the change. People can be told to change. As a result, clear communication is key to change.
	Underlying is the assumption that people are rational and will follow their self-interest once it is revealed to them. Alternately, power and sanctions will ensure compliance.
Stage 2 Junior	Beliefs: People change through powerful communication and symbolism. Change planning will include the use of symbols and group meetings.
	Underlying is the assumption that people will change if they are "sold" on the beliefs. Again, failing this, the organization can use power and/or sanctions.
Stage 3 Experienced	Beliefs: People may not be willing or able or ready to change. As a result, change leaders will enlist specialists to design a change plan, and the leaders will work at change but resist modifying their own vision.
	Underlying is the assumption that the ideal state is where people will become committed to change. Otherwise, power and sanctions must be used.
Stage 4 Expert	Beliefs: People have a limited capacity to absorb change and may not be as willing, able, or ready to change as you wish. Thinking through how to change the people is central to the implementation of change.
	Underlying is the assumption that commitment for change must be built and that power or sanctions have major limitations in achieving change and building organizational capacity.

Adapted from Miller, D. (2001). Successful change leaders. *Journal of Change Management,* (*2*)4, 383.

leadership of the organization forecast a decline in growth rates in what the organization was doing, so they shifted totally into new, but related, areas. For example, the organization delivered water treatment systems for power industries. As that market matured, the organization shifted to producing higher-quality water systems for computer makers. Eight years later they shifted to a new membrane technology that permitted integrated systems to be sold.[32]

Glegg was able to guide his organization through several major environmental shifts. A similar pattern has been observed in the revitalization initiatives of General Motors that began in the early 1990s under Jack Smith, when the firm was teetering on financial collapse.

What is really grabbing the attention of the analysts is that fact that GM is making progress across a broad front. Financially it is easing the burden of its pension liabilities . . . it has plenty of new products in the pipeline; it is catching up on Japanese standards in terms of both productivity and quality; and morale has picked up, helped by the remarkable recovery of the flagship Cadillac brand . . .

Smith, who became chief executive and then chairman in the firm's darkest hour in the early 1990s, patiently set about establishing the means for GM's recovery. He built a youngish executive team around his protégé Mr. Wagoner, who succeeded him as chairman last May. Mr. Wagoner duly brought in Bob Lutz, a 70-year-old industry veteran with a glittering career at Ford, Chrysler, and BMW, in both America and Europe, to shake things up.

The result has been an overhaul of its cautious, cumbersome committee-style management. Decisions on everything from new designs and new products to plant closures are now taken rapidly and efficiently. There is a feeling of confidence around.[33]

What is significant is the organization's ability to anticipate strategic shifts, manage that order of change, *and* continuously improve and grow between these significant changes. The levels of skill required to manage in all of these different situations are of a high order. Maintaining this is difficult. This is shown by GM's 2005 financial reports where questions are raised about its ability to manage strategic change and continuous improvement in ways that will produce the desired results.[34] The more recent move to link with Renault and Nissan is another intriguing strategic move by GM to adapt.[35]

Much of the change literature differentiates between incremental or continuous change and strategic or episodic change.[36] Episodic change is change that is "infrequent, discontinuous, and intentional." Episodic change follows Lewin's model that was outlined in Chapter 2 (unfreeze, change, and refreeze). Continuous change is change that is "ongoing, evolving, and cumulative." Weick and Quinn suggest that the appropriate model here is "freeze, rebalance, and unfreeze." That is, change agents need to capture the underlying patterns and dynamics (freeze the conceptual understanding), reinterpret, relabel (reframe and rebalance those understandings), and resume improvisation and learning (unfreeze).[37] Further, Weick and Quinn suggest that the role of the change agent shifts depending on the type of change. Episodic change needs a prime-mover change agent—one who creates change. Continuous change needs a change agent who is more of a sense maker, able to redirect the organization.

Change agents can act in "pull" or "push" ways. Pull actions by change agents create attractions that draw willing organization members to change. Often we can characterize these actions in terms of organizational vision or higher-order purposes and strategy. Push actions, on the other hand, tend to be more data based and factual and are communicated in ways that advance analytic thinking and reasoning (which pushes the recipient's thinking in new directions), or they may involve the use of legitimate, positional, and reward and punishment power in ways that change the dynamics of the situation.[38]

Table 8.3 outlines a model that relates the motivational actions of the change agent (analytical push versus emotional pull) to the degree of change needed by the organization (strategic versus incremental). The model identifies four change agent types: (1) the emotional champion, (2) the intuitive adapter, (3) the developmental strategist, and (4) the continuous improver. Some change agents will tend to act true to their type, due to the nature of their personalities and predispositions. Others will move beyond their preferences and develop greater flexibility in the range of approaches at their disposal. As a result, they are able to adopt a more contingent approach to change, modifying their approach to reflect the situation and the people involved.

The **emotional champion** has a clear and powerful vision of what the organization needs and uses that vision to capture the hearts and motivations of organization members. An organization often needs an emotional champion when there is a dramatic shift in the environment and the organization's structures, systems, and sense of direction are inadequate. To be an emotional champion means that the change agent foresees a new future, understands the deep gap between the organization and that future, can articulate a powerful vision that gives hope that the gap can be overcome, and has a high order of persuasion skills.

Characteristics of the Emotional Champion

- Is comfortable with ambiguity and risk
- Thinks tangentially

Table 8.3   Change Agent Types

Strategic Change & Incremental Change
Versus Vision Pull & Analysis Push

Source: Copyright: T. Cawsey, 2004.

- Challenges accepted ways of doing things
- Has strong intuitive abilities
- Relies on feelings and emotions to influence others

The **intuitive adapter** has the clear vision for the organization and uses that vision to reinforce a culture of learning and adaptation. Often the vision will seem less dramatic or powerful because the organization is aligned with its environment, and the change agent's role is to ensure that the organization stays on track. The change agent develops a culture of learning and continuous improvement where employees constantly test their actions against the vision.

Characteristics of the Intuitive Adapter

- Tends to embrace more moderate risks and engages in a more limited search for solutions
- Is comfortable with the current direction that the vision offers
- Relies on intuition and emotion to persuade others to propel the organization forward through incremental changes

The **developmental strategist** applies rational analysis to understanding the competitive logic of the organization and how it no longer fits with the organization's existing strategy. He sees how to alter structures and processes to shift the organization to the new alignment and eliminate the major gap between the organization and the environment's demands.

Characteristics of the Developmental Strategist

- Engages in big-picture thinking about strategic change and the fit between the environment and the organization
- Sees organizations in terms of systems and structures fitting into logical integrated components that fit (or don't) with environmental demands
- Is comfortable with assessing risk and taking significant chances based on a thorough assessment of the situation

The **continuous improver** analyzes micro-environments and seeks changes such as reengineering to systems and processes. The organization in this category is reasonably well aligned with its environment and is in an industry where complex systems and processes provide for improvement opportunities.

Characteristics of the Continuous Improver

- Is able to think logically and carefully about detailed processes and how they can be improved
- Thinks in terms of possible gains rather than great leaps
- Is systematic in his thinking while making careful gains

Note that all types of change agents could be needed, depending on the situation faced. One organization may change through a charismatic leader who pulls people into a new way of doing things. Another may engage in detailed strategic planning and dramatically shift its focus based on careful analysis. A third might transform itself over time, developing into an excellent learning organization through a focus on excellence and improvement. Finally, a fourth might engage in reengineering of systems and processes in order to change itself. All are potentially viable strategies, depending on the needs and situation of the organization.

Change agents will have their preferred styles, but, as noted earlier, some will be more able to adapt their approach and credibly use other styles, as the situation demands it. By being aware of your current level of flexibility and adaptiveness in this area, you will be in a position to undertake initiatives that will assist in the development of your capacity to adapt your approach to the situation. Alternatively, if you're concerned about your own capacity to respond, you can choose to ally with others who possess the style that a particular situation demands.

Flexibility in style will also make it easier for you to communicate with others in the organization. If you know that someone tends to be more receptive when information is data based and detailed, then communications can be tailored accordingly. For example, think about a president implementing a change that involves a major expansion. They may use their chief financial officer to talk with analysts and bankers about the financing of a proposed change. This would be different than how the sales and marketing vice president would address the change with his staff.

In Chapter 1, we briefly discussed the preferences of adaptors (those with an orientation toward incremental change) and innovators (those who prefer more radical or transformational change).[39] Kirton's work with these two orientations points out that individuals tend to have clear preferences in their orientation and sometimes fail to recognize the value present in the alternative approach to change, focusing instead on what they are most comfortable with. When this occurs, there may be an inappropriate fit of approach with the situation or the people involved. Alternatively, when individuals with both preferences are present, this can lead to disagreement and conflict concerning how best to proceed. While constructive disagreement and debate concerning alternatives is valuable, managers need to avoid dysfunctional personal attacks and defensive behavior. This again points to the importance of developing greater awareness of the different change styles and the benefits of personal flexibility. When managers lack the needed orientation and style, they need access to allies with the requisite skills. Toolkit Exercise 8.4 asks you to consider your preferences and helps you to determine your change agent style.

What Are the Differences Between Internal and External Change Agents?

Many organizations expect their managers to develop skills as change agents. As a result, those managers need to improve their understanding of internal change agent roles and strategies. Internal organization members need to learn the team-building, negotiating, influencing, and other change management skills that they need to become effective facilitators. They need to move beyond technical skills, from being the person with the answer to being the person with process management skills—the person who helps the organization find the answers and handle the complex and multivariate nature of reality it faces.[40]

Hunsaker suggests four different internal roles a change agent can play: (1) catalyst, (2) solution giver, (3) process helper, and (4) resource linker.[41] The **catalyst** is needed to overcome inertia and focus the organization on the problems faced. The **solution giver** knows how to respond and can solve the problem. The key here, of course, is having your ideas accepted. The **process helper** facilitates the "how to" of change, playing the role of third-party intervener often. Finally, the **resource linker** brings people and resources together in ways that aid in the solution of issues. All four roles are important, and knowing them provides a checklist of optional strategies for the internal change agent.

Often organizations use external change agents or consultants to promote change, as they can bring technical change management expertise to the change team. Consultants can provide a more objective external perspective on the change and can gain access to organization members in different ways than can insiders.

The risks of hiring consultants are that they often come with prepackaged solutions and are insensitive to the organization's culture or needs. The provision of ready-made answers not based in specific organizational research can be frustrating. Nevertheless, one study reports that 83% of organizations that used consultants reported they would use them again.[42]

Consultants can provide subject matter expertise and give credibility to a project that insiders might not have. However, it is crucial that line managers retain responsibility for decision making and not allow it to shift to the consultant.

External change agents can bring fresh perspectives and ideas that have worked elsewhere. Too often internal organization members are tied to the status quo unless faced with demands for dramatic change. Outsiders can avoid these traps.[43] Much can be learned from the pretested systems and procedures that others have used. At the same time, outsiders lack the deep knowledge of the political environment and culture of the organization. As a result, some organizations are moving to using change teams that embody both of these perspectives.

Change Agents and Change Teams

Often change management means the use of teams to effect change. Organizational downsizing and the increasing interest in the use of self-managed teams as an organizing approach for flattened hierarchies and cross-functional initiatives have spurred this along.[44] Teams involve people and give them the space and time to adjust their views and/or influence the change process. It moves them out of the recipient of change role to a more active and engaged one. Worren suggests that teams are important in that "employees learn new behaviors and attitudes by participating in ad-hoc teams solving real business problems.[45]

Further, he argues that as the change agent becomes immersed in the change, the role shifts from facilitator and process consultant to content expert and member of a cross-functional team as well as process consultant.[46] To this, Appelbaum and his colleagues would add the particular importance of conflict facilitation, including confrontation and the development of new agreements through dialogue and negotiation.[47]

In a benchmarking study focused on the best practices in change management, Prosci describes a good change management team member as follows:

- Being knowledgeable about the business and enthusiastic about the change
- Possessing excellent communications skills, willing to listen and share
- Having total commitment to the project, the process, and the results
- Able to remain open-minded and visionary
- Respected within the organization as an apolitical catalyst for strategic change[48]

Some of these appear contradictory. For example, it is tricky to be both totally committed and open-minded simultaneously. Nevertheless, we often find paradoxical or apparently contradictory characteristics being displayed simultaneously by skilled change managers. Keeping these paradoxes in mind helps us to both respond to and avoid difficulty. For example, the need to be both joined with and yet separate from other members of the change team in order to maintain independence of perspective and judgment is a difficult balance to maintain.[49] We see the ability to manage the paradox of commitment to stay the course with open-mindedness in Bill Gates of Microsoft. It is visible in his U-turn to strategically embrace Internet technology in 1995[50] and the shift in his corporate role from CEO to chairman and chief software architect in 2000.

Indeed, unlike other top brass who stubbornly cling to old models in the face of change, Gates is quick to learn from mistakes and embrace shifts in the marketplace. "Bill was a lifelong learner before the word became popularized. This is what makes him such an amazing guy—he is constantly coming up with new ideas, new approaches, challenging others to think outside the box," says Steve Ballmer, Microsoft CEO. "He could've sat back five or 10 years ago and said, 'OK, I've created this amazing company. I think I'll take up golf now.' But that's not the kind of person Bill is. He still is deeply committed to Microsoft and still puts in long hours here."

Microsoft's significant restructuring in 2000, when Ballmer took over as CEO, and early in 2001, when Rick Belluzzo was named president, were difficult but wise moves for Gates. "You've got to give him credit for learning to delegate, which is hard for anyone to do who has run a company for 25 years," says David Yoffie, a professor at Harvard Business School.[51]

Gates was able to develop his team in spite of a strong personality. Working with and in teams and task forces is a baseline skill for change managers. They must not only achieve the change, but they must bring the team along so that the team accepts and is enthusiastic about the change. Some believe that this requires individuals who are adept at reducing stress and strain in the team, but once again, the most effective response will depend on the needs of the situation. As an example, we can turn again to Bill Gates. While he is not known for his social skills, his capacities in the areas of vision, attracting talent and motivation of those highly talented individuals, are well recognized.

Gates rarely indulges in water-cooler bantering and social niceties that put people at ease. But while Microsoft's chairman and chief software architect is not considered a warm, affable person, he is an effective hands-on manager, says one former employee. "Bill is an exceptional motivator. For as much as he does not like small talk, he loves working with people on matters of substance," says Scott Langmack, a former Microsoft marketing manager.[52]

More recently, Gates announced that he will cease full-time work at Microsoft in order to focus on his charitable foundations.[53] His team will need to manage this transition. Teams are essential components in making change happen. Chapter 9 includes further information on using change teams. The boxed insert below describes how Federal Express systematically develops a team approach to change. Toolkit Exercise 8.5 asks you to consider your skills as a member of a change team.

Developing Change Teams at Federal Express[54]

Federal Express has developed a checklist for using change teams.

1. To ensure that everybody who has a contribution to make is fully involved, those who will have to make any change are identified and included.

2. To convince people that their involvement is serious and not a management ploy, all ideas from management are presented as "rough" ideas.

3. To ensure commitment to making any change work, the team members identify and develop "what is in it for them" when they move to make the idea work.

4. To increase the success rate for new ideas, potential and actual problems that have to be solved are identified in a problem-solving, not blame-fixing, culture.

5. To deliver the best solutions, problem-solving teams self-select to find answers to the barriers to successful implementation.

6. To maintain momentum and enthusiasm, the remainder of the team continue to work on refining the basic idea.

7. Problem solutions are presented, improved where necessary, approved, and implementation is begun at once.

8. The rough idea is refined, agreed upon, and the implementation process is planned.

Source: Adapted from Lamber, T. (2006). *Insight.* MENAFN.Com

Rules of Thumb for Change Agents

How should managers act as change agents? Several authors have proposed useful insights and wisdom from their experiences and analysis of change leaders. These guidelines, which we have integrated, combined, and added to, are listed below:[55]

• Stay Alive—"Dead" change agents are of no use to the organization. The notion that you should sacrifice yourself at the altar of change is absurd unless you truly wish it. At the same time, the invocation to "stay alive" says you need to be in touch with those things that energize you and give you purpose.

• Start Where the System Is—Immature change agents start where they are. Experienced change agents diagnose the system, understand it, and begin with the system.

• Never Work Uphill—Work with people in the system in a collaborative fashion. Don't challenge or alienate people if at all possible. Work in promising areas and make progress.

• Don't Overorganize—Plans will change. If you are too organized, you risk becoming committed to your plan in ways that don't permit the inclusion and involvement of others.

• Don't Argue if You Can't Win—Win-lose strategies deepen conflict and should be avoided wherever possible. The maxim "If you strike a king, strike to kill" fits here. If you can't complete the job, you may not survive.

• Load Experiments for Success—If you can, set up the situation and position it as positively as possible. Change is difficult at the best of times—if you can improve the odds, you should!

• Light Many Fires—High-visibility projects often attract both attention and opposition. Work within the organizational subsystems to create opportunities for change in many places, not just a major initiative.

• Just Enough Is Good Enough—Don't wait for perfection. Beta test your ideas. Get them out there and see how they work and how people react.

• You Can't Make a Difference Without Doing Things Differently—Remember that definition of insanity—"doing things the same way but expecting different results!" You have to act and behave differently to have things change. Hope is not an action.

• Want to Change—Focus on Important Results and Get Them—Not only does success breed success, but getting important results bring resources, influence, and credibility.

• Think Fast and Act Fast—Speed and flexibility are critical. Sensing the situation and reacting quickly will make a difference. Acting first means others will have to act second and will always be responding to your initiatives.

• Create a Coalition—Lone-ranger operatives are easy to dismiss. As Gary Hamel says, an "army of like-minded activists cannot be ignored."

Does Everyone Need to Be a Change Agent?

Increasingly, successful organization members will find that they need to act as change agents in their organizations. As Katzenbach suggests, the real change leader will take action—do things, try them out, and then do it again while getting better.[56]

Although this book applauds this type of initiative, remember the first rule for change agents (from above): *"Stay Alive."*

At the same time, virtually all managers will operate from the middle of the organization. That is, they will have those above attempting to direct or influence change while finding themselves trying to influence those superiors about what needs to be initiated and how best to proceed. At other times, managers will need to deal with subordinates, those who will be on the receiving end of the change, or who are themselves trying to initiate activities.

Oshry recognized the feelings of powerlessness that many of us feel when operating in the "middle" and outlined strategies for increasing one's power in these situations.[57] Problem ownership is one of the key issues. Far too often managers insert themselves in the middle of a dispute and take on others' issues as their own when, in fact, intervention is not helpful. As well, when the issue is the managers, they may refuse to use their power. They need to take responsibility, make a decision, and move on. Or they need to refuse to accept unreasonable demands from above and attempt to work matters out rather than simply acquiesce and create greater problems below. Oshry's advice to those in the middle is to do the following:

1. "Be top when you can and take responsibility for being top."

2. "Be bottom when you should." Don't let problems just flow through you to subordinates.

3. "Be coach," to help others solve their own problems so they don't become yours.

4. "Facilitate" rather than simply carry messages when you find yourself running back and forth between two parties who are in conflict.

5. "Integrate with one another" so that you develop a strong peer group that you can turn to for advice, guidance, and support.

Whether a manager acts using logic, participation, or on his or her own,[58] the message is clear: Managers are increasingly being held accountable for either taking action or helping to make change happen. Scanning the environment, figuring out what will make things better, and creating initiatives are the new rules for today's managers. This text argues that any change agent role—initiator, implementer, facilitator, or team member—is preferable to constantly finding yourself in the role of change recipient. A strategy of passively keeping one's head down and avoiding change means that the person is increasing their career risk because they will be less likely to be perceived as adding value.

Summary

This chapter describes how anyone, from any position in the organization, can potentially instigate change. It argues that becoming a change agent is a matter of who you are, your personality, but it is also a function of the situation and the vision that the change agent has. Change managers and change leaders are differentiated, and the stages of development of change agents are outlined. Four types of change leaders are described: the emotional champion, the intuitive adapter, the continuous improver, and the developmental strategist. Internal change agent roles are discussed and the use of change teams is introduced. Finally, we provide summary advice from previous experts in the field and suggest that managers all have a role to play in promoting change.

The management of change is an essential part of the role of those who want to manage and lead. It will tax a manager's skills, energize and challenge, exhaust, and depress, occasionally exhilarate, and leave managers with a profound sense of accomplishment. What it will not do is leave those managers the same person that they were.

The demands of organizations are clear: Managers are expected to play an increasingly more significant role in the management of change. Earlier this book advised managers to know themselves, assess the situation carefully, and then **take action**. The next chapter outlines action planning to assist managers in this.

Glossary of Terms

Change Agent Effectiveness—The effectiveness of a change agent is a function of the person, his or her vision, and the characteristics of the situation.

Change Leader—A **change leader** pulls people to change through the use of a powerful change vision.

Change Manager—A **change manager** creates change by working with others, overcoming resistance, and problem solving situations.

Developmental Stages of a Change Agent—Change agents can develop their change skills from a novice stage to an expert stage through successful experiences with increasingly complex, sophisticated change situations.

Types of Change Leaders—Four types of change leaders (emotional champion, intuitive adapter, developmental strategist, and continuous improver) can be identified through (a) their use of vision (pull) methods versus analytical (push) methods and (b) their orientation to change: strategic versus incremental.

Internal Change Agent—An **internal change agent** is an employee of the organization who knows the organization intimately and is attempting to create change.

External Change Agent—An **external change agent** is a person from outside the organization trying to make changes. Often this person is an outside expert and consultant.

Change Team—The **change team** is the group of employees, usually from a cross-section of the organization, who is charged with a change task.

END-OF-CHAPTER EXERCISES

TOOLKIT EXERCISE 8.1

The Interaction of Vision and Situation With Who You Are

Later in this chapter, we will explore the behaviors and attributes common to many change agents. This exercise is to have you think of your personal situation to consider why, where, and when you might become more of a change agent.

1. What purposes do you consider vital? That is, what visions do you follow for which you would make significant personal sacrifices? Review your understanding of vision from Chapter 3.

2. For many of us, there are no visions that are as powerful as we describe above. What would be a vision that could catapult you into persistent, committed, and even sacrificial (by normal standards) action?

3. How does the situation you find yourself in affect your desire to become a change agent? Think through the understanding of organizational change that you developed in Chapters 4, 5, and 6.

TOOLKIT EXERCISE 8.2

Myself as Change Agent

The following list of change agent attributes and skills represents an amalgam drawn from the previous section. Rate yourself on the following dimensions:

Attributes of Change Leaders From Caldwell	*Low* 1	2	3	4	5	6	*High* 7
Inspiring vision	1	2	3	4	5	6	7
Entrepreneurship	1	2	3	4	5	6	7
Integrity and honesty	1	2	3	4	5	6	7
Learning from others	1	2	3	4	5	6	7
Openness to new ideas	1	2	3	4	5	6	7
Risk taking	1	2	3	4	5	6	7
Adaptability and flexibility	1	2	3	4	5	6	7
Creativity	1	2	3	4	5	6	7
Experimentation	1	2	3	4	5	6	7
Using power	1	2	3	4	5	6	7
Attributes of Change Managers From Caldwell	*Low* 1	2	3	4	5	6	*High* 7
Empowering others	1	2	3	4	5	6	7
Team building	1	2	3	4	5	6	7
Learning from others	1	2	3	4	5	6	7
Adaptability and flexibility	1	2	3	4	5	6	7
Openness to new ideas	1	2	3	4	5	6	7
Managing resistance	1	2	3	4	5	6	7

Conflict resolution	1	2	3	4	5	6	7
Networking skills	1	2	3	4	5	6	7
Knowledge of the business	1	2	3	4	5	6	7
Problem solving	1	2	3	4	5	6	7
Change Agent Attributes Suggested by Others	Low 1	2	3	4	5	6	High 7
Interpersonal skills	1	2	3	4	5	6	7
Communication skills	1	2	3	4	5	6	7
Emotional resilience	1	2	3	4	5	6	7
Tolerance for ambiguity	1	2	3	4	5	6	7
Tolerance for ethical conflict	1	2	3	4	5	6	7
Political skill	1	2	3	4	5	6	7
Persistence	1	2	3	4	5	6	7
Determination	1	2	3	4	5	6	7
Pragmatism	1	2	3	4	5	6	7
Dissatisfaction with the status quo	2	3	4	5	6	7	
Openness to information	1	2	3	4	5	6	7
Flexibility and adaptiveness	1	2	3	4	5	6	7
Capacity to build trust	1	2	3	4	5	6	7
Intelligence	1	2	3	4	5	6	7
Emotional intelligence	1	2	3	4	5	6	7

1. Do you see yourself as scoring "high" on those items compared to others? If so, we think you are more likely to be comfortable in a change agent role. Lack of these attributes and skills does not mean you could not be a change agent; it just means that it will be more difficult and it may suggest areas for development.

2. Are you more likely to be comfortable in a change leadership role at this time, or does the role of change manager or implementer seem more suited to who you are?

3. Ask a mentor or friend to provide you feedback on the same dimensions. Does the feedback confirm your self-assessment? If not, why not?

TOOLKIT EXERCISE 8.3

Your Development as a Change Agent

Novice change leaders often picture themselves as in the "right" and those that oppose them are somehow "wrong." This certainty gives them energy and the will to persist in the face of such opposition. It sets up a dynamic of opposition—the more they resist, the more I must try to change them, and so I persuade them more, put more pressure on them, and perhaps resort to whatever power I have to force change.

Think of a situation where someone held a different viewpoint than yours. What were your assumptions about that person? Did you believe they just didn't get it, were wrong-headed, perhaps a bit stupid?

Or did you ask yourself, why would they hold the position they have? If I assume they are as rational and as competent as I am, why would they think as they do? Think back to Table 8.2. Are you at Stage 1, 2, 3, or 4?

Are you able to put yourself in the shoes of the resister? Ask yourself, what forces play on that person? What beliefs do they have? What criteria are they using when they evaluate the situation? (You might wish to refer to our chapter on stakeholder analysis to explore this further.)

What are the implications of your self-assessment with respect to what you need to do to develop yourself as a change agent?

TOOLKIT EXERCISE 8.4

What Is Your Change Agent Preference?

1. How comfortable are you with risk and ambiguity? Do you seek order and stability or change and uncertainty? Think of your level of comfort in higher-risk situations. Think of your degree of restlessness with routine, predictable situations.

2. How intuitive are you? Do you use feelings and emotion to influence others? Or are you logical and systematic? Do you persuade through facts and arguments?

3. Ask a significant other to reflect on your preferences and style. Does their judgment agree or disagree with yours? Why? What data does each have?

4. Given your responses to the above, how would you classify yourself? Which of the following are you?

   - An emotional champion
   - An intuitive adapter
   - A developmental strategist
   - A continuous improver

5. How flexible or adaptive are you with respect to the approach you use? Do you always adopt the same type, or do you use other approaches, depending on the needs of the situation? Which ones do you feel comfortable and competent in using? Again, check out your self-assessment by asking a significant other for their comments.

TOOLKIT EXERCISE 8.5

Your Skills as a Change Team Member

1. Think of a time when you participated in a team. How well did the team perform? Were the results positive? Why or why not?

2. Review the list developed by Prosci. Did the team members exhibit the characteristics listed by Prosci? Did you? Why or why not?

3. What personal focus do you have? Do you tend to concentrate on getting the job done—a task focus? Or do you worry about bringing people along—a process focus?

4. How could you improve your skills in this area? Who might help you develop such skills?

Notes

1. Dover, P. A. (2003). Change agents at work: Lessons from Siemens Nixdorf. *Journal of Change Management,* (*3*)3, 243–257.

2. Lattman, P. (2005, March). Rebound. *Forbes,* (*175*)6, 58.

3. Kremer, J., & McGuinness, C. (1998). Cutting the cord: Student-led discussion groups in higher education. *Education and Training,* (*40*)2–3, 44–49.

4. Mead, M. Quote reported in Webster's Online Dictionary—The Rosetta Edition, www.websters-online-dictionary org.

5. Mass, J. (2000, Fall). Leading the revolution. *Sloan Management Review,* (*42*)1, 95.

6. Zaccaro, S. J., & Banks, S. (2004). Leader visioning and adaptability: Bridging the gap between research and practice on developing the ability to manage change. *Human Resource Management,* (*43*)4, 367–380.

7. Huey, J. (1994, February 21). The new post-heroic leadership. *Fortune,* (*129*)4, 42 (5 pages).

8. Jick, T., & Peiperl, M. (2003). *Managing change: Cases and concepts* (p. 362). New York: McGraw-Hill/Irwin.

9. Tandon, N. (2003). The young change agents. In T. Jick & M. Peiperl, *Managing change: Cases and concepts* (p. 428). New York: McGraw-Hill/Irwin.

10. Kanter, R, M. (2003). The enduring skills of change leaders. In T. Jick & M. Peiperl, *Managing change: Cases and concepts* (p. 429). New York: McGraw-Hill/Irwin.

11. Hammonds, K, (2001, November). Change agents: Michael J. Fox & Deborah Brooks. *Fast Company,* 52, 106.

12. Frank, J. N. (2004). Newman's Own serves up a down-home public image. *PRweek,* (*7*)5, 10.

13. Dickout, R. (1997). All I ever needed to know about change management I learned at engineering school. *The McKinsey Quarterly,* 2, 114–121.

14. Dickout, op. cit., p. 119.

15. Francis, H. (2003). Teamworking and change: Managing the contradictions. *Human Resource Management Journal,* (*13*)3, 71–90.

16. Chilton, S. (2004). Book review of *Creating leaderful organisations: How to bring out leadership in everyone,* by J. Raelin. *Journal of Organizational Change Management,* (*17*)1, 110.

17. Katzenbach, J. R. (1996). Real change. *The McKinsey Quarterly,* 1, 148–163.

18. Doyle, M. (2003). From change novice to change expert. *Personnel Review,* (*31*)4, 465–481.

19. Kramer, R. M. (2006, February). The great intimidators. *Harvard Business Review,* 88–96.

20. Francis, op. cit., p. 85.

21. Much of this is drawn from Jick, op. cit., Module 5.

22. Ilies, R., Gerhardt, M. W., & Le, H. (2004). Individual differences in leadership emergence: Integrating meta-analytic findings and behavioral genetics estimates. *International Journal of Selection and Assessment,* (*12*)3, 207.

23. Leban, W., & Zulauf, C. (2004). Linking emotional intelligence abilities and transformational leadership styles. *Leadership and Organization Development Journal,* (*25*)7–8, 554.

24. Caldwell, R. (2003). Change leaders and change managers: Different or complementary? *Leadership & Organization Development Journal,* (*24*)5, 285–293.

25. Caldwell, op. cit., p. 291.

26. Higgs, M., & Rowland, D. (2005, June). All changes great and small: Exploring approaches to change and its leadership. *Journal of Change Management,* (*5*)2, 121–151.

27.   Higgs & Rowland, op. cit., p. 147.

28.   Bennis, W. (1989). As reported in S. Komives et al. (1998), *Exploring leadership* (p. 109). San Francisco: Jossey-Bass.

29.   Miller, D. (2001). Successful change leaders: What makes them? What do they do that is different? *Journal of Change Management, (2)*4, 383.

30.   Zaccaro, S. J., & Banks, D. (2004). Leader visioning and adaptability: Bridging the gap between research and practice on developing the ability to manage change. *Human Resource Management, (43)*4, 367–380.

31.   Patton, J. R. (2003). Intuition in decisions. *Management Decision, (41)*10, 989–996.

32.   Personal communication with the authors.

33.   Cadillac comeback. (2004, January 22). *The Economist, (370)*8359, 61–63.

34.   Taylor, A., III. (2005, April 4). GM hits the skids. *Fortune, (151)*7, 71.

35.   http://www.msnbc.msn.com/id/13630565/

36.   Nadler, D., & Tushman, M. (1989). Organizational frame bending. *Academy of Management Executive, (3)*3, 194–204.

37.   Weick, K., & Quinn, R. (1999). Organizational change and development. *Ann. Rev. Psychol,* 50, 366.

38.   McAdam, R., McLean, J., & Henderson, J. (2003). The strategic "pull" and operational "push" of total quality management in UK regional electricity service companies. *International Journal of Quality & Reliability Management, (20)*4–5, 436–457.

39.   Kirton, M. J. (1984). Adaptors and innovators—why new initiatives get blocked. *Long Range Planning, (17)*2, 137–143; Tushman, M. L., & O'Reilly, C. A., III. (1996). Ambidextrous organizations: Managing evolutionary and revolutionary change. *California Management Review, (38)*4, 8–30.

40.   Saka, A. (2003). Internal change agents' view of the management of change problem. *Journal of Organizational Change Management, (16)*5, 480–497.

41.   Hunsaker, P. (1982, September-October). Strategies for organizational change: The role of the inside change agent. *Personnel,* 18–28.

42.   Prosci Benchmarking Report. (2000). *Best practices in change management.*

43.   Saka, op. cit., p. 489.

44.   Appelbaum, S., Bethune, M., & Tannenbaum, R. (1999). Downsizing and the emergence of self managed teams. *Participation and Empowerment: An International Journal, (7)*5, 109–130.

45.   Worren, N., et al. (1999, September). From organizational development to change management: The emergence of a new profession. *Journal of Applied Behavioral Science,* 277.

46.   Worren, ibid., Table 2.

47.   Appelbaum et al., op. cit.

48.   Prosci Benchmarking Report. (2000). *Best practices in change management* (p. 12).

49.   Kahn, W. A., (2004). Facilitating and undermining organizational change: A case study. *Journal of Applied Behavioral Science, (40)*1, 7–30.

50.   Wines, L. (1996). Bill Gates: U-turn on the information superhighway. *Journal of Business Strategy, (17)*5, 34.

51.   Rooney, P. (2001, November 12). Bill Gates, chairman and chief software architect. Microsoft. *CRN,* 95.

52.   Rooney, ibid., p. 95.

53.   http://www.newswire.ca/en/releases/archive/June2006/15/c4768.html.

54.   Lambert, T. (2006, March 27). Insight. MENAFN.Com. http://www.menafn.com/qn_print.asp?StroyID=129531&subl=true.

55.   Shepard, H. (1975, November). Rules of thumb for change agents. *Organization Development Practitioner,* 1–5; Ransdell, E. (2001). Rules for radicals. *Fast Company,* 11,

190–191; Hamel, G. (2000, July). How to start an insurrection. *Ideas@Work,* Harvard Business School Press.

56. Katzenbach, J. (1996, July-August). From middle manager to real change leader. *Strategy and Leadership,* 34.

57. Oshry, B. (1993). Converting middle powerlessness to middle power: A systems approach. *National Productivity Review.* In T. Jick, *Managing change: Cases and concepts.* Homewood, IL: Irwin.

58. Howell, J., & Higgins, C. (1990, Summer). Champions of change. *Organizational Dynamics,* 40–55.

Jessica Casserra's Task Force*

Hospital Integration in the Region of Erie

Jessica Casserra stretched back from the monitor and rubbed her eyes. Technology had made it possible to be home in the evenings with her family, but as they pointed out, that didn't mean they saw much of her. For the past 2 months, most evenings and weekends had been spent poring over internal reports, briefs, governmental documents, spreadsheets, and consulting studies concerning the integration of hospital services in the Region of Erie.

The taxpayers of the region had received far more than their fair share of her time, but she wasn't sure that was translating into added value. Budgeting, control, program integration, human resource, and organizational design issues had not been resolved—they had only festered as senior hospital management, board members, and key stakeholders groups squabbled and continued to avoid making difficult decisions.

Nonetheless, the formal organizational integration of Metropolitan with five smaller hospitals and ancillary services (e.g., laundry, food services) was required to be agreed to and set in motion within 10 months. The Ministry of Health had fixed the timing. It was extremely unlikely that the provincial governing party would back down from the start date, given the political heat they had taken throughout the review process that resulted in their decision to regionalize hospital services. Jessica knew they would not want to give integration opponents additional opportunities to mobilize resistance or any hope that decisions might be reversed. They would also want this matter long past prior to the next provincial election.

Hospital Services in the Region and Their Response to Integration

The combined hospital services in the southeast region of the province responded to the needs of 250,000 people in their catchment area of approximately 30 miles by 60 miles. Metropolitan Hospital was, by far, the largest facility, with 150 beds and 700 employees or 493 full-time equivalents. Metropolitan specialized in primary care and offered a fairly full range of hospital services, from emergency to surgical, basic cancer care, and

---

* This case was prepared by Professor Gene Deszca of Wilfrid Laurier University. Copyright © G. Deszca.

dialysis. The specific services offered varied depending on the medical specialists they were able to attract to their area at any particular point in time. However, specialized needs in such areas as neonatal, advanced trauma, MRI, and more complex cardiac and cancer care interventions were transferred to a larger hospital.

Metropolitan was located in the major urban area (population = 90,000) in the region. It was surrounded by agricultural and tourist areas and a number of smaller municipalities. Five of these towns hosted 20- to 50-bed hospitals, offering limited services to residents in the immediate area.

Each of the hospitals in the region had strong local support and good reputations for the quality of care and services they provided. In recent years, this support had been tested as waiting periods for medical procedures increased and emergency care lineups lengthened. Shortages of funds and healthcare workers (nurses, specialists, and general practitioners) were stressing the system, and there was a growing concern over the future of public health care in the region.

For several years, the province had been involved in efforts directed toward reining in escalating healthcare costs through initiatives aimed at improving the efficiency and effectiveness of the hospital healthcare delivery system. This had led to provincially initiated studies of how best to rationalize and deploy services. In the southeast region of the province, this had translated into the provincially mandated integration of Metropolitan with the five rural hospitals and related ancillary services in the area.

The specific terms and conditions of the merger were yet to be determined, but the default position was clear. If the parties were unable to come to an agreement, the province would appoint an administrator who would impose the terms and conditions of the merger. In addition, de facto penalties would be imposed on the hospitals in the region, because they would be responsible for all integration costs and would lose access to provincial transitional funding support—sums that could run to $10–20 million over the next 2 to 5 years.

The prospects of the forced integration had not been met with open arms. While the Metropolitan board was largely supportive of the idea, the boards of the other five hospitals had all opposed the move. They saw it as usurping local control and as code language for the maintenance and enhancement of urban services at the expense of local services. They believed it would lead to service degradation in rural areas, culminating in the closure of some of the facilities they had worked so hard to develop and sustain. In addition, four of the five rural hospitals perceived this to be a blatant cash grab on the part of the province and Metropolitan Hospital. These four had all managed to save significant funds over the years, due to fund-raising and fiscal prudence. Metropolitan, however, found itself with a modest operating deficit ($250,000 on a $42 million operating budget). It also had an accumulated debt of $3.3 million. The smaller hospitals were free of debt.

Board members of the four hospitals with significant surpluses saw the budgetary situation as an example of urban mismanagement, whereas Metropolitan board members saw it as the result of years of overfunding of rural hospitals, combined with the fact that Metropolitan inherited the more expensive and difficult-to-manage patients.

Jessica Casserra's Appointment

Following the decision of the Ministry of Health to require the realignment of hospital service in the southeast region, Jessica Casserra was approached to lead the initiative by the chief administrative officers of three of the hospitals involved (including Metropolitan). Jessica was a former nurse with a master's in health administration, and she was a certified management accountant. She was the head of Finance, Administration, and Ancillary Services at Metropolitan. She was 47 years old and had a stellar reputation as an honest and creative hospital administrator who understood the healthcare issues of the region. When approached privately, most senior administrators at all six hospitals admitted that Jessica had, by far, the best chance of any administrator in the area of managing the integration successfully. In addition to her technical and managerial talent, she was politically astute and in possession of excellent facilitation skills.

At first Jessica had rejected the overtures. She knew this would be a very difficult assignment, she worried about the level of local support she could expect from medical and hospital staff in the region, and she doubted whether the province had the will to see it through to its conclusion. Moreover, Jessica wondered whether she had the organizational skills to take on this task. Once Jessica became convinced there would be no provincial backsliding, her professional sense of responsibility, combined with her commitment to the quality of health care in the region, moved her to agree to head the hospital integration task force.

To maintain her legitimacy in the region, she retained her responsibilities at Metropolitan. Additional help was recruited at both the hospital and task force levels to assist her with her new responsibilities, but Jessica soon found herself working 55 to 65 hours per week. This was not unexpected, but it was tiring and stressful. She was now 2 months into this assignment, with 10 months to go to the deadline. If agreements could be achieved by that point, she recognized that she would likely retain significant responsibilities for integration activities that would run for at least the next 2 to 3 years. If agreements could not be reached, Jessica would step down from her task force role and a provincial administrator would be appointed. What would happen then was far from clear.

The Task Force Design

When Jessica agreed to chair the task force, the Ministry of Health had already decided on its membership structure. In addition to the chair (formally appointed by the Ministry of Health), each hospital nominated three members, the local physicians' association nominated three members, the nurses' association nominated two members, and the member communities each nominated one member of the public. Further, the Ministry of Health appointed two nonvoting, ex-officio members to represent its interests. In addition to the chair, the task force had 29 voting members and two nonvoting members. The task force was expected to seek consensus and act in an advisory role to the involved hospitals and the province. In addition to those from healthcare professions, about a third of the task force members came from other walks of life (e.g., two farmers, one engineer, two lawyers, one pastor, two business owners, and two accountants). Jessica remembered when members had been told by the province at the first meeting that service on the task force would not unduly impair their capacity to meet their regular responsibilities. Jessica reckoned that since that first meeting, task force duties had taken 20 to 30 hours per week of her time and about 10 hours per week of the time of other members.

The task force had adequate funds to hire professional staff, consultants, and support personnel to help them in their deliberations. They had a full-time staff of eight including two hospital planners, an information systems specialist, a human resource specialist, a financial specialist, and three staff supports. These employees were hired directly by the task force through the efforts of Jessica and her staff subcommittee. In addition, consultants had received contracts from the task force to assist in the needed background work and analysis. They included two well-respected retired hospital CEOs who were contracted to investigate service structure and delivery options. Once implementation of the plan became the focus, an implementation task force would be formed. It was anticipated that most implementation task force members would be drawn from the existing hospital staff, but it had yet to be designed.

Case Study 2

The staff of the task force was housed in office space supplied by the Region of Erie, and the task force used Erie's council chamber for its meetings. In addition, there was temporary office space and a boardroom available to task force members, and Jessica had permanent office space available to her there.

Following the initial task force meeting a month and a half ago (a session hosted by the Ministry of Health), the task force had been meeting one day per week and working fairly well on exploratory matters, but they had not yet had to face difficult questions. Once the more contentious strategic and operational questions came to the table, Jessica was concerned that they might simply defer to the public positions of the various groups that had selected them for membership. This was not a recipe for success. If they were going to really add value, she believed that they had to seize this unique opportunity to reinvent hospital service delivery in the region—a tough concept to sell. Board members and representatives of other stakeholders were quick to point fingers at who needed to improve. To this point, most task force members were not prepared to publicly argue that the current system was in crisis. The preference of members seemed to be for targeted analysis and solutions that intervened in ways that preserved and enhanced the position of the stakeholder group that was recommending the tinkering.

Jessica wondered what she should do to increase the chances of task force success. How should the task force be managed, and what things should she be doing outside of the formal task force meetings? Jessica had developed a good working knowledge of the medical and managerial talent available in the hospital system in the southeast region, and she had fairly good knowledge of the various stakeholders involved. She was also a respected administrator who had developed a reputation for being a fair-minded and independent thinker who understood and cared about health care. She knew that her capacities in these areas would be taxed to the utmost.

The Strategic Questions

From a strategic perspective, Jessica continued to ponder what would be the best way to integrate hospital services and configure their management and governance structures, systems, and supports. There was a range of options, but all came with strings attached.

When thinking about the integration challenge, Jessica was very aware of the fact that Metropolitan had a well-developed strategic plan that had already contemplated some of these questions. However, she also believed these documents would likely be more of an impediment than an aid at this time. Two of the smaller hospitals had made some attempt at developing a strategic plan for themselves, while the other three had spent little time engaged in such activity. However, virtually all the hospital CEOs and their senior managers seemed to believe that they were skilled strategists who knew what the region needed. If the services offered by a newly constructed regional hospital delivery system were to be as effective and efficient as possible, Jessica knew that the hospitals would have to depart dramatically from the way they had organized themselves in the past. At present, Jessica did not have a strong sense of the strategic focus or skill set of most task force members, but it was her belief that many would be tempted to defer to the various groups that had nominated them.

Integration Options

Option A: From the perspective of the board and CEO of Metropolitan, full integration was the preferred way to approach hospital integration. This approach would rationalize services and lead to higher levels of resource use. This would mean moving to a single board and CEO, a consolidated budget and governance structure, a complete realignment of services and roles, control over all ancillary services, access to accumulated surpluses and contingency funds, and the possible consolidation of all hospital foundations into one for the entire region. This approach was seen to minimize organizational risk in the sense that all major management functions would be centralized. The fund-raising foundations were supposedly independent, but most were effectively controlled by the hospital that they were focused on. The smaller hospital foundations had combined savings of $17 million. Metropolitan's foundation controlled $15 million. In addition, the accumulated reserves and contingency funds held by the smaller hospitals themselves totaled $16 million.

The Metropolitan board salivated at the thought of what they could do with this money, but Jessica knew that any integration that was viewed by the smaller hospitals as a frontal attack would lead to protracted court battles, particularly over the control of the assets managed by the fund-raising foundations. She was told that there was a 60% chance Metropolitan would be successful, but it could take up to 5 years to conclude the legal wrangling, and the financial and organizational costs would be substantial.

She also knew that it could have a profoundly negative effect on future fund-raising activities in these communities, and she anticipated that most staff and volunteers in the smaller hospitals would view the approach very negatively. Staff resistance would likely come in the form of absenteeism, less willingness to work overtime and extra shifts, and resignations by nurses and physicians. Only the staff at Metropolitan, most of the medical specialists, and some of the GPs would be likely to view this option positively, due to their beliefs concerning the need for the infusion of funds to shore up their ability to supply new and higher-quality, leading-edge medical care to citizens in the region.

Option B: At the other end of the integration continuum was a model that would allow all hospitals to retain their independent structures and boards, with member hospitals each nominating representatives to a supraboard that would act as a planning and coordinating body. This was the option that was favored by the smaller hospitals and towns, because it allowed continued local access and control of the institutions that the smaller communities had been instrumental in developing and supporting. Neither Metropolitan not the province viewed this model favorably, because it seemed likely to perpetuate fairly siloed operations and did not seem likely to result in significant savings from consolidation and increased efficiency. These potential savings were thought to be in the order of at least $4 to $6 million per year. Given the position of the province, this would leave Metropolitan scrambling to find ways to fund an operating deficit likely to grow by $100,000 to $350,000 per year over the next few years as the population aged and the smaller hospitals continued downloading their more difficult and expensive cases.

Between these two extremes, there were many other possibilities, and Jessica knew that these needed to be narrowed, developed, and assessed. In addition, there was the wild-card issue of how to best handle chronic, long-term care in the region, but task force members and the province seemed prepared to set this issue aside for the present.

Competition

Competition was becoming more intense—somewhat surprising because this was not supposed to happen in a publicly funded system. Competition came from several sources. Private clinics had opened in or near the southeast region and were offering a number of services that had previously been supplied by Metropolitan.

Hospitals had found that these specific services were financially attractive to supply because they were relatively easy to perform; in many cases, patients (or insurers) paid for the service themselves, and in other cases, the provincial reimbursement rate greatly exceeded the costs of supplying the services. Cosmetic surgery, routine hernia treatment, rehabilitation services, CT services, and diet and lifestyle counseling were the types of services that were coming under increased competitive pressure.

Case Study 2

In addition, residents in the area could easily access private medical facilities by crossing into the United States. A number of these facilities were actively marketing their services to Canadians, and it was not unusual to find Canadian physicians affiliated in some way with these U.S. facilities. Jessica noted that the provincial government was willing to pay U.S. suppliers the provincially mandated rates for insured services. Individual patients were responsible for any differences, but for procedures such as CTs and MRIs, the provincial payments covered the majority of the bill.

Ancillary Services

Ancillary services represented both a competitive opportunity and threat. Metropolitan Hospital, in particular, was in the catering, vehicle repair, fund-raising, payroll services, security, housekeeping/cleaning, hazardous material handling, homecare, and laundry businesses, to name just a few. These were services that they could potentially commercialize and/or privatize and spin off. While Jessica had only begun inspecting these opportunities, she already knew that some were fairly efficient and effective operations—laundry, payroll services, and food services, in particular. Others (custodial/cleaning services and homecare) were less efficient and cost-effective than private-sector competitors at the present. It was not clear how she should go about structuring and evaluating these opportunities and risks. Several board members looked at such initiatives very favorably, because they saw them as a way to address deficit problems and provide funding for mainstream medical care delivery. However, a minority continued to have serious concerns about the commercialization of hospital services.

Equipment and physical plant were, on the whole, in a fairly good state of repair in the region. Equipment was never as modern or as abundant as staff would like, but overall the hospitals had managed maintenance programs well.

Jessica recognized that some of the commercialization opportunities would require significant investments in order to realize their potential. For example, the laundry facility required an investment of $13 million to allow it to take advantage of the commercialization opportunities in the area (supplying hospitals, nursing homes, the university and community college, and others in need of institutional laundry services). While the laundry, in particular, seemed to have solid economic potential, she recognized that some would argue that the resources were needed to fund hospital plant and equipment needs that more directly served the delivery of medical services.

Control and Information Systems

With the exceptions of Metropolitan's computerized accounting and payroll systems, computer information systems represented a serious point of concern. Each hospital had its own system or systems, and the systems did not communicate with each other. Some of them were clearly antiquated, and even within Metropolitan there was duplication of information entry, difficulties with information flow, and far too much reliance on paper.

Jessica knew that the issues in the areas of control system design extended well beyond software and computer concerns. Ministry of Health and Ministry of Finance requirements drove much of the activity in this area, but Jessica felt that this would be an ideal time to sort through and establish the management control information that could really benefit managers and the organization. For example, there was little to no consistency in the boundary, belief, diagnostic, or interactive control systems in operation in the various hospitals. Metropolitan's system was the most developed, but even here Jessica believed improvement was needed with both its design and use. She believed the new organization would be well served if it approached the design of the control system with an open mind and then ensured that their managers were literate in the effective use of the information emanating from it.

The critical questions concerning the control system were, what should the system be designed to do, and how should its implementation be approached? Jessica believed these would be impossible to determine in a definitive way until the fundamental strategy questions had been answered. She knew that gaining interest and approval for control system initiatives (other than those required by statute) would be a challenge. However, building the business case for control processes that went beyond historical reporting requirements would get progressively more difficult as time passed and resources tightened.

People

Managing hospital employees during the transition represented a key point of risk. Hospitals in the region were already short of nurses, and the area had been classified as underserviced by general practitioners and specialists. Little in the way of strategy had guided hospital activities, with the exception of Metropolitan, which had a fairly well-developed strategic plan. For example, 3 years earlier, Metropolitan had developed detailed and sophisticated initiatives aimed at attracting and retaining general practitioners and specialists. They had also developed initiatives to improve management practices and employee satisfaction and performance by moving to team-based management. Their efforts had met with some limited success in the areas of attraction, retention, and satisfaction, but Jessica still believed they relied far too much on hierarchy and traditional management practices. Team members still deferred to managers and physicians and engaged in few of the self-management behaviors Jessica had hoped to see.

Once integration was undertaken, the human resource challenges would escalate. Each hospital and ancillary service had its own bargaining units, and each represented a unique culture, with its own approach to financial, physical plant, and human resource management. For example, two of the smaller hospitals had served as exemplars for Metropolitan when they had begun investigating team management. They had achieved high degrees of success with the approach and were viewed as extremely well managed.

At the other end of the continuum was one small hospital that was believed to be in somewhat serious difficulty with respect to its management practices. Turnover and absenteeism were high, satisfaction was reported to be low, and efficiency and effectiveness were both well below national norms. Nonetheless, the board of that hospital was highly supportive of its practices and the performance of its senior managers. They attributed observed shortfalls to unique issues in their catchment area, but Jessica felt that this assessment didn't stand up to closer scrutiny. The fact that the hospital CEO and the head of nursing were, respectively, 62 and 60 years old might make change easier to manage at this site if they should choose to retire early.

Jessica knew that integration activities would occasion job insecurity, with its magnitude dependent on what integration approach was adopted. At present, this fear was most pronounced in middle and senior management levels, but unions had already voiced concerns about possible job losses caused by service rationalization, contracting out, and/or privatization. Until the postintegration roles of the various hospitals were clarified, staff uncertainty and anxiety were bound to escalate.

Case Study 2

Next Steps

Jessica mulled over her options but then stopped and laughed. For many years she had been a vocal advocate of strategic thinking, accompanied by action, execution, supportive management, measurement, and learning. Here she was, 3 months into her task force assignment, bogged down by tactical and operational concerns. Maybe it was time to step back and do some strategic planning for herself, but she was unclear about how best to proceed.

CHAPTER 9

Action Planning, Aligning, and Implementing Change

"Do It"—The Imperative of Action

Chapter Overview

- Change leaders need to recognize that without action, nothing happens. Take action and learn from the results. Change initiators have a "do it" attitude.
- Action planning involves making the right decisions, planning the work, organizing the team, and working the plan. "Right" decisions means approximately right, as change agents obtain feedback from action, learn, and make adjustments as they act.
- Action planning deals with encouraging people to move from initial **awareness** of the change, to being **interested**, to wanting or **desiring** the change, and finally, to taking **action** (AIDA).
- Change agents learn to specify who does what, when, and how to monitor and track their project. Responsibility charts are key tools in successful action planning.
- Successful change managers build a change team, develop detailed communications plans, and understand how to manage the change transition.

This book has a philosophical bias for taking action. However, the goal is not to take action simply to feed our need for novelty and excitement. It is to have managers do things that will increase the likelihood of positive change. Rather than passively waiting to see what others may do or complaining from the sidelines, managers need to get active. This chapter provides insights into action planning and implementation. In terms of our model in Figure 9.1, it tackles the issues of "getting from here to there"—assessing the present in terms of the future, determining the work that needs to be done, and implementing the change.

Prior to moving to action, change leaders need to have done the homework that forms the basis of successful change. They need to understand and articulate the reasons for change. They must identify the role that existing systems and structures

The Initial Organizational Analysis
**Understanding the Forces for Change and the
Organizational Situation**
Chapter 3

Why Change?
Determining the Need for Change, Determining the Degree of
Choice About Whether to Change, Developing the Change Vision
Chapter 4

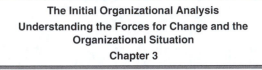

| Defining the Desired Future State |  Gap Analysis Chapters 5, 6, 7, 8 | Describing the Present State |

Action Planning and Implementation:
Assessing the Present in Terms of the Future to
Determine the Work to Be Done, Doing the Work
Chapter 9

Measuring the Change—Designing Effective Control Systems
Chapter 10

Figure 9.1   The Change Management Process

will play in promoting or diminishing change initiatives. They must recognize the likely sources of resistance and support, how those sources will respond, and how the underlying power dynamics will play out. They need to understand the levels of commitment that executives have and what their own skills and abilities bring to the change process. And all of this must be done knowing that timing and luck can seriously influence change progress.

This chapter sets out the steps for action, action that is based on analysis and a comprehension of the particular organizational dynamics facing the organization. It provides suggestions and frameworks that will help change leaders organize the change team and identify the roles they can play. The chapter provides advice on implementation tactics that lead to success. Finally, it deals with two critical aspects of change, communication tactics during the change process and transition management—keeping the organization successful during disruptive change.

Why Does This Book Adopt a "Do It" Orientation?

In the best of worlds, change agents will find that they have access to executives who will provide directional clarity, assess and approve needed changes, cultivate employee commitment for change, and offer other forms of needed support. However, this is often not the case. Some executives fail to understand the important role they have to play in this area; others will not see it as their role. Some will fear that their involvement may make things more difficult, while others will simply want to distance themselves from the change in the event that it doesn't work out.

The absence of executive support is normal during the early stages of change when the principal proponents for a new initiative may lie in middle management (or elsewhere in the organization) rather than at the top. Executives may lack awareness of the initiative, its nature and rationale, and its proponents. At other times, executive support may be invisible because of competing priorities or political realities. In these situations, change initiators may feel that abiding by formal organizational protocols around change and waiting for official support will unduly slow progress. As such, they may choose to follow the advice of Rear Admiral Grace Hopper, a pioneering female software engineer in the U.S. Navy, who is quoted to have said, "It is easier to seek forgiveness than permission."[1] Why ask questions that might lead to those in authority saying "no" when proceeding on your own is a viable option?

This approach to action planning and implementation was introduced in Chapter 5 in the sections that dealt with the use of creeping commitment, coalition building, and the bypassing of the formal approval process. As noted there, a "do it" approach does not suggest precipitous action that just gets one into trouble. It is about managers taking well-thought-out, self-initiated actions that build awareness, interest, and support in the change. It is about change agents (a) reducing the perceived risks associated with the change (e.g., via field research, experimentation, and pilot testing), (b) addressing issues of alignment, (c) challenging existing systems and processes in constructive ways, and/or (d) increasing the perceived risks of not supporting the change. Kouzes and Posner in their leadership book talk about "challenging the system"[2] to focus on the needs of customers, employees, and the organization as a whole. That is, change agents should focus on altering how they see the world, disrupting the status quo, and addressing matters related to alignment.

When it comes to "doing it," managers often believe (sometimes for good reasons) that they are constrained to the point of inaction by existing structures, systems, and supervisors. Pfeffer states that "actions count more than elegant plans or concepts," and that "there is no doing without mistakes," and what is crucial is "what is the company's response?"[3] If the organization's response to reasoned initiatives and honest mistakes is to scapegoat and blame, smart people quickly learn not to take risks that might lead to mistakes. Or they learn to cover up mistakes. Either way, the organization suffers.[*] However, beliefs about the likely organizational responses can also become a convenient excuse for inaction and the avoidance of risk taking (e.g., What if my idea really won't work or what will I do if it does work?). If such beliefs are never challenged, their stability will produce self-fulfilling prophecies.

Effective managers of change are aware of the consequences of their actions and intuitively test their organizational assumptions by engaging in an action, learning, reaction cycle. Sayles recognized this when he wrote, ". . . working leaders . . . instead of simply waiting for and evaluating results . . . seek to intervene. And the interventions they undertake require a more intimate knowledge of operations, and more involvement in the work than those of traditional middle managers."[4]

The reality of much organizational life lies somewhere between an environment that punishes those who dare to challenge the status quo and one in which all such initiatives are unconditionally embraced and rewarded. Organization members who choose not to wait on formal permission and undertake reasoned self-initiated change initiatives may experience some chastisement for not first seeking approval—particularly if the initiative runs into difficulty. However, in many organizations, they also find that this is buffered by being commended for showing initiative and trying to have a positive impact. The organization's culture and the personality of their boss (e.g., managerial style and tolerance for ambiguity) will obviously influence what response the initiator receives, but most managers value initiative—just not those that make their lives more difficult.

Clearly, initiatives that lead to the loss of a major account or create ethical and legal difficulties will be deemed unacceptable. As well, mismanagement, insubordination, or the intentional embarrassment of a senior manager is likely not going to be forgiven or forgotten. However, if an initiative represents a well-intentioned, honest, and reasoned attempt to improve the situation, forgiveness and praise may follow.

What can be done to increase the likelihood that taking action will produce desired results? The sections that follow seek to address this question by exploring a variety of action-planning tools. The purpose of these tools is to assist change leaders in designing and then managing their initiative in ways that increase the prospects for success.

---

[*]This does lead to an accountability paradox. Accountability is a needed and useful attribute. However, there needs to be a fine balance between holding change leaders accountable for what they do and encouraging the risk-taking behavior that leads to needed learning and change.

How Can We Focus on
What Needs to Happen?

... management is becoming ever more fashion-conscious. Managers implement strategies like downsizing and reengineering just because they seem like the thing to do. Managers are fashion-conscious because, in reality, 90% of running an organization is routine. Teenagers are fashion-conscious because most of what goes on at school is boring. The same goes for managers.[5]

Change agents may find it useful to pay attention to organizational ideas that are "hot" and consider how these might be applied to their organization. Such ideas may stimulate thinking, demonstrate to others that managers are keeping current, and even advance the change agenda. However, skilled change leaders avoid becoming blinded by the glossiness of the "newest" best way. Don't lose sight of what you are really trying to accomplish as an agent of change. Too often, managers become enamored with the latest fad without thinking through issues of fit, appropriateness, and need. The luster of the new technique fades quickly, along with your credibility, when it diverts attention from underlying change needs of the organization.[6] When change plans are driven by the flavor of the day rather than the needs of the firm, change leaders are headed for difficulty.

Earlier in this book, we encouraged change leaders to engage in serious analysis of their organization. Any action plan needs to be rooted in a sophisticated understanding of how the organization works and what needs to be done to achieve desired outcomes. At the same time, change managers need to recognize that there are different approaches to decision making and action taking. Mintzberg and Westley outlines three approaches: thinking first, seeing first, and doing first.[7] They believe that

1. "Thinking first" works best when the issue is clear, data are reliable, context is structured, thoughts can be pinned down, and discipline can be established as in many routine production processes.

2. "Seeing first" works best when many elements have to be combined into creative solutions, commitment to those solutions is key, and communication across boundaries is essential as in new-product development. People need to see the whole before becoming committed.

3. "Doing first" works best when the situation is novel and confusing, complicated specifications would get in the way, and a few simple relationship rules can help people move forward. An example would be when a manager is testing an approach and wants feedback about what works.

These approaches are highlighted because of the emphasis in this book on action learning. As complexity and ambiguity rise, the preferred approach shifts from Thinking First to Seeing First and then Doing First. Yes, a person should think things through, with forethought and care, and when many elements need to be combined across organizational boundaries, seeing first is needed to ensure integration and fit. However, there are always risks of failure—even with these approaches. At some point, managers need to move to action, do it the best they can, learn from the experience, and do it again, only better. If managers wait until they get it perfect, they may miss the window of opportunity. Get it approximately right, beta test it, make incremental moves when possible, and use feedback to improve upon what you have done. Doing, seeing, and thinking approaches inevitably become intertwined in major change initiatives because organizations will benefit from different approaches at different stages.

In metaphorical terms, this suggests a move from "ready—aim—fire" to "ready—fire—aim—refire—re-aim . . ."* for situations in which a "Doing First" approach to action planning is recommended. In fast-moving contexts, it is all too likely that a traditional planning process will be too lengthy and that by the time that planning is finished, the opportunity may have been missed. This metaphor recognizes that there is significant information that can be obtained from action feedback. If a change leader takes action, the surrounding organizational system will react, giving the change leader insights on how to respond and take corrective actions. Prior training and experience and a clear understanding of the purpose and vision will help change leaders to make the "generally right" decisions in these situations—ones that they then learn from and refine as they move forward.

So, what does this suggest about the action-planning and implementation process? Change must be initiated by those who are prepared to manage and lead the process; change leadership can be exercised virtually anywhere in the organization, and if you wait to get it perfect in an ambiguous and dynamic context, you may never start. Regardless of how difficult change appears to be, Confucius was right—"a journey of a thousand miles begins with a single step."[8] You need to **plan your work, organize the team, and work the plan.** These steps, properly applied, will help you keep your eye on the change goal, avoid at least some of the pitfalls, and, maybe most important, enhance your capacity to adapt effectively and learn throughout the process.

How Do We Plan the Work?

If the managers' approach to planned change has followed what this book suggests, then much planning will have already been done. Managers will have (a) diagnosed the organization, (b) clarified the vision for the change, (c) identified the gap between the present mode of operation and the desired future state, (d) understood who the key stakeholders are, and (e) recognized the critical structures and systems that will effect and be affected by the proposed change. Regardless of the change plan, change leaders need to ensure that their plan is viable, that they understand

---

*The managerial use of this metaphor is usually credited to Peters, T., & Waterman, R. H., Jr. (1982). *In search of excellence.* New York: Harper & Row. Our understanding is that its presence in its modified form has its roots in missile defense. If you are defending against incoming missiles, you don't have time to wait and plan a response. You do need to fire before you aim your missile. Then once you have things in motion, you, can re-aim your missile based on new, current information.

the change context or situation, and that they have considered major change alternatives in their approach.

Michael Beer et al.,[9] suggest a prescriptive list of "steps to effective change." (Appendix 1 contains a table that compares Beer's steps with the prescriptions of others.[10]) Beer's steps are:

1. Mobilize commitment to change through joint diagnosis of business problems.

2. Develop a shared vision of how to organize and manage for competitiveness.

3. Foster consensus for the new vision, competence to enact it, and cohesion to move it along.

4. Spread revitalization to all departments without pushing it from the top.

5. Institutionalize revitalization through formal policies, systems, and structures.

6. Monitor and adjust strategies in response to problems in the revitalization process.

For many change situations, this straightforward checklist provides valuable guidance in the development of an action plan. However, assuming a "one-size-fits-all" strategy for change can be risky. For example, the above list assumes a fundamental cooperative orientation between the organization and its employees. That is, there is sufficient commonality of goals that a shared vision is possible. The list also suggests that change should evolve and not be pushed by top management.

As well, the need for contingent thinking needs to be addressed. That is, your action plan depends significantly on the action-planning context. Planning must evolve as events unfold. As such, it is useful to remember the following saying: "No plan survives first contact."[11]

That is, while it is critical to plan and anticipate, change leaders must also recognize that planning is a means, not an end in itself. Don't ignore vital emerging information just because it does not fit with carefully conceived plans. Contingencies and alternative ways of approaching change are important contributors to enhanced adaptive capacity.

Advocates of unilateral approaches to change believe that if one changes systems and structures, behavioral change will follow and that this, in turn, will produce changes to attitudes and beliefs over time. In other words, if you change behavior, attitude changes will follow. Those who promote a more participative approach believe the opposite. They argue that you need to gain commitment in order to change behavior. Waldersee and Griffiths have examined this. They note that change initiatives have been traditionally grouped into two broad categories. Technostructural changes refer to those that are based in structures, systems, and technology. Behavioral-social changes are focused on altering established social relationships. After investigating 408 change episodes reported by Australian managers, they concluded that the unilateral approach was perceived to be more *appropriate* for technostructural change, while more participative approaches were perceived to be more *appropriate* when behavioral-social changes such as cultural change were involved.[12] When managers were asked about the perceived *effectiveness* of the change, they saw unilateral methods as more effective in bringing about successful change, regardless of the type of change. What does all of this mean for action planning? Waldersee and Griffiths suggest that

> Concrete actions taken by change managers are often superior to the traditional prescriptions of participation (Beer et al., 1990[13]). Forcing change through top-down actions such as redeploying staff or redesigning jobs may effectively shift employee behavior. With the context and behavior changed, interventions targeting attitudes may then follow. (p. 432)

While concerted concrete actions may have appeal for those who want to ensure that things are done, such an approach can be risky and needs to be managed with care. When implementation lacks sensitivity, recipients may be left feeling that their perspectives and concerns have been ignored. As noted in Chapter 7, this can result in fallout that could have been avoided: resistance and missed opportunities for valuable input.

Nohria and Khuvana have identified three generic change contexts: programmatic change, discontinuous change, and emergent change.[14] Programmatic change is traditional planned change such as the introduction of a new customer relationship system. Discontinuous change involves a major break from the past such as building a new manufacturing operation that uses revolutionary technology. Emergent change grows out of incremental change and can produce ambiguity and challenge when it fully blossoms. An organizational change to modify the organizational culture that emerges from customer and staff feedback would be an example. Table 9.1 summarizes this work. Each of these strategies is appropriate at different times and carries different risks. If the context is relatively clear and solutions are known, then programmatic change (or "thinking first," in Mintzberg's terms) is likely best. Here, one can sort through alternatives and lay out logical plans and objectives beforehand. Alternatively, if the environment is shifting dramatically and a continuation of the organization based on existing assumptions will not work, then discontinuous, top-down change might be most appropriate. Finally, if the organization is filled with a talented, knowledgeable workforce who understands the risks and possibilities, allowing emergent change could work.

Change leaders need to consider carefully what approach makes the most sense in their situation. While "do it" does get things in motion, doing something inappropriate won't build needed support for the initiative or confidence in your judgment and skill. To counteract the pitfalls of programmatic change, consider using employee engagement and feedback to connect with behavior and modularized approaches that allow for some adaptation to local conditions. The pitfalls from discontinuous change will be lessened by processes that reduce ambiguity and build support. Finally, the issues related to emergent change can be reduced through the use of field experiments, task forces to provide greater engagement, and feedback to build understanding and support.

Table 9.1   Three Generic Change Strategies

Change Type	Characteristic	Implementation	Pitfalls
Programmatic Change	Missions, plans, objectives	Training, time lines, steering committees	Lack of focus on behavior, one solution for all, inflexible solutions
Discontinuous Change	Initiated from top, clear break, reorientation	Decrees, structural change, concurrent implementation	Political coalitions derail change, weak controls, stress from the loss of people
Emergent Change	Ambiguous, incremental, and challenging	Use of metaphors, experimentation, and risk taking	Confusion over direction, uncertainty, and possible slow results

Source: Nohria, N., & Khurana, R. (1993, August 24). *Executing change: Three generic strategies.* Harvard Business School Note 494–039.

How Do We Reduce Resistance to Change?

Major Action-Planning Alternatives

While Nohria outlined different contexts for change, change leaders still need to consider how they can bring organization members "onside" with the change. There is a tendency to focus on the needed systems and structures and a failure to understand the steps to ensure that required employee support is nurtured and dysfunctional resistance is alleviated. Kotter and Schlesinger provide us with six general change strategies for dealing with people and groups in the organization.[15] These are:

1. **Education and Communication:** Often, people need to see the need for and the logic of the change. A simple lack of understanding of what is wanted and how it might work often leads to resistance. Often, change leaders fail to adequately push their message through the organization because they are under significant time pressure and the rationale "is so obvious" to them they don't understand why others don't get it. Nevertheless, this strategy takes time and energy—often well spent.

2. **Participation and Involvement:** Getting others involved will bring new energy and ideas as well as shifting people to believe they can be part of the change. Often, people can bring insights needed for successful change, particularly when others have the power to resist the proposals. This strategy works best when the change agent has time and you need to bring others onboard with the change. Participation fits with many of the norms of today's flattened organizations, but some managers often feel that it just slows everything down, compromising what is needed to be done quickly.

3. **Facilitation and Support:** Here, change managers provide resources, training, or time and support to adapt to the change. This strategy works best when the issues are related to anxiety and fear of change.

4. **Negotiation and Agreement:** At times, change leaders can make explicit deals with those resisting. This strategy can work in unionized environments where the resistance is organized. The dilemma with this strategy is that it leads to compliance but not to wholehearted support of the change.

5. **Manipulation and Co-optation:** While many managers don't like to admit the use of this strategy, the use of covert attempts to influence exists. Explicitly involving those who oppose will often co-opt them into accepting the change. If people believe they are being manipulated in a negative way, trust levels can drop and resistance increase.

6. **Explicit and Implicit Coercion:** With this strategy, as with the previous one, there is a negative image associated with the explicit use of threats and force. Nevertheless, managers often have the legitimate right and responsibility to insist that changes be done. Often, this strategy is used when speed is needed or if they believe all other options have been exhausted. Change leaders need to recognize the potential for residual negative feelings that will remain after the change.

In addition to the above, open systems analysis points to a seventh change strategy—**systemic adjustments.** At times, systemic changes can be made that address resistance in ways that are congruent with the desired changes. For example, if employee resistance has coalesced in a group of employees who were positioned in a critical function, the systemic altering of this function so that it is less critical and the reassignment of members of this group to other areas may reduce resistance markedly. However, if it is mishandled in a way that mobilizes and escalates resistance in others, it will have the opposite of the intended effect.

Toolkit Exercise 9.1 asks you to examine the methods you've seen used in organizations to overcome resistance to change.

Change managers should use a variety of resistance-reducing techniques depending on their analysis of the reasons for resistance. In general, it is wise to move as slowly as is practical. This permits people to become accustomed to the idea of the change, adopt the change program, learn new skills, and see the positive sides. It also permits change leaders to adjust their processes, refine the change, improve congruence, and learn as they go. However, if time is of the essence or if going slowly means that resisters will be able to organize in ways that will make change highly unlikely, then change leaders should plan carefully, move quickly, and overwhelm resistance where possible. Just remember, though, that it is far easier to get into a war than it is to build a lasting peace after the fighting ends. Don't let your impatience and commitment to moving the change forward get the better of your judgment concerning how best to proceed.

How Do We Engage Others as Part of the Plan?

Occasionally, change planning must be undertaken under a cloak of secrecy, such as when a merger is in the works and the premature release of information would significantly affect the price and the level of competitive risk. In general, though, the active involvement of others and information sharing have the potential to enhance the quality of action planning for most change strategies. Consider Barbara Waugh, Worldwide Personnel Manager for Hewlett-Packard Laboratories:

> Waugh's most recent campaign for change began five years ago, when Birnbaum (Director of HP Labs) asked her, "Why does no one out there consider HP Labs to be the best industrial research lab in the world?" . . . she and Birnbaum began by asking questions rather than proposing answers. Using a . . . survey, she canvassed . . .: What does it mean to be "the best" research lab . . .? The inquiry generated 800 single-spaced pages of feedback. . . . Programs: HP Labs simply had too many projects and too few priorities. People: The organization didn't remove poor performers quickly enough, and rank-and-file researchers didn't have the freedom they needed to do their jobs well. Processes: The "information infrastructure" was inadequate. . . .
>
> The feedback, says Waugh, was "800 pages of frustrations, dreams, and insights." But how could she capture and communicate what she'd learned? She drew on her experience with street theater and created a "play" about HP Labs. She worked passages from the surveys into dialogue and then recruited executives to act as staff members and junior people to act as executives. The troupe performed for 30 senior managers. "At the end of the play, the managers were very quiet," Waugh remembers. "Then they started clapping. It was exciting. They really got it."[16]

Waugh's approach is instructive because it began with an executive's question. Waugh then collected data on the issue, evoked emotional responses, and used a combination of programmatic and emergent change strategies to move organization members throughout the organization to action. It is instructive to note that this is not the first time she has nurtured change in an emergent grassroots fashion: Some of her other efforts include leveraging listening and questioning, building networks with individuals with complementary ideas, and, when needed, arranging for access to financial resources for worthy endeavors.*

Underlying planning-through-engagement strategies are assumptions regarding top-down (unilateral) versus bottom-up (participative) methods of change. Though we saw in the study by Waldersee and Griffiths[17] that unilateral implementation methods have much to offer, the success of a change is enhanced when people understand what it entails and why it is being undertaken, and what the consequences of success and failure are. All too often, technostructural changes have floundered because of design problems getting tangled up with acceptance and implementation issues that never seem to get sorted out. For example, Sobeys (a large Canadian supermarket chain) finally threw out its new enterprise software system after 2 years of implementation difficulties that culminated in a 5-day system crash that took weeks to recover from. This forced the company to take an

---

*In planning the work, the use of interviews, surveys, survey feedback, and a rigorous commitment to active listening are powerful action planning tools. They come from the Organizational Development (OD) approach to change.

after-tax charge of $50 million and revisit the issue of their information technology strategy.[18]

Regardless of the change strategy plan, the plan needs to be examined carefully for logic and consistency. The next section outlines a series of questions to improve change agents' abilities in this area.

How Do We Ensure Consistency in Our Action Planning?

Have you ever emerged from a meeting shaking your head saying, "How can they suggest taking that action given what they know of the situation?" The disconnect between your understanding of the situation and what others are doing is often evident to many except to those leaders who are guiding what is to be done. For example, faced with a loss of market share, a senior manager responds by cutting prices when customer feedback to frontline employees points to product quality and customer service as problems. Or when faced with a recurring absentee problem, management responds by requiring overtime from those who are showing up. Such disconnects are all too common and can be avoided by examining action plans with a critical eye for such inconsistencies and the unintended consequences that could result. In the first example, customers remain frustrated by quality and customer service problems but become accustomed to expecting lower prices. In the second, absenteeism and turnover may increase as employees seek to avoid being subjected to mandatory overtime.

Similarly, managers sometimes understand what needs to be done but get the sequence wrong. They might leave a meeting after a productive discussion but fail to sort out who is responsible for what. Sometimes critical steps in the plan are risky, and alternative strategies need to be considered in case things do not go as planned. At other times, they may over- or underestimate their resources or power or competence. Table 9.2 provides a checklist of questions to use when reviewing your action plans. This checklist tests the viability of the plan and asks for a rethinking of the connections between the analysis of the situation and the plan itself. Tough-minded thinking can improve the coherence and thoughtfulness of your action plans.

What Action-Planning Tools Are Available?

You have been learning about action planning throughout this book. Organizational size-up, stakeholder analysis, force field analysis—change agents use these tools to clarify what change is needed and to explore the positions and perspectives of those who will be involved in and/or affected by the change. Agents then incorporate this information with other tools (e.g., project management) to develop robust, adaptive change plans that have the greatest likelihood of producing the desired effects.

This section explores a selection of additional action-planning tools. Table 9.3 provides a partial list of tools for action planning, some of which are covered in other chapters and others that are addressed here. (Fortunately, managers use many of the approaches to action planning all the time, so much of this will be familiar to them.)

Table 9.2   Action-Planning Checklist

---

1. Is the action plan consistent with the analysis?

2. Is the plan time sequenced in logical order?

3. Is it clear who will do what, when, where, and how?

4. What is the probability of success at each step?

5. Have you developed contingencies for major possible but nondesirable occurrences?

6. Have you anticipated secondary consequences of your actions?

7. Is the plan realistic given your influence (both formal and informal) and the resources likely to be available to you?

8. Do you have the competence to implement the action steps? If not, who on your team does?

9. Who does your plan rely on? Are they "onside"? If not, what will it take to bring them "onside"?

10. Who (and what) could seriously obstruct the change? How will you manage them?

Source: Adapted from Gabarro, J., & Schlesinger, L. (1983). Some preliminary thoughts on action planning and implementation. In L. Schlesinger & J. Ware (Eds.), *Managing behaviour in organizations* (pp. 342–343). New York: McGraw-Hill.

1. *"To Do" Lists.* When managers engage in action planning, they often begin by outlining in detail the sequence of steps they will take initially to achieve their goals. That is, they make a list. To Do Lists, a checklist of things to do, is the simplest and most common planning tool. Sometimes this is all the situation requires. Don't get things complicated if a list works!

As the action planning becomes more sophisticated, simple "to do" lists will not suffice, and responsibility charting provides more control.

2. *Responsibility Charting.* Responsibility charting can be a valuable tool to detail who should do what, when, and how. As well, it can be used to help keep projects on track and provide a basis for record keeping and accountability. Table 9.4 provides an example responsibility chart. The process begins by defining the list of decisions or actions to be taken. Then, individuals are assigned responsibility for achieving or accomplishing the actions and deadlines are committed to.

3. *Contingency Planning.* Earlier, we discussed the importance of thinking through possible contingencies where events don't go as planned. Two tools, which aid us in contingency planning, are decision tree analysis and scenario planning.*

Decision tree analysis asks us to consider major alternatives we face and the possible consequences or outcome of those alternatives. We are then asked to plan

---

*Readers are encouraged to consult standard operations research texts for further information on these tools.

Table 9.3   Tools for Action Planning

---

1. To-Do Lists—A checklist of things to do.

2. Responsibility Charting—Who will do what, when, where, why, and how.

3. Contingency Planning—Consideration of what should be done when things do not work as planned on critical issues.

4. Project Planning or Critical Path Methods—Operations research techniques for scheduling work. These methods provide deadlines and insight as to which activities cannot be delayed to meet those deadlines.

5. Force Field and Stakeholder Analysis—Examination of the forces for and against change, and the positions of the major players and why they behave as they do.

    a. Commitment Charts—An evaluation of the level of commitment of major players (against, neutral, let it happen, help it happen, make it happen).
    b. The Adoption Continuum or AIDA Analysis—Examination of major players and their position on the Awareness, Interest, Desire, and Adoption continuum related to the proposed changes.

6. Leverage Analysis—Determination of methods of influencing major groups or players regarding the proposed changes.

Table 9.4   Example Responsibility Chart

Decisions or Actions to Be Taken	Responsibilities			
	Susan	Ted	Sonja	Relevant Dates
Action 1	R	A	I	For meeting on Jan. 14
Action 2		R	I	May 24
Action 3	S	A	A	Draft Plan by Feb. 17 Action by July 22

Coding: R = Responsibility (not necessarily authority)

   A = Approval (right to veto)

   S = Support (put resources toward)

   I = Inform (to be consulted before action)

Note that if there are a large number of A's on your chart, implementation will be difficult. Care must be taken to assign A's only when appropriate. Likewise, if there are not enough R's and S's, you will need to think about changes needed here and how to bring them about.

Source: Adapted from Beckhard, R. (1987). *Organizational transitions* (p. 104). Reading, MA: Addison-Wesley.

possible next actions we might take for those consequences. Such alternating action-consequence sequences can be extended as far as one thinks is reasonable. As well, probabilities can be assigned as to the likelihood of each consequence. For many applications, a simple scale (*very likely, likely, possible, unlikely,* or *very unlikely*) is probably sufficient. However, operations researchers have extended this technique and thus provide means of estimating probabilities much more exactly.

A second tool that helps managers with contingency planning is scenario planning. Here, a change strategy is formed by developing a limited number of scenarios or stories about how the future may unfold and what the implications of this would be to the organization. Change leaders typically frame these around an issue of strategic and/or tactical importance.[19] For example, if a firm producing paper forms was concerned about the long-term viability of the business, they could develop scenarios of what a paperless form producer would look like—one that was capable of adding value to medium to large organizations. Once the scenarios were developed, managers would ask themselves what would need to happen over time to make them realities and what contingencies might arise that would need to be addressed. If one or more of these future scenarios seemed worth investing in, they would develop their plans accordingly.

Scenario planning is different from forecasting. Forecasting starts in the present and uses trend lines and probability estimates to make projections about the future. Scenario planning starts by painting a picture of the future and works backwards, asking what would have to happen to make this future scenario a reality and what could we do about it.[20]

While most uses of scenario planning are at a strategy level, the principles can be applied to help you anticipate possible outcomes of change plans so that contingent actions can be contemplated in advance. Royal Dutch Shell[21] was one of the first users of scenario planning. They used it as a way to link future uncertainties to today's decisions.

4. *Project Planning or Critical Path Methods.* Project planning or critical path methods can provide valuable assistance to change managers as they think about what action steps to take. These methods have been developed into sophisticated operations research techniques to aid the planning of major projects. Critical path methods ask planners to identify when the project should be completed and to work backwards from that point, scheduling all tasks that will require time and effort. These are arranged in time sequence such that tasks that can occur simultaneously can be identified. These tasks are then plotted on a time line. Sequential tasks are plotted to determine the needed time to complete the project. With this done, managers can see if there is enough time available for the normal completion of the task. Managers can assess bottlenecks, slack, required resources, and progression paths. If there is a time problem, the project manager can add resources to speed up the project or delay the project. As well, the critical path, the path with the least slack time, can be identified and special attention can be paid to it.

Critical path methods introduce the notion of parallel initiatives. That is, managers can work on several things simultaneously. Phase 1 tasks don't have to be totally completed before beginning work on Phase 2 tasks. Care and sophistication are required with partially parallel approaches because they carry the risk of increasing confusion and redundant effort. When properly applied, though, they've demonstrated their ability to shrink cycle time. This is readily visible in areas such as new-product development. Figure 9.2 gives an example of a sequential and a parallel plan for new-product development. In the upper example, Example 1 in Figure 9.2, the tasks are plotted sequentially. In Example 2, the tasks overlap. Concept development begins before opportunity identification ends and time is saved.

5. *Force Field and Stakeholder Analysis.* Chapter 6 of this book is dedicated to understanding the change situation, with particular attention to force field and stakeholder analysis. Force field analysis asks change agents to specify the forces for and against change. Stakeholder analysis asks that the key players be identified and the relationships among players be examined. Two additional tools that are helpful when planning actions related to stakeholders are commitment charts and AIDA charts.

Commitment Analysis Charts

Managers can use commitment charts to analyze the commitment of each stakeholder. Stakeholders can be thought of as being weakly to strongly opposed (**against**) to your change project neutral (**let it happen**), slightly positive (**help**

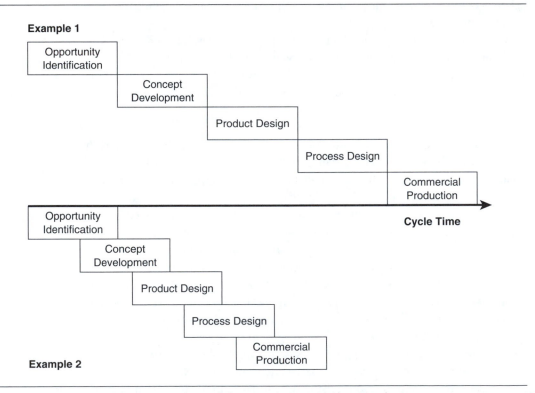

Figure 9.2   Sequential Versus Partly Parallel Process in New Product Development

Source: Shilling, M. A., & Hill, W. L. (1998). Managing the new product development process: Strategic imperatives. *Academy of Management Executive, (12)*3, 73. Copyright © 1998 by Academy of Management. Reproduced with permission of Academy of Management via Copyright Clearance Center.

it happen), or strongly positive (**make it happen**). Change leaders also need to consider the level of understanding (including its type and sources) that underpins stakeholders' commitment level. Identifying the existing level of commitment is the first step in planning tactics designed to alter those preexisting patterns. Table 9.5 provides an example commitment chart. (Note that the "X" in the table shows where the person is and the "O" shows where you want them to be.)

Table 9.5   An Example Commitment Chart

| Key Players | Level of Commitment | | | | | Level of Understand-ing (high, medium, low) |
	Opposed Strongly to Weakly	Neutral	Let It Happen	Help It Happen	Make It Happen	
Person 1		X	→O			Medium
Person 2				X	→O	High
Person 3		X	→	→O		Low

Source: Beckhard, op. cit., p. 95.

The Adoption Continuum

Often, change leaders need to think about convincing key people one person at a time. Other times, working with groups is a more viable approach. Stakeholder analysis will have identified those people who are critical to the change process. Managers need to consider how they propose to encourage individuals to move along the **adoption continuum** until the needed stakeholders have bought into the change (or at least minimized their opposition).

As noted in Chapter 6, change agents can think of the process of getting people onside with change as one of, first, creating awareness and then encouraging them to move from **awareness** of the issues to **interest** in the change, to **desiring** action, and, finally, to **action** or adopting the change. This is called the AIDA or adoption continuum. Table 9.6 provides an example of how you might map people onto the adoption continuum as a method of tracking their change attitudes.

Different individuals will often be at different points on the AIDA continuum, which makes change strategies complex. For each stage, managers need to use different tactics. For example, to raise initial awareness, managers should use well-designed general communication vehicles such as newsletters, reports, and videos. The messages should be used to raise awareness of the need for change and provide access to thought-provoking data supporting those reasons. However, if most people are already aware of what is being proposed, managers shouldn't waste efforts on general information communications.

Table 9.6   Mapping People on the Adoption Continuum

Persons or Stakeholder Groups	Awareness	Interest	Desiring Action	Moving to Action or Adopting the Change
Person 1				
Person 2				
Person 3				
. . .				

To move people to the interest phase, managers need to outline how the change will impact stakeholders personally and/or why this change should be of interest to them. Discussion groups on the issue, benchmark data, simulations, and test runs showing results can be effective in stimulating interest. Once interest is aroused, specific tactics to demonstrate and reinforce the benefits and build commitment are needed. Managers might use one-on-one meetings and direct exposure and involvement with the change. Change agents might reallocate resources or designate rewards in ways that reinforce adoption. Influencing people one at a time can be valuable if the right individuals (given their influence) are identified and the right message is communicated.

6. *Leverage Analysis.* In Chapter 6, we stated that people's position on the adoption continuum is influenced by their general orientation to change—whether they tend to be an innovator, early adopter, early majority, late majority, or laggard in matters related to change. One of the action-planning challenges for the change leaders is to sort out people's overall predisposition to change and the proposed change in particular.

Moving individuals on the adoption continuum is aided by engaging in **leverage analysis.** Leverage analysis seeks to identify those actions that will create the greatest change with the least effort. For example, if opinion leaders of a key group of individuals can be identified and persuaded to back the proposed organizational change, the job of the change leader is made easier. Likewise, if the task is to persuade senior management, one needs to identify influential individuals in this group. Identifying high-leverage methods will depend on the quality of your knowledge of the participants and your analysis of the organization and its environment.

Gladwell presents an excellent example of the notion of leverage in his book *The Tipping Point.*[22] Gladwell points out how little things can have large consequences if they occur at the right moment and are contagious or catching. As things catch on, eventually a tipping point is reached (the point where a critical mass of support is reached), the change becomes more firmly rooted, and the rate of acceptance accelerates. As Burke puts it, change agents need to find the critical few that can connect in ways that change the context and tip things into a new reality. The vision needs to be sticky, that is, cast as a story so that it will stay with people, and managers need to understand the connectors in the organization to get this message out.[23] Moore notes that one of the biggest challenges to reaching the tipping point is to build sufficient support to allow managers to cross the "chasm" between early adopters or visionaries and the early majority.[24] Once this gap has been bridged, the rate of progress accelerates because of the critical mass of supporters.

What Are Other Management Tools?

Recent work on statistical methods has added other planning and diagnostic aids: Pareto diagrams (which classify problems according to relative importance), cause-effect diagrams, histograms, benchmark and normative data, control charts (to show abnormal trends), and scatter diagrams.[25] The selection of which tools to use in this area depends on the nature of the data managers have to work with and what they want to do. In general, their real value lies in focusing attention, sorting out patterns and underlying effects, and assessing progress.

The variety of techniques and tools reported on in the popular business press continues to grow. Rigby has tracked management's worldwide use of a wide variety of tools.[26] He surveyed the use of 25 management tools in organizations and described satisfaction levels with the tools being used by more and less successful organizations. While a generic listing of tools won't necessarily help a specific change leader in a specific situation, Rigby's list of "best tools for the job" could be of interest to change leaders. Appendix 2 summarizes Rigby's results.

In summary, planning the work asks the change leaders to translate the change vision into specific actions that people can take. The plan outlines targets and dates and considers contingencies—what might go wrong (or right), how managers can anticipate those things, and how they can respond. Further, it examines how realistic the chances are and how you might increase those probabilities.

Table 9.7 outlines a checklist for developing your action plan.

How Do We Organize the Change Team?

> *Champions transform visions into realities but a committed small group*
> *of individuals can win wars and transform society.*[27]

Many years ago, a group of students at Case Western Reserve University decided that there had to be better ways of teaching organizational change and development. This small group dedicated itself to changing the system. In 2 years, they transformed parts of Case Western and created the first doctoral program in organizational development with themselves as potential graduates. They planned and plotted. They identified key stakeholders and assigned team members to each stakeholder with the responsibility of bringing that stakeholder onside—or at least neutralizing their opposition. It was the team that made the change happen. They put into practice what they were learning as students.[28]

Creating the conditions for successful change is more than having an excellent change project plan. Equally important is recognizing the different change roles

Table 9.7   A Checklist for Change

Developing Your Action Plan

1. Given your vision statement, what is your overall objective? When must it be accomplished?

2. What would be the first step in accomplishing your goal?

3. What would be milestones along the way, which will allow you to determine if you are making progress?

4. What is your action plan? Who will do what, when, where, why, and how? Can you do a responsibility chart?

5. What is the probability of success at each step?

6. Do you have a contingency plan when things go wrong? What things are most likely to go wrong? What things can you not afford to have them go wrong? How can you prevent such things from happening?

7. Is your action plan realistic given your influence both formal and informal?

8. Who does your plan rely on? Are they onside?

9. Does your action plan take into account the concerns of stakeholders and the possible coalitions they might form?

---

that need to be played and developing the change team. This section covers the different change roles that organization members can play, how you design an excellent change team, and the use of consultants as part of the change process.

What Are Possible Roles in Change Teams?*

Many change examples point out the need for a **champion** who will fight for the change under trying circumstances and will continue to persevere when others would be long gone. These change champions represent the visionary, the immovable force for change who will continue to push for the change regardless of the opposition and the resistance to change. Senior managers need to ensure that those to whom the change is delegated possess (and are seen to possess) the energy, drive, skills, resilience, credibility, and commitment needed to make it happen. If appropriate individuals are lacking, steps need to be taken to ensure that they are either developed or found in order to champion the implementation of the change.

Senior executives who act as **sponsors** of change foster commitment to the change and assist those charged with making the change happen.[29] Sponsors can act visibly, can share information and knowledge, and can give protection. *Visible sponsorship* means the senior manager advocates for the change and shows support through actions (i.e., use of their influence and time) as well as words. *Information*

---

*In Chapter 1, we discussed the roles that an individual can play: change recipient, agent initiator, and implementer. The roles here relate to change teams.

sharing and knowledge development has the sponsor providing useful information about change and working with the team to ensure that the plans are sound. Finally, sponsors can *provide protection* or cover for those to whom the change has been delegated. Without such protection, the individuals in the organization will tend to become more risk averse and less willing to champion the change.[30]

Change champions should consider two further organizing roles that are often better operationalized through the use of a team: a **steering team** and a **design and implementation team.** The steering team provides advice to the champion regarding the direction of the change in light of other events and priorities in the organization. As suggested by its name, it plays an advisory and navigational function for the change project and is the major policy-determining group.

The design and implementation team focuses on the tasks that its name implies. This is the team that plans the change, deals with the stakeholders, and has primary responsibility for the implementation. The design and implementation team will often have a **change project manager.** This person will track the change efforts and the team's progress toward change targets.

How Do We Develop the Change Team?

Developing the team can become a significant task for the change leaders. If teams can be developed until they are self-regulating or self-managed, change can be facilitated.[31] Because they operate independently, self-managed teams can reduce the management effort required in the implementation of change. Self-managed teams share an understanding of the change goals and objectives, sort out for themselves how tasks are to be differentiated and executed, and have control over the decision quality.

Wageman has identified the following seven factors as critical to team success with self-managed teams:

1. Clear, engaging direction

2. A real team task

3. Rewards for team excellence

4. The availability of basic material resources to do the job, including the individual abilities and skills of the team members

5. Authority vested in the team to manage the work

6. Team goals

7. The development of team norms that promote strategic thinking[32]

A similar list was developed by the Change Institute.[33] However, they focused more on fast action through small team numbers, compulsory attendance at meetings, and a focus on results.

The dedication and willingness to give it their "all" is the most obvious characteristic of highly committed change teams. The dogged determination to make changes regardless of personal consequences because of a deep-rooted belief in a vision creates both the conditions for victory and the possibilities of organizational suicide—the belief that what we are doing is so critical, so important, that it transcends individual consequences and results. In our earlier example at Case Western Reserve University, if the change were not successful, the individuals involved would have sacrificed several years of their lives to no organizational effect. In the case of Lou Gerstner's turnaround at IBM,[34] there was a distinct possibility that the firm would not survive and members of his inner circle would be forever known as the individuals who oversaw the collapse of this American corporate icon. Many managers don't have the fire to commit to such a degree. They lack the intensity of vision, the dedication to a cause, and the willingness to sacrifice everything to achieve change. Fortunately, most change situations do not demand that level of personal commitment and sacrifice.

In forming a change team, the personalities and skills of the members will play a significant role in the team's success. The change process demands a paradoxical set of skills:

- The ability to create a vision and the intuition to see the connections between that vision and all the things that will need to be done, including who will need to be influenced
- The ability to think positively about stakeholders while recognizing what will influence them and why they may resist you
- The ability to care passionately for an initiative and yet not interpret criticism and opposition as a personal attack
- The ability to translate broad strategy or vision into concrete change plans

A person needs to have the capacity to deal with these paradoxes, not just technical or functional expertise.

Often, organizations form teams based on functional or technical expertise. These variables are important. It is difficult to imagine a team establishing credibility if they lack such basics. However, the personalities present in the team will influence how the team interacts and performs, including its ability to manage the inherent paradoxes. While it is usually not necessary for the team to be highly cohesive, cohesion will lend strength to the change effort and focus the team's activities, because cohesion is often rooted in a shared sense of purpose or goal.

Toolkit Exercise 9.2 asks you to reflect on your experience with change teams.

How Can We Work the Plan?

De Bono describes the styles of success: energy, drive and direction, a "can do" attitude, ruthlessness, self-confidence and ego, and stamina and hard work.[35] These are the attributes of those who make things happen and who bring about change. Working the plan means that change managers need to focus, see things as opportunities, continually develop new ideas, and take on risks. At the same time, managers need to proceed ethically. Otherwise, they risk destroying credibility and the trust others have in them. Relationships can and do recover from strong disagreements, but recovery is far less likely if people feel they have been lied to or otherwise ethically abused. Most of us will know the permanent sense of betrayal that ensues when we have been dealt with unethically.

De Bono warns, "Success is an affirmation but not a learning process."[36] Chris Argyris echoes this when he claims, "People who rarely experience failure end up not knowing how to deal with it."[37] Russo and Shoemaker provide us with guidelines in managing overconfidence—in particular, they differentiate the need for confidence when one is an implementer as opposed to a decision maker. Decision makers need to be realistic; implementers can afford to be somewhat overconfident if it provides others with the courage to change.[38] However, if overconfidence interferes with their ability to interpret data or understand and deal with various stakeholders effectively, managers can impair their own ability to create successful change.

Often, managers of change must influence the key stakeholders in the organization to change their perspective and support, thereby altering the balance between forces for and against an initiative. Greiner identified four strategies of influence: (1) dealing directly with decision makers, (2) using data to convince others, (3) focusing on the needs of a target group, and (4) going around roadblocks.[39] He describes a study by Schein comparing strategies for success, which is summarized in Table 9.8.

Change leaders can influence through a combination of push and pull tactics. Push tactics are those where you overwhelm the opposition to acceptance of your plans. They consist of rational persuasion—the use of facts and logic in a nonemotional way—and pressure—the use of guilt or threats to create change. The risk of push tactics is that they lead to resistance and defensiveness. We oppose the pressure simply because it is pressure and we feel a need to defend our positions.

Alternatively, change leaders can rely on pull tactics: inspirational appeals and consultation. Inspirational appeals can arouse enthusiasm based on values or ideals. Consultation, where you seek the participation of others, appeals to the individuals' self-worth and positive self-concept and pulls them in the direction you wish.[*]

Other methods of influence include the following:

- Ingratiation: praise, flattery, friendliness
- Personal appeals: friendship and loyalty
- Exchange: forms of reciprocity
- Coalition building: creation of a subgroup to exert pressure
- Legitimating: reference to higher authority

Nutt describes four implementation tactics: (1) intervention, where key executives justify the need for change and provide new norms to judge performance; (2) participation, which involves stakeholders in the change process; (3) persuasion, which is the use of experts to sell a change; and (4) edict, which is the issuing of directives. Table 9.9 summarizes Nutt's data on the frequency of use, initial and ultimate adoption rate, and the time to install for each of these tactics.

This table demonstrates the value of a well-respected sponsor who acts as a lightning rod and energizes and justifies the need for change. The frequency of the

---

[*]These styles are described more fully in Chapter 8.

Table 9.8 Strategies for Success

		Successful	Unsuccessful
US Managers			
Using Social Networks			
	*Alliances and coalitions	57%	30%
	*Deal directly with decision makers	60%	48%
	*Contacts for information	32%	21%
Playing It Straight			
	*Using data to convince others	59%	46%
	*Focus on needs of target groups	47%	36%
Going Around the Formal System			
	*Work around roadblocks	36%	18%
	*Use organizational rules	16%	29%
UK Managers			
	*Alliances and coalitions	61%	38%
	*Use organizational rules	21%	41%

Note on interpretation: Managers reported that they used alliances and coalitions in 57% of successful changes but in only 30% of unsuccessful changes, whereas they used organizational rules in only 16% of successful changes but in 29% of unsuccessful changes.

The strategies shown here represent only those that revealed a statistically significant difference between the successful percentage and the unsuccessful percentage.

Source: Adapted from Greiner, L. (1998). *Power and Organizational Development,* (pp. 44-47). Reading, Mass: Addison-Wesley.

Table 9.9 Implementation Tactics and Success

Tactic	Percentage Use	Initial Adoption Rate	Ultimate Adoption Rate	Time to Adopt (months)
Intervention	16%	100%	82%	11.2
Participation	20%	80.6%	71%	19
Persuasion	35%	65%	49%	20.0
Edict	29%	51%	35%	21.5

Source: Adapted from Nutt, P. (1992). *Managing planned change* (p. 153). Toronto: Macmillan Toronto.

use of participation as a strategy is somewhat higher than intervention and may reflect the challenge of managing change from the middle of the organization. Adoption takes longer, but it has the second-best success rate. Persuasion is attempted more frequently than the other three tactics, but its success rate is significantly lower than participation and the time to adoption is slightly longer. Finally, it is difficult to understand the frequency of use of edict as a tactic, given its poor adoption rate and length of time to install.

Falbe and Yukl examined the effectiveness of influence tactics over 504 influence attempts. They discovered that inspirational appeals and consultation were the most effective tactics, while pressure, legitimating, and coalition tactics were least effective. Rationale, persuasion, ingratiation, personal appeals, and exchange tactics were intermediate in their effectiveness.[40]

Toolkit Exercise 9.3 asks you to consider the types of tactics used in change situations.

How Do We Communicate for Change?

In the midst of a change program, change leaders often find that misinformation and rumors are rampant in their organization. The reasons for change are not clear to employees, and the impact on employees is frequently exaggerated—negatively. In all organizations, the challenge is to persuade employees to move in a common direction. Good communication programs are essential to minimize the negative effects of rumors and to build support for the change.

In one manufacturing organization, employees were convinced that the real purpose of the organizational change plan was to get rid of employees—in spite of public assurances that the reorganization was aligning processes to service increased demand. It was not about reducing head count. Turnover reached 20% per year before leaders were able to convince the employees that the rumors were false. In a study on communications in organizations, Goodman and Truss found that only 27% of employees felt that management was in touch with employee concerns regardless of the fact that the company had a carefully crafted communications strategy.[41]

Much of the confusion over change can be attributed to the different levels of understanding held by different parties. For example, senior management may have been struggling with change issues for weeks or months and understand the need for change and what must happen. Frontline and middle managers may not have had the opportunity to reflect on the topic and lag senior management's awareness. Senior management has had time to adjust but other employees have not.

Communication plans need to be developed for three major reasons: (1) to infuse the need for change throughout the organization, (2) to enable individuals to understand the impact of the change on themselves, and (3) to communicate any structural and job changes that will influence how things are done. Perhaps the most critical reason for communication is to ensure that the rationale for change is understood broadly. This could come from a discussion of vision and purpose that pull people in new exciting directions.

An understanding of the need for change could also come from comparative data that push employees in the direction of change. Concrete but negative data that demonstrate how competitors are moving ahead of the organization can shake up complacent perspectives. Benchmark data can show a need for change. Spector demonstrates how sharing competitive information beyond top management can overcome potential conflicting views between senior management and other employees.[42]

Change managers need to understand the personal impact of change on employees. Rumors, horror stories, and gossip compete with management information and messages. Employees believe friends more than they believe supervisors. A proposed change may impact their job and future. They will have legitimate concerns that need to be addressed. Organizations and change managers have a choice: They can communicate clear messages about the nature and impact of the change, or they can let the rumors provide the basis for employee attitudes. Good communications can lessen ambivalence and resistance to change and increase the involvement and commitment of employees.[43]

Finally, communication programs are needed to convey information about future plans and how things will operate. If the organization is being reorganized, employees need to understand how this reorganization will affect their jobs. If new systems are being put into place, training needs to happen in order for employees to use the systems properly. If reporting relationships are altered, employees need to know who will do what in the organization. Thus, intentional strategies are needed to communicate this information.

What Is the Impact of Timing in Communication?

Any communication plan can be thought of in four phases: (1) prechange approval, (2) creating the need for change, (3) midstream change and milestone communication, and (4) confirming/celebrating the change success. The messages and methods of communication will vary depending on which phase your change is in. Table 9.10 outlines the communication needs of each phase.

In the prechange phase, change agents need to convince top management and others that the change is needed. They will target individuals with the influence and/or authority to approve a needed change. Dutton and her colleagues suggest that packaging the change proposal into smaller change steps helps success. Timing was crucial in that persistence, opportunism, and involvement of others at the right time was positively related to the successful selling of projects. Finally, linking the change to the organization's goals, plans, and priorities was critical.[44]

In creating the need for change, communication programs need to explain the issues and provide a clear, compelling rationale for the change. The plan and what steps are to be taken need specifying. People need to be reassured that they will be treated fairly and with respect.[45]

In the mid phases of change, people need to understand the progress made in the change program. Management needs to obtain feedback regarding the acceptance of the changes and the attitudes of employees. Change leaders need to understand any misconceptions that are developing and have the means to combat such

Table 9.10   Communication Needs for Different Phases in the Change Process

Preapproval Phase	Developing the Need for Change Phase	Midstream Change Phase	Confirming the Change Phase
Communication plans to sell top management.	Communication plans to explain the need for change, provide a rationale, reassure employees, and clarify the steps in the change process.	Communication plans to inform people of progress and to obtain feedback on attitudes and issues, to challenge any misconceptions, and to clarify new organizational roles, structures, and systems.	Communication plans to inform employees of the success, to celebrate the change, and to prepare the organization for the next change.

Source: This chart is based on Klein, S. M. (1996). A management communication strategy for change. *Journal of Organizational Change Management,* (9)2.

misconceptions. During this phase, extensive communications on the content of the change will be important as management and employees begin to understand new roles, structures, and systems.[46]

The final phase of a change program needs to communicate and celebrate the success of the program. Unfinished tasks need to be identified and discussed. The organization needs to be positioned for the next change. Change is not over—only this particular program or phase.

While change managers need to attend to the different phases in the change process, they also need to match the complexity of the communications with the method chosen.[47] Managers who need to communicate about complex issues should use person-to-person communications strategies. Goodman and others suggest using line managers and opinion leaders as lynchpins in the communications strategy, but this requires that they have been properly briefed and engaged in the change process. They also stress that change agents need to recognize communications as a two-way strategy.[48] That is, the gathering of information might be as important as telling their side.

Key Principles in Communicating for Change

Klein suggests six principles that should underlie a communications strategy:

1. Message and media redundancy are key for message retention. That is, multiple messages using multiple media will increase the chance of people obtaining and retaining the message. Too often, management believes that

since the message was sent, their work is done and it is the employee's fault for not getting the message! As one author pointed out, it takes time for people to hear, understand, and believe a message, especially when they don't like what they hear.[49]

2. Face-to-face communication is most effective. While the impact of face-to-face is highest, the cost is also higher. Face-to-face permits two-way communication, which increases the chance of involvement of both parties and decreases the probability of miscommunication.

3. Line authority is effective in communications. Regardless of the level of participative involvement, most employees look to management for direction and guidance. If the CEO says it, the message packs a punch and gets attention.

4. The immediate supervisor is key. The level of trust and understanding between an employee and his or her supervisor can make the supervisor a valuable part of a communications strategy. People expect to hear important organizational messages from their bosses.

5. Opinion leaders need to be identified and used. These individuals can be critical in persuading employees to a particular view.

6. Employees pick up and retain personally relevant information more easily than other types of information. Thus, communication plans should take care to relate general information in terms of employee impact.[50]

In summary, change leaders seldom give enough attention to communications. Change implementers and recipients often lag change leaders in their understanding of the need for and nature of the change, as well as their commitment to it. People are more likely to become involved when they understand the change and what their role will be. They need to be reassured about their future in the organization. The nature of communications depends on the stage of the change plan and what media are being used. When employees sense that there is insufficient credible communication, they search out rumors to help them make sense of the situation.

What Is Transition Management?

Change management is about keeping the plane flying while you rebuild it.[51]

In today's competitive, cost-conscious world, it is unacceptable to stop everything while making change happen. You can't just say, "Sorry, we aren't able to deliver the product we promised because we are making improvements around the place." Most organizations today have many change projects under way simultaneously. One part of the organization may be reengineering itself. Another might be introducing a quality program while another part focuses on employee empowerment. All of these must be managed concurrently while continuing to produce the service or product demanded.

Morris and Raben argue for a transition manager who has transition resources, transition structures, and a transition plan.[52] The transition manager has the power and authority to facilitate the transition and is linked to the CEO or other senior executive. Transition resources are the people, money, training, and consultant expertise needed to be successful. Transition structures are structures outside the regular organizational ones—temporary structures that allow "normal" activities to take place as well as change activities. The transition plan is the change plan with clear benchmarks, standards, and responsibilities for the change. Table 9.11 outlines a checklist for transition management.

Transition management is making certain that both the change project and the continuing operations are successful. The change leader or transition team in charge of the transition makes sure that both occur. While the change champion is visible and articulating both the need for change and the new vision, the transition manager/team is managing the organization's structural and system changes and the individuals' emotional and behavioral issues so that neither are compromised to a danger point.[53] Ackerman describes the application of a transition management model at Sun Petroleum.[54] She addresses the question, "How can these changes be put into place without seriously straining the organization?" Her solution was to create a transition manager who handled the social system requirements. Ackerman argues for a transition team that creates a transition structure enabling the organization to carry on while the change takes place. What was needed, of course, was a means for the organization to continue operating effectively while undergoing major change.

Beckhard and Harris focus on the transition details in organizational change.[55] They reinforce the importance of specifying midpoint goals and milestones, which

Table 9.11   A Checklist for Change

Transition Management

The following questions can be useful when planning transition management systems and structures.

1. How will the organization continue to operate as it shifts from one state to the next?

2. Who will answer questions about the proposed change? What decision power will they have? Will they provide information only, or will they be able to make decisions (such as individual pay levels after the change)?

3. Do the people in charge of the transition have the appropriate amount of authority to make decisions necessary to ease the change?

4. Have people developed ways to reduce the anxiety created by the change and increase the positive excitement over it?

5. Have people worked on developing a problem-solving climate around the change process?

6. Have people thought through the need to communicate the change? Who needs to be seen individually? Which groups need to be seen together? What formal announcement should be made?

help motivate the members of the organization. The longer the span of time required for a change initiative, the more important these midcourse goals become. The goals need to be far enough away to provide direction, but close enough to provide a sense of progress and accomplishment and an opportunity for midcourse changes in plans.

A second component of transition management is keeping people informed and reducing anxiety. During major reorganizations, many employees are assigned to new roles, new bosses, new departments, or new tasks. Those individuals have a right to know their new work terms and conditions. Transition managers will put systems in place to ensure that answers to questions (such as, "Will my pay be affected?" "Who is my new boss?" or "What is my new job description?") can be provided. An example of this need occurred in the Ontario Ministry of Agriculture, Food and Rural Development. As the designer of a major change in that organization, Bill Allen commented that the ministry "underestimated the importance of a well thought out transition structure and plan." Employees of the ministry had hundreds of questions about the organization change and there was no formal structure to handle these in a consistent and professional manner.[56] The transition team needs to be given the capacity to do this.

Summary

"Doing it" demands a good plan and a committed team who will work that plan. This chapter describes several generic strategies for dealing with change. It outlines Kotter and Schlesinger's proposals on how to deal with resistance to change. The chapter also lists a set of action-planning tools, which help us develop a good action plan. It outlines how we can organize for change, develop a change team, and put the plan into action. The chapter ends by considering communication and transition management.

Glossary of Terms

Generic Change Strategies—Three generic change strategies are described:

1. **Programmatic change**—Traditional planned change.

2. **Discontinuous change**—Major change that breaks from previous organizational strategies often involving revolutionary ideas.

3. **Emergent change**—Change that grows out of incremental change initiatives.

Alternatives to Reduce Resistance to Change—Seven alternatives to reducing change are outlined: (1) education and communication, (2) participation and involvement, (3) facilitation and support, (4) negotiation and agreement, (5) manipulation and cooperation, (6) explicit and implicit coercion, and (7) systematic adjustments.

Contingency Planning—Consideration of what should be done when things do not work as planned on critical issues.

Project Planning or Critical Path Methods—Operations research techniques for scheduling work.

Leverage Analysis—Identifying those actions that create the most change for the least effort.

Change Team Roles—Five roles are described:

1. **Team Champion**—The person who fights for the change.

2. **Team Sponsor(s)**—The senior executive(s) who supports the change project.

3. **Steering Team**—A group providing guidance and advice to the change agent.

4. **Design and Implementation Team**—A group making the change happen.

5. **Change Project Manager**—The person responsible for ensuring progress in the change project and for monitoring the progress of the change.

Phases in the Communications Process—Four phases in the communications process during change are outlined: (1) the preapproval phase, (2) developing the need for change phase, (3) the midstream phase, and (4) confirming the change phase.

Transition Management—Transition management is the process of ensuring that the organization continues to operate effectively while undergoing change.

APPENDIX 1: A COMPARISON OF FOUR MODELS OF CHANGE

Beer's Six Steps for Change (1990)	Kanter et al.'s Ten Commandments for Change (1992)	Kotter's Eight-Stage Process for Successful Organizational Transformation (1996)	Lueck's Seven Steps for Change (2003)
Mobilize commitment to change through joint diagnosis of problems.	Analyze the organization and its need for change.	Establish a sense of urgency.	Mobilize energy, commitment through joint identification of business problems and their solutions.
Develop a shared vision of how to organize and manage for competitiveness.	Create a vision and a common direction.	Create a guiding coalition.	Develop a shared vision of how to organize and manage for competitiveness.
Foster consensus for the new vision, competence to enact it, and cohesion to move it along.	Separate from the past.	Develop a vision and strategy.	Identify the leadership.
Spread revitalization to all departments without pushing it from the top.	Create a sense of urgency.	Empower broad-based action.	Focus on results, not activities.
Institutionalize revitalization through formal policies, systems, and structures.	Support a strong leader role.	Communicate the change vision.	Start change at the periphery, and then let it spread to other units pushing it from the top.
Monitor and adjust strategies in response to problems in the revitalization process.	Line up political sponsorship.	Generate short-term wins.	Institutionalize success through formal policies, systems, and structures.
	Craft an implementation plan.	Consolidate gains and produce more change.	Monitor and adjust strategies in response to problems in the change process.
	Develop enabling structures.	Anchor new approaches in the culture.	
	Communicate, involve people, and be honest.		
	Reinforce and institutionalize change.		

Source: This table is based on articles by Todnem By, R. (2005). Organisational change management: A critical review. Journal of Change Management, (5)4; and Beer, M., Eisenstat, R., & Spector, B. (1990). Why change programs don't produce change. Harvard Business Review, 158–166.

APPENDIX 2. RIGBY'S LIST OF THE BEST TOOLS FOR THE JOB[57]

	Impact of the Change Tool				
Type of Tool	Financial Results	Customer Equity	Performance Capabilities	Competitive Positioning	Organizational Integration
Customer Retention		++		+	
Customer Satisfaction Measures		++		++	
Customer Segmenting		++			
Cycle Time Reduction	++		+	+	
Growth Strategies	+		+		
Merger Integration Teams					+
Mission & Vision Statements					++
One-to-One Marketing	++	++	++	++	++
Pay for Performance	+				
Strategic Alliances		+		+	
Strategic Planning		+	++	++	++
Supply Chain Integration	++		++		
Total Quality Management		++			
Virtual Teams					++

+ Significantly above the mean in 1 year.
++ Significantly above the mean in every year (over 10 years).

END-OF-CHAPTER EXERCISES

TOOLKIT EXERCISE 9.1

Overcoming Resistance to Change

1. What methods have you seen used in organizations to overcome resistance to action plans? Think specifically about a change instance and what was done. When have people used

    a. Education and communication?

    b. Participation and involvement?

    c. Facilitation and support?

    d. Negotiation and agreement?

    e. Manipulation and co-optation?

    f. Explicit and implicit coercion?

    g. Systemic adjustments?

2. What were the consequences of different methods? What worked and what did not work? Why?

3. What personal preferences do you have regarding these techniques? That is, which ones do you have the skills to manage and the personality to match?

TOOLKIT EXERCISE 9.2

Change Teams in Organizations

1. Have you seen an example of an organization using teams to help implement change initiatives? If you have, what was its experience?

2. How were the teams designed (membership) and developed? What was their purpose and what was achieved?

3. If you've used teams for change, what types of teams were they, and how much authority and discretion did they have?

4. Assess the appropriateness of self-managing change teams. Under what conditions would they be appropriate?

TOOLKIT EXERCISE 9.3

Influence Tactics

1. Think specifically of change situations in an organization you are familiar with. What influence tactics did people use?

   a. Rational persuasion
   b. Ingratiation
   c. Personal appeals
   d. Exchange or reciprocity
   e. Coalition building
   f. Appeals to higher authority
   g. Dealing directly with decision makers
   h. Involving others
   i. Using organizational rules
   j. Relying on the informal system

2. How successful was each of the tactics? Why did it work or not work?

3. How comfortable are you with each tactic? Which could you use?

Notes

1. www.chips.navy.mil/links/grace_hopper/file2.htm; or www.ideafinder.com/history/inventors/hopper.htm; or www.inventors.about.com/library/inventors/bl_Grace_Hopper. htm.

2. Kouzes, J., & Posner, B. (1995). *The leadership challenge.* San Francisco: Jossey-Bass.

3. Pfeffer, J., & Sutton, R. (1999, Fall). Knowing "what" to do is not enough: Turning knowledge into action. *California Management Review, (42)*1.

4. Sayles, L. (1993, Spring). Doing things right: A new imperative for middle managers. *Organizational Dynamics, 10.*

5. Schlender, B. (1998, September 28). Peter Drucker takes the long view. *Fortune.*

6. Bunker, B. B., Alban, B. T., & Lewicki, R. J. (2004). Ideas in currency and OD practice: Has the well gone dry? *Journal of Applied Behavioral Sciences, (40)*4.

7. Mintzberg, H., & Westley, F. (2001, Spring). Decision making: It's not what you think. *Sloan Management Review, 42.*

8. http://www.everyday-taichi.com/confucius-saying.html.

9. Beer, M., Eisenstat, R. A., & Spector, B. (1990, November–December). Why change programs don't produce change. *Harvard Business Review,* 158–166.

10. Todnem By, R. (2005, December). Organisational change management: A critical review. *Journal of Change Management, (5)*4, 375.

11. Source unknown.

12. Waldersee, R., & Griffiths, A. (2004). Implementing change: Matching implementation methods and change type. *Leadership and Organization Development Journal, (25)*5, 424–434.

13. Beer, M., Eisenstat, R., & Spector, B. (1990). Why change programs don't produce change. *Harvard Business Review,* 158–166.

14. Nohria, N., & Khurana, R. (1993, August 24). *Executing change: Three generic strategies.* Harvard Business School Note 494–039.

15. Kotter, J., & Schlesinger, L. (1982). Choosing strategies for change (pp. 451–459). In *Managing organizations, readings and cases.* Boston: Little, Brown and Co.

16. Mieszkowski, K. (1998, December). Change—Barbara Waugh. *Fast Company,* 20, 146.

17. Waldersee, R.& Griffiths, A. (2004). Implementing change: Matching implementation methods and change type. *Leadership and Organization Development Journal, (25)*5, 424–434.

18. Software crash hits Sobeys hard. CBC News, January 25, 2001, http://www.cbc .ca/news/

19. http://www.valuebasedmanagement.net/methods_senario_planniong.html.

20. Noori, H., Munro, H., Deszca, G., & McWilliams, B. (1999). Developing the right breakthrough product/service: An application of the umbrella methodology, Parts A & B. *International Journal of Technology Management, 17,* 544–579.

21. Wylie, I. (2002, July). There is no alternative to . . . . *Fast Company,* 106–110.

22. Gladwell, M. (2002). *The tipping point.* New York: First Back Bay.

23. Burke, W. (2002). *Organization change: Theory and practice* (pp. 274–280). London: Sage.

24. Moore, G. (1999). *Crossing the chasm.* New York: Harper-Business.

25. Imai, M. (1986). *Kaizen: The key to Japan's competitive success* (p. 239). New York: Random House.

26. Rigby, D. (2001, Winter). Management tools and techniques: A survey. *California Management Review, (43)*2.

27. Source unknown.

28. H. Sheppard, personal communication with T. Cawsey.

29. Webber, A. M. (1999). Learning for change (an interview with Peter Senge). *Fast Company, 24,* 178.

30. Senge, P. M. (1996). The leader's new work: Building learning organizations. In K. Starkey (Ed.), *How organisations learn* (pp. 288–315). London: International Thompson Business Press.

31. Zawacki, R. A., & Norman, C. A. (1994, Spring). Successful self-directed teams and planned change: A lot in common. *Organization Development Network,* 33–38.

32. Wageman, R. (1997, Summer). Critical success factors for creating superb self-managing teams. *Organizational Dynamics,* 49–61.

33. As quoted in Johnston Smith International. 2000 Change Management Conference, The Change Institute, Toronto, November 22, 2000.

34. Gerstner, L. (2002). *Who says elephants can't dance: Inside IBM's historic turnaround.* New York: HarperCollins.

35. De Bono, E. (1984). *Tactics: The art and science of success* (ch. 2). Toronto: Little, Brown and Co.

36. De Bono, op. cit., p. 41.

37. Argyris, C. 1991, May–June). Teaching smart people how to learn. *Harvard Business Review,* 104.

38. Russo, J. E., & Schoemaker, P. J. H. (1992, Winter). Managing overconfidence. *Sloan Management Review,* 7–17.

39. Greiner, L. (1998). *Power and organizational development* (pp. 44–47). Reading, MA: Addison-Wesley.

40. Falbe, C., & Yukl, G. (1992). Consequences for managers of using single influence tactics and combinations of tactics. *Academy of Management Journal, (35)*3, 638–652.

41. Goodman, J., & Truss, C. (2004, September). The medium and the message: Communicating effectively during a major change initiative. *Journal of Change Management, (4)*3, 234.

42. Spector, B. (1989, Summer). From bogged down to fired up: Inspiring organizational change. *Sloan Management Review.*

43. Goodman, op. cit., p. 217.

44. Dutton, J., et al. (2001, August). Moves that matter: Issue selling and organizational change. *Academy of Management Journal, (44)*4.

45. Klein, S. (1996). A management communication strategy for change. *Journal of Organizational Change Management, (9)*2, 37.

46. Klein, ibid.

47. Daft, D., & Lengel, R. H. (1984). Information richness: A new approach to managerial behavior and organizational design. In B. Staw & R. Cummings, *Research in organizational behavior* (Vol. 6, pp. 191–233). Greenwich, CT: JAI Press.

48. Goodman, op. cit., p. 218.

49. Duck, J. D. (1993, November–December). Managing change: The art of balancing. *Harvard Business Review,* 4.

50. Klein, op. cit., p. 34.

51. Source unknown.

52. Morris, K. F., & Raben, C. S. (1999). The fundamentals of change management. In D. Nadler et al., *Discontinuous change* (pp. 57–58). San Francisco: Jossey-Bass.

53. Duck, op. cit., p. 9.

54. Ackerman, L. (1982, Summer). Transition management: An in-depth look at managing complex change. *Organizational Dynamics,* 46–66.

55. Beckhard, R. (1987). *Organizational Transitions,* p. 47. Reading, MA: Addison-Wesley.

56. Personal correspondence with W. Allen, Ministry of Agriculture, Food and Rural Affairs, Ontario Government.

57. Rigby, D. (2001, Winter). Management tools and techniques: A survey. *California Management Review, (43)*2. Copyright © 2001 by The Regents of the University of California. Reprinted with permission of The Regents.

CHAPTER 10

Measuring Change

Designing Effective Control Systems

What gets measured is what gets done.

Chapter Overview

- Measures are critical components of the control system that guides the change and integrates the initiatives and efforts of various parties.
- Control systems can facilitate change if designed properly.
- Four types of control systems exist: diagnostic/steering controls, belief systems, boundary systems, and interactive controls. Different parts of each system are needed as the change project shifts from the planning to implementation phases.
- Four measurement tools are presented: the balanced scorecard, strategy maps, the risk exposure calculator, and the Duration, Integrity, Commitment, and Effort (DICE) model.

What gets measured affects the direction, content, and outcomes achieved by a change. Measurement influences what people pay attention to and what they do.[1] All too often, the measures needed to help frame and guide the change are not sufficiently thought through. Managers generally acknowledge that such measurement is important but are reluctant practitioners when it comes to its use.[2]

Many reasons are offered for why measurement and control are given short shrift, including concerns over the complexity of the change, inability to measure what is important, ambiguity as to what exactly the change will look like as it takes shape over time, and concerns that measures may be unable to adapt to changing conditions.[3] As well, managers and employees will be concerned about their own futures and careers. Measurement that enhances accountability may leave some managers of change feeling vulnerable. They may worry that critics will use the measures to second-guess the initiative and even undermine the manager.

Nevertheless, well-thought-out measures and control processes can provide change leaders with valuable tools. With the information from these measurement systems, change managers will be able to more effectively monitor the environment, guide the change, gauge progress, make midcourse corrections, and bring the change to a successful conclusion.[4] A key managerial change skill resides in being able to identify such measures, build them into one's change, and adapt them, as needed.[5] In the case of RE/MAX (described below), we see the impact of a new measurement system that focused on attracting and retaining superior agents.

> For RE/MAX, the Denver, Colorado, based real estate franchise network, a redefinition of customers away from industry norms has been crucial. Cofounder and Chairman David Liniger says that the firm's success has resulted from the simple idea that RE/MAX customers were the real estate agents themselves, not the buyers and sellers of real estate. More specifically, RE/MAX targets high-performing agents who represent just 20% of the entire pool of real estate agents but account for some 80% of all sales.
>
> RE/MAX's focus on these agents originally consisted of changing the industry's traditional 50-50 fee split between broker and agent to a franchise system, in which agents kept all commissions after a management fee and expenses. In some cases, that boosted commission retention rates as much as 85%. Additional services followed, including national marketing, training by satellite, and coordinated support.
>
> The results are impressive: According to Liniger, the average RE/MAX agent earns $120,000 per year on 24 transactions, versus an industry average of $25,000 on seven transactions. "The customer comes second," he says, but hastens to add, "If your emphasis is on having the best employees, you're going to have the best customer service."[6]

At RE/MAX, management achieved strategic realignment with a shift in measures or metrics from fee splitting related to sales to ones based on a franchise model. This example demonstrates that what is measured and rewarded can have a major impact on what outcomes are achieved. Sometimes these measures are a simple matter of personal choice, as in the case of an athlete who links training metrics to performance goals and then celebrates the small steps that lead to the accomplishment of milestones along the way. In other situations, measures grow out of expectations and/or requirements established by others, such as just-in-time measurement placed on suppliers by automobile firms.

When employees accept organizational measures, they are more supportive of the organization in general and have less work stress, more job satisfaction,

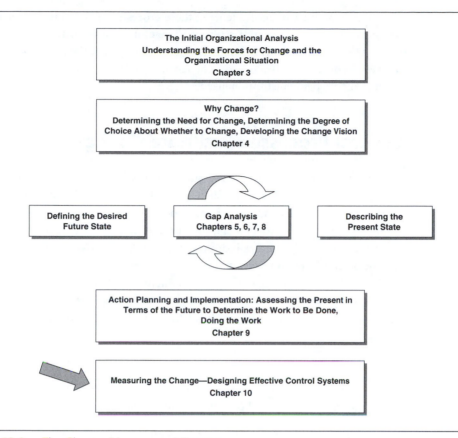

The Initial Organizational Analysis
Understanding the Forces for Change and the
Organizational Situation
Chapter 3

Why Change?
Determining the Need for Change, Determining the Degree of
Choice About Whether to Change, Developing the Change Vision
Chapter 4

Defining the Desired
Future State

Gap Analysis
Chapters 5, 6, 7, 8

Describing the
Present State

Action Planning and Implementation: Assessing the Present in
Terms of the Future to Determine the Work to Be Done,
Doing the Work
Chapter 9

Measuring the Change—Designing Effective Control Systems
Chapter 10

Figure 10.1   The Change Management Process

improved job performance, better work and family balance, less absenteeism, less job burnout, and more organizational commitment.[7] RE/MAX appears to have been successful in this, as seen by its success in attracting and retaining real estate agents who exceed performance levels in the industry.[8] With RE/MAX, integration and coordination came through support services that were wrapped around the realigned franchise relationship that targets successful realtors (rather than home purchasers) as RE/MAX's primary customers.

In this chapter, we begin by looking at the role of measurement in change management and how it influences people's behavior. We examine a variety of issues with respect to the development and use of measures and the impact of measures that send misleading information. The role of measurement and control in the management of risks related to successful completion of the change are then discussed, as is the question of "what to measure" at different stages in the life cycle of the change. Finally, Kaplan and Norton's balanced scorecard approach is used to address the question of how to align the measures in the same direction to increase the prospects of success.

Figure 10.1 shows where the topic of measurement and control is in the change model. While measurement is identified as occurring at the end of the change process, the role goes well beyond scorekeeping and auditing functions used to assess how we did. Change leaders use these processes throughout change projects to help define the change need, steer the change, and assess whether the plan is producing the desired results. Change managers will attend to the feedback received to make midcourse corrections to the change project and to assess the extent to which their plans are being institutionalized.[9]

How Can Control Processes Facilitate Change?

Often, change leaders focus on measurement systems and how they impede the change that the managers want. Change leaders need to understand the impact of measurement systems and alter them to benefit rather than impede change. The challenge is to redefine and realign measures so that they are internally congruent with the vision and to utilize indicators that can help guide the change process as it moves from inception to fruition.

Below is a case example, Control Production Systems,[*] where change agents modify the control process. In this example, the change agents benefit from consultation with key participants[10] and focus their efforts by collaborating with diverse groups.[11]

A Case Study in the Value of Realigning Measures[12]

Control Production Systems (CPS), a medium-sized firm that designs, manufactures, sells, and services customized production control systems, had noticed an erosion of their market share to competitors. Declining customer loyalty, greater difficulty selling product and service updates, and an increased reliance on price to win the business were shrinking margins and making competitive life more difficult, even though the innovativeness and quality of their product and service offerings were strong. The firm possessed a fairly strong and positive culture that reflected the values of innovation, quality, and open communications, but recent setbacks had shaken its confidence.

As the result of a town hall meeting called to discuss corporate results, the CEO acted on the suggestion that a cross-functional task force be formed to assess the situation and recommend a course of action. The change team involved sales agents and customer support staff in both the diagnosis and the design of a change program. The team was led by the director of sales and service. It reported to the senior management team on a monthly basis, with the expectation that the initial analysis and the framing of recommendations would be completed within 2 months, followed by implementation activities. An intranet Web site was created to facilitate communications about the change, and transparency, candor, and no reprisals were the watchwords for the change team's approach. Finally, sufficient resources were allocated to the team to allow it to get on with its task.

---

[*]Firm's name is disguised.

Prior to the change, sales agents were organized on a geographic basis and paid on a salary-plus-commission basis. After a sale, they handed off responsibility to customer support staff to address order fulfillment and post sales servicing. The customer support staff were rewarded on the basis of cost control and throughput. If customers never contacted the organization for help, that was viewed as a good thing because it generated no cost and pointed to satisfaction. Shorter calls were seen as better than longer ones, due to cost implications, and standardized responses and online help provisions were preferred over troubleshooting over the phone, for the same cost reasons. No systematic record of customer calls was stored, and customer response was on a first-come, first-serve basis.

However, analysis by the change team showed that customers who had minimal contact with the customer support staff were less likely to develop a relationship with the firm, were likely to be deriving less value from their purchase, and were less likely to be aware of innovations and applications that could benefit them. In other words, the very activities that drove short-term costs lower were hurting customer loyalty and longer-term profitability.

After the investigation, the team concluded that there was a need to change the way they dealt with and serviced their major customers. They determined that the way to increase sales and profitability was to ensure that customers saw the company as a trusted partner that could assist in finding ways to enhance their productivity and quality through improvements to their control systems.

This required the company to undertake a major realignment in how it dealt with its customers. Sales and customer support services were brought together and were given a portfolio of customer accounts in a particular industry. They were to be experts in these accounts and to manage them on a continuing relationship basis. The vision was one of a customer-focused partnership, in which one-stop shopping, customer intimacy, service excellence, and solution finding would frame the relationship, rather than simply selling and servicing in the traditional manner.

During the change, measures focused on employee understanding of the new service model, skill acquisition, customer pilot test results, and employee commitment to the new approach. Further, measures were developed to ensure that service failures in areas of delivery, response time, quality, and relationship management were identified and dealt with quickly if they were beginning to occur during the transition period. Steps were taken to ensure that such data surfaced and were dealt with. This was done through encouraging its generation, focusing on the search for systemic causes and the development of remedies, celebrating openness and experimentation, and avoiding finger-pointing. Milestones for the change were established, and small victories along the transition path were identified, monitored, and celebrated.

Once changes were initiated, performance measures were brought into alignment by focusing on such factors as customer satisfaction with the breadth and depth of services, response time, customer referrals, repeat sales, and margins. The reward system shifted from a high commission base for sales personnel and salary plus a small bonus for those in customer service to one that was focused on salary plus a team-based performance incentive, constructed around a set of measures that included customer satisfaction, retention, share of the customer's

(Continued)

(Continued)

business in their product and service area, and customer profitability over time. In the three years since the change, there have been significant improvements in all the targeted measures, and feedback from customer service has become an important influencer of product refinement and development.

The case example demonstrates many of the principles of effective change management.

On the front end of the change process at CPS, change leaders used measurement to help in problem identification, root cause analysis, the development of awareness of the need for change, and the vision. They recognized the disconnect between existing measures that reinforced cost reductions in servicing clients (first-order effects) and the desired but unrealized longer-term outcome of customer loyalty and customer profitability over time. During the change process itself, measurement was instrumental in aiding in the development and fine-tuning of the change. Change leaders communicated throughout the change process using analysis derived, in part, from measures that people trusted. Smaller accomplishments along the way, as assessed through the achievement of the milestones, were acknowledged. In the end, significantly greater client satisfaction with the products and services (e.g., the first-order effects) gave rise to customer loyalty, follow-up purchases, and profitability over time (second-order effects), which they had previously been unable to achieve.

To make the question of the impact of measures and control processes all the more real, consider a change you are familiar with and complete Toolkit Exercise 10.1.

How Do We Choose What Measures to Use?

There is no shortage of possible indicators—cycle time, machine efficiency, waste, sales per call, employee satisfaction, waiting time, market share, profitability per sale, cost of sale, customer retention, to name just a few. If we try to measure everything, we are likely to end up paying attention to nothing very well. To focus attention, we need to be clear about where we are in the change process and what dimensions are important to monitor at this stage, given the desired end results. Here is a list of criteria to help change managers determine which measures should be used.

Focusing on Critical Factors

Measures influence what people pay attention to and choose to do, even when they believe those actions are ill-advised. This is particularly true when they believe that those in power and/or whose opinions they value see the measures as important and base decisions about resources and rewards on them.[13] Consider the all too common practice of trade loading—the notoriously inefficient and expensive practice of unloading excess inventory onto distributors and retailers in order to make the manufacturer's numbers look better in the short term.[14] For years, staff at Gillette knew that the practice of trade loading was having a negative effect on pricing, production efficiencies, customer relations, and profitability. Trade loading meant that unsold inventory was hidden from Gillette's eyes in the distribution channels and that price discounting was eroding margins (distributors quickly learned how to time purchases to take advantage of such discounts). In spite of the widespread awareness that this practice was ill-advised, it continued until new leadership, dialogue, active analysis, and the realignment of strategy, tactics, measures, and related system finally brought an end to an unhealthy practice.[15]

Using Measures That Are Perceived as Fair

Peoples' perception of the appropriateness and fairness of the measures is driven as much by the process used to develop them as by the outcomes they deliver.[16] Procedures need to be established for addressing measurement and control issues in a manner that reduces resistance through utilizing communication processes that enhance understanding, provide opportunities for input and feedback, build trust and support, and avoid punishing people for taking reasonable action, based on their understanding of the change goals and what is expected of them. The measures chosen are often accepted if the process used in arriving at them is seen as reasonable and fair, even when the implications of those measures are not particularly positive for those being measured. This matter of fair process was discussed in detail in Chapter 7 (The Recipients of Change).

Avoiding Mixed Signals

Measurement systems related to change often produce conflicting signals, and it is not unusual to find firms saying one thing but signaling another through the measures and the related rewards. For example, an organization may develop measures and initiate changes aimed at enhancing quality and customer satisfaction but then require the shipment of flawed products in order to meet just-in-time delivery metrics and avoid exceeding their internal scrap and rework targets. They do this even though they know that substandard products will increase warranty work, require customers to do rework, and put the firm's reputation with the customer at risk. The fundamental problem in this example is that measures are not in alignment. An auto parts firm initiated such a quality program and reinforced it with a gigantic display board preaching "Quality is important because General Motors demands it!" However, next to this sign sat pallets of completed parts with supervisory tags that approved shipment, overriding quality-control inspection reports that had ordered rework prior to shipment.[17] The inability to deal with quality problems led to the loss of the GM contract and, ultimately, the closure of the plant approximately 18 months after the display board was first unveiled.

Employees are very aware of such conflicting messages. Confusion, frustration, sarcasm, and eventually alienation are the natural consequences. When such inconsistencies are built into a change initiative and go undetected or unaddressed by the change agent, cynicism about the change and its advocates increases, and the change process flounders. Kerr's well-known paper "On the Folly of Rewarding A, While Hoping for B" explores many of the issues around measurement and the production of unintended consequences.[18]

Modeling the Desired Behavior—"Walking the Talk"

To help ensure that measures and the related control processes have the intended effect, change leaders need to be seen as "walking the talk," while using sound communication practices when dealing with questions related to what to measure, who to engage in discussions about measurement and control, how to deploy the measures, and how to interpret and use the data effectively to manage the change. Approaches designed to reinforce perceptions of the fairness and appropriateness of the measures and their proper application and use are advanced by such leader behavior.[19]

Ensuring Accurate Data

Employees, customers, and others will supply accurate data when they trust the measurement system. Excessive rewards, pressure, and/or sanctions for success and failure can lead to flawed information from the most carefully designed set of measures.[20] If deliverers of bad news are shot, and good news is put on pedestals, it is likely that you will receive data that tell you what you want to hear, rather than what you need to hear.

Keeping the Measures as Simple as Possible

When measures related to change management and control are being developed, due regard needs to be given to both their cost and value. We can overinvest in systems unnecessarily. The general rule of thumb is the simpler the better.

Matching the Precision of the Measure to Environmental Stability

Change managers need to match the precision of measures to the environment. If the environment is predictable and the change is significant, they can devote time and money to developing precise, sophisticated measures. However, if the environment changes rapidly, approximate measures are more appropriate.[21] Table 10.1 looks at the nature of the change context and considers what types of measures are likely to be more appropriate.

What Types of Control Systems Exist?

Robert Simons, an expert in the area of management control systems, believes that managers focus too much on traditional diagnostic control systems. He argues that managers need to think about four types of control levers:[22]

1. **Diagnostic/steering controls**—the traditional managerial control systems that focus on key performance variables, for example, sales data responding to changed selling efforts.

Table 10.1   The Change Context and the Choice of Measures

Change Context:	Choose More Precise, Explicit, Goal-Focused Measures	Choose More Approximate Measures, Focus on Vision and Milestones, and Learn as You Go
When Complexity and Ambiguity Are:	Low	High
When Time to Completion Is:	Short	Long

2. **Belief systems**—the structure of fundamental values that underpin organizational decisions: for example, the stated organizational values that often accompany the vision and mission.

3. **Boundary systems**—the systems that set the limits of authority and action and determine acceptable and unacceptable behavior: for example, limits to spending authority placed on managerial levels. These tend to focus on what is unacceptable and identify not only what is prohibited but also the sanction.

4. **Interactive controls**—the systems that sense environmental changes that are crucial to the organization's strategic concerns: for example: market intelligence that will determine competitor actions.

Each of these systems can help in promoting the change. Clear **diagnostic control systems** means that change agents will understand critical performance variables and can modify systems to encourage new, desired behaviors while discouraging dysfunctional ones. An understanding of **beliefs systems** allows the change leader to appeal to higher-order values of individuals and the core values of the organization to motivate behavior and overcome resistance to change. Understanding of **boundary systems** means that change leaders know their limits and the risks to be avoided. If they choose, they can test those boundaries explicitly to push in new directions. Finally, change initiators will be sensitized to environmental shifts and strategic uncertainties and the impact of these on the change project by **interactive control systems.** This will allow the change initiators to modify change plans. (See Figure 10.2.)

Table 10.2 sets out the different elements of the control system and relates them to the measures used at different stages of the change process. As the change progresses from initial planning to wrap-up and review, the control challenges and measurement issues also shift. The key is to align the controls and measures to the challenges posed by the stage that the change is at and prepare for the next. This helps to ensure that change leaders have the information and guidance they need to assess matters, make decisions, and manage their way forward.

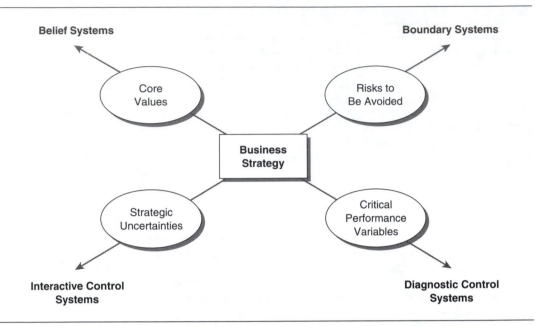

Figure 10.2   Strategy and the Four Levers of Control

Controls During Design and Early Stages of the Change Project

At the commencement of a major change, mission and vision (i.e., belief systems), interactive control systems (e.g., environmental assessment), and boundary systems play particularly important roles in clarifying overall direction, as options and potential courses of action are explored. Data from secondary research, exploratory discussions, preliminary organizational assessments, and initial experimentation can be helpful at this stage because they allow projects and alternatives to be considered in a more grounded manner than would otherwise be the case. Information from these sources is used to sort out what should be done next and to make initial "go/no-go" decisions on whether to continue to proceed in the development of the initiative.

In the early stages, change leaders need to have systems that will identify whom to talk to—who will tell them what they "need to hear," not what they "want to hear." Enthusiasm and commitment on the part of change leaders are beneficial to the change but can create serious blind spots. As "go/no-go" decisions are made, managers need to develop and refine the directional and steering control measures and specify important milestones. Project-planning tools such as the critical path method can play a useful role (see Chapter 9).

Controls in the Middle of the Change Project

Indicators that define the overall purpose, direction, and boundary conditions (what actions are acceptable and unacceptable) for the change are still important in helping to clarify what change is intended. However, diagnostic and steering

Table 10.2   Control Systems, Measures, and the Stage of the Change

	Controls When Designing and Planning the Change	*Controls in Beginning Stages of the Change Project*	*Controls in Middle Stages of the Change Project*	*Controls Toward the End of the Change Project*
Belief System (What are our beliefs and values? What is our purpose?)	Assessing congruence with purpose of the change project.	Congruence assessment.	Congruence assessment.	Congruence assessment.
	Communicate how the change relates to the core values and mission.	Appeals to fundamental beliefs to overcome resistance.	Reaffirming core values through the change project.	Reevaluation of core values based on shifts caused by the change project.
Diagnostic and Steering Controls (Focusing resources on targets; Measuring progress; Taking corrective action and learning as we go)	Assessment of the impact of existing controls on the change project.	Development of milestone measures.	Evaluation of progress against milestones.	Determination of project completion.
	Considering what diagnostic systems will have to be developed and/or altered under the change.	Developing tactics to alter control systems as needed.	Are systems and processes working as they should?	Confirmation that new systems are appropriate.
			Modification of milestone measures as needed.	Project evaluation to develop learning on how to improve change processes.
Boundary System (What behaviors are *not* ok?)	Limits to the change set by the organization's values and beliefs.	Go/no-go guidance as to appropriateness of actions.	Go/no-go guidance as to appropriateness of actions.	Reevaluation of boundary limits.
	Testing the limits of what is acceptable.		Reassessment of risks.	
			Reestablishment of boundaries.	
			Testing of new boundaries.	

(Continued)

Table 10.2 (Continued)

	Controls When Designing and Planning the Change	Controls in Beginning Stages of the Change Project	Controls in Middle Stages of the Change Project	Controls Toward the End of the Change Project
Interactive Controls (Environmental scanning; Assessing possible paths and targets)	Assessing opportunities and threats; considering possibilities.	Affirming that the change project is aligned with environmental trends.	Ongoing monitoring.	Obtaining feedback from others regarding the success of change activities.
	Testing the viability of existing vision, mission, and strategy given the environmental situation.	Assessing how to use environmental trends to increase the chances of change success.	Involving others in change targets and plans. Confirming that environmental signals support the change.	Ongoing environmental scanning and assessment of organizational strengths, weaknesses, opportunities, and threats (SWOT).

controls (e.g., budgets and variance reports, project schedule data) play an increasingly important role as the change moves forward. Managers need to recognize whether the information produced leads or whether it lags the actual situation. As in the example of CPS, discussed earlier in this chapter, customer satisfaction was a lead indicator, while repeat sales and profitability were lag indicators of the improved situation. If this had not been recognized, initiatives undertaken to improve customer satisfaction may have been discontinued because there was no immediate improvement in sales. Change leaders also need to consider how measures can help organizations adapt to unforeseen situations.

Change leaders need to develop milestones and road markers through project-planning and goal- and objective-setting activities and use these milestones to track progress with the change and reinforce the initiative of others by recognizing their achievement. For example, if a firm were implementing a new performance management system, the (a) completion and sign-off on the design of the system, (b) completion of the training schedule, (c) achievement of needed levels of understanding and acceptance of the system (as assessed by measures of comprehension and satisfaction with the system), and (d) completion of the first cycle of performance reviews (with system evaluation data from those using the system) are possible road markers.

At important milestones, go/no-go controls once again enter the picture, with conscious decisions made about refinement of the change and decisions about the appropriateness and desirability of proceeding to the next stage. If milestones are not being achieved, change leaders need to refine or redefine the measures or the time line.

Controls Toward the End of the Change Project

As the end of a planned change approaches, diagnostic and steering measures begin to be replaced by more concrete outcome measures. What was accomplished and what has been the impact? How do the results compare with what we had expected to achieve? What can we learn from the change project? Change leaders need to capture the observations and insights of those involved in the change, as it will help in future changes.

Toolkit Exercise 10.2 asks you to apply Simons's control systems model and the above notions.

Measurement Tools

Measurement and controls systems will vary greatly depending on the change situation. Four tools that can assist in planning and deploying change in ways that enhance internal consistency, alignment, and aid in assessing risk are specifically helpful in thinking about change. These are (1) the strategy map, (2) the balanced scorecard, (3) the risk exposure calculator, and (4) the "DICE" model. These are described briefly below.

The Strategy Map

Once change leaders have developed their vision and strategy for the change, they can then develop a visual representation of the end state that they have in mind with what Kaplan and Norton call a strategy map. They recommend starting with financial measures and then define the paths that will produce those outcomes. To achieve the financial objectives, what objectives have to be accomplished from the customer perspective? To achieve these customer objectives, what must be accomplished from an internal business process perspective? Finally, to accomplish the internal process objectives, what must occur with employees from the learning and growth perspective? The assumption underlying strategy maps is that financial outcomes are the end points that the organization is focused on and that other objectives support and lead to financial outcomes. In essence, the cause and effect that produces the desired financial results is from the bottom up (i.e., commencing from the learning and growth perspective).

This visualization can prove useful in helping people to understand what is being proposed and why, including the clarification of cause-effect relationships and how they contribute to the desired outcomes. It can also help change leaders to identify gaps in their logic, including missing objectives and measures. When Mobil used this method, it helped them to identify gaps in the plans of one of their business units, where objectives and metrics were missing for dealers—a critical component for a strategy map focused on selling more gasoline.[23] Figure 10.3 describes the major components of a generic strategy map and their place in the hierarchy.

To give you a sense of how a strategy map can be used to help, one is set out in Figure 10.4, involving the change discussed earlier in this chapter for Control Production Systems, a firm that designs, manufactures, sells, and services customized production control systems.

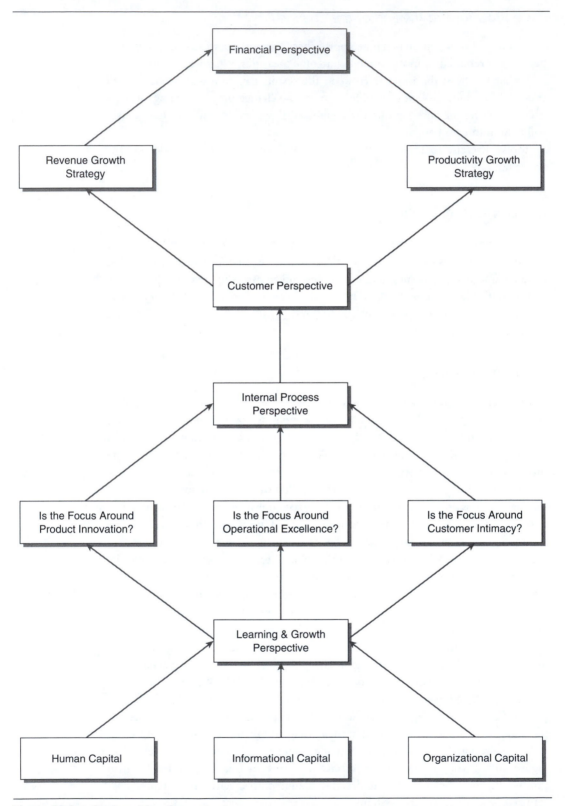

Figure 10.3 Strategy Map Components

The Balanced Scorecard

Once change goals have been established, milestones highlighted, and measures articulated through the strategy map, managers of change face the challenge of integrating them into a coherent whole. Kaplan and Norton argue that it is important to pay attention to the environmental context and select measures that will provide a more balanced, integrated, and aligned perspective concerning what needs to be done to produce the desired outcomes.[24] This is why approaches like the balanced scorecard are helpful.

Kaplan and Norton believe that the measures used in control should include customer measures, internal process measures, and employee learning and growth measures as well as financial measures. Some of these indicators will be lead indicators, while others will lag. For example, improvements in service levels such as the response time to a customer inquiry could be a lead indicator of improvements in customer satisfaction. However, this may not immediately translate into new sales and increased profitability. Improvements in such measures will often be lag indicators of improvements in service levels because of the nature of the purchase cycle involved. The balanced scorecard recognizes that not all effects are immediate. By setting out your assumptions concerning what leads to what, it makes it easier for the change manager to test assumptions, track progress, and make appropriate alternations when necessary.

When developing a balanced scorecard for a change initiative, remember that the relevant customers may be employees in other departments of the organization. Kaplan and Norton argue that the likelihood that multiple measures will all mislead senior executives at the same time and in the same direction is much less than if they rely on a single indicator. Figure 10.5 outlines the balanced scorecard for a change project.

Mission for CPS:

Design, manufacture, service, and support industry leading production control systems that enable them to enhance the efficiency and effectiveness of their production processes beyond what is possible through other means. Customer loyalty and long-term profitability are built on a foundation of excellence in these areas.

Vision for the Change in Customer Orientation:

Our valued industrial clients will achieve results that outpace industry averages through the use of superbly designed and expertly installed and configured production control system equipment and software. We will support our customers through technically competent account representatives who are focused on the challenges and needs of specific industries and customers, and committed to ensuring that their success is significantly enhanced through the value derived from the production control systems. Our product leadership combined with superb customer care and excellent technical support will result in highly loyal and committed customers who look to CPS for all their more sophisticated control system needs.

Strategy Map for CPS:

Figure 10.4   Strategy Map for Control Production Systems

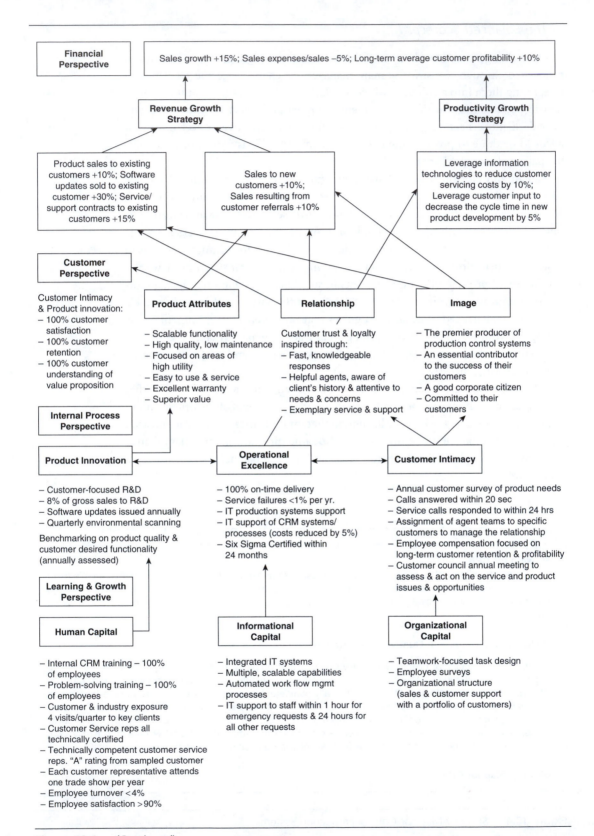

Financial Perspective

Sales growth +15%; Sales expenses/sales −5%; Long-term average customer profitability +10%

Revenue Growth Strategy

Productivity Growth Strategy

Product sales to existing customers +10%; Software updates sold to existing customer +30%; Service/support contracts to existing customers +15%

Sales to new customers +10%; Sales resulting from customer referrals +10%

Leverage information technologies to reduce customer servicing costs by 10%; Leverage customer input to decrease the cycle time in new product development by 5%

Customer Perspective

Customer Intimacy & Product innovation:
− 100% customer satisfaction
− 100% customer retention
− 100% customer understanding of value proposition

Product Attributes

− Scalable functionality
− High quality, low maintenance
− Focused on areas of high utility
− Easy to use & service
− Excellent warranty
− Superior value

Relationship

Customer trust & loyalty inspired through:
− Fast, knowledgeable responses
− Helpful agents, aware of client's history & attentive to needs & concerns
− Exemplary service & support

Image

− The premier producer of production control systems
− An essential contributor to the success of their customers
− A good corporate citizen
− Committed to their customers

Internal Process Perspective

Product Innovation

− Customer-focused R&D
− 8% of gross sales to R&D
− Software updates issued annually
− Quarterly environmental scanning

Benchmarking on product quality & customer desired functionality (annually assessed)

Operational Excellence

− 100% on-time delivery
− Service failures <1% per yr.
− IT production systems support
− IT support of CRM systems/processes (costs reduced by 5%)
− Six Sigma Certified within 24 months

Customer Intimacy

− Annual customer survey of product needs
− Calls answered within 20 sec
− Service calls responded to within 24 hrs
− Assignment of agent teams to specific customers to manage the relationship
− Employee compensation focused on long-term customer retention & profitability
− Customer council annual meeting to assess & act on the service and product issues & opportunities

Learning & Growth Perspective

Human Capital

− Internal CRM training – 100% of employees
− Problem-solving training – 100% of employees
− Customer & industry exposure 4 visits/quarter to key clients
− Customer Service reps all technically certified
− Technically competent customer service reps. "A" rating from sampled customer
− Each customer representative attends one trade show per year
− Employee turnover <4%
− Employee satisfaction >90%

Informational Capital

− Integrated IT systems
− Multiple, scalable capabilities
− Automated work flow mgmt processes
− IT support to staff within 1 hour for emergency requests & 24 hours for all other requests

Organizational Capital

− Teamwork-focused task design
− Employee surveys
− Organizational structure (sales & customer support with a portfolio of customers)

Figure 10.4   *(Continued)*

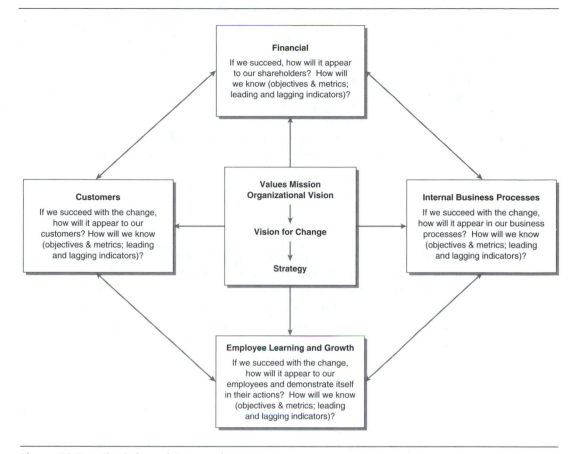

Figure 10.5   The Balanced Scorecard

Source: Kaplan, R. S., & Norton, D. P., (1996, January-February). Using the balanced scorecard as a strategic management system. *Harvard Business Review,* 76. Copyright © 1996 by the Harvard Business School Publishing Corporation, all rights reserved. Reprinted with permission.

A systemic approach to the selection and application of metrics in Kaplan and Norton's four categories can be used to help us align change metrics with the vision, mission, and strategy of the firm. Change leaders can examine the effects of the change against critical objectives and metrics. They can see how the metrics translate when looked at through the eyes of employees and customers, against business processes, and against financial lenses. Alignment approaches like the balanced scorecard help ensure that interventions are assessed for internal consistency and the capacity to advance the organization's agenda.

Figures 10.3, 10.4, and 10.5 show the strategy map and the balanced scorecard. Toolkit Exercise 10.3 asks you to construct a strategy map and balanced scorecard for a change that you are familiar with. In doing so, view the customers as those who will be the recipients of the outcomes of the change. As such, the customers can be internal to the firm as well as external.

The Risk Exposure Calculator

Bob Simons has developed a risk exposure calculator for use in assessing the level of risk associated with a company's actions.[25] It focuses primarily on internal rather

Table 10.3   The Risk Exposure Calculator

Factors Leading to Increased Risk:

1. ***Change Pressure***—When change leaders feel significant pressures to produce and accomplish the change, when there are high levels of ambiguity, and when the leaders have little experience with change, risk is increased.

2. ***Change Culture***—When the rewards for risk taking are high, when senior executives resist hearing "bad" news, and when there is internal competition between units, risk is increased.

3. ***Information Management***—When the situation is complex and fast changing, when gaps in diagnosis exist, and if decision making is decentralized, risk is increased.

than external environmental risks. Although it is designed for use on the overall organization, it can be modified to assess the risk exposure related to a particular change initiative as well as the status quo. Table 10.3 outlines Simons's risk exposure calculator.

Simons argues that risk is related to the rate of growth of the company, its culture, and how information is managed. In a change project, if the change leader is under significant pressure to produce, if there is a great deal of ambiguity, and if employees are inexperienced in change, then the risks associated with the change initiative will be higher. Further, if the culture pushes risk taking but executives resist bad news and there is internal competition, risks will be higher. Finally, if the change situation is complex and fast changing, if there are gaps in diagnostic change measures, and if decision making regarding change is decentralized, then risks will be elevated. Of course, the reverse holds. That is, if there is little pressure to produce, and so on, then the risks are lower. Managers who take too little risk may run into as much difficulty (although of a different type) as those who take on too much risk. If this risk calculator had been applied to Enron by individuals who were knowledgeable about internal operations, scores indicating very extreme risk would have been recorded. The environment at Enron was complex, fast moving, and highly ambiguous; many senior managers lacked experience with what sorts of change they were trying to accomplish; risk taking and competition were pushed to the extreme; and the bearers of concern and bad news put themselves at risk within the firm.

Change leaders can take advantage of the risk calculator by using the information from it to make the risks more manageable during the planning and deployment stages. For example, ambiguity can be reduced by emphasizing the change vision or by creating explicit milestones. Risks related to inexperience can be moderated by adding experienced managers to the change team. Toolkit Exercise 10.4 sets out a risk calculator based on Simons's work and allows you to calculate a risk score indicating whether the project is in a safety zone or not.

*The **D**uration, **I**ntegrity, **C**ommitment, and **E**ffort (DICE) Model*

A more process-oriented approach to assessing and managing the risks associated with change projects is offered by Sirkin, Keenan, and Jackson. Based on empirical data, they have developed a four-factor model for predicting the success of a change initiative. They refer to this as the Duration, Integrity, Commitment, and Effort (DICE) framework.[26] The higher the score on the model, the riskier the change effort and the greater the likelihood of failure.

The "D" refers to duration and asks about how frequently the change project is formally reviewed. If the frequency of formal review is less than 2 months, it receives a score of 1. A score of 2 is awarded when the frequency is from 2 to 4 months, a 3 for a frequency of between 4 and 8 months, and a 4 for time intervals in excess of 8 months. The message is that the risk of failure increases as the time between formal reviews rises.

The "I" relates to the integrity of performance. The first part of this measure asks about the team leader's skills and credibility, and the second part asks about the skills, motivation, and focus of members of the change team. If the team leader has the skills needed and the respect of coworkers, if team members have the skills and motivation to complete the project on time, and if at least 50% of the team members' time has been assigned to the initiative, then a score of 1 is recorded. If the change team and change leader are lacking on all dimensions, a score of 4 is recorded. If the factors lie somewhere in between, scores of 2 or 3 are allocated.

The "C" refers to commitment and is a two-stage measure. The first part assesses senior management commitment. If the words and deeds of senior managers regularly reinforce the need for change and the importance of the initiative, a score of 1 is given. If senior managers are fairly neutral, scores of 2 or 3 are recorded. When senior managers are perceived to be less than supportive, a score of 4 is applied.

The second part of the "C" scale evaluates employee or "local level" commitment. If employees are very supportive, a score of 1 is given. If they are willing but not overly eager, the score shifts to 2. As reluctance builds, scores shift to 3 and 4.

"E" is the final factor in the DICE model and refers to the level of increased effort that employees must make to implement the change. If the incremental effort is less than 10%, it is given a score of 1. Incremental effort of 10% to 20% raises the score to 2. At 20% to 40%, the score moves to 3, while additional effort in excess of 40% raises the score to 4.

The overall DICE score is calculated in the following fashion. First the Integrity score and the Senior Management Commitment score are weighted more heavily in the model, with each being multiplied by 2. This is because the scores on these factors have been found to be more significant drivers of risk. Then the scores are added together:

Overall Dice Score = Duration + (2 × Integrity of Performance) + (2 × Senior Management Commitment) + Local Level Commitment + Effort

Their research shows that change projects with scores of between 7 and 14 have a high likelihood of success. A score that is higher than 14 but less than 17 falls into what the authors refer to as the worry zone. Projects are classified as extremely risky when the overall score exceeds 17. They refer to this as the woe zone. Change projects with scores in excess of 19 have been found to be very unlikely to succeed.

This model is useful in assessing risk and in also pointing to concrete things that can be done to make the risks much more manageable during the planning and deployment phases. For example, risks can be reduced by having more frequent formal project reviews and by the staffing of change initiatives with more competent and credible team leaders and members. Likewise, increasing local- and senior-level commitment and allocating sufficient time to those change managers will also help.

Toolkit Exercise 10.5 asks you to apply the DICE model to a change you are familiar with.

Summary

Care taken in the selection of measures and control processes helps focus energy and effort. It also saves change managers a great deal of time later on because it enhances the efficiency and effectiveness of the change, provides an early warning system of problems, and thus leads to faster attention to needed areas and appropriate midcourse corrections. It also forces change leaders to be honest with themselves and others about what will be accomplished and what it will take to bring these things to reality. There is an old management adage that makes a lot of sense: "It is far better to underpromise and overdeliver than to overpromise and underdeliver."

The careful selection and use of metrics can be used to enhance ownership of the change through how the measures are selected (i.e., who participates in their selection) and through ensuring that those involved receive the credit for what is accomplished.

Glossary of Terms

Control and Measurement Systems—The measures and control processes developed to focus, monitor, and manage what is going on in the organization.

Control Systems: Diagnostic/Steering Controls—The traditional managerial control systems that focus on key performance variables: for example, sales data responding to changed selling efforts.

> **Belief Systems**—The structure of fundamental values that underpin organizational decisions: for example, the stated organization values that often accompany the vision and mission.

> **Boundary Systems**—The systems that set the limits of authority and action and determine acceptable and unacceptable behavior: for example, limits to spending authority placed on managerial levels. These tend to focus on what is unacceptable and identify not only what is prohibited but the sanction.

> **Interactive Controls**—The systems that sense environmental changes crucial to the organization's strategic concerns: for example, market intelligence that will determine competitor actions.

Strategy Map—The visualization of how the vision and strategy can be systematically brought to fruition. Strategy Maps begin with **financial perspective** and then define the paths that will produce those outcomes. To achieve the financial objectives, what objectives have to be accomplished from the **customer perspective**? To achieve these customer objectives, what must be accomplished from an **internal business process perspective**? Finally, to accomplish the internal process objectives, what must occur with employees from the **learning and growth perspective**? The assumption underlying strategy maps is that financial outcomes are the end points the organization is focused on and that other objectives support and lead to financial outcomes.

Balanced Scorecard—An integrated set of measures, built around the mission, vision, and strategy. Measures address the financial perspective, customer perspective, internal business process perspective, and learning and growth perspective. As such, they provide a balanced perspective on what is required to enact the strategy.

Simons's Risk Calculator—An assessment tool that considers the impact that certain factors may have on the risk levels faced by the firm.

> **Change Pressure**—When change leaders feel significant pressures to produce and accomplish the change, when there are high levels of ambiguity, and when the leaders have little experience with change, risk is increased.

> **Change Culture**—When the rewards for risk taking are high, when senior executives resist hearing "bad" news, and when there is internal competition between units, risk is increased.

> **Information Management**—When the situation is complex and fast changing, when gaps in diagnosis exist, and if decision making is decentralized, risk is increased.

DICE Method of Assessing Risk—A process-oriented approach to assessing and managing the risks associated with change projects.

Duration measures how frequently the change project is formally reviewed. As duration increases, risk increases.

Integrity of Performance is a two-part measure. The first part asks about the team leader's skills and credibility, and the second part asks about the skills, motivation, and focus of members of the change team. As skills, credibility, and motivation decrease, risk levels increase.

Commitment is a two-stage measure. The first part assesses senior management commitment. The second part evaluates employee or "local level" commitment. As commitment decreases, risk levels increase.

Effort measures the level of increased exertion that employees must make to implement the change. As the amount of incremental effort increases beyond 10%, risk levels increase.

END-OF-CHAPTER EXERCISES

TOOLKIT EXERCISE 10.1

Reflecting on the Impact of Measures and Control Processes on Change

Think of a change initiative that you are familiar with:

1. What measures and control processes were employed in tracking and guiding the change initiative? Were they consistent with the vision and strategy of the change? Were they viewed as legitimate by those who would be using them?

2. How was the measurement information captured and fed back to those who needed to use it? Was it a user-friendly process and did the information arrive in a useful and timely form?

3. Did the change managers consider how the measures might need to evolve over the life of the change initiative? How was this evolution managed? By whom?

4. Were steps taken to ensure that the measures used during the change would be put to proper use? Were there risks and potential consequences arising from their use that would need to be managed?

5. Were goals and milestones established to plot progress along the way and used to make midcourse corrections, if needed? Were the smaller victories celebrated to reinforce the efforts of others when milestones were achieved?

6. What were the end-state measures that were developed for the change? Were they consistent with the vision and strategy? Were they viewed as legitimate by those who would be using them?

7. How was the end-state measurement information captured and fed back to those who would need to use it? Was it a user-friendly process?

8. Were steps taken to ensure that the measures would be put to proper use? Were there risks and potential consequences arising from their use that would need to be managed?

TOOLKIT EXERCISE 10.2

Application of Simons's Control Systems Model

Consider a change you are familiar with:

1. Describe the control processes and measures that were used with the change (i.e., the belief, interactive, boundary, and diagnostic controls). When and how were they used and what was their impact?

   a. During the earlier stages of the change initiative

   b. During the middle stages of the change initiative

   c. During the latter stages of the change initiative

2. Were there forbidden topics in the organization, such as questions related to strategy or core values? Were those limits appropriate and did anyone test those limits by raising controversial questions or concerns? Were small successes celebrated along the way?

3. What changes could have been made with the control processes and measures that would have assisted in advancing the interests of change?

TOOLKIT EXERCISE 10.3

Aligning the Change With Systems and Building the Balanced Scorecard for the Change

Think about a change you are familiar with:

1. State the mission, vision, and strategy for the change.

2. Consider the mission, vision, and strategy of the organization:

    a. Is the proposed change consistent with these?

    b. If not, what needs to be done with the change or the existing mission, vision, and strategy to bring them into line?

3. Financial Component of Scorecard: If you succeed with the change vision, how will it appear to the shareholders or those responsible for funding the change? How will you know (objectives and metrics)? Are some of these leading indicators while others are lagging indicators?

4. Customer Component of Scorecard: If you succeed with the change, how will it appear to your customers? How will you know (objectives and metrics)? Are there leading and lagging indicators here?

5. Internal Business Processes Component of Scorecard: If you succeed with the change, how will it appear in your business processes? How will you know (objectives and metrics)? Are there leading and lagging indicators here?

6. Employee Learning and Growth Component of Scorecard: If you succeed with the change, how will it appear to your employees and demonstrate itself in their actions? How will you and they know (objectives and metrics)? Are there leading and lagging indicators here?

7. Lay out the scorecard you've designed for your change and seek feedback from a classmate.

8. Can you show how the different components are connected to each other by developing a strategy map for the change?

TOOLKIT EXERCISE 10.4

Using the Risk Exposure Calculator

Consider a change initiative that you know is currently being considered for adoption and apply the risk exposure calculator to it.

				Score
Change Pressure	Pressure to Produce Low High 1–2-3–4-5 Score:	Level of Ambiguity Low High 1–2-3–4-5 Score:	Experience With Change High Low 1–2-3–4-5 Score: (Note: High & Low anchors are reversed for this item)	Out of 15 ___
Change Culture	Rewards for Risk Taking Low High 1–2-3–4-5 Score:	Executives Resist Bad News Low High 1–2-3–4-5 Score:	Internal Competition Low High 1–2-3–4-5 Score:	Out of 15 ___
Information Situation	Situation Is Complex and Fast Changing Low High 1–2-3–4-5 Score:	Gaps Exist in Diagnostic Measures Low High 1–2-3–4-5 Score:	Change Decision Making Decentralized Low High 1–2-3–4-5 Score:	Out of 15 ___
Total Score =				

Using scoring criteria consistent with that developed by Simons, if your score is between 9 and 20, you are in the safety zone; between 21 and 34, you are in the cautionary zone; and between 35 and 45, you are in a danger zone.

1. Does the organization have an appropriate level of risk taking, given the nature of the business they are in? Does it play it too safe, about right, or does it take excessive risks?

2. Is the overall score helpful to you in thinking about risk and what factors may be contributing to the overall risk levels?

3. Do the findings help you to think about what can be done to make the levels of risk more manageable?

Based on Simons, R. (1999). How risky is your company? *Harvard Business Review, (77)*1, 85–94.

TOOLKIT EXERCISE 10.5

Applying the DICE Model

1. Consider a change initiative that you know is currently being considered for adoption and apply the DICE model to it.

   - Duration score ____

   - Integrity of performance ____

   - Senior management commitment ____

   - Local-level commitment score ____

   - Effort ____

$$\text{The DICE score} = D + 2I + 2 \text{ Sr. Mgmt Commitment} + \text{Local-level Commitment} + E$$

2. What score did the change project receive? Was it in the low-risk category (7 to 14), the worry zone (between 14 and 17), or in the high-risk area (over 17)?

3. Do the findings help you to think about important sources of risk to the success of the project?

4. Do the findings help you to think about what can be done to make the levels of risk more manageable?

Notes

1. Fred, E. (2004). Transition in the workplace. *Journal of Management Development,* (*23*)10, 962–964.

2. Ford, M. W., & Greer, B. M. (2005). The relationship between management control system usage and planner change achievement: An exploratory study. *Journal of Change Management,* (*5*)1, 29–46.

3. Ford & Greer, op. cit.; Schreyogg, G., & Steinmann, H. (1987). Strategic control: A new perspective. *Academy of Management Review,* (*12*)1, 91–103; and Preble, J. F. (1992). Towards a comprehensive system of strategic control. *Journal of Management Studies,* (*29*)4, 391–409.

4. Kotter, J. P., & Schlesinger, L. A. (1979). Choosing strategies for change. *Harvard Business Review,* (*57*)2, 106–114; Lorange, P. M., Morton, S., & Goshal, S. (1986). *Strategic control.* St. Paul, MN: West; Simons, R. (1995). *Levers of control.* Boston: Harvard Business School Press.

5. Kennerley, M., Neely, A., & Adams, C. (2003). Survival of the fittest: Measuring performance in a changing business environment. *Measuring Business Excellence,* (*7*)4, 37–43.

6. Brant, J. R. (2003, May). Dare to be different. *Chief Executive,* 188, 36.

7. Szamosi, L. T., & Duxbury, L. (2002). Development of a measure to assess organizational change. *Journal of Organizational Change Management,* (*15*)2, 184–201.

8. Harkins, P., & Hollihan, K. (2004). *Everybody wins: The story and lessons behind RE/MAX.* New York: John Wiley & Sons.

9. Miller, D. (2002). Successful change leaders: What makes them? What do they do that is different? *Journal of Change Management,* (*2*)4, 356–368.

10. Weber, P. S., & Weber, J. E. (2001). Changes in employee perceptions during organizational change. *Leadership and Organizational Development Journal,* (*22*)5–6, 291–300.

11. Nauta, A., & Sanders, K. (2001). Causes and consequences of perceived goal differences between departments within manufacturing organizations. *Journal of Occupational and Organizational Psychology,* 74 (Part 3), 321–342; Cooke, J. A. (2003). Want real collaboration? Change your measures. *Logistics Management,* (*42*)1, 37–41.

12. G. Deszca. Personal experience.

13. Denton, D. K. (2002). Learning how to keep score. *Industrial Management,* (*44*)2, 28–33; Anonymous. (2002). Materials management benchmarks easy to find, but often measure wrong things. *Hospital Materials Management,* (*27*)3, 3–4.

14. Sellers, P. (1992, October 5). The dumbest marketing ploy. *Fortune,* (*126*)7, 88 (5 pgs).

15. Kanter, R. M. (2003). Leadership and the psychology of turnarounds. *Harvard Business Review,* (*81*)6, 58–67.

16. Kim, W. C., & Mauborgne, R. (2003). Fair process: Management in the knowledge economy. *Harvard Business Review,* (*81*)1, 127–139.

17. T. Cawsey & G. Deszca, personal experience.

18. Kerr, S. (1995). On the folly of rewarding A, while hoping for B. *Academy of Management Executive,* (*9*)1, 7–14.

19. Lawson, E., & Price, C. (2003). The psychology of change management. *The McKinsey Quarterly, Special Edition:* Organization. www.mckinseyquarterly.com.

20. Higgins, J. M., & Currie, D. M. (2004). It's time to rebalance the scorecard. *Business and Society Review,* (*109*)3, 297–309.

21. Eisenhardt, K. M., & Sull, D. N. (2001). Strategy as simple rules. *Harvard Business Review,* (*79*)1, 106–116.

22.   Simons, R. (1995). Control in an age of empowerment. *Harvard Business Review,* (*73*)2, 8–88.

23.   Kaplan, R. S., & Norton, D. P. (2000). Having trouble with your strategy? Then map it. *Harvard Business Review,* (*78*)5, 167–179.

24.   Kaplan, R. S., & Norton, D. P. (1996). Using the balanced scorecard as a strategic management system. *Harvard Business Review,* (*74*)1, 75–85.

25.   Simons, R. (1999). How risky is your company? Harvard Business Review, (*77*)3, 85–94.

26.   Sirkin, H. L., Keenan, P., & Jackson, A. (2005). The hard side of change management. *Harvard Business Review,* (*91*)9, 108–118.

Oshawa Industries[1]

Although Mark Talbot knew that he was developing a reputation as a quick technical and managerial understudy, he never thought he'd be promoted to plant manager at Oshawa Industries (OI) after just 6 months as assistant plant manager at the electroplating plant. He wondered how a relative "greenhorn" like himself could effectively manage the complicated situation at the plant. In the 6 months since he joined the plant, Talbot had found a product pricing system that didn't readily appear logical, inconsistent senior management behavior, labor-management relations and employee morale that were close to rock bottom, outdated equipment, declining sales, and deteriorating customer service. Convinced by the vice president, Roger Sutherland, that he was the person for the job and that this was the "opportunity of a lifetime for a young manager," Talbot wondered how he should tackle the situation—given that he had accepted the job.

Oshawa Industries and Oshawa Holdings Limited

Oshawa Industries was a subsidiary of Oshawa Holdings, a company of over 25 automobile parts manufacturing, metal finishing, and electroplating plants. For many years, Oshawa Holdings grew under the leadership of Dean Carter (CEO), his brother Jack (Executive VP Manufacturing Operations), and Chet Wainwright, the executive vice president (EVP) who provided technical leadership. Roger Sutherland was in his forties and had joined the firm approximately a year ago as vice president of Administration. As a seasoned manufacturing executive with an MBA, he provided managerial skills and was responsible for administrative systems, human resource systems, industrial relations, and senior management development at the time that Dean and Jack Carter and Chet Wainwright began to consider retiring.

There were other senior executives at the OHL headquarters (e.g., the chief financial officer, the VP Computing and Information Systems, the VP Marketing and Sales), but Dean, Jack, Chet, and Roger were the senior decision makers. Much of the past growth was attributable to Dean's entrepreneurial and administrative skills and Chet's technical capacities, augmented by Jack's people-oriented focus and much more recently by Roger's managerial skills and strategic outlook.

Although Oshawa Industries was a subsidiary of Oshawa Holdings, the cultures were very

---

[1]All proper names have been disguised. This case is based on the original Oshawa Industries by T. Cawsey and R. McGowan, copyright the Laurier Institute.

different. The OHL Corporate Profile identified three guiding principles: entrepreneurially focused factories, the pursuit of joint ventures, and an emphasis on quality in both employee relations and products and services (see Exhibit 1). OHL was a Tier 1 manufacturer to the automotive industry. All but 2 of the 21 Oshawa Holdings operations (averaging approximately 100 employees per plant) were nonunion, had gain-sharing plans, were profit sharing, and operated under participative management principles to encourage employee productivity and loyalty. Plant managers were given a fair degree of autonomy in how they operated their plants but were held accountable for key performance indicators (measures related to cost, profitability, customer satisfaction, and employee satisfaction).

The commitment of OHL's plant management to the above principles was evident in the high esteem in which they were held by both customers and employees. Consistent superior profitability and growing volumes flowed directly from plant actions. Dean Carter commented that the role of head office was to act as the bank and auditor for OHL plants, to be the deal maker involving new plants or joint ventures, hire well, and to then get out of the way and let the plant managers run their operations. Oshawa Industries' (OI) culture and organization, however, were a very different matter.

Oshawa Industries was comprised of a single plant, with OHL's head offices located in adjacent single-story buildings in a heavily industrialized section of Oshawa. The OI plant, built 25 years ago, specializes in electroplating and metal finishing for steel manufacturers and automotive plants, where OI is a Tier 2 supplier. This plant electroplates many different types of products, ranging from fasteners to auto parts to 10-ton steel rolls for steel producers.

Plant equipment in the electroplating division was a mixture of equipment installed in the 1980s and updated electronic quality-testing equipment. The plant housed vats of caustic chemicals, automated racks (which suspend metal parts for coating and heat-treatment ovens), and equipment capable of chrome plating up to 10 tons of material at a time. During the past decade, processing lines were added or existing ones were expanded within the original facilities, which themselves were not expanded (see Exhibit 2 for the plant floor layout).

The plant's dedicated, continuous process lines operate with cycle times of up to 1 hour. Automated overhead racks raise and lower the parts in the solutions as well as transport them along the processing line. Most processing lines consist of a series of tanks containing solutions formulated to degrease, clean, and electroplate the parts. At the electroplating tank, an electrical current was introduced to the solution, causing ions in the solution to be deposited on the parts. After plating, some parts were heat-treated to increase the life span of the finish. OI had recently installed a "state-of-the-art, high-tech" electrolysis-less nickel metal-plating process that added 17% to its productive capacity, at a cost of $750,000. Because it offered a superior finish at a lower cost, OI was looking to this process for competitive advantage, but Sutherland did not believe this had yet to materialize.

Most plating jobs involved a standard set of procedures, and OI was quality registered to meet the demands of the auto industry. This registration was the product of the efforts of OHL staff who understood how to obtain and retain standards and who had been instrumental in ensuring that OI met minimum conditions. However, when employees were faced with orders for unique finishes or those involving nonstandard metals, they relied on Wainwright's expertise or, in his absence, one of two senior plating technicians. To those who knew Wainwright, it seemed that he believed that plating was an "art" directed by the plater and implemented by semiskilled workers. Wainwright's hands-on approach meant that most employees had received little formal training in plating or advanced technology. Such process specifications were not documented for the nonstandard jobs that made up approximately 25% of the production, and process problems were often solved by Wainwright or one of the two senior plating technicians through trial and error. However, Talbot discovered that special written instructions from Wainwright were increasingly being overridden by workers who were experiencing confusion as to how to put them into practice and still meet production targets. Talbot also noted that trends that started in 2002 were continuing: Late deliveries were increasing, productivity was decreasing, and margins were becoming thinner.

The hazards of an electroplating plant were well known to the employees and to Dean Carter. Acid burns, cyanide poisoning, electrical shocks, crushed fingers, and scalds were common injuries. An improved ventilation system was recently installed at OI to enhance the quality of the air, which previously had been tainted by propane and combustion products from forklifts, vats, and furnaces. Aging pipes, tanks, and spill pails containing chromic, sulfuric, and nitric acids and caustic oils were sources of employee concern. In many areas of the plant, natural and artificial light were blocked by equipment, both stored and operational, and the noise level was sometimes considerable. Employees often joked that OI had a climatically controlled plant—the outside climate controlled the plant's environment!

Cost, finish quality, and delivery have traditionally been key success factors in the electroplating industry, and OI has had a solid reputation in these areas. Meeting or exceeding customer plating specifications for corrosion resistance, appearance, uniformity of deposit, hardness, wear resistance, and finish has been critical to acquiring and maintaining customer contracts. Increasingly, however, product quality differences between plating firms have disappeared, and OI has found that it is increasingly necessary to focus on cost, order fulfillment (just-in-time delivery was particularly important to firms supplying the automotive sector), and service/responsiveness as differentiators.

One competitor, in particular, had become a serious threat to OI. The local plant was part of a large multinational firm that specialized in the automotive sector and was one of four electroplating operations that it owned. In addition to services similar to OI, they offered two substitute processes (electrodeposit point and nitride finishes) that OI did not offer. Certain key customers were reporting that this firm was steadily becoming more cost competitive and were providing equivalent or superior coating finishes and better on-time performance. OI had experienced the loss of two existing plating contracts to them in the past year that had represented 15% of their total business volume. They were further eroding OI's position as a local market leader through their recent successes involving contracts for the electroplating of components for two new automotive programs. With the exception of the recently installed metal plating process and quality instrumentation mentioned earlier, new technologies and applications for metal finishing had not been aggressively pursued by Wainwright or OI.

OI's customer base was located within a 200-mile radius, because of their customers' desire to control the transportation and handling costs related to heavier products that needed electroplating. There were 11 firms competing for business in OI's market area, but the top three accounted for 80% of the business (based on billings), with OI at 45%, down from 50% a year ago. OI's primary focus was automotive and steel industry applications, and they did not compete in such sectors as semiconductors, jewelry, and medical applications.

The industrial electroplating industry in North America was undergoing consolidation, was in the mature stage, and was showing signs of decline as firms switched to the use of plastics and composite materials that did not require electroplating, reduced weight and in some cases costs, and reduced environmental concerns related to the electroplating process. Technical innovations in electroplating were focused on improving quality and cost-effectiveness and addressing environmental hazards associated with the process, but traditional approaches still dominated the sectors that OI served. Up until now, OI's customers had demonstrated little appetite for integrating most electroplating applications into their manufacturing facilities, because of environmental and health and safety risks, plus their belief that their needs in this area were best addressed by outsourcing to experts in the field. One exception involved the location of electrodeposit paint lines in certain larger plants.

Management of OHL and OI

For the first 18 years of his employment with OI and OHL, Chet Wainwright was the general manager (GM) and then the executive vice president, reporting directly to Dean Carter. The two men formed the nucleus of OI/OHL. Wainwright's "technical genius" in electroplating and automotive manufacturing processes led to his central role in OI's operations and his subsequent position as a consultant to OHL's joint ventures and executive vice president of OHL. OI was their first operation but now represented less than 2% of their total billings.

Early in OI's history, Dean Carter was constantly involved in the commercial and technical aspects of the electroplating plant—it was "his" plant. This constant involvement in the plant became a burden for the technical GM (Wainwright) and other managers. Eventually, employees avoided Carter and the information trickled rather than flowed upward. This didn't bother Carter, who saw it as "his" plant and he could do as he wished. Carter loathed unions but one was certified at OI 12 years ago, following an organizing campaign by the International Auto Workers (IAW). Carter was known to act decisively, seldom changed his decisions, and developed a reputation as a tough negotiator. He continued to support charities many years after initial contributions, and he was loyal to his staff, most of whom never left the company.

Wainwright knew a lot of people in the industry, and a lot of people knew him. As one manager said, "Wherever you went they seemed to know Wainwright—even in the States and abroad." Wainwright's technical prowess, savvy, extensive travel experience, and a knack for storytelling made him a "legend" of sorts in the industry. It was often Wainwright's reputation that gained OI and OHL access to new customers or market opportunities.

Wainwright knew how to read Carter. He knew when to challenge one of Carter's bids and when not to. In the latter case, Wainwright would move "heaven and earth" to make sure the job was done. For the last several years, Wainwright's energies were consumed with bringing on new plants for OHL, and this meant that Wainwright was away from headquarters for extended time periods and did not maintain close contact with OI. When he went to OI meetings with major customers (which was now occurring infrequently, involving relationship management and damage control), he often had to rely on his background knowledge, internal reports, and long-term relationships.

In the mid 1990s, Wainwright became EVP, moved to the role of a consultant to OI, and spent even less time at the plant. The first post-Wainwright plant manager (James Horkey, the former assistant OI plant manager) was replaced 2 years later (for health reasons) by Gerry Pawlawsky, who assumed responsibility for the plant's daily operations. In addition to Wainwright and Pawlawsky, there were Quality (Jim Lavin), Production (Brian Miller), and Maintenance managers (Robert Harcourt) overseeing the plant's approximately 40 production employees (see Exhibits 3 and 7 for the production employee breakdown and organizational chart). The OI Office Administrative Manager (Arlene Matthews) also managed the Fabrication operations. Matthews was originally hired by Dean Carter's father immediately after she received her high school diploma and had remained with the firm ever since. OI, in fact, had been the only place she'd ever worked. Excluding already mentioned managers, there were approximately 10 nonunion office staff employees at OI.

Employees and Management/ Union Relations

All plant employees at OI were members of the IAW. There were also two unionized plants within the OHL group of companies. The unionized workers at OI were hourly-paid employees, whereas all management positions were salaried. Gain sharing and profit sharing were not part of the compensation scheme at OI. Carter knew most of the employees by name, either from involvement in their hiring or from his physical presence over the years. Most employees had been with OI for 15 to 20 years, and everyone earned similar wages.

Union/management relations were brittle at best. Union members felt that the recent plant managers were relatively powerless and that their decision making was dictated by Dean Carter. Following Wainwright's promotion to EVP, the plant manager role had changed hands a couple of times, and Talbot had heard rumors of a shop floor pool betting on his expected departure date. The union contract was ambiguous as illustrated by the following excerpt from the contract regarding seniority:

> It is agreed that each employee shall have a measure of job security and job opportunity based on his length of service and his ability to perform the work available.
>
> This, in effect, means that the employee with the greatest length of service shall have the greatest seniority rights to such work as is available, provided the employee is qualified to properly perform the work available.

Office/supervisory staff and plant workers rarely mingled. During lunch, office staff and supervisory personnel usually ate lunch at their desks, while the plant floor workers ate in the small lunchroom at the front of the plant. Although anyone could eat in the lunchroom, it was usually used by only the shop room workers. With its Spartan furnishings—a rectangular table and soft drink-, coffee-, and snack-dispensing machines—its appeal was that it was "close to work." OI's seven designated parking spaces were reserved for the plant manager, assistant plant manager, quality control manager, office manager, and three visitors. Other OI employees parked their cars precariously on a first-come, first-serve basis along the side and back areas of the property, leaving only narrow access corridors for delivery trucks.

Finance

OI's financial affairs were controlled through OHL by Dean Carter and OHL's staff accountant, Al Simpson. Financial statements were developed on a consolidated basis for OHL. After 6 months at OI, Talbot had little feel for OI's financial position or cash flow. For example, net 30/2% was a common term for customers, but Talbot did not yet know their compliance rate.

Products or process lines were selected according to the degree to which management believed they affected the contribution to overhead. If there were no parts to finish, the lines would be shut down. Profitability of OI as a whole, rather than that of individual products or plating lines, was the concern. Equipment was seldom removed from the plant floor. Carter's perspective was that equipment that had been bought and paid for should be operated, regardless of its relative efficiency.

It was not clear to Talbot how prices were developed. It seemed that Carter and Wainwright or the plant manager of the day would basically quote whatever price was necessary to get the customer. Product pricing seemed to be based on the following criteria used either individually or in some combination:

1. How many dollars per hour can the machine generate?

2. What price can the market bear?

3. Where do you want to hold direct and indirect labor and overhead costs? This frequently depended on what management thought Dean Carter wanted to see.

4. What are the plant's average costs? Hold the average and force it down if possible!

5. How many sales do I want?

6. What do we think it's going to take to get the job?

This approach led to pressure on quality and service. Increases in the costs of labor and raw materials were passed on to established customers when it was felt that they would accept such an increase. Otherwise, OI would be forced to swallow the increase and senior managers would try to figure out how costs could be pared further.

There were systems for tracking major variables on a daily basis: labor, raw materials (e.g., chemicals), sales, payables, and so on; however, the inventory system for supplies/raw materials was not well developed, and there was no specific tracking of utilities or raw materials directly to the processing lines and production runs that used them. Each line was charged an average rate for utilities, chemicals, and other overhead costs. These were normally allocated on a percentage-of-sales basis. Talbot knew that the lines' usage of water, electricity, and chemicals varied considerably, but all allocations of those costs to the customer were considered "flexible" and allocated as needed to make the statement "look right."

The game was always to make money. Budget statements were finalized through an iterative process, often going through a number of revisions before they "were right." Financial statements and profitability information were compiled monthly for OI (see Exhibits 4 to 6 for financial information on OI).

Sales

Historically, OI had boasted a 65% market share in the Oshawa region, but this had slumped to 45% and recent sales growth had been flat. Carter was aware that recent sales were primarily to customers with long-standing loyalties both to OI and to himself or to Chet Wainwright personally and realized that OI was starting to lose "old" customers (internal advocates were retiring or exiting their purchasing roles) without attracting new ones. Purchasing relationships built on personal friendships and loyalties were becoming passé, and new purchasing managers were being held accountable for increasingly stringent measures. Cost competitiveness was an important challenge for OI, but so too were product quality and on-time delivery. Recent investigations at OI revealed that oil and grease had occasionally dripped onto newly plated parts, and some defective parts were being buried in the middle of bins, ready for shipment to the customer.

It seemed to Talbot that the firm talked about customer service but operated with a production orientation, with no clear understanding of what customer service meant. Lines were run "when it was convenient" for the shop rather than for the customer. Often orders lingered at the production manager's desk for a week or more. Talbot could see that in an environment driven by just-in-time production, OI was not meeting customer needs. Talbot knew that customer service meant meeting clients' needs when they needed it and doing it better than the competition.

Environmental Issues

With public concern for environmental issues on the rise, government pressure on electroplating firms was increasing. Under the Ontario Environmental Protection Act, almost everything to do with the electroplating industry was classified as hazardous because the processes are laden with acids and heavy metals. The old "solution to pollution by dilution" had become increasingly unacceptable, and pollution-control equipment was very expensive. One consultant estimated that purchasing and installing adequate pollution-control equipment at OI would cost almost $450,000. OI had allocated $200,000 for the direct purchase of 90% of the required tanks, pumps, and meters and decided to install the equipment themselves but had not yet undertaken the work.

Decision to Hire Mark Talbot

In the mid 1990s, it became apparent to Carter that Wainwright needed a plant manager to oversee the OI plant's daily operations, since much of Wainwright's time was spent on the road, managing new plants and visiting customers. He also noticed that emerging metal-finishing technologies were beyond the scope of Wainwright's interest. Wainwright also recognized the need for a plant manager as well as a successor and was more than willing to assist any new recruit in learning the processes involved in the electroplating industry.

Pawlawsky was the second plant manager promoted by Carter and Wainwright. Pawlawsky found that although he was "responsible" for management of the plant, he still had to get approval from either Wainwright or Carter for any operational changes or expenditures. During his first few 2 years, Pawlawsky identified several problems within the plant and questioned a number of business practices, but he never developed a strong relationship with Carter or Wainwright. He was unable to persuade them to accept and implement most of his proposed changes. Relationships, especially between Pawlawsky and Carter, faltered. Carter was very concerned about Pawlawsky's inconsistent management style with employees. One moment he

pushed quality and the next he pushed output. Carter eventually deemed Pawlawsky unsuitable for the position of plant manager, and he was demoted to assistant plant manager.

Shortly thereafter, the quality manager quit over a salary dispute, and 1 month later Roger Sutherland joined as vice president. One of Sutherland's first jobs was to fill the vacant plant manager and quality manager positions. When no acceptable replacements were found from among staff at OI and OHL, it was decided that an "outsider" would be hired and trained. Over a period of 4 months, Wainwright and Sutherland interviewed eight candidates for the plant manager job and seven candidates for the position of quality manager. Talbot, a 28-year-old engineering graduate with 3 years of manufacturing experience, was the sixth candidate for the latter position. Sutherland was very impressed and began to wonder if he might not be a good candidate for the plant manager position.

Sutherland quickly arranged a series of OHL interviews for Talbot. When Wainwright first interviewed Talbot, he asked him about his career goals, and Talbot indicated that his goal was to have Wainwright's job. After receiving positive reports on Talbot from Wainwright and Sutherland, Carter was curious to meet this bold candidate. When Carter interviewed Talbot, he was impressed by Talbot's drive and nerve. He thought that Talbot might be the candidate with the needed technical and entrepreneurial skills and who would not be afraid to "take the bull by the horns and get the job done" in order to bring OI's operations in line with the guiding principles of OHL.

Talbot was equally impressed with what he heard during the interviews with Sutherland, Wainwright, and Carter and admired Sutherland for his apparent management abilities. Carter stressed the company's focus on quality, his desire for OHL to be an industry leader in the coming decade, and his concern for the employees. Carter stressed that OHL was just an advisory board and would not interfere with OI's operations, and that he believed in autonomy for competent general managers. Carter also alluded to the possibility that "for the right man," the plant manager position could lead to that of general manager or even to becoming a VP/technical consultant of OHL. There were no salary negotiations, but Carter presented Talbot with a job offer for employment at OHL.

Talbot accepted and started in January 2002 at Brockville Enterprises, a new offshoot company of OHL. He was hired to install new plating equipment, and for the next 6 months, he learned plating from the ground up. Sutherland developed a close relationship with Talbot during this period.

By June 2002, Wainwright and Sutherland felt that Talbot was ready to move to OI to assume the position of assistant plant manager. The position of assistant plant manager was curiously named because OI did not have a plant manager at the time. So in effect, Talbot had no direct reporting relationship to anyone other than Wainwright. Six months earlier, Pawlawsky had expressed the desire to be transferred out of his role as assistant plant manager and become the quality manager at OI. His request for the transfer was honored with the arrival of Talbot.

Talbot's First 6 Months as Assistant Plant Manager

Sutherland wanted to expose Talbot to both new and existing customers, the full range of OI's products and services, and the opportunity to prove himself in a position where any mistakes made would be small. Sutherland felt that Talbot was bright, but his lack of management and operating experience was a shortcoming. He felt it particularly important that Talbot learn as much as possible from Wainwright.

Talbot's first task after joining OI was to identify new sales opportunities for the company since sales growth had fallen during the previous year. His initial goal was to attract new sales equivalent to 300% of his annual salary.

In addition to his sales function, Talbot was Wainwright's technical apprentice because OI needed to decrease its dependency on Wainwright's technical expertise.

During Talbot's first 6 months, the relationship between himself and Wainwright, though intermittent, prospered. Carter also felt a growing confidence in Talbot's ability to assume the role of plant manager. Talbot was a quick study and able to draw on his chemical engineering degree and technical background to learn the intricacies of electroplating. Talbot asked a lot of questions, but he was never perceived as a threat by Wainwright. By January, the situation had started to change. Operating procedures and business practices that had previously been taken for granted by Wainwright and the plant staff were under scrutiny by Talbot. Talbot was beginning to take a more active role in managing the plant, often bypassing Wainwright's approval and initiating and implementing small changes to the manufacturing process on his own. Talbot also found that the quality, production, and maintenance managers continued to talk directly to Wainwright, rather than to him.

Although Talbot seemed to be slowly winning the support and cooperation of some plant personnel, Talbot felt that some of his approaches were earning him a reputation as a "stubborn purist" on issues such as quality. Talbot's unwillingness to ignore problems or to accept shortcomings in either the operations or in people's performance and his "take charge" attitude and questioning style resulted in some tensions between himself, Wainwright, and other managers in the plant. That was why he was surprised when he heard through Carter that Wainwright recommended his promotion to the position of plant manager under Wainwright 12 months ahead of the original plan. If a firm offer of promotion materialized, he thought that he would take it but wondered what he should do. How would he manage the people, production and marketing, and corporate issues at OI?

Exhibit 1   Guiding Principles of Oshawa Holdings Limited*

Joint Venture

Oshawa Holdings' policy is to form joint ventures with its major customer. Such a policy allows each party to contribute, in an organized way, to improve die operations of the company, such as sharing technology and production methods. Oshawa Holdings tried to reduce or at least maintain the cost of the product to die customers by cost-improvement programs or increases in volume. In this way, long-term stability and market penetration can be obtained.

Oshawa Holdings joint venture companies operate completely independently. Each has a chief executive officer and is an autonomous entrepreneurial company. Oshawa Holdings only monitors their operations and makes sure that the shareholders' interests are being developed and protected. Our experience is that, if monitored properly, an independent entrepreneurial company, with the proper chief executive officer, will prosper. Because Oshawa Holdings does not get involved in the day-to-day operations of its joint ventures, it is able to be involved in a number of them.

Employee Relations

To create a quality culture, the most important thing is to have a happy family relationship among all employees and to have the employees enjoy their jobs. To do this, it is critical to have employee involvement in the management of the company. All employees must be involved in the objectives of the company such as quality, production levels, methods of production, and capital spending. This emphasizes that all employees are of equal importance and contribute equally to the company's success. When employees are involved in the management of the company, their jobs are more secure, interesting, and varied, and they care more about the company and are happier. Every effort is made to avoid laying off permanent employees and to increase job security. In Oshawa Holdings' companies, the employees also share in the profits of the company through gain sharing or other forms of profit sharing. These policies ensure that the employees of Oshawa Holdings will remain company oriented and work as a team without outside interference.

Statistical Process Control

To have a quality culture, it is also necessary that each plant must be under complete statistical process control. Machine and process capability studies must be constantly performed, and statistical inspection and charting of the production must be done. Many of Carter's companies have reduced acceptable production tolerances to 50% of print specifications. At Oshawa Holdings' companies, the machine operators are the inspectors, and machines are repaired and rebuilt based on machine capability studies. Records must be kept so that complete traceability of production can be done. All employees must attend SPC seminars every 2 months to update their knowledge, and new employees must attend a 2-week course on SPC. Oshawa Holdings's objective is to eliminate final inspection audits by statistical machine and process control and operator inspection and charting.

Small Entrepreneurial Focus Factories

Oshawa Holdings believes that small, entrepreneurial focus factories are the best type of organization for North America to produce quality products efficiently. Its policy is to create small companies with a limited number of technologies, which are managed by technically qualified people. This enables each technology to be fully developed and controlled and to be operated at its optimum. Each of these companies searches for new materials, conducts research and development, and develops new production and process equipment. Along with Oshawa Holdings, they also are committed to diversification. This type of organization is very efficient and keeps production and overhead costs low.

Source: Oshawa Holdings Limited Corporate Profile, 1988.

Exhibit 2 Plant Floor Layout

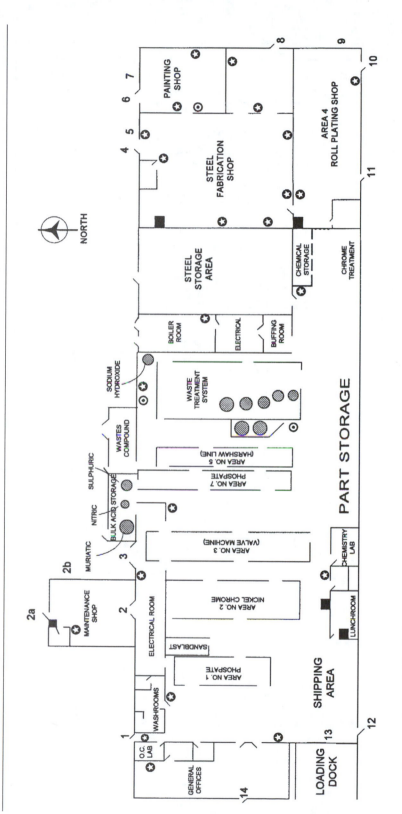

OSHAWA INDUSTRIES

PLANT LAYOUT

✪ FIRE EXTINGUISHER

◎ EMERGENCY SHOWER/EYEWASH

■ FIRST-AID STATION

SCALE

0   5m   10m

NORTH

Case Study 3

Exhibit 3   Employee Distribution

Classification	Number of Employees	Plant Seniority Number / years	Wage Rate $ / hour
Steel Shop			
Welding & Layout	3	1 @ 28; 2 @ 13	22.98
Welding & Fitup	2	1 @ 7; 1 @ 6	22.84
Plating Department			
Plater Special	5	1 @ 36; 1 @ 34 2 @ 20; 1 @ 12	23.12
Plater 1	15	1 @ 31; 5 @ 13 7 @ 12; 1 @ 8 1 @ 2	22.60
Plater 2	7	3 @ 12; 1 @ 9 2 @ 7; 1 @ 2	22.12
Maintenance Department			
Maintenance (ticketed)	2	1 @ 19; 1 @ 1	25.00
Maintenance (nonticketed)	2	1 @ 35; 1 @ 20	22.60
Chemistry Department			
Chemist	1	1 @ 20	23.12
Shipping Department			
Shipper	1	1 @ 20	23.12
Tractor Trailer Driver	2	1 @ 17; 1 @ 16	23.12

Case Study 3

Exhibit 4   Oshawa Industries Balance Sheet, December 31

Account	1998	1999	2000	2001
Current Assets				
Cash	$52,908	($77,190)	$452,132	$243,340
Accounts Receivable	1,001,014	1,105,324	992,116	1,487,726
Inventory	406,162	351,684	325,466	398,928
Prepaid Expenses	48,700	72,590	38,634	29,554
Deferred Exchange	4,600		109,820	198,912
Total Current Assets	$1,513,384	$1,452,408	$1,918,168	$2,358,460
Investments				
Intercompany	$1,450,134	$252,788	$493,350	$560,880
Investment in Europe	1,381,710	718,000		718,000
Total Investment	$1,450,134	$1,634,498	$1,211,350	$1,278,880
Total Fixed Assets	$3,740,600	$4,081,824	$4,339,060	$4,799,874
Accumulated Depreciation	2,820,124	3,032,472	3,193,540	3,487,596
Net Fixed Assets	$920,476	$1,049,352	$1,145,520	$1,312,278
Other Assets	$820			$0
Total Assets	$3,884,814	$4,136,258	$4,275,038	$4,949,618
Current Liabilities				
Accounts Payable	$537,842	$548,934	$553,926	$639,316
Accrued Payroll	32,558	38,698	11,308	20,084
Pension Plan Payable	2,374	65,676	85,466	48,126
Accrued Staff Benefits	115,118	102,374	118,542	128,702
Taxes Payable				
Payroll Tax	96,104	95,668	126,714	132,894
Sales Tax	794			0
Income Tax	124,372	(162,546)	434,496	323,742
Operating Loan		890,000		11,056
Other Liabilities	95,946	113,238	605,206	349,538
Total Current Liabilities	$1,005,108	$1,692,042	$1,935,658	$1,653,458
Long-Term Liabilities				
Bank Loans Payable	$40,000	$430,000	$24,000	$18,000
Sales Contract	130,558	320,220	251,744	179,844
Customer Deposits	51,752	30,538	22,656	9,624
Shareholder Loans		850,156	850,156	2,437,036
Deferred Income Taxes	296,842	248,200	248,200	244,200
Total Long-Term Liabilities	$519,152	$1,879,114	$1,396,756	$2,888,704
Shareholder Equity				
Common Shares	$200	$200	$200	$200
Current Retained Earnings	1,542,086	1,944	313,230	(69,450)
Accumulated Retained Earnings	790,722	556,800	623,038	472,336
Total Equity	$2,333,008	$558,944	$936,468	$403,086
Auditor's Adjustment	$27,544	$6,156	$6,156	$4,370
Total Liabilities and Equity	$3,884,812	$4,136,256	$4,275,038	$4,949,618

Exhibit 5   Oshawa Industries Statement of Income and Expenses for Periods Ending December 31

Description	1999	2000	2001
REVENUES			
Steel Division	$950,500	$907,784	$1,259,586
Plating Division	$8,406,524	$8,746,344	$8,693,478
TOTAL SALES	$9,357,024	$9,654,128	$9,953,064
LESS			
Sales Discounts	$31,884	$33,268	$39,018
Credit Notes	$13,890		
Adj. Work in Progress	($16,490)	($12,610)	($22,844)
NET SALES REVENUES	$9,294,760	$9,608,248	$9,891,202
EXPENSES			
Labor	$3,162,470	$3,149,156	$3,254,016
Benefits	775,438	817,024	881,636
Materials	2,391,534	2,294,548	2,364,098
Shipping	605,494	649,836	905,198
Utilities	846,280	800,490	772,476
Fixed-Asset Expenses	327,378	382,854	425,312
Marketing and Administration	397,116	355,300	442,086
TOTAL EXPENSES	$8,505,710	$8,449,208	$9,044,822
OPERATING PROFIT (LOSS)	$789,050	$1,159,042	$846,380
OTHER SALARY EXPENSE			
DEFERRED EXCHANGE			
OTHER INCOME	4,246	54,038	23,950
INTEREST INCOME (CHARGES)		(99,842)	(28,920)
TOTAL PROFIT (LOSS)	$793,296	$1,113,238	$841,410
TOTAL INCOME TAXES	$349,200	$490,200	$369,200
AFTER-TAX PROFIT (LOSS)	$444,096	$623,038	$472,210
REVENUES, STEEL	$934,010	$895,142	$1,236,742
REVENUES, PLATING	$8,360,768	$8,713,106	$8,654,460
EXPENSES, STEEL	$952,154	$967,376	$1,160,678
EXPENSES, PLATING	$7,553,554	$7,481,832	$7,884,144
PROFITS, STEEL	($9,920)	($37,230)	$44,058
PROFITS, PLATING	$454,018	$660,268	$428,152

Case Study 3

Exhibit 6   Oshawa Industries Financial Analysis

Ratio	1999	2000	2001
Current Ratio	0.86	0.99	1.43
Quick Ratio	0.65	0.82	1.19
Return on Total Assets	10.74%	14.57%	9.54%
Return on Stockholder Equity	79.45%	66.53%	117.15%
Net Profit Margin	4.78%	6.48%	4.77%
Current Liabilities to Inventory	481.13%	594.73%	414.48%
Sales to Inventory Ratio	26.43	29.52	24.79
Average Collection Period (Days)	43.41	37.69	54.90
Cost to Sales Ratio	87.24	84.24	86.97

Industry Standards

Ratio		1999	2000	2001
Current Ratio	Upper Quad.	2.3	2.5	1.3
	Median	2.0	1.7	1.3
	Lower Quad.	1.2	1.1	1.2
Quick Ratio	Upper Quad.	N/A	2.6	0.9
	Median	N/A	1.3	0.9
	Lower Quad.	N/A	1.0	0.5
Return on Total Assets	Upper Quad.	28.6%	23.9%	13.1%
	Median	17.0%	21.8%	10.1%
	Lower Quad.	13.3%	17.8%	5.0%
Return on Stockholder Equity	Upper Quad.	57.6%	48.9%	38.1%
	Median	49.5%	31.4%	26.3%
	Lower Quad.	25.7%	24.6%	18.6%
Net Profit Margin	Upper Quad.	10.7%	13.4%	8.6%
	Median	6.7%	9.0%	7.3%
	Lower Quad.	6.1%	7.2%	4.0%
Current Liabilities to Inventory Ratio	Upper Quad.	N/A	99.2%	144.1%
	Median	N/A	179.2%	265.8%
	Lower Quad	N/A	287.3%	644.4%
Sales to Inventory Ratio	Upper Quad.	N/A	88.6	21.5
	Median	N/A	74.3	12.7
	Lower Quad.	N/A	17.8	8.5
Average Collection Period (Days)	Upper Quad.	N/A	40.1	27.7
	Median	N/A	62.8	42.6
	Lower Quad.	N/A	69.8	72.5

Note: Industry Standards were obtained from Dun and Bradstreet Canadian Norms and Key Business Ratios, SIC 3471. Costs to sales ratio averages about 77% for comparable industries.

Case Study 3

Case Study 3

Exhibit 7 Organizational Structure of OHL and OI

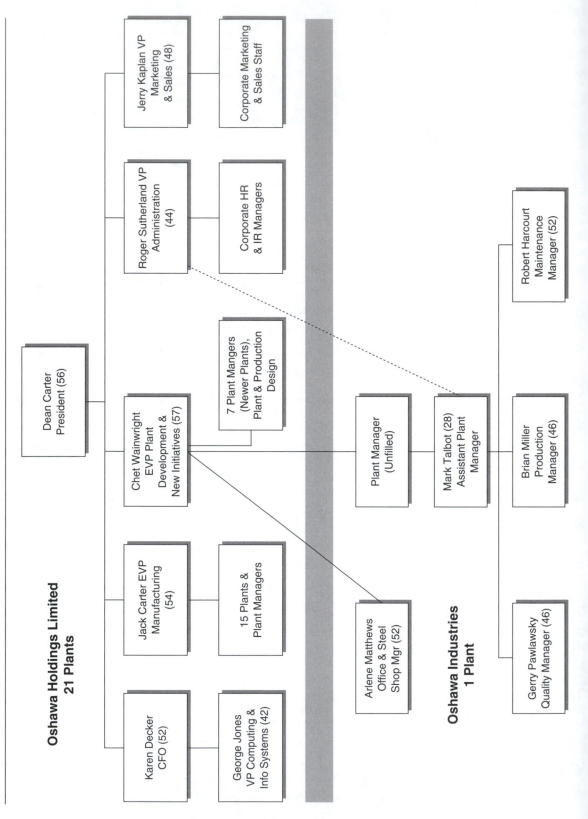

**Oshawa Holdings Limited
21 Plants**

Dean Carter President (56)

Karen Decker CFO (52)

George Jones VP Computing & Info Systems (42)

Jack Carter EVP Manufacturing (54)

15 Plants & Plant Managers

Chet Wainwright EVP Plant Development & New Initiatives (57)

7 Plant Mangers (Newer Plants), Plant & Production Design

Roger Sutherland VP Administration (44)

Corporate HR & IR Managers

Jerry Kaplan VP Marketing & Sales (48)

Corporate Marketing & Sales Staff

Arlene Matthews Office & Steel Shop Mgr (52)

**Oshawa Industries
1 Plant**

Plant Manager (Unfilled)

Mark Talbot (28) Assistant Plant Manager

Gerry Pawlawsky Quality Manager (46)

Brian Miller Production Manager (46)

Robert Harcourt Maintenance Manager (52)

Questions for Class Discussion

1. Use the congruence model to describe Oshawa Industries. What is happening in its environment? What has been its implicit strategy prior to Talbot's arrival? Is the strategy in line with Oshawa's inputs? Are the transformation processes all aligned well with its strategy?

2. When you evaluate Oshawa's outputs at the organizational, group, and individual levels, do you see anything that might identify issues that your organization should address? What key congruencies and incongruencies exist?

3. Are there some aspects of how Oshawa works that you have difficulty understanding? If so, identify the resources you can access to help with this analysis.

4. Identify one set of dynamic, nonlinear interactions from Oshawa Industries that demonstrates Sterman's concepts.

5. Using Quinn's competing values model, what has been Oshawa's value emphasis? What does it need to do more of? Less of?

6. What phase does Oshawa appear to be going through using Greiner's model for organizational growth?

CHAPTER 11

Summary Thoughts on Organizational Change

Once you fall in a river, you're no longer a fisherman, you're a swimmer.

—Gene Hill

Chapter Overview

- This chapter presents an expanded summary model of organizational change and applies the model to a case situation.
- The future of organizational change and organizational change agents is discussed.
- Individuals wishing to become organizational change agents need to recognize that two main routes exist: sophisticated technical specialists and strategic generalists.
- Several paradoxes in the field of organizational change are summarized.
- The chapter ends with questions on how to orient oneself to organizational change and what questions change agents need to ask.

Writing a concluding chapter on organizational change is paradoxical. How does one conclude something one sees as ongoing? In some ways, a conclusion violates the orientation of this book. We see change as normal, pervasive, everyone's responsibility, and a necessary skill for all managers. Change is not something you deal with and then move on. Rather, it is a continuing process of learning and accomplishment. Nevertheless, in this chapter, we present two major sections: a summary of the key concepts as applied to a case situation and concluding thoughts about how organizational change will evolve. We end with key questions for organizational change.

What Is Our Summary Model of "How" to Change?

Throughout this book, we have argued for an explicit model for change. Figure 11.1 outlines the summary model. This model suggests that change agents move systematically from awareness of the need for change, through initiation, planning and

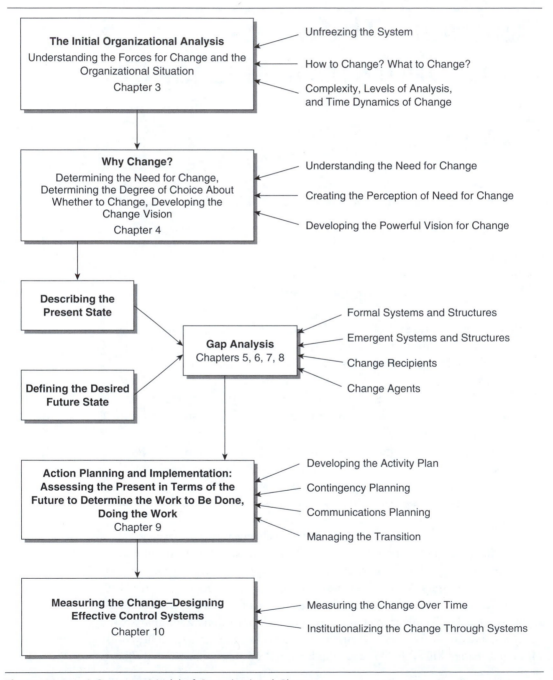

Figure 11.1 A Summary Model of Organizational Change

implementing the change, to measuring and confirming the change. A summary Checklist for Change is given in Appendix 1 at the end of this chapter.

A review of this model is given below using the case of "Harry and the Company Takeover." Each of the concepts—"Initial Organization Analysis," "Why Change?" "Gap Analysis," "Action Planning and Implementation," and "Measuring the Change"—is evident in Harry's actions. The purpose of the review is to demonstrate the usefulness of the explicit model on which this book is based.

Harry and the Company Takeover

When Harry decided to help his cousin salvage his business, he had no idea things were in as bad a shape as they were. He knew that the banks had called their demand notes that would put the company into receivership, but he was shocked at the number of issues he found that needed to be dealt with. In his mind, the company's business model was straightforward: renting out specialized heavy equipment (either with or without operators) to a relatively easily identified set of customers. Straightforward, maybe, but there was no question that things were a mess.

Harry's cousin had founded the firm 15 years ago. He had grown it steadily through the first 10 years, followed by accelerated growth through most of the past 5 years. The bankruptcy of a key competitor and unprecedented growth in the area had resulted in a robust market. Staff levels had more than doubled during the past 5 years to 57 employees. Fifteen employees were located in the office area, handling administrative, accounting/finance, and sales functions. The remainder were in the repair shop, yard, or on the road, dealing with maintenance, delivery, and equipment operation roles.

Sales had flattened and moved to a modest decline over the past year. Other financial indicators showed worrying trends. For 2 years, operating expenses had risen significantly. While Harry wasn't certain why, he thought that equipment purchases had led to higher interest charges and that labor costs had risen significantly. It was as if the firm had lost its capacity to manage the growth.

Things had gone from difficult to worse in the past 2 years. His cousin had varied his management approach from requesting to pleading and finally to avoiding issues at work. Employees referred to him as Waldo (from the children's book *Where's Waldo?*), because he was usually impossible to find when guidance was sought or a decision needed to be made.

Harry agreed that he would try to turn things around in return for his cousin's consenting to turn over decision-making power and control while focusing on what he knew best—things related to operations and the equipment. His cousin had grown up with a love for heavy equipment, and family members said that the only reason he was in business was so that he could have newer and bigger toys to play with. He had specialized knowledge about which equipment was suitable for which jobs, and prior to the past 2 years, he had been adept at developing relationships with customers that generated repeat business.

The terms were agreed to, but Harry's arrival did not reverse his cousin's disappearing act. He continued to appear depressed and distant, with little appetite for assuming a more active operational role in the business.

(Continued)

---

*This case is based on personal experience of the authors.

(Continued)

Harry believed that the business had solid prospects and should be able to sustain a more than adequate return on the investment. However, it certainly was not doing so now. He met with the bank and presented a turnaround plan. Based on his reputation as a successful entrepreneur and his willingness to make a significant investment to improve liquidity, they agreed to renegotiate the operating loan and line of credit. This would provide the firm with the breathing space needed to execute the turnaround.

Harry moved into his cousin's office and began to actively take control of the management of the firm. He was shocked to find a culture of permissiveness, waste, and tolerance for corruption. As he walked through the parts and maintenance areas, he found parts, tools, and equipment scattered about. Grease on the floor made walking a risky proposition. Pizza boxes, pop tins, and bottles were littered around. He thought he smelled liquor on some employees. He observed that lateness and absenteeism were problems. No one seemed to be doing anything about them because the labor market for mechanics and operators was tight and supervisors were afraid that people might quit.

The housekeeping within the office/administrative area was somewhat better than other parts of the operation, but it still left much to be desired. Some employees smoked in work areas, despite no-smoking rules. While the accounting and finance area appeared to be somewhat better organized, they often had difficulty providing the managerial data Harry requested.

After reviewing sales information, Harry also found himself wondering about the source of orders. Most orders came from brokers rather than directly from users of the equipment. He wondered why and guessed that the brokers were taking 15% to 25% off the top for the orders.

In an inspection of the operations shortly after his arrival, Harry found seven brand-new tires and rims stashed behind a building. When he checked purchasing invoices, he learned that nine had been bought the week before. On further investigation, he was told that no new tires had been mounted on any equipment. Harry could not locate two tires and rims worth over $1,500 each.

One of the first things that Harry did was to walk around the operation and talk to people. He would look them in the eye and say, "I want to make money here. What do you want?" At the same time, he started insisting that if someone came to him with a problem, they should also come with what they wanted out of the situation—a solution to the issue. When they did, he would listen intently, take time to discuss things thoroughly, voice appreciation and support, and approve action, when appropriate, with the words "Great—let's get on with it. Let me know if you need anything and keep me in the loop with how it goes." The consistent message from Harry was that this operation will be a success and everyone will win, if we exercise more discipline and if everyone shows initiative and contributes to improvements needed to make this operation a winner.

Harry realized that many members of the firm probably wanted to do a good job. That was the sense he got as he visited departments, talked with individuals one-on-one, and heard about their frustrations. Some employees seemed to come and go as they wished—three even brought their dogs to work. He had listened to one customer's complaint about late delivery of equipment and learned that the person delivering the machinery had stopped for 3 hours en route. The driver's excuse was lunch and engine problems that had miraculously been resolved. Morale was in the toilet but turnover had yet to become a problem.

Harry called the employees together during his first week to introduce himself; address the need for improvement; solicit their cooperation, ideas, and effort; and to let them know that he planned to be around regularly. Harry also put up flipchart sheets in the office during the first week and began listing every issue or problem that he or others identified. His list contained 93 items by the end of the third week. However, by the third week, he had also approved four employee-initiated improvement plans.

During his first week, Harry smelled alcohol on the breath of an employee who appeared to be under the influence. He fired him on the spot. He told employees that new rules on attendance would be enforced.

During the third week, Harry called people together for a second plant meeting and summarized some of the problem areas that had been identified as needing attention. He also announced the initial change recommendations that employees had advanced and publicly thanked the initiators. He stated that new rules on work scheduling would be implemented. He stated that housekeeping in both the plant and office had to improve. He said that the business had the potential to be a first-class operation and that it was time for it to quit looking like a pigsty. The shop floors would be degreased, the walls would be repainted, and tools and equipment should be properly stored. If people wanted pizza or anything other than a donut or muffin with their coffee, they would be expected to eat it in the lunchroom or not at all. Major cleanup activities were undertaken over a 3-week period, with floor degreasing and painting occurring during the weekends.

During his third week, Harry went into the workspace of the people with dogs and said, "What are these? Employees or pets?" They vanished from the workplace. After further investigation of the tires he had found stashed, Harry concluded that the person who had signed the purchase order for the nine tires was selling them out the back door, and on the Wednesday of week three, he escorted him off the premises.

During the fourth week, Harry had an opportunity to follow up on his hunch that the company was losing margin by relying on brokers. He phoned one of their customers who regularly used their equipment but who went through a broker and asked why they were not placing orders directly. "Because you never called us before" was the answer. Before he ended the conversation, he had a $50,000 work order placed directly. When Harry relayed this conversation and its results to the sales staff, they were at first defensive. Further conversation, combined with his now standard question ("We want to make money—do you want to be part of it?"), elicited affirmative responses, although they still seemed unsure as to how they should change their sales approach. Harry made a note to himself that they would need further training and guidance or need replacement.

Harry recalled similar conversations with other employees. For example, in a conversation with a truck driver, Harry said, "We make money when you are delivering equipment to clients. If you stand around when orders are pending, we don't make money. People who work hard and get more equipment to clients are going to make more money. Do you want to be part of this or not?" "I'm in" was the response.

(Continued)

(Continued)

During the fourth week, Harry noticed that certain pieces of equipment that had been in for repair in week one were still inoperable. He asked why and was told that the maintenance supervisor was in a dispute with the field service foreman and sales staff over the allocation of repair and maintenance charges, and as a result, needed repairs had not been undertaken. This had resulted in lost rental sales. The argument had been going on for over a month, and he was told that this was not the first time. Harry reacted with frustration. He called an immediate meeting of those involved, ordered the equipment repaired as soon as possible, and stated that this was no way to resolve conflicts. He added "unclear responsibilities" to his list of issues on the flipchart.

During Harry's sixth week on the job, he announced that he wanted a system that would give him a profit and loss statement for each piece of equipment. "Why do you want that?" was the response. When he explained why to the employees in accounting, they understood, but operational employees saw it as more paperwork that might get in the way of sales and servicing.

When he began to explore equipment repair invoices during week six, he noted that many expensive repairs had been done onsite at their clients. Much of the work looked routine but was made much more expensive because of the location and because the company had to negotiate with the client over operating losses while the machine was down. Harry wondered why that equipment hadn't been serviced prior to leaving the shop. When he inquired further, he discovered that there was no formal preventive maintenance program established for the equipment.

By week seven, the cleaning and painting of the office area and workplace had been completed and it helped to spruce up the environment. Employees were reacting positively to the improved workplace, as reflected in comments Harry received during his many walks through work areas each week. Little additional action seemed to be needed from Harry to maintain the improvements. Even the paperwork in the office area seemed to be better organized now, but Harry wondered whether it was simply being put into boxes and hidden from view. When he told employees in the plant that he thought that swearing was unprofessional conduct at work, they just looked at him.

Things seemed to be getting better, but much more needed to be done. He went down his list, noting some of the most pressing items:

1. No formalized preventive maintenance systems.

2. Questionable inventory management system, missing parts in some areas, excess inventory in others, and a significant volume of obsolete parts that were held in inventory.

3. Missing tools and equipment, including some bigger-ticket items such as a $35,000 loader and a $25,000 compressor.

4. Sales relationships not actively managed, clients not phoned in a timely manner, customer complaints not acted upon until threats were invoked.

5. Logistics/scheduling, customer delivery and pickups, onsite servicing of equipment not handled well. Customers complained about their ability to predict when things would be done and downtime.

> 6. Lags between order filling and client billing, slow payment of accounts payable.
>
> 7. Poor relations with suppliers of parts and equipment, due in part to slow payment, disagreements of terms and conditions, and lack of supplier responsiveness to emergency requests.
>
> 8. Finally and important, the role his cousin would play after the company had been revitalized.

As one can surmise from the case, Harry's *initial organizational analysis* provided extensive evidence of **what** needed to change. The list was long: from employees drinking on the job to sloppy shop cleanliness, the potential theft of valuable equipment, low performance expectations, a lack of needed systems and processes, and the absence of a disciplined approach to interpersonal conduct and dispute resolution. **How** to change was not as clear, as the culture of the organization reinforced the negative dynamics. Clearly, Harry needed to change the systems and culture to get things back on track—assuming, of course, that the bank would give him the time to turn the operation around.

The answer to the question (see Figure 11.1) "Why change?" was evident to Harry and to the bank but was not evident to all the employees. Harry needed to "unfreeze the situation." The initial behavior of some employees indicated complacency, resignation, and, in some cases, a desire to milk the company for as long as it lasted. He dealt with the bank by giving them a plan and putting in his own money. This and his reputation as a skilled owner-manager persuaded the bank to work with him. Harry tackled the culture of permissiveness by making his expectations clear to employees (Are the dogs "employees or pets"?). While some of this was unorthodox, the communication was clear. As well, Harry understood that actions counted. By firing people who were abusing the organization, he was making the strongest statements possible about what was not acceptable. Because he was in charge of the operation, he had the power to do this. Note that Harry's cousin also had the formal authority to take such actions, but he had chosen not to act. Over time, Harry's cousin had come to be perceived as powerless.

Harry's *vision for change* was clear and simple: "I want to make money. This will take individual initiative, discipline, and systems and processes that can support our work. What do you want?" The strategy was to service clients with the rental equipment they needed in a timely and profitable manner. One could argue over the nature of the appeal, but the vision was clear and appropriate to the company's situation. At the same time, Harry seemed to have an implicit vision for the longer term. His actions to clean up the workplace; stop employees from swearing and smoking; empower employees to engage in active problem solving; become more customer, cost, and performance focused; and act on their improvement ideas, all suggest a new vision for the workplace.

The list of 93 issues was his *gap analysis*. In his view, there would be employees who would want to work and who would welcome being part of a successful company. Those employees he appealed to directly, by outlining how they could make more money by helping the company succeed. Those who resisted strongly were fired if their behavior was illegal or unethical or if they failed to meet standards. Harry tried to recognize and reinforce employees who began to embrace the change. Implicitly, the message was that they could be viewed as change agents working in the employee group. Harry recognized that there was an absence of formal structures. The reporting lines and procedures were unclear, as shown by the dispute between the maintenance supervisor and the general foreman and sales staff. Formal systems either were faulty or didn't exist. For example, the accounting system could not track usage and profitability by machine, and there was no preventive maintenance system. Harry dealt with key stakeholders in priority: the bank, the employees, and key clients. The aftermath of these contacts created initiatives that raised expectations, began to improve performance, and helped to generate hope for the future.

The case example demonstrates nicely the *dynamics of action planning and implementation*. The operation was relatively simple, and his plan consisted explicitly of dealing with the list of issues needing attention. He discussed specific issues with employees and demanded that others take action to deal with the issues. As he learned about the ambitions and competencies of employees, he encouraged them. He also fired those who were engaged in inappropriate behavior or who failed to meet reasonable performance standards. His communications plan was personal, constant, and direct.

Finally, because of the size of the operation, Harry was able to *measure the changes* directly. Some changes he could see. The plant was cleaner. The dogs were gone. Others he could track by looking at sales figures and profit margins. At the same time, he knew that the systems he wanted, such as a system to track profits per piece of rental equipment and a preventive maintenance program, would take longer to install.

The case example above illustrates the change process outlined in Figure 11.1. Toolkit Exercise 11.1 provides a detailed step-by-step summary for planning a change project. While change agents need a model for change, they also need to understand how organizational change will develop in the future. The chapter now considers these shifts.

How Will Future Organizations Affect Organizational Change?

In Chapter 1, we presented Barkema's views on the changes organizations face and how they would need to adapt.[1] In his view, all organizations will need to be global in orientation. Small and medium-sized firms will access global markets through the Internet in low-cost/high–information transmission ways. Others will form organizational networks, partnering with others to complete the value chain. Some will be large, focused global firms with worldwide activities.

Barkema states that organizations will have autonomous, dislocated teams. That is, organizations, large or small, will require motivated teams to coordinate their activities across borders and cultures. At the same time, structures will be "digitally enabled." They will have the electronic systems to facilitate coordination. Scanning systems will transmit sales data from stores and warehouses anywhere to manufacturing facilities in real time and will be used to determine future production levels. Personal communications devices such as the BlackBerry will mean that people can communicate anytime, all the time. Such dispersed systems facilitated by almost instantaneous communications will make it easy for competitors to respond to each other's actions. The world will move faster.

Such changes will mean that organizations will need tight/loose controls both within and between firms. Within organizations, critical strategic variables will be closely monitored and controlled. Visions will be articulated and adhered to. At the same time, rapid environmental shifts will demand local responses that vary by region, as well as responses that are broader in their geographic reach. What works in one country won't necessarily work in another. Think of the regional differences in the formulation of branded products such as Coke and McDonald's, and this reality becomes clearer. Consequently, managers will need to have the autonomy and loose controls to respond to local needs within the critical boundaries of the firm.

Between organizations, networks of firms will be linked to allow for needed information exchange. What is shared will vary from the purely transactional to the strategic, depending on the levels of trust and intimacy existing between firms. At the same time, these firms will maintain their independence on key strategic dimensions viewed as proprietary and/or sources of competitive advantage critical to their longer-term success.

Galbraith suggests that strategy and structure of organizations will continue to be closely tied.[2] Organizations will come in an enormous variety of forms and complexity. Straightforward work that is repetitive and easily understood will disappear and companies will organize around opportunities and resources. The key management tasks will involve innovation and the mastering of complexity. Galbraith classifies potential strategies and suggests matching structures.

According to Galbraith, organizations in the 21st century will become more customer oriented or more focused. In the customer-oriented organization, organizations will have three major organizational parts: business units, international regions, and customer accounts. These parts will be linked with lateral processes: teams and networks. Focused organizations will have subunits focused on different key criteria: costs, products, or customers.

Malone argues that tomorrow's organizations will have the benefits of both the large organization and the small organization.[3] Digital technologies will enable economies of scale and knowledge while preserving the freedom, creativity, motivation, and flexibility of smaller organizations. There will be a shift from traditional centralized hierarchies to organizations of loose hierarchies, democracies, and marketlike organizations.

- Loose hierarchy example: Wikipedia, a free online encyclopedia that anybody can edit, and when errors occur, others will spot and correct them.
- Democracy examples: W. L. Gore, where you become a manager by finding people who want to work for you, or Mondragon, where employees elect a board of directors to make decisions.

- Market example: An Intel proposal, where plant managers propose to sell futures on what they produce and salespeople buy futures for products they want to sell. Prices fluctuate and will determine what products get produced at what plants and who gets to sell the products.

The above is not intended to be comprehensive but rather to suggest the variety of thinking on how organizations will evolve in the future. As a result of these and other trends, organizational change and organizational change agents will need to shift as well. Table 11.1 is based on the forecasts in Chapter 1 and summarizes these potential changes. The table indicates that change agents will have a set of generalist capabilities providing basic competencies. As well, specific change skills of pattern finder, organizational analyst, mobilizer, empowerer, enabler, enactor, disintegrator, and integrator need to be developed. Finally, specialist roles for change agents could be developed. For example, change skills in information technology or in mergers/acquisitions are two likely specialist areas.

In summary, those involved with organizational change, if they have not already done so, need to develop the following:

- A stronger strategic and global perspective for small and large companies.
- Knowledge of networks and emergent organizational forms and how they work.
- Skills in risk management and knowledge management.
- Understanding of the impact of Web-enabled communication, change-related blogs, and fast-response capacity.
- The ability to communicate worldwide while maintaining a human face.
- Perceptiveness of different cultures and norms and how they affect change.
- The capacity to deploy empowered but bounded teams operating with a vision focus. The boundaries come from the vision and agreed-to expectations concerning performance, modes of operation, and other predefined standards and shared commitments.

As the environment evolves, the roles of change agents will shift. All change agents will continue to need basic skills in facilitation, influencing, negotiation, and visioning. They will need to understand project management and to be able to implement projects. In addition to the generalists, some change agents will specialize and add value through their intimate knowledge of a particular industry, sector, or change target. Specializations, such as those listed below, will evolve further:

- Merger and acquisition specialist
- Joint venture and alliance specialist
- Organizational integration specialist
- Business-stage specialist: early-stage growth, maturity, decline, renewal

Table 11.1   The Impact of Organizational Trends on Organizational Change and Change Agents

Organizational Trend	Organizational Change	Change Agent
Globalization—be big, or be specialized and excellent, or be acquired, squeezed, or eliminated	Strategic global perspective for both large firms and niche SMEs	Pattern finder Vision framer
Virtual and networked organizations	Knowledge of networks and emergent organizational forms	Organizational analyst and aligner
Loose/tight controls	Knowledge and risk management	Mobilizer, empowerer, enabler, enacter
24/7 response requirements		Disintegrator and integrator
Cost and quality focus, outsourcing, and supply chain rationalization	Web-enabled communication, change-related blogs, fast response capacity with a human face	Corporate gadfly and trend surfer
Shortening product life cycles and increasing customer expectations	Negotiation and network development, quality, cost leadership, and/or customer focus	Generalist capacities: facilitation, influencing, negotiating and visioning skills, project management expertise
Increasing focus on integrated customer services and knowledge management	Creativity, innovation, and deployment	Specialist roles, related to expertise needed for specific change initiatives. For example, software system integration, customer relationship management, flexible manufacturing, organizational integration following acquisition
Technological change fundamentally alters industry structures, both in terms of the "what" and the "how"	Empowerment, teams, and process focus	
Changing demographic, social, and cultural environment		Capacity to develop and sustain the trust and confidence of multiple stakeholders
Political changes are realigning alliances and the competitive environment		

- Large-scale or disruptive change specialist
- Crisis management specialist
- Information technology system integrator
- Organizational structure specialist
- Supply change integrator
- Cross-cultural specialist by specific culture
- Interorganization specialist including government or industry relations
- Multiparty negotiation specialist

In addition to specialist areas, new "generalist" skills will be needed. Skilled change agents will be increasingly sensitive to what is happening in the organization's environment—"trend surfers" perhaps, who recognize and give voice to factors that represent potential opportunities and threats. They will help manage the complexity of organizational change by developing skills in recognizing and understanding patterns within organizations. They will understand how to mold disparate perspectives into a compelling vision and know which actions provide significant leverage within the organization. Their abilities to mobilize others will be grounded in empowerment and enabling skills. They will be able to both disintegrate and integrate parts of the organization as needed. That is, they will know both how to separate organizational units into self-directed entities and how to link disparate parts into an integrated whole. Finally, they will need to manage their activities and actions with integrity, so that they will be able to develop and sustain the trust and confidence of multiple stakeholders.

Many would argue that these represent skill areas that have always been important. While this is true, the pace of change and the speed of competitive responses have made these skills even more critical to sustained organizational success. As a result, the value to both the change agent and the firm has increased.

How Do You Become an Organizational Change Agent?

For many change agents, their initial involvement with the design and/or implementation of change typically begins when they are asked (or volunteer) to join a team or task force or otherwise assist with a change initiative. Invitations arise for a variety of reasons. Individuals may have been noticed because they exhibited interest in a project, or someone may believe they would be helpful because of their skills or perspective.

Change skills tend to fall into two broad categories. First, there are the technical skills that develop from functional training and experience. Change implementation often requires the involvement of individuals who possess specific technical skills and abilities in order to advance the project. If the change involves the deployment of new software or a new approach to customer relationship management, individuals with appropriate technical competencies will need to be involved with the implementation. Second, there are the more broadly applicable general management skills that grow out of experience with the framing, approving, and implementing of change initiatives and include the development of interpersonal competences that facilitate change.

Some change agents will choose to remain more focused on particular technical/functional areas, with those skills becoming increasingly more sophisticated with the passage of time. Their initial involvement could be the provision of computer training to support a system upgrade. Gradually, these change agents could be involved in more sophisticated technical changes. Their expertise would grow, and they might become an expert in an area such as large-scale software system integration. Likewise, the person who begins doing job design and group development work might develop, over time, into an organizational integration specialist. Technically oriented individuals will require some competence in more general change management skill areas (e.g., interpersonal communications). However, it will be their technical expertise that will be sought when the initiative lies within their domain.

Those who choose to orient their development around more general change management skills initially may start their careers in technical/functional change management. However, these individuals may develop more sophisticated general change management competencies such as organizational analysis, leadership, interpersonal communication and influence, negotiation, project management, and implementation skills. The management of more complex change initiatives benefits from those who possess these more broadly applicable change management skills.

When we first become involved with change, our change skills are usually at an early stage of development. They become increasingly sophisticated and well honed in either

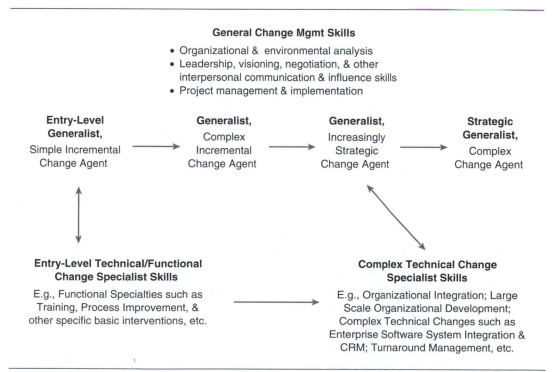

Figure 11.2   Change Management Skill Development

a technical/specialist stream or a broader generalist stream. Each stream will provide interesting and useful career opportunities. (Figure 11.2 outlines these streams.)

Paradoxes in Organizational Change

The field of organizational change today has a set of underlying paradoxes that change agents struggle with. Just as quantum physics now considers an electron as both a particle and a wave,* some aspects of organizational change have two perspectives. Both aspects are important and neither should be rejected. Several of these paradoxes are outlined below.

For example, the management of organizations will become more complex as the strategic focus of all organizations develops a global perspective. Organizational change will need to evolve tools and processes that encourage the systematic management of a wide number of elements (organizational systems, structures, emergent organizations, cultures, leadership, technology, organizational design, etc.) while maintaining the speed of change. Clearly, a challenge will be to handle the complexity without being overwhelmed and frozen by it. Organizational change as a field needs to handle the paradox of how to maintain the momentum of change (something that may require simplification) while not dismissing the complexity of an organization's environment.

A second paradox involves an organization's need to be simultaneously centralized and decentralized. Organizational change needs to learn how to help organizations understand this paradox and to evolve better mechanisms of handling this tension.

As organizations become skilled in promoting decentralized initiatives, they will face the challenge of handling multiple change initiatives simultaneously. Organizational change needs to consider which change initiatives will block or run counter to others and which ones will support and facilitate others. These consequences and interaction effects are not always self-apparent, and sometimes initiatives that look like they are supportive of other activities in the short run may have adverse consequences over the longer term. How can organizational change help an organization institutionalize or finish one project while continuing multiple other ones, and how can it assist in identifying unintended side effects?

Organizational change involves both incremental/continuous and radical/discontinuous change. Which does your organization need, or does it need both? Can we avoid radical organizational change and the disruptions involved by developing adaptive, flexible organizations? Organizational change as a field needs to develop further insights into this paradox.

Finally, our digital world and the rise of the knowledge worker shift the territory of organizational change from a hierarchical frame to a democratic, participative one. But the essence of a change project is that there is a direction that, in the end, is perceived as better, and that direction often is mandated, nondemocratically,

---

*Under certain circumstances, the electron looks like a particle and has the characteristics of a particle (mass, solidity, etc.). Under other circumstances, the electron seems to be a wave. It has a frequency and other wave characteristics. This paradox is resolved only by accepting an electron as both.

from above. Most change projects need input but also some degree of central management. While the value orientation of organizational change toward the worth of people is reinforced as organizations move toward more egalitarian modes, the pressure for movement in specific directions creates potential paradoxes.[†]

Given these paradoxes, change agents must develop a positive orientation to change that permits them to deal with what seem to be inherent contradictions.

How Should You Be Oriented to Organizational Change?

Everyone is a participant in organizational change. You will find yourself in any of a number of the roles: initiator, implementer, facilitator, and recipient. Change is just part of living, and opportunities will emerge that will allow you to act as a change leader or change agent. Given this, several lessons stand out that help provide a useful orientation:

1. Gain perspective and insight by recognizing the dynamism and complexity of your organization. What connections exist between parts, and how do they work?

2. Recognize that people's perceptions are critical. The perception of benefits and costs determines a person's reaction to a change proposal.

3. Understand that your perception is only one of many. Your view is neither right nor wrong. It is just your point of view of how things are.

4. Gather people as you go. There are multiple ways to achieve your change, but the ways that bring friends with you are easier and more fun.

5. Pull people to what you think is needed with a powerful change vision. Push people through argument and rewards when you need to, but gaining support through their hearts is often the better way.

6. Get active in pursuit of your vision. If you do something, you will get responses and you can learn from those. Not doing anything cuts you off from learning.

7. Have a plan oriented around your change vision. Having an explicit plan means your thinking can be discussed and challenged. Know that your plan won't last when you start implementing it, but it will certainly be useful in starting a discussion and gaining commitment.

8. Do things that are positive. Actions that suck energy from you and the system are difficult to sustain. Growing your energy as change agent is important.

[†]Organizational change will need to be prepared for blogs that discuss openly the issues surrounding change initiatives. Can change leaders accept and deal positively with open criticism that may show up on such blogs?

9. To start meaningful change, you need only a few believers. To continue, you need to develop momentum until a critical mass of key participants are onside. Some will never join in and that's okay unless they attempt to sabotage or otherwise disrupt agreed-to initiatives.

10. There are many routes to your goal. Find the ones with the least resistance that still allow you to proceed with integrity.

What Are the Critical Questions?

We wish to end this book with a highlighting of the critical questions that are valuable to ask yourself about change. They can serve as checkpoints for the multiple points in the change process that need to be tracked—from environmental awareness, to planning, implementation, and preparation for next phases. Generalizations in matters related to change can prove difficult to apply to specific situations, but the following questions should provide guidance.

1. What is the environment telling you prior to, at the beginning, during, and following the implementation of the change? In particular:

   a. What is the broader environment telling you about future economic, social, and technological conditions and trends?
   b. What are your customers or clients (both inside and outside the organization) telling you?
   c. What are your competitors doing, and how are they responding to you?
   d. What are the partners within your network doing, and how are they responding to you?
   e. What do the people who will potentially be the leaders, managers, and recipients of change want and need?

2. Why is change needed? Who sees this need?

3. What are your purpose and agenda? How does that purpose project to a worthwhile vision that goes to the heart of the matter?

4. How will you implement and manage the change?

   a. How will you resource the change initiative?
   b. How will you select and work with your change team?
   c. How will you work with the broader organization?
   d. How will you monitor progress so that you can steer and alter speed and course, if necessary?
   e. How will you ensure that you act (and are seen to act) ethically and with integrity?

5. What have I learned about change, and how can I remember it for the future? How can I pass on what I learned?

6. Once the change is completed, what comes next? The completion of one change simply serves as the starting point for the next.

That's it. It's an evolving list, and its further development is up to you. You've been reading and thinking about how to develop your skills as an agent of change. It's time to deploy those ideas; see what works when, where, why, and how; and learn as you go—no excuses. If you want to make things happen, you will have to learn to live with the frustration, excitement, uncertainty, loneliness, and personal development that come with being a change agent. The learning lies in the journey, while joy, a sense of accomplishment, and feelings of fulfillment accompany the completion of milestones and the realization of changes that have a positive impact on the lives of others.

> *And the day came when the risk it took to remain tight in a bud was more painful than the risk it took to blossom.*

> —Anais Nin

Appendix 1: A Summary Checklist for Change

Initiating Change

- Understanding the need for change
- Creating the perception of need for change
- Developing the powerful vision for change

Planning Change

- Having an organizational model
- Differentiating **how** to change and **what** to change
- Structures and systems: approval of change, facilitating and hindering change, developing adaptive structures for change
- Informal systems: resistance to change, power dynamics, the role of perceived impact, force fields, stakeholders (commitment, adaptiveness)
- Recipients: reactions (negative, ambivalent, positive), recipients' adaptation (anticipation, denial, anger, acceptance)
- Change agents: leading and managing, change agent types, change teams

Doing the Change

- Engaging others
- Developing the activity plan
- Contingency planning
- Commitment planning
- Communicating the change
- Managing the transition

Measuring and Confirming the Change

- Measuring the change
- Changing the measures over the life of the change project

END-OF-CHAPTER EXERCISES

TOOLKIT EXERCISE 11.1

Action Planning for Change

Toolkit Exercise 11.1 applies the tools from all chapters and asks you to develop a complete change plan. See Toolkit Exercise 4.2 for an exercise to create a powerful vision statment.

Small-Group Discussions

Your assignment is to begin the development of an action plan for a change you want to make happen. This will be broken into four parts:

1. The development of a sequence of action steps and the arrangement of them into a critical path with a clearly defined end goal, intermediate targets, and specific first step.

2. The consideration of contingencies—What might go wrong? How will these things be handled?

3. A responsibility chart. That is, who will do what, where, when, and how?

4. A transition plan including a communications plan. How will the transition be managed? Who will make the innumerable decisions required to handle the details? Who will provide information to those affected? As well, how will the change be communicated to organization members?

The Action Plan

Begin the development of an action plan.

- What are the critical steps that must be accomplished?
- What sequence should these occur in?
- Can some be done simultaneously?
- Who needs to become committed to the project?
- Where are key players on the adoption continuum?
- Are they even aware of the change?
- If aware, are they interested, or have they moved beyond that stage to either desiring action or having already adopted the change?
- What will it take to move them along the continuum, in the direction of adoption?

The AIDA Continuum

Key Player Name	Aware?	Interested?	Desires Action? Change?	Adopter?
_____	_____	_____	_____	_____
_____	_____	_____	_____	_____
_____	_____	_____	_____	_____
_____	_____	_____	_____	_____
_____	_____	_____	_____	_____
_____	_____	_____	_____	_____
_____	_____	_____	_____	_____

What is the commitment to the "adoption" of those who have reached the adopter stage? That is, are they at the "let it happen" stage, the "help it happen" stage, or the "make it happen" stage?

How can the commitment levels of key stakeholders be increased?

The Measurement of Change

How will you know that your goal or change project is successfully implemented? (At times, success will be obvious—for example, a new system in place. At other times, success will be more difficult to measure—for example, attitudes toward the adoption and acceptance of a new system.)

What intermediate signals will indicate that you are making progress? What is the first step or sequence of steps?

Our end goal is:

We can measure it by:

Intermediate measures and milestones are:

The first step is:

The Critical Path

Arrange your action steps in sequence. What should go first, second, and so on? What activities cannot begin or should not start until others are completed? What time lines should you observe? Often it is useful to begin at the "end" of the project and work backwards to "now."

Contingency Planning

Remember "O'Brien's Law"*? Well, it holds and things will not go as planned. But we can plan for the unexpected.

What are the critical decision points? Who makes those decisions?

What will you do if the decision or event does not go as planned? What plans can you make to account for these contingencies? If you can, draw a decision tree of the action plan and lay out the decision-event sequence.

Responsibility Charting

Who will do what, where, when, and how? Often a responsibility chart can be useful to track these things.

Actions or Decisions	Person #1	Person #2	Person #3	Person #?
Action #1				
Action #2				
Decision #1				
Action #3				
. . .				

Coding: R = Responsibility (not necessarily authority)
    A = Approval (right to veto)
    S = Support (put resources toward)
    I = Inform (to be consulted before action)

Note that if there are a great number of A's on your chart, implementation will be difficult. Care must be taken to assign A's only when appropriate. Likewise, if there are not enough R's and S's, you will need to think about changes needed here and how to bring them about.

---

*O'Brien's Law states: Murphy was an optimist.

Notes

1. Barkema, H. G., et al. (2002, October). Management challenges in a new time. *Academy of Management Journal,* (45)5, 916.

2. Galbraith, J. R. (2005, August). Organizing for the future: Designing the 21st century organization. Strategy and structure. The process will continue. *Academy of Management Journal.* http://www.aom.pace.edu/odc/2005/galbraith.pdf.

3. Malone, T. (2005, August). Inventing organizations. *Academy of Management Journal.* http://www.aom.pace.edu/odc/2005.html.

4. Refer to Beckhard, R. (1987). *Organizational transitions* (p. 104). Reading, MA: Addison-Wesley, for a further discussion on responsibility charting.

Self-Managed Work Teams at South Australian Ambulance Service[1]

Ray Main pondered the box of questionnaires received from the ambulance officers (AOs). Normally, a 45% response rate would be a good response to a survey. But in 35 out of the 60 stations, less than half of the AOs in the team responded. Without the input of more than half of their team members, he didn't feel he could provide representative feedback to the station teams.

Next Wednesday, the Empowerment Strategic Task Force was meeting to hear his report on the survey. He knew they would want recommendations regarding the next step in moving South Australian Ambulance Service (SAAS) to an empowerment culture.

South Australian Ambulance Service

SAAS provides emergency paramedic and advanced life support services as well as routine ambulance transfers throughout the state of South Australia on a self-funding basis. The service is provided by 600 full- and part-time staff and some 1,100 volunteers in areas difficult to service.

Emergency calls go to 1 of 4 communications centers that pass the message to 1 of 19 metro teams in Adelaide, to one of the 20 rural teams or to 1 of the 60–70 volunteer teams.

Until the late 1980s, SAAS was an integral part of St. John Ambulance Service (under the St. John Priory) and was staffed by both full-time AOs and volunteers. Full-time employees worked Monday to Friday from 9 A.M. to 5 P.M. Volunteers handled all evening and weekend work.

One manager described the old culture in strong terms:

> SAAS was a traditional, hierarchical organization with 9 managerial levels for approximately 650 employees and 1,500 volunteers. We were very inward looking in our approach. It was lots of "jobs for the boys," and as long as you were obedient and followed orders you were okay.

A senior executive described SAAS as a "militaristic" organization with "an extreme number of levels: regional superintendent, assistant regional superintendent, regional director, assistant regional director, station officer, assistant

---

[1] This case was prepared by Professor Tupper Cawsey of Wilfrid Laurier University. Copyright © T. Cawsey.

station officer." Most decisions were made by three managers at the top of the organization who then had difficulty getting things implemented because of the powerful middle managers and station officers.

In 1989, a strike by the full-time employees led to the professionalization of the service and the beginning of its separation from the St. John Ambulance Service. After the strike, the use of volunteers was minimized, and full-time employees operated the service 24 hours per day, 7 days per week.[1] This change required an influx of several hundred new AOs and an increase in their professionalism and training. All full-time AOs were now required to complete a 3-year program leading to a diploma through the TAFE college system.[2]

In 1992, a new CEO, Ian Pickering was appointed to reorganize the service and complete the separation of SAAS from the St. John Priory. His mandate was to improve the clinical expertise in SAAS and to make it the best ambulance service in Australia. Shifting the organization from the old military model to an empowerment one was a key part of his strategy to achieve excellence.

The South Australia government passed legislation on March 16, 1993, changing the nature of SAAS. On March 17, 1993, Pickering restructured SAAS. Nine levels of management were reduced to four. All middle and lower-level managers were invited to apply for the new positions that were created, but there were no job guarantees. Retirement packages were offered and many managers took them. The day lives in organizational memory as "the St. Patrick's Day Massacre."

At the same time, all employees were organized into the teams mentioned earlier, 19 metro AO teams, 20 rural AO teams, 20 support staff teams, and 60+ volunteer teams. (See Exhibit 1 for a partial organizational chart.) The team leader positions often went to younger, better-qualified, and newer employees,[3] since many older employees needed to retrain in order to be qualified for team leader positions.

In 1993, a strategic plan was developed. As one manager put it, "It was the first time we asked ourselves, 'What was our mission? Why are we here?' Never before had we defined patient service (as opposed to patient care)."

This strategic plan was reworked in 1995 (see Exhibit 2 for a summary of the vision, mission, key objectives, and major strategies). The plan included a commitment to "an empowered and accountable workforce." Seven cross-functional project teams were established to help implement the strategic plan: (1) the Workforce Empowerment Team, (2) the Workforce Development Team, (3) the Information Technology Team, (4) the Commercial Team, (5) the Structure Team, (6) the Volunteer Team, and (7) the Business Development Team. Chris Lemmer, regional director (Metro), headed the Workforce Empowerment Team with Ray Main seconded full-time as project coordinator.

By 1997, SAAS had changed significantly. Paramedic courses had been run for the first time, and 35 AOs had received this higher-level qualification. An Advanced Life Support qualification had been developed as an intermediate step between basic AO training and paramedic training, and many AOs had completed this qualification. Clinical performance improved dramatically. Survival statistics for ventricular fibrillation arrest, for example, improved from 4.1% in 1994 to 26% in 1997. Performance measures can be found in Exhibit 3 and financial statements in Exhibit 4.

The 1995–1996 Annual Report stated that "a restricted patient transport license was granted to another patient transport service" for non-emergency ambulance transfers, which introduced a competitive threat to SAAS. The St. John Priory continued to withdraw its links with SAAS. And a new amalgamation with the SA Metropolitan Fire Service was under way.

---

[1] Full-time employees provided ambulance services except for difficult-to-serve rural areas. South Australia has vast areas of outback with few people. Providing service to these areas is costly.

[2] TAFE is a community college system.

[3] One senior manager speculated that the really good AOs did not apply for the team leader position initially because they wanted to become paramedics first.

Exhibit 1   Partial Organizational Chart—SA Ambulance Service

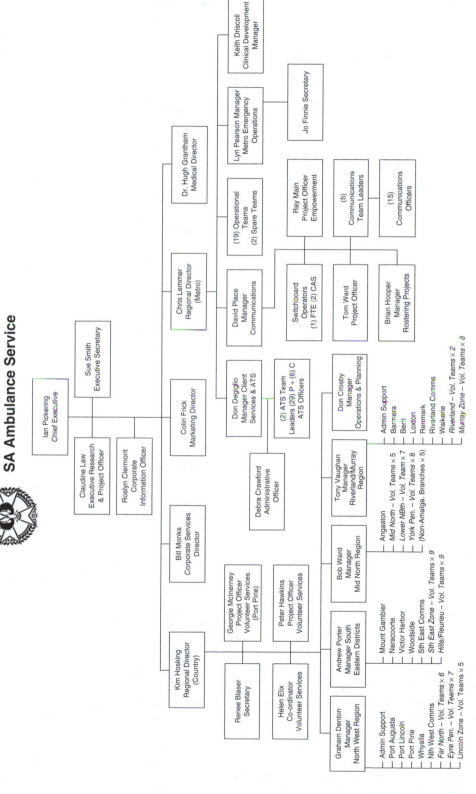

SA Ambulance Service

Ian Pickering
Chief Executive

Sue Smith
Executive Secretary

Claudine Law
Executive Research
& Project Officer

Roslyn Clermont
Corporate
Information Officer

Bill Monks
Corporate Services
Director

Colin Frick
Marketing Director

Chris Lemmer
Regional Director
(Metro)

Dr. Hugh Grantham
Medical Director

Keith Driscoll
Clinical Development
Manager

Lyn Pearson Manager
Metro Emergency
Operations

Jo Finnie Secretary

Don Degiglio
Manager Client
Services & ATS

(2) ATS Team
Leaders (29) P + (6) C
ATS Officers

David Place
Manager
Communications

(19) Operational
Teams
(2) Spare Teams

Ray Main
Project Officer
Empowerment

Switchboard
Operators
(1) FTE (2) CAS

Tom Ward
Project Officer

(5)
Communications
Team Leaders

Brian Hooper
Manager
Rostering Projects

(15)
Communications
Officers

Debra Crawford
Administrative
Officer

Don Crosby
Manager
Operations & Planning

Tony Vaughan
Manager
Riverland/Murray
Region

— Admin Support
— Barmera
— Berri
— Loxton
— Renmark
— Riverland Comms
— Waikerie
— *Riverland – Vol. Teams × 2*
— *Murray Zone – Vol. Teams × 8*

Bob Ward
Manager
Mid North Region

— Angaston
— *Mid North – Vol. Teams × 5*
— *Lower NBth – Vol. Team × 7*
— *York Pen. – Vol. Teams × 8*
— (Non-Amalga. Branches × 5)

Andrew Porter
Manager South
Eastern Districts

— Mount Gambier
— Naracoorte
— Victor Harbor
— Woodside
— Sth East Comms
— *Sth East Zone – Vol. Teams × 9*
— *Hills/Fleurieu – Vol. Teams × 9*

Kim Hosking
Regional Director
(Country)

Georgie McInerney
Project Officer
Volunteer Services
(Port Pirie)

Peter Hawkins
Project Officer
Volunteer Services

Renee Blaser
Secretary

Helen Elix
Co-ordinator
Volunteer Services

Graham Denton
Manager
North West Region

— Admin Support
— Port Augusta
— Port Lincoln
— Port Pirie
— Whyalla
— Nth West Comms
— *Far North – Vol. Teams × 6*
— *Eyre Pen. – Vol. Teams × 7*
— *Lincoln Zone – Vol. Teams × 5*

Case Study 4

Exhibit 2 SA Ambulance Service—Strategic Plan 1996 to 2000

Vision

> Our aim is to provide the best Ambulance Service in the Asia Pacific region and maintain this position into the 21st century.

Mission

> The SA Ambulance Service is committed to the provision of total quality clinical care and transportation of patients.

Guiding Principles and Values

> We will be focused and responsive to the needs of our patients and customers in both clinical and commercial terms.
>
> In all things we do will maintain our leadership and expert status on all pre-hospital patient care matters and be recognized as the best by both our peers and the community.
>
> We will be innovative in our approach to business and strive to add value to the services we provide to our patients and clients.

Implementation

> The implementation of our plan depends on all of us. Implementation is being carried forward by seven project teams.
>
> Workforce   Information Technology
> Structure   Commercial
> Volunteers   Structured Communications
> Diversification
>
> The teams are implementing our Strategic Plan, using Continuous Quality Improvement principles, bringing together the results of our detailed organizational assessment.

Key Objectives

> 1. We will have an empowered and accountable workforce (that is committed to achieving the vision).

> 2. We will ensure our selection, placement, competencies, and personal development of staff matches the challenges facing the organization.

> 3. We will support our volunteer ambulance services in all aspects of the business.

> 4. We will investigate issues associated with the withdrawal of St. John Priory and amalgamation with the Metropolitan Fire Service.

> 5. We will implement structural changes associated with amalgamation with the Metropolitan Fire Service being cognizant of cultural issues.

> 6. We will have IT systems to support our new structure and processes.

> 7. We will have a cost effective service.

> 8. We will effectively manage our assets—replace, maintain, upgrade.

> 9. We will have a well informed public and staff.

> 10. We will retain and expand existing revenue generation.

> 11. We will establish a Trust for securing funding of development initiatives.

> 12. We will diversify our business.

Case Study 4

Exhibit 2

Major Strategies
1. Creating an understanding and commitment to the team concept which will include processes for staff awareness and staff development. Identifying and implementing the most appropriate structure to support and enable teams and to define relevant roles and responsibilities.
2. Identifying the competencies and/or educational requirements of all positions within the structure identified in the empowerment review. In cooperation with teams, overcome obstacles that restrict the development of team performance. Reviewing selection and promotion procedures.
3. Creating an awareness of the state-side Ambulance Service which incorporates career and volunteer staff. Creating an awareness of the value of volunteers to the organization. Linking the Country Volunteer structure to the empowerment goal as part of our workforce objective. Ensuring that all strategic objectives apply to country volunteer systems.
4. Researching and developing an understanding of relevant legislation including the Ambulance and South Australian Metropolitan Fire Service Acts. Define and recommend to the Minister for Emergency Services and Ambulance Board our future status.
5. Developing an understanding of each other's culture. Preserving our identity and promoting our culture. Including amalgamation in Enterprise Bargaining negotiations.
6. Developing, understanding, actively lobbying, and promoting the service needs and timetables for Whole of Government initiatives. Resourcing and supporting the IT plan. Ensuring the IT plan is updated to meet any new objectives.
7. Developing business units to perform within a commercial environment. Training leaders in business issues.
8. Developing an asset management policy (cognizant of the SA Government Strategic Asset Management Plan). Recommending to Government, asset strategies that support the best interest of the Service. Optimizing the location of our assets.
9. Reviewing and improving our internal communication systems. Obtaining commitment from the Executive and the Ambulance Board to continue to fund commercially justifiable marketing initiatives.
10. Obtaining government funding commitment for 5 years. Identifying specific areas in SAAS for the responsible allocation of cost savings in a timely manner. Advising the Minister for Emergency Services and Ambulance Board of the most commercially viable fee rates.
11. By setting up a Trust structure. Developing guidelines for funding of development initiatives.
12. Financing a Research and Development Study of market opportunities. Developing an action plan based on outcomes of study. Implementing a business development plan.

Case Study 4

Exhibit 3   Performance Measures for SAAS

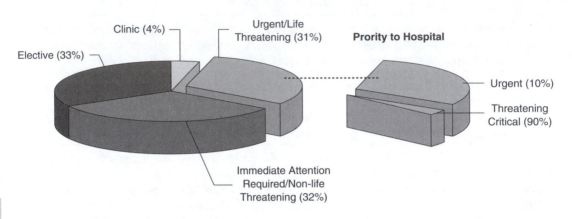

Ambulance Reponse to Patients by Priority

Clinic (4%)
Urgent/Life Threatening (31%)
Elective (33%)
Immediate Attention Required/Non-life Threatening (32%)

Prority to Hospital

Urgent (10%)
Threatening Critical (90%)

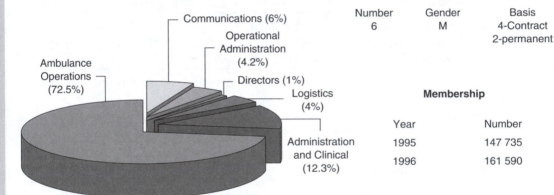

Number of Staff Employed

Communications (6%)
Operational Administration (4.2%)
Ambulance Operations (72.5%)
Directors (1%)
Logistics (4%)
Administration and Clinical (12.3%)

Career Staff (Executive)

Number	Gender	Basis
6	M	4-Contract 2-permanent

Membership

Year	Number
1995	147 735
1996	161 590

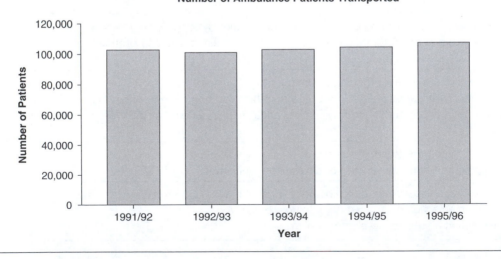

Number of Ambulance Patients Transported

Number of Patients (y-axis: 0 to 120,000)

Years: 1991/92, 1992/93, 1993/94, 1994/95, 1995/96

Priority One Response Times

Criteria
Metropolitan:
- 50% responded to within 7 minutes
- 95% responded to within 14 minutes
Country:
- 50% responded to within 8 minutes
- 95% responded to within 18 minutes

Performance

SA Ambulance Service's performance is as follows:
Metropolitan:
- 50% of cases are responded to within 7.62 minutes
- 95% of cases are responded to within 13.88 minutes
Country:
- 50% of cases are responded to within 5.45 minutes
- 95% of cases are responded to within 22 minutes

country performance figures are influenced by a few very long distance transports

Patients Transported by Region

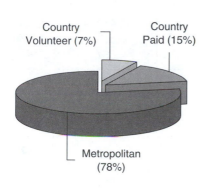

Emergency Casetypes

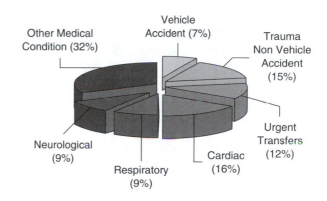

Revenue 1995–96

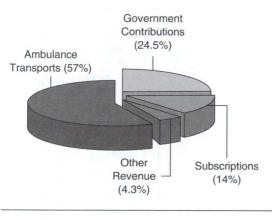

Expenses 1995–96

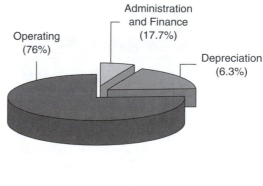

Case Study 4

Exhibit 4   Financial Statements for the Year Ended June 30, 1996

Operating Statement for Year End of June 1996	1996 $ ' 000	1995 $ ' 000
REVENUE		
Ambulance transport	24,385	24,731
Subscriptions	6,052	5,699
Government contributions	10,502	9,371
Other revenue	1,918	1,962
	42,857	41,763
EXPENSES		
Operating	32,482	32,007
Administration & finance	7,606	6,170
Depreciation	2,687	2,968
	42,775	41,145
Operating surplus before abnormal items	82	618
Abnormal items		(620)
Operating surplus after abnormal items	82	(2)
Accumulated surplus at the beginning of the financial year	2,616	2,523
Aggregate of amounts transferred from reserves	567	971
Total available for appropriation	3,265	3,492
Aggregate of amounts transferred to reserves	908	876
Accumulated surplus at the end of the financial year	2,357	2,616

Statement of Financial Position as of June 1996	1996 $ ' 000	1995 $ ' 000
CURRENT ASSETS		
Cash	8,658	8,232
Receivables	2,990	2,977
Investments	412	419
Inventories	169	166
Other	718	944
Total current assets	12,947	12,738
NONCURRENT ASSETS		
Investments	29	
Property, plant, and equipment	8,432	8,334
Total noncurrent assets	8,461	8,334
Total assets	21,408	21,072

Case Study 4

CURRENT LIABILITIES		
Creditors	1,236	1,800
Provisions	4,042	4,050
Unexpired subscriptions	2,028	1,805
Total current liabilities	7,306	7,655
NONCURRENT LIABILITIES		
Creditors	60	—
Provisions	2,260	1,717
Total noncurrent liabilities	2,320	1,717
Total liabilities	9,626	9,372
Net assets	11,782	11,700
EQUITY		
Capital	6,298	6,298
Reserves	3,127	2,786
Accumulated surplus	2,357	2,616
Total equity	11,782	11,700

Note: The Statement of Cash Flows is to be read in conjunction with the notes to and forming part of the financial statements.

The Job of the Ambulance Officer

Two ambulance officers were assigned to each vehicle. In the Metro area, most stations had two emergency vehicles plus one or two routine transfer vehicles. Each station had kitchen facilities, a lounge, sleeping areas for night shifts, and exercise rooms. When an AO began his or her shift, assuming the previous crew was in the station, they would ensure that the vehicle was ready for a call. A lengthy, detailed list of supplies had to be checked. Materials used had to be replaced.

A typical Metro morning shift is described in Exhibit 5.

Getting to a call was considered urgent and was carried out at speeds up to 100 kph. On arrival,

AOs unloaded the emergency equipment (in the cases above, oxygen and an electro-cardiograph and stretcher) and entered the house. One AO took the lead in each case, making decisions on the immediate response demanded by the patient's condition (e.g., if blood pressure was down, should a saline drip be attached?).

AOs prided themselves in their clinical skills. They had developed sophisticated medical protocols to assist in the diagnosis and were skilled in asking relevant questions about the individual's medical history. Paramedics had eight or nine drugs at their disposal to help deal with cardiac patients where speed was essential. As one paramedic described, "We can do everything an emergency room can do, only we do it sooner. If we can't help the patient, they won't survive."

Exhibit 5   A Typical Morning Shift for a Metro AO Team

0800	Arrival
0800–0830	Checking and restocking vehicle
0830–0840	Relaxation
0840	Communications moves the vehicle to a central location in the service area
0840–0900	Wait at location
0900 (approx.)	"Shortness of breath" call
0900–1030	Travel at high speed to call, attend patient, take patient to hospital
1030–1100	Travel to SAAS workshop to have air-conditioning switch replaced
1100–1215	Assist a second AO team in a pickup
1215–1245	Return to station, quick lunch
1245	"Fainting patient" call
1245–1400	Travel at high speed to call, attend patient, take patient to hospital
1400 . . .	Continue

While AOs were trained to present themselves as confident professionals to reassure anxious patients and relatives, they were also able to listen closely to the patient and any others present to understand the circumstances of the patient's difficulty in order to improve the diagnosis. Often, prior to any treatment, the AO would carefully explain what they were going to do and its consequences. For example, if an AO was attaching a saline drip, she would state why she was doing this ("With your blood pressure a little low, you need some fluids and we are just going to give you some."). She would describe what to expect and the consequences of her actions ("I need to inject this needle. It will hurt but only for a moment. By giving you fluids, it will help your blood pressure and you won't feel so dizzy.").

Friday evenings and holiday weekends were often the most stressful times to be an AO. Major car accidents occurred, and some family disputes became violent. AOs then dealt with people with severe injuries. In car crashes, extraction of the injured could be a problem. In family disputes, violence could continue during their intervention. SAAS had counselors available to help AOs deal with the trauma they faced.

AOs had complained for years that they dealt with emergency situations, made life-saving decisions, and could commandeer thousands of dollars of equipment (including helicopters) in an emergency, but couldn't order a shirt for themselves if one was ripped. Someone "in authority" had to authorize it.

By 1997, SAAS had evolved a customer service orientation. Its definition of success went beyond the survival rate of its patient to include thoughtful treatment of relatives, effective relations with hospital medical staff, and considerate patient care. In terms of emergency services, the aim was to have "a patient ready for ongoing treatment delivered in the best possible condition with accurate information about the patient's health." Exhibit 6 shows the cause-and-effect chart leading to having a patient ready for ongoing treatment.

Key performance indicators were developed with success measures for each of the indicators as shown in Exhibit 7.

The Evolution of Team Management

A key component of the strategy articulated for SAAS was an empowered workforce. Pickering changed the structure of the organization as one of his first and one of his most dramatic moves. The transition to team management was sudden and the organization was not fully prepared. As one manager put it, "The catchword was *empowerment*. We didn't know what it meant, but we told everyone."

Ian Pickering articulated the reasons for team management in an address to a community group. (See Exhibit 8 for a summary of the speech.) One enthusiastic supporter stated, "Team is the only way I will survive. One peer of mine is looking so old. He does things I just won't. For example, he drove hundreds of miles just to discipline a person, to tell them off. My aim is to be an invisible manager, to influence, and to be a facilitator and let the teams do their own thing. It seems to be working as I spend most of my time educating, encouraging, and modeling."

In the Metro area, teams had 10–13 members, organized by stations. Some larger stations had two teams of 10–13 members each. The rationale for this was that it took that many people to operate two ambulance teams 24 hours per day, 7 days per week, including, as well, time off for vacation, illness, training, and other absences. Because of the shift schedule, it was very difficult for Metro teams to meet. As one AO put it, "We suffer from a tyranny of roster that prevents us from really forming and acting as a team." (See Exhibit 9 for an example roster rotation.)

Country AOs on the other hand had considerable time together. Calls were not as frequent. As one manager described it, "If someone wants to study and learn, then they should come to the country as there is lots of time if you use it. I got books and a laptop and began to improve myself."

Several teams "raced ahead" in acting as empowered teams and then became frustrated when they couldn't operate as they felt was appropriate. For example, one team immediately decided to assign team members all the responsibilities previously held by the station officer. The team met and made decisions and individual team members carried them out. Unfortunately, SAAS organizational systems were not prepared for this, and team members were refused service or stores because they did not have the correct authorizing signature.

Another team decided to do away with the team leader (TL). As one would expect, leaders emerged anyway. Interpersonal issues arose that the team couldn't resolve. Factions developed and the team couldn't handle these resulting conflicts. As well, health and safety regulations require an individual with formal responsibility for these areas—assigning the responsibility to the "team" was illegal.

Other teams decided to choose their team leaders by voting. It became a popularity contest. One team dismissed their team leader because "they didn't like him." In this case, the union played a significant role in reconciliation. They asked the team how they would feel if management dismissed one of them because they didn't like that person. In this case, the TL did resign—he felt he could not be effective without the support of the team. But the union intervention was critical in increasing the employees' understanding of the responsibilities that went with empowerment.

Case Study 4

Case Study 4

Exhibit 6   Cause-Effect Chart for "Patient Ready for Ongoing Treatment"

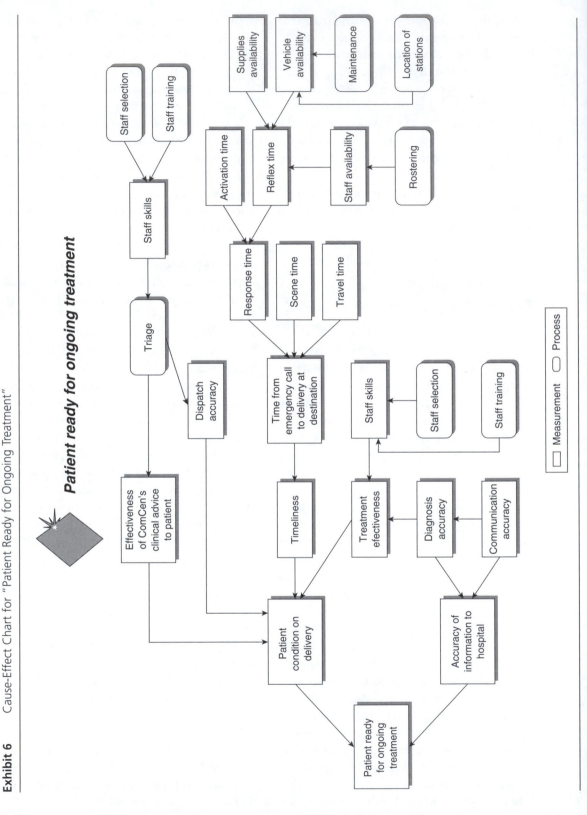

Patient ready for ongoing treatment

☐ Measurement   ◯ Process

Exhibit 7   Key Performance Indicators and Success Measures

Key Performance Indicator	Measurement	Method of Measurement
Patient Ready for Ongoing Treatment	• Patient condition on delivery • Accuracy of information to hospital	• Monthly sample of cases by peer audit and hospital feedback • Monthly sample of cases by peer audit and hospital feedback
Timeliness	• Time from emergency call to arrival at hospital • Delay in meeting Ambulance Transport Service commitments	• Response time + scene time + transport time for each trip • Contracted time minus actual time for each trip
Communication With Patients	• Communication with patients	• Sample of cases by patient and hospital feedback on interpersonal skills, etc.
Cost	• Cost relative to best practice	• Monthly figures from each department
Revenue	• Revenue	• Monthly revenue
Preparedness for Disasters	• Preparedness for disasters	• Rolling 3-month survey to rate staff knowledge of roles and availability of equipment and supplies
Community Awareness	• Community confidence rating	• Annual community survey
Staff Satisfaction	• Employee satisfaction rating	• Annual survey of staff and volunteers

Bernie Morellini, the staff development officer, held workshops on the concepts of empowerment and quality management. In these 2-day workshops, teams developed vision and mission statements and began identifying key objectives for their team. (See Exhibit 10 for an example team vision-mission-goals statement.) While these seminars were greeted with enthusiasm, AO's often left them uncertain about exactly how to translate these ideas into their operations. Who had what authority remained unclear.

Nevertheless, SAAS developed increasing confidence in itself with the introduction of paramedics. It had taken considerable skill on Pickering's part to convince the Medical Advisory Committee to accept the need for and usefulness of paramedics.

A major marketing campaign was created to announce the change in SAAS. The launch was at the Adelaide Festival Theatre with major television coverage. Uniforms were redone, ambulance vehicles repainted, all to symbolize

Case Study 4

Exhibit 8   Summary of Address Given by Ian Pickering

Address by:
Chief Executive Officer
Mr. Ian Pickering
SA Ambulance Service

Imagine... you are looking to buy a business.

Imagine . . . you are looking to buy a business. This business is a parcel pickup and delivery service. You may be required to pick up parcels from different locations at the same time. However, no parcel can be left longer than 10 minutes or it may be ruined. Not only that, you will be seriously criticized in court if you fail in this mission.

You will get no warning of the need to pick up these parcels. Sometimes people will call you to pick up parcels that are dropped in the street. Even if it is dark and raining you have to go. You will not know the size or condition of the parcel until you arrive. You will have to wrap the object before you pick it up. It may be dirty—it may be leaking—it may swear at you or even attack you.

You will have to make sure someone of above-average intelligence sits with the parcel and keeps checking in case it deteriorates in transit. There is no use by date to let you know how delicate the situation is.

It is acknowledged that it will cost you a lot of money to do this but people think you should do it for nothing. Does this sound familiar? Would you buy this business?

It's all a matter of perception. Perceptions can be deceiving.

I contend you cannot run a business such as this on a paramilitary-style structure. If you are honest with yourself, you will agree that the majority of decisions that impact on the desired outcomes of an ambulance service are made by the crew of an ambulance. Therefore, it follows that the endeavors of an ambulance organization should be directed at supporting a well-educated and empowered workforce at the sharp end so those decisions are timely and appropriate. Not a series of approval processes that both delay and dilute critical decisions.

Ambulance services of today operate in an increasingly competitive environment in which the medical and community expectations demand the continual identification, definition, and improvement of the most appropriate levels of care and service. Today's ambulance officers are better educated, different in culture, work history, and work ethic than their predecessors.

So, what did we see when we took a long hard look at ourselves? PROBLEMS.

The SA Ambulance Service has introduced radical changes to their management principles, moving away from a paramilitary culture, to a culture that is based on quality of service, best practice, empowered work teams, an organization that is able to continually look at itself and the way it goes about its business, so that it learns from its experiences.

What did we do?

The outwardly obvious strategies included the adoption of a "Commercial Charter," the introduction of new-style uniforms (dispensing with rank markings) and redesigned vehicle livery, together with a public awareness campaign based on a "Going Green" theme.

Case Study 4

However, the major culture changes had to come from within. The priority is to develop an organization that recognizes and values the importance of constantly striving for a cost-effective best-practice ambulance service, while at the same time tangibly acknowledging the fact that the majority of decisions affecting the core business of the service (i.e., saving lives) are made by two officers crewing an ambulance.

Fundamental to our plan is the belief that all of our people should have the opportunity to influence decision making and be able to confidently accept the accountability that comes with empowerment.

Empowerment is a "buzzword"—misused in many instances—it is not handing over the budget for chocolate biscuits. It means being treated like intelligent adults who are capable of making reasonable decisions given the parameters in which to operate.

SA Ambulance Service has a vision—and we believe we know how to get there.

the change to more professional empowered services. Unfortunately, changes at the political level prevented the complete implementation of the plans. This failure encouraged the cynics who "had seen change attempts before and nothing really would happen."

Teams improved their clinical practices with the introduction of a case card audit.[4] The case review process protected AOs from individual liability. It was assumed that the AOs did the best that was possible under the circumstances.

Progress Toward Self-Management Across SAAS Teams

The progress toward self-management varied considerably across teams. Summaries of interviews with four teams are given below.

Team Hodgson[5]

Team Hodgson declared that "the team is us."

In the first year, our team had some personnel problems. The team leader was a nice guy, but he didn't seem to be working for the team. He expected us to come up with concepts, and when we did, he would say, "That's a silly idea." Or when we brainstormed, he would say, "That's not going to work!" There were some personal issues as well. He kept an "I'm all right, Jack" attitude when it wasn't. For example, he would do all the administrative work without help. He would be in here until all hours of the night working. And even then, the paperwork didn't get done on time. He would ask our opinion and then change things. He and one of the other team members started annoying each other, and this put this team member under a lot of pressure. Finally, this team member couldn't handle being questioned, and he would start yelling at

[4] A case card audit is a review of the write-up (the card) of each case dealt with by the service. That is, after each call, a case card describing the situation and what was done is produced. The audit is a team review of these cards in order to learn and improve.

[5] All team names are fictitious.

Exhibit 9   Rotating Roster for Metro Region

This roster assumes four groups, each with 4 days on and 4 days off.
Nine members are needed to operate the team. One person would be on annual holidays, one person would be on other duties, and one or two persons are spare, ill, or have other responsibilities.

Team A	Day	Day	Night	Night	Off	Off	Off	Off
Team B	Off	Off	Day	Day	Night	Night	Off	Off
Team C	Off	Off	Off	Off	Day	Day	Night	Night
Team D	Night	Night	Off	Off	Off	Off	Day	Day

Examining this chart shows the amount of interaction between members and the difficulty in getting together as a team of 11–13.

other team members and demanding details of any calls. We weren't sure what was going on until after the TL had left. We were too close to the situation.

Once the TL had left, there was a bit of a vacuum. We decided to take a step "back" and we had three team meetings. During them, we were spending too much time on "in-house" activities and not enough on developing the team. We spent a lot of time on maintenance activities—who is going to clean up the station; sheets aren't being signed like they are supposed to.

The person who was in a dispute with the TL has been much better since the TL left.

Finally, we got rid of the station running stuff and moved on to learning and improving. But there were no measures for each thing we were doing, so we drew up our practices manual and focused on three areas: human factors, customer service, and cost. We have to revamp this now as only a few of us were here when the original planning was done.

The process started when we had a day session with Bernie. This got us going but we needed another day to really put together some plans. We realized that if we want something, we have to cost it and put a proposal together. If we want a training day per month, we have to show how it helps and how to get it done. If a member

wants time off, we decide. Soon we will have the training plan for next year finalized. We will have it finished by the end of the year.

We wrote our station work practice manual so it contained a statement of team focus, a vision, mission statement, guiding principles and values, and key objectives in the three critical areas.

(See Exhibit 11 for the set of clinical care objectives.)

Team Boulder

The idea and concept is good but getting there could have been better. Two years ago, they started the team concept. We thought it was "about time" as we had hinted long ago we shouldn't have a boss. We were all sort of lost when teams started. We were told to document what we did, make up the rules. So, we said "ok" and began meeting once each week. Perhaps we needed more education to make the transition easier.

There was some attempt to educate us. Each center sent one person to a course. But by the time he got back, the message was confused. Most AOs had been here a long time and were confused by what was taught.

We are starting with our own mission and vision and standard operating practices. We are starting to make our own rules. It used to be that a computer would arrive and we would wonder "why and when." Now we talk about what we need and put it in a budget. Before, the attitude was we don't care where money went as long as I get paid. Now we are accountable for budgets. So if we put a hole in the wall, we have to pay for fixing it. We are allowed to talk to DMs as humans and get respect.

We meet monthly or every 6 weeks or so. We put the holiday list up and get input. This year, we got joint input on the budget. Next year, individuals will do subbudgets.

Next year, we will really have a clear picture of the team concept and fully understand it and be comfortable operating as a self-directed team. Sometimes we lacked confidence and expected to get a "no." Instead, we were asked, "What took you so long to ask?"

We worry about vehicle maintenance as a team. The usage of the station is our responsibility, and we get others to use it. We have set our

vision and mission, and now we are just working on how to specify objectives and how to achieve them.

I'm sure that we can become pacesetters.

Team Crossover

We always ran as a team. The old station officer (SO) discussed things with us and we had input. When the SO went away, one of the team got to see the administrative work he did. Now we all see some of it and get a bigger picture. Now there is more input.

At our team meetings, we solve problems. For example, we had a communications problem in the region and decided the best solution was a satellite phone (which wasn't budgeted for). So at the team meeting, we figured out how to get support and raised $3,000 of the $4,200 cost.

We work on documenting our procedures. This gives us a benchmark against which we can

Exhibit 10   Example Vision-Mission-Goals for a Team: Ambulance Team—Strategic Plan 1997–2004

Vision

The aim of the Waikerie Ambulance Team is to be the best team within the SA Ambulance Service and to maintain this position into the 21st century.

Mission

The Waikerie Ambulance Team is committed to the provision of clinical care and customer and community service.

Guiding Principles and Values

1. We will be focused and responsive to the needs of our patients and community.
2. In all things we do we will maintain our knowledge, skills, and attitude to ensure a professional relationship with our peers and our community.
3. We will strive to lead, compete for, and deliver a service that is innovative and value adding to our patients and our community.

Implementation

The implementation of our plan depends on all of us. We are implementing our Strategic Plan using the principles of Continuous Quality Improvement principles.

Exhibit 11 Team A: Clinical Care Objectives

We will ensure that our knowledge, skill base, and attitudes are being continuously developed to provide total quality clinical care to our patients.

ALS

- We will all be fully ALS-qualified by the completion of 1998.
- If appropriate or required, the cost of training will be incorporated into the next financial year.
- Knowledge and skill maintenance will be incorporated into the station-based study plan and skill practice plan.

Paramedic

- We will have at least one team member paramedic qualified by the end of the year 2000.
- As part of the station study plan, we will incorporate knowledge that will guide us toward paramedic status.
- The cost of paramedic training will be budgeted into the appropriate fiscal year.

Tools

- We will maintain and upgrade our existing station library.
- We will subscribe to associated periodicals.
- We will subscribe to the Internet.
- We will build a medical-associated CD library.
- We will develop an "Adopt-a-Doc" program.
- We will ensure the maintenance and availability of training equipment. This may be coordinated through the CTL.
- We will utilize the resources of the Ambulance Service Education Unit.
- We will involve the district manager and CTL appropriately.
- We will have an annual review of the acceptability and relevance of current tools.

Continued Education Program

- We will develop a program for each module to meet the needs of the CEP in consultation with the CTL.
- This program must meet the individual needs of each team member.
- At the end of each module we will review the effectiveness of the program.

Study Plan

- We will develop a yearly plan, based on our teams' aims and objectives for the coming year.
- The plan will consist of monthly and weekly topics. These topics will be value adding to our knowledge.
- The plan will incorporate a series of short and long written questions. The appropriateness of these questions will be determined by the team.
- The effectiveness of the plan will be reviewed bimonthly at team planning days.
- This plan may be reinforced by the CTL through station visitations.
- We will develop a review program that incorporates:

1. Identifying key performance indicators
2. Conducting monthly case reviews
3. Conducting continuous case card audits
4. Recognition of measurable results
5. Six-month review of station-based and associated clinical training
6. Ensuring the CTL is programmed into our station-based program to provide regular useful feedback

Skills Practice

- We will develop a monthly review program that incorporates skill not included in the current CEP. This will be done in consultation with the CTL.
- We will develop a program that fosters integration and skills review with our volunteer sub-branches.
- We will develop a program that encourages skill sharing with allied health professionals, for example, doctors, nurses, district nurses, CAFHS nurses.
- We will initiate a clinical placement program with the Health Services.
- We will maintain a skill log book recording protocols as they are performed in the field and in practice.

improve out practice. We create graphs and track our performance. Work practices have been developed for 32 of our procedures. Other teams have asked for copies, but we have refused. If they just took ours, they wouldn't own them. You can see on the wall our system for duty roster. We organize it by week with a list of responsibilities for each job that has to be done, and the person checks them off when they are done.

We are concerned as we have just had two new members added to our team, and we need to figure out how to include them in the team. We aren't certain how comfortable the new members are with the team concept. We sure hope that we get along as well as previously. We need to make certain that we don't assume too much. We have planned a team-building day where we will get to know one another and then we can discuss how we want to operate. Only after all this will we look at the 32 work practices to see if changes should be made.

We think we can handle most things. We did have to get help with a team dispute that got out of hand—but we did try our procedures first. We do most things. We develop and implement our own training program. Our budget is zero based, and we spend a lot of time figuring out what we need and how that should be budgeted for. For example, we figure out how much to budget for tires based on the condition of the tires—head office could never figure that out.

Team Carleton

We are not sure what we are supposed to do with this team management stuff. We think we do a good job as AOs—our clinical performance is excellent, we think. And that's what our job is.

We are on the road most of the time responding to calls. That keeps us busy. I don't know what they expect us to do—come in on our days off to build a team with people I never see from one week to the next? Most of the guys don't want to do that. And how will the Ambulance Transport Service AOs fit in? They don't even do the same job that we do.

We are out there dealing with people who need our help. I find that by the time I am finished my shift—particularly if it is a Friday night—I just want to leave this place and escape. Some of the things we have to deal with are pretty gruesome and I want to get out of here. The last thing I need is to spend time talking about something that isn't important.

If it will affect our clinical practice, then we should be trained properly. If it isn't part of our clinical practice, why are we doing it?

They tell us to manage our own budget, but there's nothing in there that helps pay for overtime so we can meet. If we wanted to get together as a full team, we would have to ask for money for it and it's not worth it.

The Role of the Team Leader

As was mentioned earlier, many team leaders were uncertain of their role. Some team leaders became adept at talking team and empowerment language but not doing it. AOs were used to making decisions on the spot and continued doing so as team leader. Old autocratic habits died hard, particularly when a station officer switched roles and became a team leader. In one team, the station officer had been particularly dominant. That person continues that behavior. The team continues to look at him and ask, "Is this okay?" even though there was encouragement for the team to take responsibility.

One station officer who became team leader completely reversed his style. He wouldn't do anything without team input. This slowed all decisions and frustrated the AOs. He believed that everyone had to be "nice" to each other and agreeable. It took a while before he realized that teams and team leadership didn't mean being nice; rather, it meant using teams and team skills to improve service.

Another team leader saw his role as being a facilitator and providing guidance when a team needed it. If the team has a problem, the team leader helps them to solve it rather than solve it for them. He describes his role as follows: "Often, I present the team with new and different alternatives to broaden their thinking. Or I ask some questions to get them to consider aspects of an issue that I think they haven't covered. Much of my role is ensuring that I learn and then pass that on to the team. So I have been taking courses and have taught them about Pareto charts, fishbone analysis, and PDCA (plan, do, check, act). This gives them the tools to improve their own performance.

A more typical response was simple confusion over the team leader role. One team leader commented, "I had little experience and education about working in a team. And there doesn't seem to be any support for me when I need help. I know the vision and what we were trying to do, but I don't feel I have the tools to get there. I think some team leaders have no idea whether they are doing well or not—they have nothing to refer to."

One team leader questioned how he was to operate. "I can't get my team together because of the shifts we are on. How can I get team decisions? My guys want to do good AO work, and they aren't certain how this empowerment stuff fits in. Finally, I just rented a hall and had everyone come to a session where we talked about team issues. I just sent them (management) the bill and said, 'Pay it.'"

One team leader went to a team referred to as "Jurassic Park" because the AOs had been there so long. Many of the misfits had gravitated to this team, and most managers predicted that this individual would not be able to make things work at that location. However, he listened and got stuff done. He convinced the team to be patient for changes and always explained why he was doing things.

This team leader was frustrated enough to summarize his feelings in a memo to AOs in March 1996:

The honeymoon is over!! Team members feel that the team concept is failing—dismally. Team members believe that the new Clinical Team leaders are station officers with a new title. The team does not believe they are empowered to make any team-based decisions. . . . Empowerment implies ownership. Ownership implies responsibility. Responsibility implies that there is no one else to blame. If the team accepts empowerment, they also accept the responsibility.

How does my team become empowered?

Team meetings will be held with the district manager and Clinical Team leader. The purpose of these meetings is to establish what station activities the teams are willing to take responsibility for. Once these areas are identified, the team and team members are locked into a commitment to ensure that those tasks are undertaken. . . . It should be noted that teams will not be forced to accept responsibility if they so desire. . . . As stated previously, having items such as time sheets and leave approvals signed by the Clinical Team leader is somewhat questionable. Under the team empowerment concept, these and many other tasks would become the responsibility of the team. This would allow the Clinical Team leader to perform the function that they were employed to do—that is, facilitate the training requirements as identified by the teams and to provide clinical support.

The Workforce Empowerment Implementation Team

This cross-functional team headed by Chris Lemmer, Metro regional director, was created as a result of the strategic planning sessions in 1995. Members had been chosen because of their expertise and their interest in the project. Nine people were on the team, representatives from all key areas of the organization (two team leaders from operations, two district managers, and a rep from the training college, from the communications team, from the workshop, and from administration). Initially, the team met biweekly. Now with the survey being tabulated, it had been about 2 months since the last meeting. At each strategic planning review, each task force team has to report on its progress.

The Workforce Empowerment Implementation Team stated its mission as: "We are committed to the development of systems, processes, and resources to enable work-teams to become self-managed."

The task force believed that the first stage in moving to an empowered culture was the structure change that had occurred. The second stage entailed teaching the workforce about "empowerment." In order to develop a "base line" for the change, the workforce survey was developed (see Exhibit 13). Exhibit 13 shows a sample feedback sheet that could be made available to the teams.

The Implementation Team believed that an education program for team leaders and then teams was necessary. The workforce survey would provide information to assist the design of an education package and would enable a "remeasurement" after training in order to judge the progress toward self-managed teams.

Ray Main, as mentioned earlier, had been seconded to the team as project Coordinator for 2 years. His responsibilities included developing and implementing the program of education mentioned above, in concert with the Implementation Team. A preliminary allocation of $165,000 for the 1997 year had been set up to support the Implementation Team's activities.

Ray Main's Dilemma

As a previous team leader, Ray had been frustrated by the apparent lack of systems and support for the move to an empowered culture. Now he was in a position to create that support. But where to begin? Should he work with the teams that want to evolve as a team and help them develop plans? What should be done about the teams who have ineffective team leaders? Should that be the district manager's or the regional manager's responsibility? How can the Metro teams be helped when they can't even meet?

As he sat there, he pulled the pile of surveys over and wondered how these could be best used.

Exhibit 12   Team Development Survey

**SA
Ambulance
Service**

**Strategic Plan Implementation
Workforce Empowerment Team**

Team Development Survey

August 21,1997

Dear Staff Member,

One of the key objectives of the SA Ambulance Service 1996–2000 Strategic Plan is the achievement of an 'empowered workforce'. As outlined in BWT (July 22nd), the Workforce Empowerment Implementation Team has the responsibility to guide and support teams through the transition to a team-based work environment. In order to provide the most appropriate support, there must be a determinant of how far *your* team has moved along the road to 'empowerment', if at all.

Help us to help you by completing this survey.

Individual answers will be collated with those from the other members of your team and results will be fed back to you in the form of a composite team profile. Please return the completed questionnaire in the reply-paid envelope supplied by **Friday, September 12th, 1997.** Thank you for your help.

Yours sincerely,

Ray Main
Project Coordinator
Workforce Empowerment
ph   (08) 8274 0405
fax   (08) 8272 6230
pager   (016080) 6812100
E-mail   raymain@senet.com.au

on behalf of the Workforce Empowerment Implementation Team.

Question 1
Please indicate the team (work-unit) that you belong to.
(For example: Campbelltown; Revenue; Berri Comcen; Fleet.)

_____

Question 2.
How many members are there in your team (including the team leader)?

_____

For the remaining questions, please mark the box ☑ which best represents your response to each question. All individual survey results are confidential.

Question 3.
To what extent has your team set a team focus (commonly called a mission, goal, or purpose)?
- ❑ Our team has developed a focus.
- ❑ Our team is in the process of developing its focus.
- ❑ We have not commenced developing a team focus. (Please go to Question 5)

Question 4.
To what extent do you refer to the team focus when making work-related decisions?
- ❑ Most of the time I refer to the focus when making work-related decisions.
- ❑ I sometimes refer to the focus when making work-related decisions.
- ❑ I am aware of the team focus, but it has no impact on my daily work.

Question 5.
Do members of your team have clearly defined roles or functions?
- ❑ Yes. Each member has an identified and assigned role within the team.
- ❑ Our team is in the process of defining and assigning appropriate roles.
- ❑ No. We have not identified or assigned specific roles to team members.

Question 6.
Does your team have a set of ground-rules that have been agreed upon by the whole team?
- ❑ Yes. We have a set of rules that we refer to, especially in meetings.
- ❑ There are rules, but they have not been openly agreed upon.
- ❑ No. We have no ground-rules.

Question 7.

Are you satisfied . . .	Yes	Partly	No
– with the way your work-unit functions as a team?	❑	❑	❑
– that members in your team have the knowledge and skills necessary to build an effective team?	❑	❑	❑

Question 8.
Does your team have an improvement plan in place?
- ❑ Yes. Our team has a specific planning procedure that we refer to when we have a goal to achieve.

(Continued)

Case Study 4

Exhibit 12 (Continued)

❑ There is a certain way that we do things, but I could not say that it is a plan known by all team-members.

❑ No. We have not developed a recognized team plan for achieving goals and objectives.

Question 9.
How do team members behave when they get together for a meeting?

❑ Team members try hard to create an open, supportive environment for team discussions.

❑ Most members participate, but to different degrees.

❑ Some peoples' behavior make our meetings hard-going.

Question 10.
When team members have differences or conflicts, how are they handled?

❑ Conflicts are discussed openly and resolved.

❑ Conflicts are resolved sometimes.

❑ Conflicts are ignored, or people are told not to worry about them.

Question 11.
In your opinion, how does your team go about achieving goals or objectives?

❑ If the outcomes of our efforts affect others of the team, members always refer to our team's planning procedure.

❑ Our team has a certain way of going about the achievement of goals, but we do not *always* do it that way.

❑ Members usually try to solve problems or achieve results by relying solely on their own experience.

Question 12.
In team meetings and day-to-day discussions:

❑ team-members feel comfortable to express themselves openly and honestly.

❑ there are times when members say what they truly feel, but it is not the norm on our team.

❑ team-members often speak behind others' backs and feel uncomfortable confronting others with issues that trouble them.

Question 13.
In your opinion, at your team meetings, do team-members ...

	Always	Sometimes	Rarely
Speak clearly?	❑	❑	❑
Avoid long anecdotes and examples?	❑	❑	❑
Listen actively?	❑	❑	❑
Explore, rather than debate each speaker's ideas?	❑	❑	❑
Avoid interrupting and speaking over others?	❑	❑	❑
Contribute equally to team discussions?	❑	❑	❑

Questions 14.
During team-meetings or get-togethers, are you aware of non-verbal communication occurring within the group?
(eg, mood, attitude, body-language)

❑ Yes

❑ Sometimes

❑ No

Question 15.

In your opinion …	Yes	Sometimes	No
Are decisions affecting your team, made by the whole team?	❏	❏	❏
Are team members sensitive to the needs of others in the team?	❏	❏	❏
Do you have a feeling of team pride and spirit?	❏	❏	❏
Does your team regularly communicate or network with other teams to learn from each other's successes and failures?	❏	❏	❏

Question 16.

Does your team use data as the basis for decision making?

❏ Yes
❏ Sometimes
❏ No

If 'No', please indicate why not:

_____

_____

_____

_____

Questions 17.

To your knowledge, does your team …	Yes	Don't know	No
– measure team performance from the customer's point of view?	❏	❏	❏
– collect data linked to organizational improvement goals?	❏	❏	❏
– set objectives using data obtained from measuring team effectiveness?	❏	❏	❏
– review data at team meetings and take improvement actions?	❏	❏	❏
– observe change when they make improvement efforts?	❏	❏	❏

Question 18.

Do you think your team has the appropriate level of authority to make the decisions that affect your team?

❏ Yes. Our present level of authority is satisfactory.
❏ Not sure.
❏ No. We require more decision-making authority.

Question 19.

How would you describe your team leader's management style?

❏ S/he is participative – is part of the team.
❏ S/he is consultative – consults with us but has the final say.
❏ S/he is authoritarian – runs things his/her own way.

Question 20.

Given your knowledge of your team leader's management style and skills, do you believe s/he is capable of building your group into an effective team?

❏ Completely capable.
❏ Somewhat capable.
❏ Not capable at all.

Case Study 4

Exhibit 12 (Continued)

Question 21.

At your team meetings ...	Always	Sometimes	Never
Is an agenda distributed before the meeting?	❑	❑	❑
Do you follow the agenda closely?	❑	❑	❑
Are minutes recorded?	❑	❑	❑
Is there a facilitator or chairperson?	❑	❑	❑
Do meetings start on time?	❑	❑	❑
Do meetings finish on time?	❑	❑	❑
If members cannot attend, do they put in an apology?	❑	❑	❑
Do you make an action list of tasks to be completed before the next meeting and assign them to people?	❑	❑	❑
Are adequate facilities available for your meetings (meeting room, white-board, etc.)?	❑	❑	❑

Question 22.

Does you team measure the results of its efforts in terms of Key Performance indicators (KPI's) or Key Result Areas (KRA's)?

❑ Yes

❑ Not sure

❑ No

If 'Yes', please give examples:

_____
_____
_____
_____
_____

Question 23.

Have you had any training or experience working in the team environment?

❑ Yes

❑ No

If 'Yes', in what form did you receive this experience or training?
(e.g. – in previous employment, team training days etc.)

_____
_____
_____
_____

Question 24.

Have you experienced any difficulties with team building or the team environment?

❑ Yes

❑ No

If 'Yes', please give examples.

_____
_____
_____
_____

Case Study 4

General Comments on Team-building and Empowerment

Please use this space to make any comments on team-building and empowerment in SAAS. Due to the anonymous nature of your replies, we will be unable to respond to you personally (unless you include your name here) but your experiences and observations will help the Workforce Empowerment Implementation Team to develop an education and support service that will best meet your needs.

_____

_____

_____

_____

_____

_____

_____

_____

_____

_____

_____

_____

Thank you for your time.

Please post the completed survey in the stamped reply envelope by **Friday, September 12th, 1997.**

Ray Main

Case Study 4

Exhibit 13   Sample Feedback Sheet for Team on 13 Dimensions Compared to SAAS

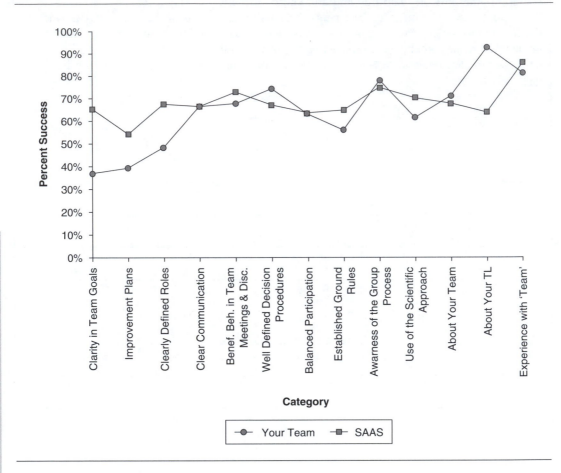

Index

About the Authors

Tupper Cawsey is Professor of Business, Wilfrid Laurier University, Waterloo, Ontario. He has been Associate Dean of Business at Wilfrid Laurier University, MBA Program Director, Director of the Laurier Institute, and Area Coordinator of the Management and Organizational Behaviour Area in the School of Business and Economics. Cawsey was recognized nationally in 2001 as one of Canada's top five business professors by receiving the Leaders in Management Education award, sponsored by PricewaterhouseCoopers and the National Post.

Cawsey created the Case Track for the Administrative Sciences Association of Canada, a peer-review process for cases. He is author or coauthor of more than six books and has published and/or presented more than 80 papers, monographs, and technical papers. He has received "best case awards" for several cases. In 2005, he received the Christiansen award from the Kaufman Foundation and the North American Case Research Association.

Gene Deszca is Professor of Business Administration, Wilfrid Laurier University, Waterloo, Ontario, Canada. He is a past Director of the MBA program and is currently the Area Coordinator of Management and Organizational Behavior. He has published and/or presented over 100 papers, monographs, and technical papers and three books. Three examples of the coauthored pieces are *Canadian Cases in Organizational Behaviour* (2005), *Canadian Cases in Human Resource Development* (2002), and Driving Loyalty Through Time-to-Value, *International Journal of Service Technology and Management, 17,* 3, 277–296.

His current research and consulting involves organizational change, the development of high-performance organizations, and the management of networks in SMEs. He has been instrumental in the development of the Society of Management Accountants of Canada's post-university professional accreditation programs and serves as a Director on their national board.